Present Sense

Present Sense

A practical guide to the SCIENCE of measuring performance and the ART of communicating it with the brain in mind.

Steve Morlidge

Copyright © 2019 Steve Morlidge

The moral right of the author has been asserted.

Apart from any fair dealing for the purposes of research or private study, or criticism or review, as permitted under the Copyright, Designs and Patents Act 1988, this publication may only be reproduced, stored or transmitted, in any form or by any means, with the prior permission in writing of the publishers, or in the case of reprographic reproduction in accordance with the terms of licences issued by the Copyright Licensing Agency. Enquiries concerning reproduction outside those terms should be sent to the publishers.

Matador
9 Priory Business Park,
Wistow Road, Kibworth Beauchamp,
Leicestershire. LE8 0RX
Tel: 0116 279 2299
Email: books@troubador.co.uk
Web: www.troubador.co.uk/matador
Twitter: @matadorbooks

ISBN 978 1838591 090

British Library Cataloguing in Publication Data.
A catalogue record for this book is available from the British Library.

Printed and bound in Malta by Gutenberg Press Ltd
Typeset in 11pt Adobe Garamond Pro by Troubador Publishing Ltd, Leicester, UK

Matador is an imprint of Troubador Publishing Ltd

Table of Contents

Introduction: What?   ix

    WHAT IT IS NOT   XI
    WHO?   XII
    WHY?   XIII
    WHY ME?   XV
    APPROACH   XVI
    STRUCTURE   XVIII

part 1: **The Need**
Rethinking the process of performance reporting

1. Why Do We Need To Change The Way We Do Stuff?   3

    I explain why traditional approaches – especially variance analysis – fail as a way of making sense and communicating performance and how technology has sometimes become part of the problem rather than the solution.

        INTRODUCTION   3
        SOME HISTORY   8
        VARIANCE ANALYSIS: RIGOROUS BUT WRONG   13
        THE BOTTOM LINE   20
        WHY TECHNOLOGY WON'T SAVE US   21
        THE SOLUTIONS AND HOW TECHNOLOGY *CAN* HELP US   25

part 2: **Sense**
The Science of Extracting Meaning From Data

2. Performance Reporting:
   What is it and What Has it Got to Do With Brains? 31

   In which we will explore the concepts of 'performance' and 'reporting' and how an appreciation of the way that the brain functions can help us design better tools and more effective strategies for understanding and communicating performance in a world of Big Data

WHAT IS PERFORMANCE?	31
WHAT IS REPORTING?	35
WHAT HAS THIS GOT TO DO WITH BRAINS?	36
OUR BRAINS: A REPORT CARD	40
HOW THE BRAIN DOESN'T WORK	43
HOW THE BRAIN ACTUALLY WORKS	44
WHY THIS IS IMPORTANT	52
WHAT IS THE PROCESS OF PERFORMANCE REPORTING?	53

3. Direction: Performance as Flow 63

   In which I describe how adopting a dynamic perspective helps set the context to help frame meaningful explorations of performance and provide some simple techniques to help understand and present trend information and analyse causality and risk.

PAINTING THE BIG PICTURE	63
ORGANIZATIONS AS DYNAMIC SYSTEMS	66
THE CONVENTIONAL PERSPECTIVE	68
THINKING ABOUT THINKING	71
THE DYNAMIC PERSPECTIVE — SIMPLE AVERAGES	76
SMOOTHED AVERAGES	78
SEASONALITY	81
MOVING TOTALS	84
THE ARGUMENT FOR DYNAMIC MEASURES	86
OTHER APPLICATION OF MATS	88
A REAL-LIFE EXAMPLE	94
SUMMARY	99

Table of Contents

4. Uncertainty and Predictability:
   Big Data and the Weak Signal — 103

   In which I explain how variation is an important attribute of performance and why we need to understand it to be able to make meaningful inferences from data. I also describe some simple tools that help information professionals effectively engage with it.

SIGNALS, NOISE AND THE MANAGEMENT OF VARIATION	103
OUR BRAINS AND NOISE	111
THE CHALLENGE OF NOISE IN REAL LIFE	113
THE SOLUTION	115
SEQUENCE	116
SIZE	122
CONTROL CHARTS	122
SETTING UP A CONTROL CHART	125
INTERPRETING CONTROL CHARTS	128
CONTROL CHARTS IN FINANCE	129
CONTROL CHARTS: RISK AND PERFORMANCE	133
CONTROL CHARTS AND CONTINUOUS IMPROVEMENT	134
SUMMARY	139

5. Level: What Does
   'Good' Look Like? — 143

   In which I describe a method to enable performance to be tracked dynamically, taking account of noise, and explore the nature of targets, how they can be set and whether they are required at all.

TRACKING PERFORMANCE	144
WE NEED TO TALK ABOUT TARGETS	149
WHAT IS A TARGET?	155
WHAT KINDS OF GOALS ARE THERE?	157
A SYSTEM OF TARGETS	161
TARGETS AND MOTIVATION	165
TARGETS AND PERFORMANCE REPORTING	167
DO WE NEED TARGETS? (ONE MORE TIME)	167

What Have We Learned So Far? — 173

HOW TECHNOLOGY CAN HELP – AND WHY IT ISN'T *THE* SOLUTION	177

part 3: **Present**
The Art of Communicating by Visual Means

6. Communicating by Visual Means — 185

In which I explain how the brain interprets visual stimuli and how this underpins visual literacy. I also describe a process to help design reports that communicate performance more efficiently and effectively.

GRAPHICAL GRAMMAR	185
COMMUNICATION	189
WHY THIS IS IMPORTANT	193
VISUAL THINKING PROCESSES	194
HOW DO WE SEE?	196
DESIGNING REPORTS FOR BRAINS – THE BASICS	204
PUTTING IT ALL TOGETHER	221
PULLING IT ALL TOGETHER: A CASE STUDY	237

What Have We Learned? — 244

part 4: **Action**
Putting ideas to work

7. Reporting is Reporting (Not Storytelling) — 249

In which I argue that information professionals should model themselves on news reporters, not storytellers.

8. Now What? — 257

In which I share a practical framework to help readers work out how best to facilitate changes in their organization.

Epilogue: A Reflection — 267

Reading List — 269

ACCOUNTING, MEASUREMENT AND GOALS	269
COGNITIVE SCIENCE	270
DATA VISUALIZATION	271
OTHERS	271

End Piece — 273

introduction

What?

Sometimes the character of a book reveals itself to its author only after many painful hours spent labouring over the manuscript. Other times it is obvious from the outset.

With my previous book it was only after the text was written and me and my co-author were approaching the publication date that we hit upon the title. We stumbled about a lot before we found a way of articulating our hazy ideas and discovered the powerful yet subtle idea that defined what we were trying to express.

That book was about forecasting, so it was about the future. However, we wanted to avoid making clichéd claims about prediction or foresight because the key message was that the future is unknowable but that the act of looking forward – in structured and intelligent manner – helps prepare you for possible futures by sharpening reflexes and priming perception. To be prepared and ready we do not need to be able to predict, we simply need to anticipate. That's where the title *Future Ready* came from.

This book is different. Forecasting is an exercise in speculation: producing information about possible futures. The current is about how to make sense of data that we already have about the past. It is focussed on how to go about extracting information from data – not how we can manufacture credible information in the absence of data. This provided the word 'Sense' for the title of this book.

The second word in the title – 'Present' – reflects not only the time frame that I am interested in but also the second major theme in this book. Information has no value by itself. It has to be communicated to other people who then use it to inform their actions. The person charged with extracting meaning from data – the information professional – therefore has not only to cultivate analytical skills but also the ability to communicate it effectively to his or her audience. They need to *present* meaning in an effective manner.

So, the title *Present Sense* alludes to both these two interrelated strands that weave through this book. It is about creating meaning by making sense of the present (what one might call 'current history') and finding ways to communicate it – to present it to the intended audience.

There are two apparently different and challenging tasks for the analyst charged with this task.

First, to make sense of what, in most modern businesses, is a super abundance of data that is noisy, messy and often poorly structured.

Second, having derived some meaning from the data, to find ways to communicate it effectively to others. Particularly those who do not have the capability or the time to make sense of it for themselves but nevertheless are charged with making decisions.

The challenge for the people tasked with doing this – and for me the fun – is that it requires two different kinds of skills, neither of which they are routinely trained to do.

To elicit meaning requires the ability to scientifically reveal patterns – to unearth the signals buried in the noise. To be able to communicate meaning demands a mastery of the techniques that exploit this understanding. In practice, this involves the use of graphical design principles, a facility that is almost literally an art.

So, there is some science in this book and there is also art. But there is one thing that links these two things together: the brain. The brain helps us uncover meaning. And communication requires the transfer of this meaning to other brains. As the ideas for this book matured it seemed to me that I couldn't tackle either of these subjects without understanding the role that the brain plays in this drama.

Extracting meaning from data is not a mechanistic process. It requires the analyst to build and test hypotheses. Rather than set up an arithmetical system and simply crank the handle, we need to learn about how to gather and interpret evidence. This is based on our brain's ability to identify patterns in the data and find creative ways to understand and explain what they reveal about the nature of reality. To do this job effectively information professionals have to understand how the brain does its job. They need to appreciate the things that the brain does really well and learn how to exploit these strengths and use tools and techniques to overcome its weaknesses.

Neither is communication purely a matter of aesthetics. The way that the human brain takes in information is rooted in the physiology of the brain and how it assimilates the meaning of the sensory data sitting on a piece of paper or a computer screen. Communicating effectively must involve developing an appreciation of how to present information in a way that your audience's brains will grasp your intended meaning quickly and faithfully. Which, because we are an animal dominated by our sense of sight, means understanding how to best visualize data.

So, *Present Sense* is about scientific enquiry – simple mathematics and biology – and it's a book about the art and craft of visual communication.

The challenge for me as an author is that the words 'science' and 'art' are scary terms for many people.

'Science' conjures up images of lab coats and complex formulae and, for most people, 'art' brings memories of our pathetic attempts at school to create a likeness of the simplest everyday objects. If that is the way you are feeling right now let me reassure you.

The only science involved in the analytic techniques I will introduce you to in this book is pitifully simple and straightforward. It's just that you have never been told about it. And if you think you have no artistic ability, I hope to show you that anyone can produce reports that look slick and professional (and perhaps even cool!) by following a simple set of guidelines. And I'm living proof of this because I'm not a scientist by training, and I'm not turned on by art.

So, *Present Sense* is for normal human beings, not Hawkings or Hockneys. Specifically, it is for practitioners in business; those people charged with the analysis of performance data and the production of reports and those responsible for managing them.

This is therefore an intensely practical book focussed on needs of business users. But, along the way, as we explore the principles that underpin what might otherwise be regarded as a prosaic business activity, I hope that it helps the reader to see the world with fresh eyes – creating new meanings that they can exploit in other aspects of their work.

WHAT IT IS NOT

It is equally important for me to be clear about what this book is not.

I will *not* be talking to you about *what* specific variables to measure, other than they should relate to performance and viability (which I will define in detail). This book only addresses how to measure – not what to measure. I recognize that this goes against recent trends, which have seen an industry grow up around performance metrics. Almost every business has its own 'Balanced Scorecard' (BSC), 'dashboard' or 'management cockpit'. And there are thousands of books on the market about 'killer Key Performance Indicators' (KPIs).

I will not be adding my voice to this noisy debate about what should be measured. It seems to me that what you choose to measure will be specific to your part of your business and to its situation. I will assume that the reader of this book already has a pretty good idea about what metrics are most relevant for him or her, and if they don't that they know where to go to get advice.

What this book aims to do is to provide practical guidance on how to make sense of performance data, *whatever you choose to measure*. This is possible because the fundamental questions we need to answer are generic and *not* context specific. Questions such as: 'Is this good performance or bad performance?', 'Are things getting better or worse?', 'Has anything significant just happened?', 'What is driving performance?' and so on apply equally to any kind of organization in any context.

Neither will I be describing fancy new data visualization techniques or telling you the best way to lay out a table of numbers. Again, there is a lot of traffic in this space already, but I also don't want to be too prescriptive about what you should do in any particular set of circumstances. Instead I will explain why some things work and why others don't and so provide you with the ability to make good design choices for yourselves, whatever you are seeking to communicate.

So, this is more a *how* book than a *what* book.

If that's not what you were expecting, sorry. Perhaps you should ask for a refund!

WHO?

My background is in finance[1] – it is what I know best – and so the primary audience for this book are the members of this profession, both the doers in and the managers of financial performance management processes. If you are one of this number my aim is to help you do a better job, in ways that will be easily recognized and appreciated by non-experts. Quickly, starting tomorrow.

But the primary audience for this book is finance folk. The approaches I describe can be applied by anyone responsible for analysing or presenting any sort of performance data, and not just those in corporate or head office roles.

The job of analysing and communicating financial performance management information lies at the heart of the traditional role of a management accountant. It did when I qualified in 1981 and it still does. Today you might find these roles performed in departments with the name FP&A (Financial Planning and Analysis) but there are similar roles in many other parts of organizations, and a lot of the people in them will not have a finance background. So, throughout this book I will refer to the 'analyst' or 'information professional' to reflect the broad scope and applicability of the concepts I describe.

'Information worker' roles have always been important, but never more so than now.

For the first time in the history of business data is not in short supply, but although data is super abundant, powerful insights are still hard to come by – arguably it has become harder. The ability to extract meaning from data and use it effectively to run a business is an important source of competitive advantage in a way, and to a degree unimaginable even a decade ago. Sitting at the nexus between business operations and decision makers in the business, and with access to enormous amounts of data, information professionals have a pivotal role to play.

They are not merely 'quants', number crunchers or PowerPoint jockeys. They are not worker drones in a number factory or a passive conduit through which information flows. I believe that their responsibility for extracting and communicating meaning gives information professionals a key role in helping to create a shared corporate consciousness – the sense a business has of the world and its place in it. A job that requires a different order of expertise than most of us have been trained in.

---

1. Here, and elsewhere in this book, I use the word 'finance' in the broadest sense of the word, to describe someone who works with information that is denominated in a currency. This includes people who work in the financial services industry but most 'finance' people do not.

WHY?

Performance reporting is an established part of corporate life and there is already an industry around so-called 'Big Data' and 'data visualization'. What can this book add, and why now?

While the importance of performance reporting and analysis has always been recognized, the tools and techniques that are commonly used have not changed to reflect the information-rich environment that business inhabits or to exploit the technology now available to make sense of it.

There has been an explosion in the reliability and quantity of data, but, in most organizations, performance is analysed in the same way it always has been – by comparing the actual for a defined period in time with a target – what accountants call 'variance analysis'.

For reasons that will become clear, this simple, crude approach fails to capture important features of the quality of performance and provides little help to managers drowning in an ocean of turbulent data.

The opportunities, and the challenges, that we now face in our world of superabundant data is a relatively recent phenomenon. A decade or so ago, before integrated ERPs (Enterprise Planning Systems) came on the scene, a common lament of managers I heard when I spoke at conferences was 'we don't have enough data'. Just a few short years later I hear the same people complaining that they are overwhelmed with it. The reality, however, is not that they have too much data but that the tools that they use to analyse it and the thinking associated with them have not evolved to deal with the changing environment.

Unsurprisingly, the advent of Big Data has been accompanied by an explosion in interest in sophisticated analytical and data visualization software.

Organizations can now do things that would not have been possible only a few years ago, such as using sophisticated algorithms to analyse granular purchase data to customize adverts or make suggestions to individual consumers. But, as yet, these analytical technologies have made little contribution to the job of performance measurement and management. This is because the nature of the performance data and the complexity of the management decision-making do not easily lend themselves to sophisticated mathematical analysis. But it is also because – up until now – the software has been too sophisticated and too costly for the process and for the people running it.

Tools that enable users to produce arresting graphics quickly and easily are gaining real traction in organizations. Anything that makes information more accessible, and therefore actionable, has to be a good thing, but unless this is backed up by analytical techniques with substance the risk is that these visualizations are no more than attractive packaging that can just as easily mislead as inform.

Software has a critical role to play in this brave new world, but my aim is not to sell some technologically-driven utopian vision. So, forget your dream of becoming like a latter-day James T Kirk on the bridge of the Starship Enterprise throwing questions and challenges at data scientists glued to their space age instrument panels. Information technology (IT) is an important enabler of the approach I advocate in this book but there is nothing completely novel in this book from a technological point of view.

Instead I will draw on a wealth of insights, approaches, tools and techniques that have been developed in this and related fields, many of which have been around for a long time. The solutions are largely already out there but practitioners are largely ignorant of them and how they can be used because their perspective on their job and how to do it is so narrow. Partly due to the relentless pressure to 'get things done', but also because of the way that managers are trained and learn to think about what they do and how they should do it. I hope this book will fill in some of these gaps.

If there *is* anything truly new in this book – for a management audience – it is the recognition of how important it is to understand how the human brain works in order to do a better job of analysing and communicating performance information. The mechanistic approaches to analysing and reporting performance that I and my contemporaries were taught give no consideration to how our brains make sense of data and assimilate information – which goes a long way to explaining why they often don't work too well.

True, artificial intelligence (AI) and machine learning are hot topics right now, but much of the debate is fixated on the prospect of them replacing rather than helping human beings. Technology is developing at a breath-taking pace but the complexity of many of the tasks that we accomplish with ease and what neuroscientists are learning about the way our brain makes sense of the world makes it clear – to me at least – that while technology can support and guide us it will always be no more than a tool – albeit a very sophisticated one – rather than our master.

For the next few decades at least, our job is to learn how to use these tools effectively, not to start planning for being replaced by robots. This starts with understanding what our brains do so well, but also where they need technological support to compensate for their shortcomings. Crucially we need to learn how to design digital tools so that the 'brain–computer' interface works as well as possible. After all, until someone made the first stone axe by designing a handle for our hands to create an effective 'body–tool' interface the only technology we had to chop down trees were unwieldy lumps of rock.

In summary, the traditional methods we have learned fail to equip us for the challenges of making sense of organizational performance and communicating this to decision makers in the 21st century. Nor do they help us exploit the wealth of data or the powerful technologies we now have at our disposal.

The aim of this book is to learn from advances that have been made in statistics, process analysis, cognitive science, data visualization and graphic design. To adapt them to our purposes and to package them in a simple and practical form to provide information professionals with a simple, coherent and scientifically grounded toolkit for everyday use.

What?

WHY ME?

Any author of a book like this has a challenge to convince a reader that their point of view is well informed, authoritative and worth listening to. It isn't always absolutely necessary that the author has first-hand experience of what he or she is writing about. Peter Drucker, arguably the most influential management author of this century, only ever worked as a journalist, and many other management gurus have worked solely in academia or consulting. But if an author has personal experience of the issue that he or she writes about it brings a certain credibility with it.

In my case, my interest in the subjects I write about flow directly from my experience as a finance professional in a major multinational company. The biggest part of the jobs I did involved preparing plans and analysing performance. By working closely with people from other functions at many different levels over many years I developed a rounded perspective of what was involved in managing a complex business.

Most of the time, like everyone else, I just got on with the job, doing things as they had always been done without giving too much thought to what I did and why. But over time I increasingly became aware that many of the things that I and my team did or didn't do felt wrong or just pointless, and this gradually eroded my confidence in the results of my work and my job satisfaction.

For example, over a period of ten years my team and I built the financial infrastructure of the company from scratch, and because of my position in the business and my experience of it I *know* that no other single person had better access to information than me, or a better understanding of how the business worked. And yet, as the business grew and became more successful, I got increasingly more uncomfortable as I realized that I didn't really understand why. When I was asked, it wasn't difficult to come up with a story that would convince anyone who knew less than me, but I wasn't personally convinced it was the 'truth'. The way I had been taught to make sense of data simply couldn't answer the important questions in a way that convinced me.

Then I got lucky. A chance introduction to Jeremy Hope and Robin Fraser, founders of the Beyond Budgeting Round Table, gave me an opportunity to discover how other organizations worked. Breaking out from the confines of my day job kicked off a new life of learning for me. I've now spent nearly two decades learning about things I wished I had known when I had a 'proper job'. That is great for me personally, but this knowledge only has value if I can share it, ideally with as many people like my old self as possible, which is my motivation for writing this book.

My encounter with Beyond Budgeting (where I was European chairman of the organization) ultimately led to me being involved in helping to set up Unilever's Finance Academy. Our first job was to build, from scratch, a strategy for the finance function, dubbed 'Finance of the Future'. With this came the opportunity to travel the world speaking to any and every expert that we thought might be able to help us. And after the new strategy was adopted by the finance leadership team, I led the project tasked with bringing Beyond Budgeting principles into Unilever – an organization with about a quarter of a million employees working in over 100 countries.

In a role like this, however compelling your arguments for change, it is not long before people start asking, 'That's all fine and dandy, but what should we *do*?' At this point vision and rhetoric have to make room for hard and practical things like processes, tools and techniques. And this kicked off a new cycle of learning for me as it became clear that many of the methods and techniques that were associated with budgeting needed to be rethought and replaced.

The first fruits of this labour manifested themselves in the book *Future Ready* and led to me starting a software business (CatchBull) to fill a gap in the forecasters' tool set.

Present Sense is a further extension of this work, and it is also informed by it. For example, the process of developing the CatchBull software has helped me develop an understanding of how to sort, sift and analyse large volumes of granular data to extract actionable insights into the performance of the forecast process. This knowledge and some of the techniques we use can also be applied to the analysis of actual data, as can the tricks of effective graphical communication of statistical information that we use in our software.

This book is also part of the continuing process of helping practitioners move away from traditional bureaucratic top-down budgeting processes towards a management model that is more flexible, externally focussed and less prone to political game-playing. Many practitioners find it difficult to let go of budgeting even if they are convinced of the need to change. Their management tools are predicated on having a budget; therefore they do not have a choice.

But you don't have to commit to abandoning budgets to benefit from the insights and techniques set out in this book. Reducing the reliance on traditional variance analysis and finding ways to exploit the opportunities presented by Big Data will pay dividends even if you don't change your performance management model. And learning how to present and communicate better visually is a universally useful skill.

If by the end of the book you have had your eyes opened and want to explore the idea of Beyond Budgeting further, I have written a short guidebook called *The Little Book of Beyond Budgeting* that you can find at all good (large, American, online) booksellers.

APPROACH

My goal has been to produce a book that is useful and accessible; practical and thought-provoking.

I'm very sceptical of case studies in business books. It's not difficult to tell an engaging story by selecting the facts that fit your theory, but that doesn't make it true.[2] Instead, I hope I will be able to convince you with the power of my logic and by appealing to your own experiences, using simulations or mock-ups to simplify or illustrate a point.

To make the content as widely applicable as possible, I only advocate approaches that are capable of being executed using tools that every reader will have on their PC or laptop – products like Microsoft Office, particularly Excel – and I will assume no special programming skill. If you want to deploy the practices demonstrated widely you may need specialized software, but I think it is important that you should be able to try things out for yourself and pilot potential solutions on a small scale rather than taking my word for it. Then, if and when you decide to make an investment in a more robust technology, you can do so with knowledge of what you want and the confidence that it will work.

Also, although what follows is grounded in science, you don't need any specialized knowledge or skills. Although some of the techniques will be unfamiliar, the level of mathematical ability required to use them is no higher than any information professional already possesses.

Also, because I didn't want to produce a worthy but dull textbook, I have tried to tell a story and pepper the narrative with observations and anecdotes to keep your interest. Occasionally some mathematics or a numerical exercise will unavoidably break into the narrative flow. It is important to get to grips with these to be able to put the ideas into practice, but feel free to jump over the mathematics if you don't have the energy or inclination to engage in it and come back to them later when the time is right. Personally, I always skip over technical details in books the first time round and return to them when I need to engage at a practical level. I have designed the book with this in mind, so don't feel guilty if you find yourself jumping about.

Learning anything new involves having to unlearn first and I hope and expect that what I have to say will lead to you having a different perspective on familiar subjects. So, if I am successful, your patterns of thought will begin to change.

This will be uncomfortable at first because you are not practised in them and because letting go of learned habits that you have come to rely on is tough. This is inevitable and natural. I have tried to make it easier to re-orientate your ideas by using analogies from everyday life, but don't expect everything to be easier on day one – particularly if you need to bring other people with you. Persevere and try and resist the temptation to fall back into old bad habits. In time it will be the old habits, not the new things, that will seem perverse and unnatural.

Finally, as I have already mentioned, this book is pulled together from a range of disparate sources. Rather than attempt to dazzle you with the breadth of my knowledge and clutter up the book with a lot of derivative ideas I have included references to other sources where specific topics are tackled in more depth but in the same spirit. If anything that I have written is not sufficiently clear, or if you need to gain a deeper understanding, I encourage you to consult these primary sources.

2. Phil Rosenzweig's book *The Halo Effect* is a highly recommended expose of how 'case studies' and other pseudo-scientific approaches to explaining business performance not only deceive and mislead readers of popular business books but also their authors, even if they are written by academics who aspire to high standards of proof.

STRUCTURE

The book is structured as follows.

In Part 1 I set out the problem with traditional approaches to measuring and communicating performance information. Part 2 describes better ways of making sense of performance and Part 3 how to present to decision makers in a more effective way. Finally, the subject of implementation is tackled in Part 4.

The 'meat' of the book is contained in Parts 2 and 3. Ironically, although the subject matter of Part 2 will be unfamiliar to most readers, you are likely to find it an easy read since the practices I describe will be intuitively easy to grasp. Part I, on the other hand, will be much more challenging because it requires the reader to deal with a familiar subject in unfamiliar ways.

Specifically, this is what you will learn from each chapter:

PART 1: THE NEED

Chapter 1. Why Do We Need to Change the Way We Do Stuff?

- Why we shouldn't confuse data with truth.
- How targets can be unhelpful as a guide to performance.
- Why traditional 'actual to target' comparisons are an unreliable guide to performance.
- Why tables of numbers are not effective at communicating performance information.
- How traditional approaches fail to guide intervention by decision makers.
- Why these long-standing weaknesses have now become a major problem for organizations.
- Why attempts to simplify using tools like 'traffic lights' are dangerous.
- Why pairwise comparisons between actuals and forecasts are helpful.
- How Big Data makes things worse not better.
- Why sophisticated mathematical techniques will not provide the solution.

PART 2: SENSE

Chapter 2. Performance Reporting: What is it and What Has it Got to Do with Brains?

- How to define 'performance'.
- Why it is difficult to assess the level of performance.
- Why an appreciation of trends is an important component of performance.
- How and why variation is relevant to measuring performance.
- What 'reporting' is and how it differs from analysis.

What?

- What role performance reporting performs in organizations.
- What data is and how it differs from information.
- How understanding the way that our brains work helps us do a better job.
- Why our existing tools are deficient from a neurological perspective.
- What lessons we can learn from the way our brains make sense of the world.
- What implications the brain model has for the role of information professionals.

Chapter 3. Direction: Performance as Flow

- Why it is important to measure the dynamics of organizational performance.
- How accountants have lost the plot.
- How tables of numbers fail as a means to communicate patterns of performance.
- Why information professionals need to understand the difference between thinking fast and thinking slow.
- How averages help us make sense of trends.
- Why cumulative and rolling averages are deficient as a means of measuring trends.
- How smoothed averages are calculated and why they are effective.
- Why moving annual totals (MATs) are a powerful tool for making sense of performance.
- How MATs can be used to understand causality and risk.

Chapter 4. Uncertainty and Predictability: Big Data and the Weak Signal

- What noise is.
- Why noise is important.
- What qualities of noise make it inherently difficult to deal with in a performance reporting context.
- Why human beings struggle to deal with noise in assessing organizational performance.
- What we need to take into account when we are making statistical inferences based on data.
- How to increase the level of confidence when making probabilistic inferences.
- How to use patterns to detect a change in the signal in a noisy data series.
- How to use data values to detect a change in the signal in a noisy data series.

- Why understanding the level of variation in a data series is important for measuring and managing performance.

Chapter 5. What Does 'Good' Look Like?

- How to continuously track actual performance against a moving target.
- The benefits that accrue from the ability to continuously track performance.
- How targets shape organizational culture.
- How conventional fixed targets can make things worse.
- How we define a target.
- What reference points goals require.
- How goals might be expressed with reference to time.
- What different ways there are for expressing the desired value of a variable.
- When a goal can be changed.
- What kind of aspiration the desired value of a goal represents.
- How different goals relate to each other.
- What role goals play in motivation.
- What role goals play in organizational performance.
- How technology can enhance performance reporting.
- Why machine learning will not replace human beings in the performance reporting process.
- Why *insight* is not enough.

PART 3: PRESENT

Chapter 6. Communicating by Visual Means

- Why it is important to learn to use graphical grammar.
- What characterizes effective communication.
- How reports can fail to communicate.
- How reporting differs from analysis.
- Why digital dashboards have not replaced paper-based reports.
- How Business Intelligence software can enhance reporting.
- Why visualization works for reporting.
- When visualizations do not work.
- How the brain 'sees'.
- What implications the perception process has for how visualizations are used in reporting.
- How to design effective reports.
- How to decide what a report should contain.
- What needs to be considered when structuring a report.

What?

- The qualities that are required in a well-designed visualization.

Chapter 7. Reporting is Reporting (Not Storytelling)

- Why 'storytelling' is a bad analogy for performance reporting.
- The principles that should guide the actions and behaviour of performance reporters.

PART 4: ACTION

Chapter 8. Now What?

- How to go about creating the conditions for successful change.
- What process to follow in managing a successful change project.
- How to tackle the process of changing performance reporting when you don't have an explicit mandate.
- In what order changes should be made.
- In Summary: the Big Idea in This Book

This list will give you an inkling of the 'big idea' behind this book, but it is always helpful to get a proper sense of where you are headed before you set out on any journey as it helps you to re-orientate yourself if at any point you become lost.

Let me do this by telling you something more about my own journey.

It has been clear for me for many years that the traditional approach to performance reporting, based on a simple comparison of the actual for a period and a target, doesn't work.

I found the idea that you could specify in advance what 'good' looked like absurd, particularly if the business environment was unpredictable and working at a detailed level. It was also clear that the actual for any single period could be affected by any number of unpredictable factors. So, how much faith could you have that the difference between the two conveyed any useful information? Traditional variance analysis was like a stool with only two legs, both of which were broken.

Over the years I adopted a set of new 'tools' that worked to fill the information gap, but I was aware that something important was missing.

What I didn't have, which made me hesitate at putting pen to paper until now, was a 'theory' – something that explained why the things that I had learned to do worked where variance analysis did not, and which guided my efforts to find other tools that filled in the gaps in my armoury.

Scientists call what I was searching for a 'paradigm'. A paradigm is a set of concepts or thought patterns, which help structure work in a field and guide the choice of methods that are used to acquire knowledge.

It became clear to me that the fundamental problem I had with the traditional approaches to measuring performance was that it was based on an inappropriate paradigm. A paradigm that was a product of the era into which they were born – the age of machines and mass production. The unstated assumption behind what I had learned to do was that the world was known and predictable and that organizations should respond to these external stimuli in a predictable way. The old tools worked only if these conditions were met, which they weren't.

The world I worked in was complex, dynamic and messy. For most of the time it was really difficult to work out what was really going on. Not only didn't we have the answers – it was sometimes difficult to work out what questions to ask. The kinds of tools I needed were those that helped to reduce the level of uncertainty and to focus attention on those things that really matter – the things that required people to act.

Over the years it became clear to me that this was a world where solutions inspired by biology rather than engineering were more likely to achieve. After all, a good working definition of 'life' is the ability for an entity to survive in and adapt to a dynamic and unpredictable environment.

The more I thought about it, the clearer it became that this wasn't just a philosophical idea.

If performance reporting is about looking for meaning to guide action, then I should be looking at the entity that nature had designed specifically to do this job – the brain. So, at a very practical level, I needed to understand and learn how the human brain makes sense of overwhelming amounts of complex and ambiguous information and use it to design more effective strategies for making sense of performance data. And, given that our brains couldn't do this job in the artificial environment of organizations unaided, I should be looking for tools that exploited its strengths and – where it was being asked to do a job it hadn't evolved to do well – compensated for its weaknesses.

But it doesn't stop with sense-making. Reporting requires us to transfer meaning from our brain to other brains, as quickly and faithfully as possible. Which means that we also need to design tools that are built on an understanding of how human brains assimilate information. Communication tools that are much better than tables of numbers that our brains have not evolved to 'consume'.

So, this is the *big idea*. We need to approach the task of reporting on performance from a biological perspective. Specifically, we have to appreciate that it is a cognitive process that requires us to help our brains make sense of the environment and communicate meaning to other brains. And the tools that we use, like all good tools, need to both amplify our inherited capabilities and work in a way that 'fits' with our brains so that they feel like they are part of us, rather than like a badly fitting prosthetic.

That's the thinking behind the book, but before we go any further let me lay out where I plan to take you, starting with a rather fundamental question, which I think is too frequently assumed away rather than answered.

'What is performance'?

An organization can be said to be performing when it is successfully fulfilling its purpose. We report on it to determine to what extent it is performing on three dimensions – level, trend and variation – and to help establish what if any intervention is required.

Information professionals are charged with assimilating and making sense of data and communicating it to decision makers, who normally act collectively.

There is a huge amount of sensory data available to organizations, which grows exponentially with every passing month, and its nature reflects the increasingly volatile, uncertain, complex and ambiguous environments that organizations operate in.

Given these conditions, this job cannot be performed mechanistically, in the way that we have learned, with simple comparisons between a data point and a target. Instead the information professional needs to adopt a method of enquiry akin to that used by scientists – by forming and testing hypotheses. Since this has proven to be the most effective way of building knowledge it is no surprise to find that our brains, guided by millions of years of evolution, have adopted a similar strategy to perceive and make sense of the world.

In a nutshell, we can't *process* data to extract meaning; we have to *interact* with it, in the same way that scientists do when they are attempting to unlock the secrets of nature and every one of us does in every moment that we are awake and aware. Information professionals can therefore be seen as gatekeepers of organizational consciousness. And performance reporting is analogous to the process of perception, guided by purpose – that is, what we are seeking to achieve.

To perform this role effectively requires tools that help exploit the strengths and mitigate the weakness of the information professionals' own brains. And to communicate what has been learnt we need to understand how best to present information in a way that enables the brains of our particular audience to assimilate it, quickly, easily and with the minimum amount of ambiguity.

This book provides information professionals with a set of tools and methodologies, based on solid scientific insights into the process of perception in the human brain. I hope you, the reader, find that you can use them to help you do a better job. At the very least, given that so much of what we do at work we have learned by rote, I hope that it will cause you to pause and to think.

For me, that would be a little triumph.

That's the big idea. But, before we can think big, we need to get a proper understanding of why and how the current system is broken. And that means we have to dive into the detail.

It is a truism that the only way to learn is by making mistakes, and that it's more efficient to learn from other people's failures rather than your own. So, let's start with a story about one of mine.

Enjoy!

part 1
The Need
Rethinking the process of performance reporting

need

/niːd/
noun: **need**; plural noun: **needs**

1. circumstances in which something is necessary; necessity.
2. a thing that is wanted or required.

chapter 1

Why Do We Need To Change The Way We Do Stuff?

> I explain why traditional approaches – especially variance analysis – fail as a way of making sense and communicating performance and how technology has sometimes become part of the problem rather than the solution.

INTRODUCTION

It was 1996 – the year that the Spice Girls split up and Dolly the sheep was cloned. I was the Financial Controller for a large unit of a highly respected multinational company, and I had just made my own personal breakthrough – the final piece of the jigsaw was in place.

Performance reporting at the touch of a button; burned straight onto acetate. The wonders of modern technology!

Whatever next?

And I couldn't wait for my next board presentation where I could show off my new baby.

But when I came to unveil my new innovation to the senior team I was swamped by a tidal wave of indifference. Deflated by my disappointment, I cornered the Sales Director as he grabbed a dose of nicotine and quizzed him about it. I knew him well and liked him. He was charismatic and funny but blunt; a quality that he chose to share with me at this moment.

'What a load of old b*******' was the gist of his opinion on my efforts.

'OK, so volume in Tesco was up by half a million against budget in March and prices were down by £300k. So what?' He shrugged and walked off. He clearly didn't, as I had hoped, feel obliged here or in the board meeting to provide a blow by blow analysis of how this had come about or mount a defence of his sales team. He didn't even seem to think it was worth explaining his analysis of my presentation, probably because I had just demonstrated what an idiot I was, so it wasn't worth the effort of stating the obvious.

As I reflect back on this experience now, I wonder how is it possible to be so wrong on so many levels? How could an intelligent, experienced professional be so unconsciously incompetent?

Before I explain why I came to appreciate the extent of my ignorance and stupidity conclusion, I need to describe what I had done, and how I came to make the mistake. This might make some readers from a conventional finance background uncomfortable because I'm sure that most of you have done – or are doing – the same kind of thing.

Let's start with some background.

In 1992 when I was given the job of Financial Controller in a new business, I found my department in the throes of a meltdown. Thirty of the original complement of 120 people had just been 'released', along with my predecessor, and the people left were unsurprisingly not the most motivated bunch I have ever met. The financial accounts, which ran on an old IBM System 360 computer (a design dating back to 1964), were months out of date and the bank account hadn't been reconciled for the last two quarters. The asset accountant, who had 30 years' experience under his belt and was charged with the task of trying to find the reason for a multimillion-pound hole in his accounts (using an old manual calculator he was fond of), had just revealed that he was number dyslexic. This meant he couldn't tell the difference between the numbers 6 and 9, which went some way to explaining the hole. And my 'colleague' who headed up the management accounts part of my empire had already decided that I was his mortal enemy and was doing everything possible to help me fail in my new job.

You don't have to know anything about accountancy to appreciate that this was not a good place to be.

Four years down the line we had turned everything around and I was justifiably proud of what my team had achieved, and over confident as a result. We had implemented an integrated ERP system (we were SAP's first customer for its new client–server software in the UK). We had introduced fast close processes and integrated the management and financial accounts to produce a single 'version of the truth', complete with forecasts within a day after the bookmonth end. This meant that the senior team had a beautiful and colourful report pack on their desk within five days of the end of the period. And if they had any kind of query, we could drill down from the report data to individual invoices and tell them who had made the entry, when and the name of their pet dog (I made up the last bit – SAP doesn't have this as a field in their master records). As far as modern, 'best practice' finance processes were concerned, we had therefore ticked every box.

So, what went wrong when I presented my slick set of acetates to the board?

My first big mistake was to assume that the difference between a target and an actual for a period provided useful information about performance. It didn't and it usually doesn't. This might sound an outrageous thing to say given that most business performance reports work on this premise, and not just in finance.

Let me explain what I mean by imagining what my Sales Director might have said, had he taken the trouble.

> Look, we both know that the budget number was just a 'made up number' produced over a year ago. We had no idea, and we never will, what a 'good' number for sales would be in Tesco in March because we don't know how fast the market is going to grow, and how much share they are likely to have of it. Nor do we have any idea what our competitors will do or whether we will want to defend our share of Tesco's market, if they attack us, or increase our take if we spot a vulnerability. And you are kidding yourself if you think there was any science behind the target for the year. I negotiated it with the CEO – we just haggled and agreed on a number. And remember both our bonuses are tied to the number we agree to – so we were actually negotiating my pay. He wanted a high number and I wanted a lower one, so we met in the middle. And then your accountants took the number we agreed on and spread it across the months and played around with it so that the total business had a profit number for the first quarter that the guys in head office would wear.

What the imaginary sales director is telling me here is that whenever there is uncertainty or volatility in the business environment any target that is set in advance can never be more than a 'good guess' or a statement of aspiration. It is not a realistic estimate of an achievable level of performance.

Also, because it doesn't take account of the actual business context, it might drive the wrong behaviour. To use a military analogy, a commander of an army might want to advance on all fronts but if the enemy is throwing all of their forces at your position, you might be doing very well just to hold it.

Finally, target setting is often highly politicized, which makes them an even more unreliable guide to performance. In such circumstances, targets are really just a tool used by participants to try to get people to do what they want (pay me more money, pull out all the stops) rather than a foundation for the rational analysis of performance.

My imaginary conversation didn't end there.

> Also, Steve, you have to remember that we had a big promotion at the beginning of the month, so sales we would expect to make in March were booked in February because we had to stock up Tesco stores in advance. But the cost of securing the deal was booked to March because that is when we ran the promotion, so your conclusions about March performance was false.
>
> And, even in a normal month, we know that a lorry full of product breaking down or being turned away from the warehouse on a Saturday night at the end of the month can make a significant difference to the numbers – and that's before I make allowance for somebody's Aunt Nellie being on holiday.
>
> So that's why I don't take any notice of your numbers, and why I would be nuts to use them to take any decisions.

To translate: in any single period, there are a host of things that can distort 'reality' as recorded in the books. Some of these are knowable and could allow for them if we are prepared to put in the effort and make some educated guesses. But some of the things that distort the numbers we can never know about. Some will affect the timing of when we record a value; others are just random events that distort the picture. In other words, any measurements we make, even if they are indisputable statements of fact, will contain an unknowable level of 'noise'. And the more detail we go into the more this noise will obscure what is really going on. To paraphrase, we will just see trees – not the wood. When we assess performance, we need to be able to discount the noise so we can focus our attention on the signal. Only then can we begin to extract meaning and decide the best course of action.

In summary, my mistake was that I had compared a single data point (containing an unknown amount of random noise) with a target (which was a politically motivated guess made 12 months before) and assumed that the difference was meaningful. When you put it in those terms it doesn't sound too clever, does it?

But with the benefit of hindsight, I can see that I made even more errors.

For example, the 'information' that I had presented to the board looked something like Table 1.1.

Table 1.1:
An example of the sort of table I presented to the Board

A typical traditional performance report, in this case reporting on sales compared to budget.

Sales (£k)

	Q3				Variance v Budget			
Product Groups	**Budget**	**April Estimate**	**July Estimate**	**Actual**	**April Estimate**	**July Estimate**	**Actual**	**%**
Product A1	£ 184.9	£ 185.9	£ 171.7	£ 176.1	£ 1.0	-£ 13.2	-£ 8.8	-4.8%
Product A2	£ 214.3	£ 226.7	£ 214.1	£ 214.7	£ 12.4	-£ 0.2	£ 0.4	0.2%
Product A3	£ 123.3	£ 117.7	£ 115.0	£ 110.4	-£ 5.6	-£ 8.3	-£ 12.9	-10.5%
Product Group A	£ 522.4	£ 530.2	£ 500.7	£ 501.1	£ 7.8	-£ 21.7	-£ 21.3	-4.1%
Product B1	£ 156.8	£ 161.2	£ 156.2	£ 151.9	£ 4.4	-£ 0.6	-£ 4.9	-3.1%
Product B2	£ 162.2	£ 175.5	£ 163.8	£ 163.8	£ 13.3	£ 1.6	£ 1.6	1.0%
Product Group B	£ 319.0	£ 336.7	£ 320.0	£ 315.8	£ 17.7	£ 1.0	-£ 3.2	-1.0%
Product C1	£ 195.7	£ 200.5	£ 201.0	£ 193.1	£ 4.8	£ 5.3	-£ 2.6	-1.3%
Product CX	£ -	£ -	-£ 13.5	£ -	£ -	-£ 13.5	£ -	
Product Group C	£ 195.7	£ 200.5	£ 187.5	£ 193.1	£ 4.8	-£ 8.2	-£ 2.6	-1.3%
Total Product Groups	£ 1,037.1	£ 1,067.4	£ 1,008.2	£ 1,010.0	£ 30.3	-£ 28.9	-£ 27.1	-2.6%

Tables of numbers are still the data analysts' default mode of presentation in business. It is not difficult to see why.

You can cram a lot of 'information' into a small space, so can use them to answer many of your audience's questions. And they are easy to generate. You don't have to put much thought into it.

But, on the downside, it can be hard work trying to make sense of the data in tables.

Because of the shortcomings of targets, it might be difficult to answer basic questions like, 'Is this good performance?' And it is also almost impossible to work out whether things are getting better or getting worse.

If the numbers for previous periods are not displayed on the page (which they often aren't because it takes up too much space) the reader has to somehow reconstruct them in their head based on what they were able to remember from previous periods. Even if history was presented in the table, it is very difficult to determine trends from a limited subset of raw numbers; it requires a lot of cognitive effort and it is easy for two people to arrive at different 'answers'. To my mind it is like throwing a handful of jigsaw pieces on a table and saying to your audience 'there you go, now go work out what the picture is'.

Finally, it is also very difficult for the audience of decision makers to answer the question, 'Has something significant happened in the period that I should pay attention to?' The 'something significant' might be a 'one-off' problem with a process that requires remedial action or something that may provide early warning of a change in performance, good or bad.

If the recipients of reports like this can't make sense of them, or – perhaps worse – come to different interpretations of the facts, then the next steps in the decision-making process will be difficult, fraught and misguided.

The point I am making here is not that 'tables are bad' but that information professionals need to pay more attention to what information their audience really needs and how best to present it to ensure that they collectively get the right message, quickly and easily.

Once your audience has a clear and consistent understanding of the reality of performance, they can then do their job – bringing together their disparate knowledge, experience and skills to understand the reasons why things happened and to work out what to do for the best. And, because we human beings have very advanced visual pattern-recognition skills, we need a good understanding of how to effectively present information in a graphical form. Lists and tables of numbers just won't work.

This story illustrates the two themes in this book.

First, in order to do a better job, information professionals like the 'me' of 20 years ago need to improve our methods of communicating information – in this case reporting on performance to teams of decision makers.

This is the 'Present' of the book's title. It is a kind of 'art', and analysts are not recruited for their artistic skills. But the good news is that while there isn't a 'right' answer there are many practices that are clearly wrong, and by learning to avoid these even the most artistically challenged amongst us can quickly improve our work. I can vouch for that because I have successfully applied these ideas in my own business, and I'm no artist.

Second, we need to do a better job of extracting meaning from data. We have to do more than merely process data. We must develop an ability to understand trends and spot other meaningful patterns in performance by learning how to separate signals from noise. This accounts for the 'Sense' in the title of the book. The good news here is that, while this requires developing a bigger repertoire of analytical skills, most of the basic requirements can be fulfilled using a handful of very simple tools that every competent information analyst can easily and quickly master. They are tried and tested approaches that have been used in other walks of business life for many years that I wish the 'me' of 20 years ago had known about.

My objective in writing this book is to package this knowledge so that every practising professional can apply it in their own business as soon as they put the book down. This is why I have chosen to describe and demonstrate these approaches using the tool that every reader will have access to – Microsoft Excel – rather than reference any one of the Business Intelligence (BI) or visualization tools out there on the market. To the frustration of every software vendor in this field, Excel is still the tool of choice for analysing and reporting on performance, but also using common tools enables you to quickly try it for themselves. You don't have to 'take my word for it'. And by experimenting with these ideas yourself you can produce something you can immediately benefit from and become a better-informed purchaser of software when and if you decide to exploit these ideas and insights in a more sustainable way.

You have now heard my confessional, but don't worry about me – or beat yourself up if you find yourself in a similar position. It's not our fault. The sad fact is that none of us have ever been taught how to do things any other way, which is quite remarkable considering how far and how fast IT has advanced over the last few decades.

In my case I qualified as a management accountant in the early 1980s, and then, as now, performance reporting was regarded as the central pillar of the profession. Also, then as now, if you picked up the examination syllabus and looked for performance reporting the key technique that you are expected to have mastered is 'variance analysis'.

To better understand why this is, and why there is a need to change, let us get a handle on exactly what has changed in the 'information space' in the 30 or so years since I started work.

SOME HISTORY

Back in 1980 the computer hadn't made it out of the payroll office of most businesses. In my first 'real job' I generally added up numbers by hand, but if the list was too long or I didn't have the time I took them to one of the 'girls' (usually a formidable lady of advancing years – my mother-in-law used to be one!) operating a comptometer – a device like a manual calculating machine that you operated using all your fingers simultaneously. After a year or so I got my first electronic calculator but only after I submitted a capital proposal and had it duly recorded as an asset in the balance sheet!

Where computerized data did exist, there was not very much of it, and it was usually highly unreliable. In those days all computer systems were bespoke; customized, full of bugs and interfaces with other systems that were notoriously prone to failure and error.

In the days where data was in short supply and unreliable and where the world moved at a slower pace, analysing variances made some kind of sense. It allowed us to squeeze a lot of information out of a small amount of data and provided a mechanism to highlight problems in the data. Back then we didn't worry about the conceptual flaws in the target-setting process, our inability to understand the dynamics of performance and separate signals from noise, because *these were not the problems we then had*. And in the days when any information published within an organization was produced on a manual typewriter there was no alternative to tables of numbers.

Fast forward 30 years and the data problems we used to suffer have largely disappeared. Integrated ERP systems now provide users with copious amounts of reliable 'internal' data about our organizations, stored in huge data warehouses, and in more recent times this has been supplemented by a torrent of external data about the marketplace, our customers and competitors.

It's difficult to quantify the scale of this change, so I will use the cost of data storage as a proxy measure for the quantity of data available to businesses. In 1981, it cost roughly $700,000 to purchase a gigabyte of hard disk storage capacity. By 2014 a gigabyte cost about 3 cents – roughly a 25,000,000-fold plus reduction![1] And this number doubles every 14 months, following the same trajectory as Moore's Law, which describes the rate of change in computing processing power.[2]

Cloud technology and the mediation of so many transactions through the web has supercharged the trend towards ever greater data storage, so my guess is that we could probably add at least an extra zero to this number. IBM estimates that we are generating 2.5 quintillion bytes of data each day, more than 90% of the data that has *ever* existed was created in the last two years. You can provide your own adjective to describe the scale of this change, so long as it means 'something really big'.

The year 1981 was also when IBM sold its first ever PC. It cost the equivalent of $15,000 but ran something like 500 times slower than today's equivalent machine.

But it is not only the scale and quality of the data about the world and our technological ability to process it that are different. The world that we are seeking to understand is itself changing at an increasing pace – largely as the result of the same technological processes.

The military use the acronym VUCA to describe the volatile, uncertain, complex and ambiguous world we now inhabit. But, while the military has evolved

[1] To get a sense of the scale of this change and its implications for the way that we process data, imagine that in 1981 we had one orange and that we used a manual juice extractor to squeeze all the information we possibly could get out of this single fruit. But by 2015 we have 25 million oranges, which would fit in about 200 large articulated lorries. If all these lorries were lined up it would create a traffic jam 4 kilometres long. So, the good news is that we have a lot more oranges than we used to have. The bad news is that we are still using the 'one orange at a time' manual juice extractor.

[2] Source: http://www.mkomo.com/cost-per-gigabyte

to meet these new challenges and to exploit the huge volumes of intelligence and cheap computing power available to them, performance management professionals have barely changed their approach at all. Variance analysis is over 100 years old but in 2016 it is still promoted by professional accounting bodies as the 'gold standard' approach to performance analysis.

The only significant change in performance management practice over the last 30 years is the increased attention given to non-financial measures, or KPIs. This shift followed the 1987 publication of *Relevance Lost: The Rise and Fall of Management Accounting* by Bob Kaplan and Tom Johnson, in which they criticized traditional finance performance measures as 'too little, too late and too aggregated'. After *Relevance Lost* Kaplan teamed up with David Norton to write *The Balanced Scorecard*, which described a technique that kicked off what has been called 'the performance measurement revolution'.

The increased focus on, and use of, non-financial information that the BSC brought about was undoubtedly right and valuable. The battle to introduce different perspectives into traditional financially dominated performance reporting has now largely been won. But it has done nothing to address the other problem that was beginning to emerge at about the time Kaplan and Norton's book hit the shelves. If anything, it has made matters worse. As I mentioned earlier, when I started regularly speaking at business conferences the complaint I heard most frequently was 'we don't have enough data'. But we are no longer data impoverished – in fact, we are now overloaded with data, and adding new metrics makes this problem more acute. So, I now hear 'we have too much data'. For the first time in our history mankind is facing problems of data abundance and evolution has not equipped us to deal with it.

THE BALANCED SCORECARD

The Balanced Scorecard (BSC) is the best-known example of a performance management framework that attempts to integrate financial and non-financial metrics. It has four perspectives that contain different attributes of performance that are taken to be causally linked. So, financial performance is the result of certain aspects of the customer experience that are in turn determined by the performance of important (internal) business processes. Finally, according to this framework, business processes are made more effective and efficient though a process of learning.

The example of a BSC for a regional airline shown in Figure 1.1 illustrates how one is constructed. First, the critical attributes in each perspective are identified and the causal links between them plotted on what Kaplan and Norton call a strategy map. Then key measures for each of these attributes are defined and targets set. Improvement is achieved through initiatives, which, if successful, will be reflected in the level of financial performance.

STRATEGY MAP

MEASURES   TARGETS   INITIATIVES

Financial Perspective

- Market value
- Seat revenue
- Plane lease costs

- + 25% pa
- + 20% pa
- -5% pa

- Optimise routes
- Standardize planes

Customer Perspective

- On time rating
- Customer ranking
- Customer numbers

- Rank no 1
- 98% satisfied
- +25% pa

- Quality management
- Customer loyalty programme

Internal Perspective

- On ground time
- On time departure

- <25 minutes
- >90%

- Cycle time reduction programme

Learning Perspective

- % ground crew shareholders
- % ground crew trained

- 100% stockholders after 5 years
- 100% in year 1

- Stock ownership plan
- Training programme

Figure 1.1:
A Balanced Scorecard

An example of what a BSC could look like for an airline company.

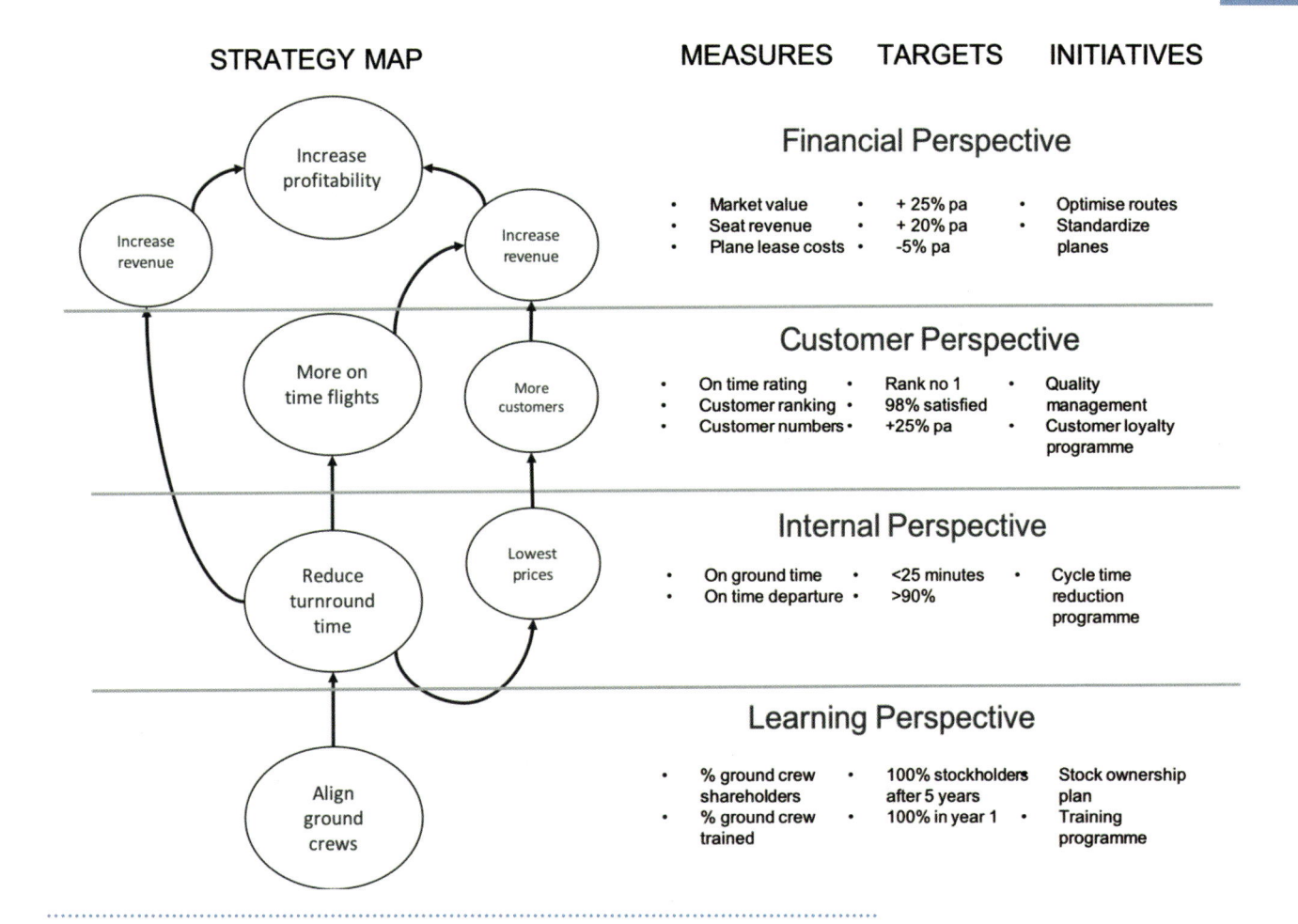

I see some parallels with the issue we face with food in the developed world.

In the distant past our ancestors didn't have access to enough calories so our bodies evolved to gorge on energy intensive foodstuffs like sugars and fats whenever they became available, which was infrequently. But things are different now. In many countries these 'unhealthy' foodstuffs are no longer in short supply but still our bodies crave more, because we can't turn off genetically programmed mechanisms. As a result, the developed world has an obesity crisis.

I think we now have the same problem with data – we think we have too much because we don't know what to do with it. Our organizations have therefore become bloated and slow moving and suffer from a range of weight related diseases – but the craving for more doesn't go away. We somehow feel that by consuming just a little bit more our hunger will be assuaged – but it never is.

Is the problem really that we have too much data? Or is it that the methods we use to process it are too crude to exploit these newfound riches? Do we need to cut back on our intake or should we upgrade our metabolic processes so that we can consume more of what we 'eat'?

I'm sure that a lot of data is captured 'just because we can' with no clear idea of how it can be used, but my belief is that we should focus more on the latter. Our real problem is not that we have too much data – it is our impoverished ability to make sense of it.

The BSC helped usher in an era when the range and nature of things that we measured expanded enormously, but the issue of how to analyse the resulting data has never been addressed. It was taken for granted that the way to analyse non-financial numbers was to compare them to a target at the end of a financial period. Where did the target come from? Nobody said: which left unchallenged the questionable assumption that any difference between the measure and the target, or any change in the measure, is meaningful and therefore grounds upon which action should be taken.

It is a similar story when it comes to communicating performance information. While everyone now seems to agree that graphics and visualization are 'a good thing' that we should do more of, there is little structured guidance about how to use graphical techniques to present and communicate performance information in an effective way.

So, while the amount of reliable data that businesses have at their disposal has expanded exponentially, as has the computational power potentially available to analyse and communicate it, the techniques that we use evolved in an era of data scarcity and have not changed at all.

The other thing that hasn't changed is the bandwidth of the human brain. We are no cleverer than we were 100 or 1,000 years ago. If anything, the challenge facing communicators has become bigger due to the fact the capacity available for performance information has shrunk because of the increase in the demands on our attention from other parts of our densely connected digitized world. And the intolerance for anything that is difficult to digest has increased.

Unsurprisingly the call now is for 'simplification'.

The 's' word is often used to support moves to focus attention on a narrower range of metrics – the 'vital few' – or to use high-level aggregates or averages. Because the human brain is finite and the demands on it are potentially infinite some form of selection is inevitable. But, if this is done unscientifically, we risk throwing away or systematically ignoring information that has been carefully and expensively collected. To paraphrase Stafford Beer, the great systems thinker, ignorance is the ultimate form of simplification.

The urge to simplify is the driver of probably the only 'innovation' in data analysis or presentation that has made it into mainstream use in the last 30 years. RAG charts, sometimes called traffic lights, use red, amber and green colour coded icons or numbers to signify whether something is good, bad or indifferent. In principle the idea is great, but if there is no scientific rationale behind the classification of values (which in my experience there rarely is) all we do is hard code our ignorance and make it more visually attractive. Attractive, that is, to everyone except that 10% of the male population who are red–green colour blind. And any member of the audience coming from parts of the world where red signifies something 'good' rather than 'bad' is likely to be totally confused.

There is no doubt that in order to extract sense from our superabundant data we need to find some way to filter out what is irrelevant or distracting so that we can focus our limited attention on that small proportion of our data sets that contain actionable insights. We then need a way of communicating this quickly and effectively in a manner that preserves this meaning. The problem is that the tools we traditionally use – especially in Finance – are incapable of performing this role.

I started this chapter with a story about a turning point in my career when I first realized that what I had been doing was completely inadequate. If you already 'get it' or are impatient to get to the meat of the book you might want to skip the next section because I am going to drill down into the problem some more. But the assumption that performance can only be understood by comparison with targets is so deeply embedded that I expect many readers will need more persuasion before they are prepared to leave behind the comforting assumptions of a working lifetime.

Simple 'actual to target' pairwise comparisons are ubiquitous in organizational life, but I suspect that accountants will be more reluctant to acknowledge their limitations. The edifice of financial performance management is built on what we call variance analysis – which is an 'actual against target' comparison on drugs.

Variance analysis takes the difference between target and actual and breaks it down into its constituent parts thereby – so the theory goes – exposing the reason for the deviation. Except that it doesn't. It just creates the illusion of insight.

Understand how variance analysis works and you understand the reason why we finance guys struggle to extract and communicate information in a way that other members of the organizational community find meaningful and useful.

VARIANCE ANALYSIS: RIGOROUS BUT WRONG

It is easy to forget that the commonplace 'furniture' of working life, barely noticeable because we are so familiar with it, hasn't always been there. Variance analysis is one such piece of social technology. And it wasn't 'discovered', it was invented to help people deal with a particular set of problems at a certain time. Only when we appreciate the specific problems that it was designed to fix can we begin to recognize its shortcomings when faced with a different set of problems of the sort that we now have.

Prior to about 1900 variance analysis didn't exist in its current form. The first book on the technique was published in 1918 and initially it was used to analyse costs using targets based on the material standards developed by engineers for production control purposes. Prior to the 20th century most businesses were run by owners rather than professional managers or by engineers focussed on manufacturing operations. However, the 1920s was an era of rapid industrialization, when the first multidivisional companies were born, initially in the motor industry – the 'high-tech' sector of the time. The complexity of these large diversified businesses and the separation of ownership from day-today management meant that new ways of measuring and managing performance were needed.

The market was therefore primed for the idea of exercising control through budget-based analysis and a young Chicago Business School professor called James O McKinsey duly obliged by publishing the first book on the topic in 1922. When he went on to found the world's first consulting company budgetary control became the world's original consulting 'product'.

McKinsey and his peers advocated managing by setting detailed targets (budgets) for every financial component of a business and subsequently controlling performance by analysing variances from budgets. The expectation was that performance could be steered back to the predetermined plan in the same way that a manufacturing plant could be directed to fulfil its production quota.

Given the rudimentary state of business record keeping and computation technology at the time this approach was a considerable advance on the alternative – an amalgam of financial accounts and production records. Although the process of creating a budget is often time consuming and tedious the process of analysing performance by referring to budgets – once they have been set – is straightforward, so it is easy to see why the idea caught on. So simple and obvious in fact that it can blind us to its shortcomings.

I will use a very simple sales example, in Table 1.2, to illustrate these shortcomings.

Table 1.2:
Simple Sales Variances

A simple variance analysis example. But how meaningful is it?

Revenue	January	February	March
Actual	25	40	45
Budget	30	35	48
Variance	-5	5	-3
%	-20%	13%	-7%

As you can see, in Table 1.2 sales revenue is lower in January than in the other months in the first quarter, but the fact that the budget is lower for the month might suggest that this is unavoidable – perhaps the result of a post-Christmas dip. Revenue in March is marginally higher than in February, but the budget was set even higher. So, as a result, the variance against budget in March was negative. That suggests that performance is better in January and February than in March.

But is that right? How sure can we be of this? Are these variances instead the result of a flawed process of target setting or perhaps just a manifestation of random fluctuations in revenue around a stable long-term trend? The uncomfortable truth is that with a simple pairwise comparison of a single period value and a target set using an unknown process we simply can't answer any of the basic 'big' questions we have about performance with any confidence.

Why Do We Need To Change The Way We Do Stuff?

- Is this good performance or bad?
- Is it getting better or worse?
- Has anything significant happened that requires action to be taken?

But accountants don't stop here. They need more detail, and they like tidy arithmetical processes.

If you pick up any textbook on budgetary control, you will probably find somewhere in the section on performance analysis a picture like the one in Figure 1.2.

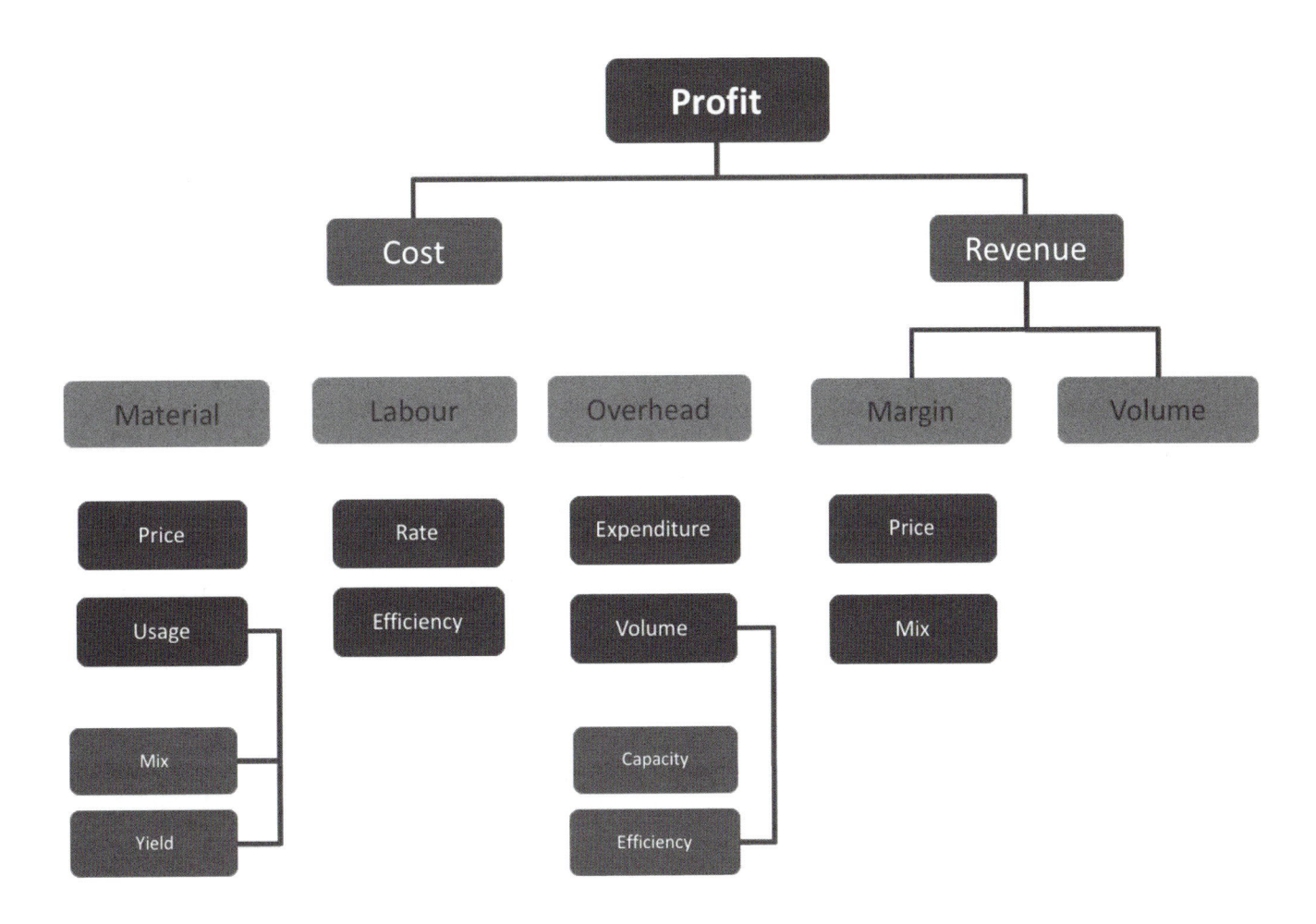

You can understand the appeal of the variance tree. It is logical and structured. There appears to be no escape from the forensic glare of the controllers in finance. But its apparent rigour is also its weakness.

One of the reasons why accountants like budgets is that they are arithmetically coherent – they add up neatly. Because budgets are built from the bottom up, we can drill down from a high-level variance to lower-level ones to uncover the 'root cause' – or so they would like to believe. In Table 1.3, for example, I have broken down the revenue variance into two constituent parts: price and volume.

Figure 1.2:
Variance tree

This demonstrates how a high-level profit variance can be broken down into the various contributory factors to provide a comprehensive breakdown of the reasons for the deviation from target or plan – assuming that every element of the plan is reasonable and every measure is free from noise, which is unlikely ever to be the case.

Revenue	January	February	March
Actual	25	40	45
Budget	30	35	48
Variance	**-5**	**5**	**-3**
%	-20%	13%	-7%

Breakdown

Actual			
Price/unit	5	5	5
Volume (units)	5	8	9
Budget			
Price/unit	5	5	6
Volume (units)	6	7	8
Variances			
Price	0	0	-9
Volume	-5	5	6
Variance %			
Price	0%	0%	-20%
Volume	-20%	13%	13%

Table 1.3:
Revenue variance broken down into price and volume

A worked example showing how 'comprehensive' variance analyses can be misleading.

Now our variance analysis in Table 1.3 is telling us that the volume performance in March was better than the other two months and that the negative revenue variance in March is the result of a price rise that we assumed for March that didn't take place.

Does this now make the performance in March good – a continuation of a favourable upward trend in sales? Or is it bad because we failed to get the price increase through? Or was the price increase a guess made six months ago when the budget was set or a 'plug' figure somebody used to make the total budget come back to the numbers that head office wanted to see?

Again, we just don't know. More detail generates more questions not more answers. And the more granular the data gets the more noise swamps any signals that the data may contain. We become overwhelmed by data about individual events and so lose sight of the patterns that convey meaning and insight, in the same way that we lose a sense of the picture on a TV screen when we focus on individual pixels. Too many trees but no wood. All content, but no context.

To be clear, I am not arguing that variance analysis can never work – just that it is wrong to use it to try to understand the performance of a business as a whole rather than, say, to use it to control product costs.[3] Why?

[3]. I don't mean to imply that targets work perfectly in a production environment either! Indeed, one of the approaches to performance management that avoids the use of arbitrary targets originated in manufacturing, as we will discover later in the book.

1. To produce a meaningful variance analysis, you need meaningful targets to start with. The manager of a manufacturing operation can do this because she can refer to a product specification that defines exactly what materials should be and in what quantities. But the manager of a sales force can only speculate about the behaviour of his customers or competitors, which makes for unreliable targets.
2. It also assumes that every piece of data is a pristine manifestation of the truth, unsullied by chance or random factors. Production processes are explicitly designed to minimize variation. Raw materials have to conform to specifications and production processes are tightly defined. Other business processes are unavoidably more open to the outside world that cannot be controlled in this way, so randomness and noise have a much bigger impact on the data. As a result, no single data point represents 'the truth'.
3. Finally, conventional variance analysis assumes history is largely irrelevant. It is understood that all the information you need to interpret performance and to determine the appropriate course of action is contained in a single variance number. But life is not like that – it is a continuum. What you measure today is a product of actions taken in the past and an exclusive focus on a single period obscures the play of cause and effect and the direction of travel of the business – good or bad. A single piece of data is a snapshot in time, like a frame in a film. To understand performance – the behaviour of a system in time – we need to stitch the snapshots together. Variances do not give us the information we need to make decisions because every image in our performance movie is distorted by noise and the myriad of false and arbitrary assumptions made in setting targets and is presented to us one frame at a time.

The bottom line is that while variance analysis might be simple and provide us with neatly packaged answers, we should treat the results with a great deal of caution. Instead of simplifying the task of analysing performance, variance analysis makes it more complex, and more reliant on personal interpretation.

And, the more granular the level of analysis the bigger the problems become. More detailed analysis requires that more targets be set, which makes the process more bureaucratic and the targets more arbitrary. Greater detail also means that noise has a bigger impact on the data. So, instead of providing clarity, variance analysis creates irrelevant and misleading information. And by supressing the time dimension it makes it more difficult to see data in its historical context – the 'bigger picture'.

Finally, the obsession with targets and variances makes the whole process of performance reporting laborious and time consuming, but it also can make the business less responsive. As we have seen with the March price increase in the example in Table 1.3, targets that might have made sense when they were set quickly become out of date but the interconnected nature of the budgeting system makes changing targets difficult and disorientating because single changes cascade through the whole network.

In conclusion, while simple pairwise comparisons of actuals and targets to analyse performance met an important need in the formative years of professional management when data was scarce and communication difficult, it leaves us poorly equipped to tackle the challenges and opportunities faced by 21st-century managers. And while full-blown variance analysis of the kind shown here is a less common feature of financial performance management than it used to be, the target-driven performance management culture is in rude health right throughout organizations, despite its manifest weaknesses.

VARIANCES ARE NOT ALL BAD

My criticisms of variance analysis are directed at its use to analyse performance. This shouldn't be taken to mean that I believe all forms of comparison are invalid. Quite the contrary.

A number in isolation signifies nothing. It has to be compared to something else to mean something – the issue is what should it be compared to and what conclusions can be drawn from this? Indeed, Part 2 of this book will go on to advocate methods based on comparing numbers from the **same data series** to:

- Expose patterns of behaviour
- Help spot changes in the level and nature of performance
- Quantify the level of noise and so by exception detect signals buried in the data

Also, in my previous book (**Future Ready**) I strongly advocated systematically comparing actuals with forecasts, not to judge performance but as a means of testing and improving the models and assumptions on which the forecasts were based. Variances between actual and forecast are a reflection of the reliability of the forecast **not** the quality of performance.

Finally, I have devoted a lot of space to decrying the way in which targets are set and how they are compared to actual data, but there are ways to do both of these things that avoid most of the problems associated with simple variance analysis, as we will discover later.

Variance analyses have gripped the corporate imagination because they are simple to calculate and to understand. They are also a seductive tool for senior executives since they offer the prospect of being able to direct performance without having to get involved in the management of the business: you just set targets once a year and administer systems of rewards and punishments to encourage compliance. You can see why that might be popular!

But perhaps another reason why variance analysis took hold in the 1920s was that the results could easily be communicated using the technology available at that time – paper and typewriters. Tables of numbers are easy to produce and compress a lot of information into a relatively small space whereas charts had to be drawn manually and take up a lot of real estate on the page.

Why Do We Need To Change The Way We Do Stuff?

Tables are an efficient way of cramming pieces of numerical data, like variances, onto a single sheet of paper, and all other things being equal the less space that you use the better. But does that make them an effective device for communicating information about performance?

Let me answer this question using another example. Table 1.4 gives a summary of the simulated performance of a simple one-product company XYZ Ltd that I created for this book, using variances shown in a conventional table format.

	Quarter 4				Year to Date				2017	
	Actual	Budget	Variance	v Last Year	Actual	Budget	Variance	v Last Year	Budget	v Last Year
Turnover	245	262	-16	-4%	944	970	-26	5%	989	5%
COS	131	139	8	3%	506	527	20	-4%	539	-7%
GP	114	123	-9	-4%	438	443	-6	5%	450	3%
Gross Margin %	47%	47%	0%	0%	46%	46%	1%	0%	45%	-1%
A&P	36	37	1	2%	141	141	-0	-2%	140	1%
Overheads	39	40	1	-5%	139	148	9	-4%	136	2%
Profit	38	46	-7	-14%	157	154	3	11%	174	11%

Table 1.4:
Performance of XYZ Ltd

Note: COS = Cost of Sales, GP = Gross Profit and A&P = Advertising and Promotional expenditure.

How easy is it to make sense of the analysis of performance in this table. Put yourself in the position of the recipient of this report and use it to analyse the performance of XYZ Ltd. Try to answer these questions:

1. Is this good or bad performance?
2. Is it getting better or worse?
3. Has anything significant just happened?
4. How credible is the budget for next year?

How did you find it?

If you are used to analysing numerical information you will probably find it easy to come up with some answers, but you might be less sure in them than you would have been before you read my criticisms of variance analysis. And I'm confident that if you share this table with someone you will find that they come to slightly different conclusions than your own.

The other thing that I'm sure that you will have noticed is that trying to make sense of all this is hard work. You will have had to really concentrate in order to answer the questions I posed, and you might have noticed your eyes jumping around the table comparing one number with another as you tried to build up a picture of what was going on. If you weren't aware of this take another look at the table and retrace the path that your eyes took.

Any lack of confidence you might have in your conclusions and the sense of effort you experienced is not because the task I set you is inherently difficult. My 'toy' company is hugely less complex than anything that you deal with in real life. These uncomfortable sensations are a sure sign that I chose a very poor way to communicate information. It simply isn't a good fit with the way that our brains work.

The human brain has evolved over millions of years to efficiently assimilate information from our natural environment. This is why our visual perception is so much better developed than any other of our senses and why it is particularly good at spotting patterns and movement – provided information is presented in a way that appeals to our eyes.

In contrast, the symbolic systems we use in the West for communicating numbers emerged only 500 years ago when Leonardo Fibonacci introduced Arabic numbering systems into Europe.[4] We are born with highly-developed visual circuitry, but we have to laboriously train our brain to use numbers, which is why so much of our formal education is devoted to it, and – even then – some 'well-educated' people fail to acquire more than the most basic level of numeracy. But even if you are highly numerically literate you will find it much more effortful to assimilate the numbers in the tables in this chapter than if the same data was presented visually. And while two people may come to different conclusions about the meaning of a set of numbers there is much less chance of them perceiving the same shape in a different way, for the same reason: it is 'easy' and 'more natural'.

And yet, despite our unsatisfactory personal experiences with tables and the ubiquity of computing power at our fingertips, performance reporting in business – particularly that produced by finance people – is still hugely reliant on tabular presentations and on decks of paper.

In summary, thanks to technological advances our capability to collect data, to analyse it and to communicate information to an audience has increased enormously over the last few decades. But our chronic addiction to approaches created to solve the problems faced by the first professional managers nearly a century ago severely limits our ability to exploit this potential. This is wasteful and it imprisons our minds. Our world is colourful, rich and full of life and ambiguity, but the 'pictures' of it that we create in our head are no better than bad caricatures.

The problem is clear. The challenge is to work out what to do differently.

[4]. In fact, the Arabs imported the idea from India. It should really be called the Hindu numbering system.

THE BOTTOM LINE

To summarize, there are four main problems associated with traditional approaches that we need to overcome if we are to make the process of understanding and communicating performance fit for the modern world.

Too static
Performance is continuous but conventional approaches present us with a series of snapshots separated in time. As a result, trend information is blurred, and patterns of cause and effect are hard to detect.

Failure to distinguish between signals and noise

Data carries signals but is also unavoidably infected with noise. Conventional approaches do not enable us to distinguish between the two. Because we do not recognize the existence of noise, we falsely assume that *any difference between two numbers is meaningful*. And by acting on corrupted information we often amplify the noise, hence making it even more difficult to distinguish fact from fiction.

Confuse variance with performance

Comparing 'point' targets to actual outcomes is an unreliable guide to real performance because of the existence of noise and because targets are usually set without any sense of context many months in advance, often by an arbitrary or politically-driven process.

Do not take account of the brain's processing limitations and strengths

Our capacity to collect data is unlimited but the bandwidth of our brains is fixed and subject to ever-increasing demands. Conventional approaches to analysing and communicating performance, using numbers alone, are difficult for brains to process. This is inefficient and increases the risk of confusion and misinterpretation.

WHY TECHNOLOGY WON'T SAVE US

However, you might be thinking, what about the things that we hear so much about these days when we go to conferences or read business blogs? The media is full of stories about Big Data, data analytics, data visualization, dashboards and more recently AI. Surely, they will have solved these problems?

It goes without saying that better software tools are clearly *good things*. But it would be wrong to assume that there is a technological silver bullet out there that will solve all our problems for the same reason that buying a Stradivarius is unlikely to improve your fiddle playing. Tools carry potentiality; they don't deliver any results on their own. It takes hours of practice to play a violin and as far as data analysis is concerned most of us are still in kindergarten. Also, overplaying the technological card blinds us to the beautiful music we can make right now on our desktop machines, if we only knew how. But there are other more fundamental reasons why I'm sceptical about some of the technological hype out there.

Big Data is a new word that describes a phenomenon that is not new. But it has come to assume a much more prominent and important place in our everyday lives for good reason. We had lots of data back in the 1990s but what we are faced with now is a whole new ball game:

1. Volume. There is a lot more data than there ever has been, and it is growing at an exponential rate. For example, IBM estimates that we are generating 2.5 quintillion bytes of data each day, more than 90% of which was created in the last two years.

2. Velocity. The data is available much more quickly particularly if it is sourced from the Internet or smart devices like our phones or the sensors in our car.
3. Variety. It is available in many forms. Traditionally data was highly structured – classified and organized – but today a lot of data is unstructured, particularly if it takes the form of text (e.g. tweets), sounds or images.

BIG DATA ISN'T NEW – THE FUTURE HAS ALREADY HAPPENED

If you think that I am making too much of this Big Data stuff – that it is either not going to happen or that somehow technology will sort this out for us when it does – or that I am exaggerating when I say that the risk is that we will simply ignore this, let me tell you a story.

I can't remember exactly when, perhaps around the end of the 1990s, the retailers that my old company sold to started sharing their EPOS (electronic point of sale) data with us. Think of it – every day (or even more frequently) we had records of how much we had sold and in which store.

Think of it.

How useful would it be to be able to track the sales of our products on a daily basis? We could spot emerging trends almost instantly and work out how well our interventions (promotions/advertising/product innovations) were working. With the retailers' support we could carry out trials in limited areas to find out what worked and what didn't before pouring huge sums of money in. In theory, we could dispense with an enormous amount of expensive market research, which was necessarily less reliable because it was based on consumer intentions not their actual behaviour. And we could check that our customer did what they promised to do when we handed over cash to pay for prominent displays in their stores.

But what actually happened?

Every day the files landed with a big electronic thud on the company's servers and just sat there, neglected and unloved.

Why? Because, although the potential benefits were obvious, no one had any idea how to extract meaning from such a huge volume of fast-changing, noisy and messy data. So we just ignored it.

The future has already arrived and is waiting for us to hop on the bus. Get on or get left behind.

Just having data is of course of little value, and this is where data analytics come in. To convert this data into information we need to structure the data and then look for patterns in it. In theory these patterns represent information that we can do something with.

Unfortunately, it is not quite that simple.

The first problem we face is our friend noise. The more granular and unstructured data is the more noise it contains. And as anyone who has ever looked up at a cloud and seen a rabbit (or Elvis) knows, it is possible for us to detect patterns in noise and, as it turns out, computers are prone to this as well. This was recognized a long time ago, by Johnny von Neumann the brilliant mathematician. 'With four parameters I can fit an elephant,' he said, 'and with five I can make him wiggle his trunk.' What he meant was that the more data we have and the greater the sophistication of our techniques the better the chance of coming up with something that is complete nonsense.

I can't express this any better than Nate Silver did, in his book *The Signal and the Noise: The Art and Science of Prediction*. Silver is famous for his ability to analyse complex real-world process, like elections, and make stunningly accurate predictions based on the application of mathematical technique, so he is no luddite.

> "This is why our predictions may be more prone to failure in the era of Big Data. As there is an exponential increase in the amount of available information, there is likewise an exponential increase in the number of hypotheses to investigate. For instance, the U.S. government now publishes data on about 45,000 economic statistics. If you want to test for relationships between all combinations of two pairs of these statistics– is there a causal relationship between the bank prime loan rate and the unemployment rate in Alabama? – that gives you literally one billion hypotheses to test. But the number of meaningful relationships in the data–those that speak to causality rather than correlation and testify to how the world really works–is orders of magnitude smaller. Nor is it likely to be increasing at nearly so fast a rate as the information itself; **there isn't any more truth in the world than there was before the Internet or the printing press. Most of the data is just noise, as most of the universe is filled with empty space**." (my emphasis)

Silver refers to the complexity that is an inevitable consequence of scale – the unimaginable number of mathematical combinations. But, even if it were not complex, it is easy to demonstrate why the real world cannot be understood through simple mathematical association alone. For example, a computer might notice a correlation between the sales of men's shorts and ice cream, but it cannot know whether the ice cream sales cause the sale of shorts (perhaps because the ice cream drips on bare legs rather than on fabric) or vice versa. And it takes a human being to spot that both are caused by something else altogether, which might not appear in the data set at all – temperature.[5] The difficulty of spotting causal patterns in data is complicated further when we have to factor in the time dimension as well. Something that we observe now might be the result of actions taken one month, one quarter or even a year ago, and the key event might even not have been captured as 'data' at all – like 'that's when we started using cute animals in our TV adverts'.

[5]. Arguably we only know for sure that a relationship is causal rather than purely a correlation through action – when we do something and get the response we expect. Analysis alone simply provides us with a plausible hypothesis to test.

I could go on, but you should have got the message by now. This technological stuff might be great for letting you know that 'people who order this item also bought...' but, because this 'insight' is the product of a relatively simple correlation, I wouldn't use it to do anything complicated like choosing what meal to cook for my in-laws this evening.

Likewise, there has been an explosion of interest in data visualization – the use of graphics to help us understand complex phenomena. This is undoubtedly a good thing since it exploits the visual pattern-seeking power of our brains and the processing capabilities of computers. But there is a downside to this potential. Fancy software is not cheap and not only is it complex to use but achieving good results requires a degree of design skill that it is unreasonable to expect from the average analyst who probably can't tell the difference between a Rembrandt and a regression analysis. Ultimately, only brains can understand how brains work and it takes a skilled brain to work out how best to design something that generates the right response in another individual's brain.

Dashboards go some way to solving this problem for us. They are specifically designed to help us make sense of performance data and come with a pre-packaged set of design templates and graphical tools. But they have a couple of downsides.

Firstly, their ability to convey insights is limited by the ability to extract meaning from data. So, if you do not know how to separate noise from signal you could be doing the equivalent of saying 'look at the rabbit' rather than 'it's a cloud, just ignore it'. Communicating meaningless noise in a compelling fashion is not what we should be aiming for.

There is a second, more profound reason that I think can easily be overlooked in our understandable excitement with what this kind of technology can do.

Performance reporting is embedded in a social process we call decision-making. Computerized dashboards are, however, designed for individual use. They are tools for personal productivity and enlightenment. This is not a bad thing, but because everyone will use them differently, they do not help create the shared collective consciousness necessary for effective organizational action.

This was brought home to me forcibly recently when I got a request from a user of the forecast performance reporting dashboard that my own software company sells. 'You know these charts you have on the top right-hand corner of the home page?' he asked me. 'Is there any easy way to copy a bunch of these for different accounts into PowerPoint?' My first reaction was unprintable, along the lines of 'That's not the point you dummy! We built this thing so that you could do everything on screen: zoom in and out, up and down, slice and dice – anything you want. You can't do that with PowerPoint you…*****!!!'

On reflection, however, I realized that I was the dummy. Our client was reporting on forecast performance to his company's leadership team, made up of people from other functions, such as sales, all of who had an input into the forecasting process. Quite properly, he wanted to use a specific subset of the charts for our tool to influence the behaviour of his colleagues in a very particular way. He had a specific message that he wanted to communicate so it was important that the target audience saw the same charts at the same time along with the same contextual commentary that he – as an expert – was able to supply.

The point I had failed to realize is that dashboards are designed to help an *individual* make sense of things for herself, but that they are unsuited for the task of reporting, communicating a distilled and crafted message to a *group* of decision makers. Reporting is a social process not a personal one, so we need a tool that can broadcast information to an audience not help individuals to generate it for themselves.

The implication of this insight is that we should not think of information professionals as being like plumbers who design and maintain data pipework (although this is important). They have responsibility for content as well. They are not authors of fiction or public relations (PR) professionals spinning a story for their clients. Their – your – role is closer to that of a serious journalist, responsible for presenting a clear, concise and balanced view of the world, without disguising its complexity and ambiguity.

In this role technology is your friend but it's not a silver bullet that will make all your problems disappear. You need to learn how it can best serve you by desk learning and careful thought. But there is no substitute for the experience that comes from experimentation with simple tools like Excel that you already know how to use. While it is unlikely to be the final destination, experimenting with spreadsheets will make us better-informed consumers when it comes to buying and using more sophisticated tools.

THE SOLUTIONS AND HOW TECHNOLOGY *CAN* HELP US

So far, I've focussed on problems. From now on it's about solutions.

I have tried to ensure that the solutions I recommend are conceptually and scientifically robust but also practical and easy to apply. And rather than using rhetoric or spin stories based on artfully edited case studies to win you round I will show you how to do a better job and encourage you to try things out for yourself.

The solutions I will demonstrate mirror the problems I have defined.

Dynamic – to expose trends
Performance is a pattern of behaviour that cannot be captured by focussing on individual data points. We need to measure and analyse performance in a way that exposes trends and trajectories.

Filtered – to deal with noise
We must to be able to separate the wheat (the signal) from the chaff (the noise) to focus our limited attention, knowledge and intellect on the right things and avoid being distracted by – or worse reacting to – randomness. Simple arithmetic can't so this for us. We need to view data through a probabilistic lens and use statistical filters to help us extract insights from big noisy data sets.

*Reframe the meaning of performance –
to reflect its complex multi dimension*

We need nuanced targets or comparators that are less arbitrary than the targets produced by traditional processes like annual budgeting and better reflect the actual business context and performance potential. They have to help us track performance *over* time, rather than being anchored on points *in* time, and help us filter out the influence of noise.

Communicate more effectively – to exploit the capability of our brains

It is imperative for us to develop a better understanding of how to communicate meaning effectively to an audience of decision makers with differing knowledge, experiences and capabilities. This needs to be based on an understanding of how the brain processes information and a grasp of good design principles that exploit its capabilities.

I have argued that we should not look to technology as a silver bullet that will solve all our problems for us. But it is equally clear to me that we will not be successful in achieving any of these goals without the help of technology. However, we first need to learn how to best exploit it.

All of the techniques and approaches I describe in the following pages can be deployed using paper and personal calculators if you want to adopt a 'back to nature' approach to performance measurement. This would be perverse, so I expect and encourage you to experiment using desktop productivity software such as spreadsheets. Excel will, however, only get you so far. To implement methods that I recommend at scale and at speed in real life you will most likely need specialized software – but having experimented using simpler, more forgiving technology you will have developed a good grasp of what will work best in your organization and what you want from a specialized software solution.

I have also explained that I do not believe that dashboards are the solution to the problems of communicating meaning – primarily because they are designed to support personal understanding and enquiry not the social process of decision-making. Enormous progress has, however, been made in the last few years in understanding and codifying good practice in dashboard design and graphical communication, led by pioneers like Edward Tufte and Stephen Few. And these principles can be applied directly to the design of performance reports even if they continue to be produced in Excel or PowerPoint and distributed on paper. Again, I encourage you to practice with these ideas and experience for yourself the impact they can make. And what you learn can then be applied to customizing the dashboard software you have already got or are minded to buy.

That's enough of the preamble to this book – let's start ambling.

Why Do We Need To Change The Way We Do Stuff?

Learning	Reason
Why we shouldn't confuse data with truth.	All data contains noise, as well as a signal. It requires more than one data point and a scientifically robust inference process to enable us to detect the difference between the two.
How targets can be unhelpful as a guide to performance.	Fixed targets assume that you can know in advance what represents 'good performance', which is often difficult in a fast-moving world. Also, the process of target setting is often political and, particularly at a granular level, somewhat arbitrary.
Why traditional 'actual to target' comparisons are an unreliable guide to performance.	Comparing a single data point infected with an unknown level of noise with a target of unknown validity is more likely to confuse and misdirect actions than enlighten or promote wise interventions.
Why tables of numbers are not effective at communicating performance information.	The human brain struggles to assimilate information presented in a numerical form and tables present data in a way that requires a lot of effort to isolate relevant information.
How traditional approaches fail to guide intervention by decision makers.	Because numbers either represent single data points or are highly summarized it is difficult to distinguish between what is 'normal' to be ignored and what is abnormal, requiring an intervention.
Why these long-standing weaknesses have now become a major problem for organizations.	The volume of data, the pace of change and the shortened attention span of decision makers makes the failure of traditional methods to assess and communicate performance information effectively a major problem.
Why attempts to simplify using tools like RAG 'traffic light' charts are dangerous.	Attempts to classify performance without any scientific rational for making distinctions is unhelpful at best and positively misleading at worst.
Why pairwise comparisons between actuals and forecasts are helpful.	Deviations between actuals and forecasts should not be used to judge performance but they are essential to ensure that forecasts are a reliable guide to the future.
How Big Data makes things worse not better.	The ratio of signals to noise declines as the amount of data increases. So, while the potential for greater insight exists it is more difficult to extract meaning.
Why sophisticated mathematical techniques will not provide the solution.	Mathematical techniques rely on correlation, so at best they can do no more than spot patterns that may or may not be the result of causal relationships.

part 2
Sense:
The Science of Extracting Meaning From Data

sense

/sɛns/
noun

1. a faculty by which the body perceives an external stimulus; one of the faculties of sight, smell, hearing, taste, and touch.
2. a feeling that something is the case.

chapter 2

Performance Reporting: What is it and What Has it Got to Do With Brains?

> In which we will explore the concepts of 'performance' and 'reporting' and how an appreciation of the way that the brain functions can help us design better tools and more effective strategies for understanding and communicating performance in a world of Big Data.

WHAT IS PERFORMANCE?

Let's start at the beginning.

What comes to mind when you hear the word 'performance'?

Performance is one of those words that we might think we understand but is as slippery as a bar of soap when we try to pin it down. For example, the word performance is used in the context of businesses to describe the acting out of a play, the discharge of obligations under the terms of a contract, or the characteristics of a car. What – if anything – do all these uses of the word performance have in common?

I think the quality shared by all these uses of the word performance is that they relate to *purposeful action.*

Something has been performed when its intended purpose has been fulfilled and performance describes the act of fulfilment. So, when we describe something as a 'good performance' we are saying that the intended purpose has been fulfilled.

For example, top speed and acceleration are the most important performance attributes of a sport car, so that is the criteria we apply when we judge its performance. Whereas for a family saloon we would place greater weight on fuel efficiency and comfort. Because these two types of car were designed to fulfil different purposes, the definition of 'good performance' differs as well.

For a business organization the purpose will differ depending on things like the ownership structure, its industry and its strategy, so it is difficult to define performance in a way that is equally relevant to them all. However, what almost all businesses share is the need to survive – that is, to be a going concern.[1]

So, we cannot judge performance based on a single variable. We need to take account of a range of numbers. At least one of them must be a financial variable, such as profit or cash, since an organization cannot survive if it is not financially viable – even a sports car needs fuel. But it is very unlikely that financial variables alone will suffice.

WHAT IS PURPOSE?

The topic of 'purpose' is subject to lively debate in the business world at the moment - and one that we don't have the time or space to go into in any detail in this book. But given that it is so central to the idea of performance I cannot ignore it altogether either.

For the last decade or so in business the subject has been treated as though it was settled because business orthodoxy was in the grip of the Friedman doctrine.

This is named after the famous Chicago School economist Milton Friedman who, in his 1964 book *Capitalism and Freedom*, opined: 'there is one and only one social responsibility of business - to use its resources and engage in activities designed to increase its profits so long as it stays within the rules of the game, which is to say, engages in open and free competition without deception or fraud'.

Over subsequent years this view came to dominate mainstream thinking and led to the development of concepts such as shareholder value, often tied to massive incentives in an attempt to align the interests of managers (agents) with those of shareholders (the principals).

In practice it has not turned out to be quite as straightforward as its advocates hoped. The exclusive focus on shareholders and it has been blamed for everything from short termism in business, egregious behaviour that sometimes tipped over into outright fraud and the creation of divisions and inequalities that erode the foundations of the liberal societies that provided capitalists with the freedoms they enjoy.

But there were always other views on the purpose of organizations, most notably those articulated by Peter Drucker. In 1954 he wrote: 'there is only one valid definition of business purpose: to create a customer...It is the customer who determines what a business is. For it is the customer, and he alone, who through being willing to pay for a good or for a service, converts economic resources into wealth, things into goods. What the business thinks it produces is not of first importance–especially not to the future of the business and to its success.'

More recently, there has been a tendency to conceive an organization having a purpose that transcends the merely economic relationships between it and its shareholders or customers. Two of the most successful business books of recent years, *Reinventing*

[1]. The exception to this are single purpose entities, for example, businesses that are set up to build a major piece of infrastructure that will be wound up when the job is completed.

Organizations by Frederick Laloux and *Start with Why* by Simon Sinek, are based on this premise.

But, while the idea is attractive and no doubt inspiring for those people who believe they are working in an organization that has a higher goal, the notion that this can be simply defined or created by words is, to my mind, simplistic.

I believe that what really counts is not what people say but what they do. 'Purpose' is therefore what people infer from observed behaviour not what people say the purpose is. After all, Enron claimed that 'we treat others as we would like to be treated ourselves...we do not tolerate abusive or disrespectful treatment. Ruthlessness, callousness and arrogance don't belong here'. And purpose is probably not a simple, one dimensional thing that is independent of context.

My sense is that it is better to think of it as a hierarchy of needs that shapes behaviour differently based on the prevailing circumstances – rather like Maslow's famous hierarchy. If you are in danger of going out of business, your behaviour is motivated by the need to stay solvent, so economic needs (physiological in Maslow's terms) will appear to be the purpose. At the other extreme if economic needs have been fulfilled, higher-level goals (such as self-actualization) may be the primary driver of behaviour and thus be what people experience as 'the purpose'.

So, purpose is not a simple thing, but that doesn't invalidate the need to imbue work with meaning – as we shall discuss later in the context of targets and motivation. As articulated by Argyris and Shoen we should constantly strive to bring our enacted values – those that drive behaviour – in line with our espoused values – what we say we believe is important.

But while the subject of purpose is not simple there are two things we can say with confidence:

- If an organization is insolvent it cannot fulfil any kind of purpose. So, while financial considerations are rarely **the** purpose of an organization, they are always relevant to the assessment of its performance
- If targets drive the behaviour of people within an organization, then the nature of the targets will become the enacted purpose of the organization...not what anyone says the purpose is.

Let's now turn to the attributes of performance variables.

Level

The most obvious dimension of performance is its level. We expect sports cars to be quick – the faster the better. Measuring the level of a variable should enable us to answer the question, 'Is performance good or bad?'

Traditional performance reporting systems, like variance analysis, really only address the question of the level of performance, which is taken to be the gap between the actual value of the variable and the target. But this only works if the target is a meaningful expression of the purpose of an organization, which is trickier than it sounds.

One reason why it is difficult to express purpose in quantitative terms is that it is a relative concept. What passes for good performance in a sports car or a family saloon depends on the attributes of other cars, which is changing all the time. Similarly, a publicly quoted company needs to at least match the performance of its peers if it is not to be consumed by them. And, while you can speculate, it is impossible to know in advance how other organizations will perform, not least because they are trying to outperform you!

This fundamental paradox makes 'objective' target setting so difficult, a fact that traditional performance management systems gloss over. And this difficulty is compounded by the fact that the vast majority of variables that we measure have a very indirect and complex relationship with the small numbers of variables that are critical to the purpose of the organization. Even if we know that we need to deliver a return on equity of 'x', translating this to a meaningful target for the cost of part of a business like, say, the accounting department, is not straightforward.

Level is a key attribute of performance, but it is not the only one.

Trend

Our common-sense definition of performance also includes trend. We expect a sports car to be capable of going quickly, but if it takes an hour for it to reach its top speed, we are unlikely to call it high performing.

This is because, unlike plays or contracts, businesses do not have a defined ending, so we can never really say that a business *has been performed* – we can only say that a business *is performing* if it is behaving in a way that is consistent with the need to survive and prosper. And it is not just company management that need a dynamic perspective. Investors and other stakeholder groups are mainly interested in what has happened in the past because it reflects the ability of a business to generate returns in the future. Most of the value of a listed company is based on expectations for the future, which in turn are based on the trajectory of performance. So, the results for any single period only have meaning in the context of what has gone before, which is something that traditional variance analysis, with its narrow focus on a single data point, ignores.

Trends provide the context necessary to make a meaningful assessment of performance. A '100mph' performance means something different if the speed for the preceding periods was 80mph than if it was 120mph. In addition, only by looking at results over time can we distinguish between the impact of one-off events that are down to good or bad luck and genuine performance.

So, assessing performance requires us to understand the trend as well as the level of a variable. But there is a third dimension of performance, which is usually completely overlooked.

One of the other flaws of traditional variance analysis is that it assumes that any difference between an actual value and a target is potentially meaningful. In other words, it assumes that there is no randomness or chance in the output of the systems or how we measure it.

We know this is wrong. Noise is an avoidable fact of life, and to be able to make judgements about whether the trend is up, down or stable, or whether a deviation from a target is meaningful, we need to be able to measure the level of noise in order to filter out its effect.

Variation

But noise, or the variation of the value of a variable around its true level, is not just an impediment to measurement – it is also an important dimension of performance itself. A product, or a company, that consistently performs well is more valuable than one that is inconsistent or unreliable. Consistent results, in line with our needs, is after all how we define quality.

In summary, here is my definition of performance: a pattern of behaviour over time in those variables that are pertinent to the intended purpose. In the case of business organizations this means those variables that relate to the viability of an organization – its ability to survive and thrive. And there are three important dimensions of performance:

1. Level
2. Trend
3. Variation

WHAT IS REPORTING?

Having come up with an operational definition for performance we now need one for the word 'reporting'.

One way to do this is to describe what reporting is not.

Reporting, in the sense that I will use it in this book, is not the product of ad hoc analyses of aspects of performance, even if (confusingly) they are contained in documents that are called reports.

The definition of reporting I will adopt is: the process of communicating information on a regular basis in a standardized format to a group of decision makers in order to help them determine whether and how to intervene.

The key words in this definition are: 'information', 'regular', 'standardized', 'group of decision makers' and 'intervene'.

This definition includes exception reporting, where alerts and alarms are generated when something occurs that needs to be attended to immediately. Although the content of exception reports varies (by definition), the process for generating is routine, so it falls within the scope of this book.

This doesn't mean that other, ad hoc ways in which information is disseminated are unimportant – on the contrary. In fact, it is unusual for problems and opportunities identified in performance reports to be acted upon *without* further analysis.

But I am choosing to focus upon routine performance reporting because it is the pivot around which all other forms of information management revolve.

It focusses the attention of management on the small subset of the potentially infinite number of issues that are important for the health of the organization at a given point in time as a precursor to more detailed investigation and, potentially, action. Think of performance reporting as being like all the things that you can do to monitor your health – weight, blood pressure, heart rate, blood sugar levels and so on. Analyses, by contrast, comprise all the detailed tests that a medical professional might perform to determine the cause of an abnormal reading prior to making a detailed diagnosis and prescribing an intervention.

Another reason for focussing on performance reporting is that the really big decisions in business are normally taken collectively; and most of the smaller ones are informed by the context set by the shared perception and interpretation of performance communicated through routine performance reports.

Finally, because routine performance reporting is a 'set piece' process it is relatively easy to come up with principles to inform and guide information workers. And it has the unique challenge of communicating to groups, which makes it interesting.

So, we now are in a position to answer the first question in the title of this chapter: 'what is performance reporting?' It is:

A routine process of producing information to direct the attention to patterns in organizational behaviour that are relevant to its health and to the achievement of its purpose that may require interventions to be made by decision makers. Let's now turn to the second question.

WHAT HAS THIS GOT TO DO WITH BRAINS?

The subtitle to this book is *A Practical Guide to the Science of Measuring Performance and the Art of Communicating it With the Brain in Mind*. You might be wondering at this point why 'the brain' gets such a big share of the billing. The fact that we use our brains to analyse and communicate is not news, so why make a big deal out of it?

When I started writing this book my aims were limited – I simply wanted to provide an antidote for the tendency of traditional textbooks and technically-orientated works on the topic to overlook the flaws and foibles of our mental processes and the challenges of communicating with less numerically literate people who do not share the world view of information professionals.

One of the unexpected pleasures of being an author though is that you learn as you write, even when you thought you knew exactly what you were going to say before you started. You discover holes or weaknesses in your logic and your narrative. Also, in the act of packaging your thoughts for consumption by other people you begin to see a familiar subject from novel angles. In particular, you become aware that how you have learned to think about things is based upon a questionable series of assumptions that you weren't even aware that you had made.

And as I wrote I was reminded of the upheavals in economics as we have become more aware of how the rigorous mathematical models of neoclassical economics have been built on a series of assumptions about the way people behave that simply does not match our personal everyday experience.

The so-called 'Homo Economicus' of classical economic theory has unlimited access to information and behaves perfectly rationally in order to maximize his or her personal utility. But everyone is aware that, in reality, we all exist in a state of partial or complete ignorance and Spock-like rationality is something that (happily) only exists in science fiction. Indeed, whole branches of management – such as sales and marketing – are built on a recognition that consumer choice is heavily (perhaps predominately) based on the emotional criteria that we often do not behave rationally in the purely logical sense of the word. For example, why should it make much difference whether a product is priced at £4.99 or £5.00? But we all know that it does.

Yet, despite the fact that this is 'common knowledge', it took Daniel Kahneman and Amos Tversky, psychologists working in the academic backwater of the Hebrew University of Jerusalem, to formally bring this to the attention of the intelligentsia; work for which Kahneman was awarded the Nobel Prize for economics and that has spawned the whole field of Behavioural Economics.

We are all prisoners of the assumptions we make about the world, most of which we are never aware of, or choose to ignore even when we know they are false. And that includes nearly all the economists who won the Nobel Prize before Kahneman.

As I wrote it struck me that, just like classical economists, our view of the process of analysing and disseminating information assumes away the characteristics of real human beings, and that only by surfacing and challenging these assumptions can we truly learn and improve. And, as we will learn, the mental mechanisms that Kahneman believes underpin our pseudo-rational economic behaviour also feature in the way we assimilate data in the context of performance reporting.

But I'm getting ahead of myself. Let's return to our starting point.

I believe that most traditional practising information professionals – and that included the 'me' of two decades ago – are trapped in a mental cage. This mental prison is based on the assumption that our brains are passive recipients of data that we subsequently process in a simple linear fashion. Traditional variance analysis, whereby we mechanistically compare data to a predetermined comparator, is simply one tangible manifestation of this way of thinking. This world view affects what we do in our day-to-day job in ways that we do not recognize. In this world our mental processes look something like those shown in Figure 2.1.

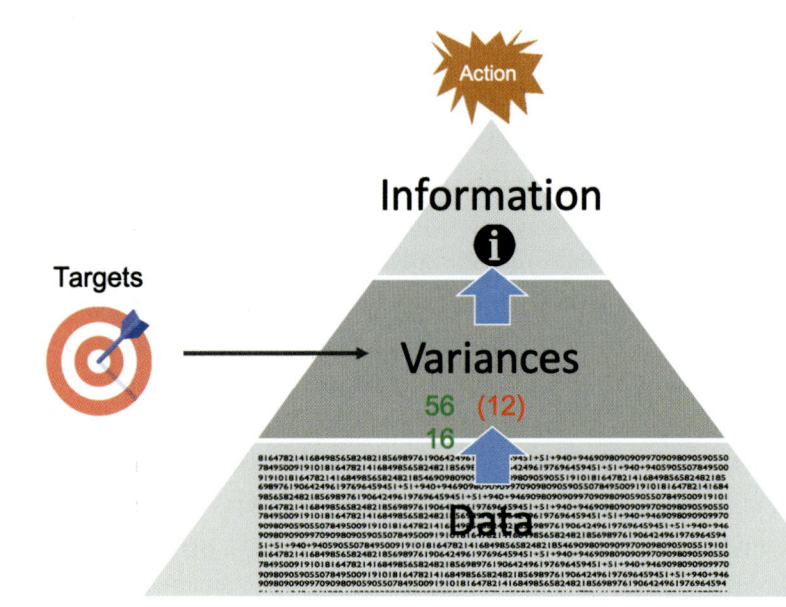

Figure 2.1:
Traditional model of data processing

Traditionally we have assumed that information is the output of a simple linear process whereby data is collected, sorted and analysed by reference to externally determined targets.

Earlier I described the process of performance reporting in simple linear terms, in a way that will be very familiar to most readers.

In this familiar world we first collect facts about the world that we call data. We apply analytical tools, like variance analysis, to process this data to generate information. We then report it to decision makers who take action that changes something in the world.

As I wrote it seemed increasingly clear to me that, at best, this picture was incomplete. And that by focussing exclusively on tools and techniques I too was at risk of completely missing the role played by the human brain in selecting what to measure, how to make sense of the data and in communicating insights to other brains that subsequently interpreted it for themselves.

I knew from what I had read about recent advances in cognitive science that what really goes on when we assimilate sensory data from our environment is much less straightforward than the picture painted here. It was also clear that this has significant implications for the way that information professionals think about and do their job, which a book like mine needed to address.

Firstly, the act of choosing what to measure and how is not a 'given'. It is based on a theory of the world – which in this case is what we believe is important for the health of our organization. So having goals related to our sense of purpose are important not just because they help us determine what is 'good' performance, but also because they help us to distinguish what data may be relevant, and what can safely be ignored.

Having collected data we have then to choose what to pay attention to and what to ignore, never more so than in the era of Big Data when the capability to collect facts vastly outstrips our ability to 'process' them.

Information professionals then have to attribute some meaning to the selected data, which implies understanding its significance in the context of decisions that might be made.

Finally, these insights – almost literally seeing something 'in' data – then need to be communicated, quickly and with no loss of meaning, to other human beings who may choose to take action based on them.

Each stage of this process requires tools – methods, techniques and technologies – since our brains cannot accomplish all of these tasks unaided. But tools are not neurologically neutral. The best tools are those that best bridge the gaps between the capability of our brains and the job that needs to be done. So, in designing tools and choosing which ones to use and when, we need to understand both what we are trying to achieve and the installed capabilities of our brains – both the things we do well that we should leverage and the shortcomings we need to mitigate. Our tools should be designed to fit us. Unless we have no other options, we should not be asking people to do things that our brains haven't evolved to accomplish with a minimal amount of effort. And yet I believe that is what most of us currently do.

The way that our brains work is a product of our shared evolutionary history. Human beings evolved in an environment where the biggest threats to our survival were immediate and obvious.

But the world that we now inhabit is very different. It is infinitely more complex and varied and the relationship between cause and effect is often obscure and indirect.[2] Our stunning evolutionary success as a species is a result of our ability to reprogram the software in our brains (a process we call learning) but also our skill in creating tools to do what our bodies and brains cannot do unaided. Indeed, the ability to manufacture tools is the key mark of the emergence of modern humans by palaeontologists. And how do they know that the rocks and boulders that they find in Olduvai Gorge and other sites of early human activity are tools made by man? It is because of the sharp edges that make them capable of cutting but also, crucially, the fact that the rocks *fit the human hand*.

Effective tools bridge the gaps between our innate capabilities and the task that needs to be accomplished, and the best tools are those that get the job done and fit our bodies and brains so intimately that when we use them they feel like an extension of us rather than an alien prosthetic. This is why I passionately believe that we have to explicitly take account of the way that our brains function in working out how best to make sense of the world and communicate this effectively to others.

To summarize, we use our brain to make sense of data, and the recipients of the reports we produce do the same with the information they receive. Clearly, the ability to make sense of data varies between individuals, and as information professionals you need to be keenly aware of this when communicating the results of your analysis. However, what are just as important but often overlooked are the strengths and weaknesses that we all share. The fact is that all our brains are very good at some things and very bad at others, and this should be the most important consideration, not our idiosyncratic capabilities. What are the qualities that we share?

2. Homo Sapiens has been around for around 100,000 generations, of which only about 10 have been since the start of the industrial revolution.

OUR BRAINS: A REPORT CARD

Unlike many other animals that use a broad range of senses our mental processes are dominated by one: sight. Smell, sound and touch are subordinated to sight. Around 70% of all our sensory receptors are in our eyes and it is estimated that image-processing accounts for half of the energy consumed by our brains.[3] In particular, we are very good at distinguishing shapes and, at a higher level, the patterns that are formed by groups of shapes. Our brains are also very sensitive to movement, which we can detect in our peripheral vision even when our gaze is focussed elsewhere.

From an evolutionary perspective, in a world where you kill or be killed, it is easy to see why visual skills would have been important to survival. It therefore seems sensible to utilize our dominant and most sophisticated cognitive capability to help make sense of data as well as to communicate it to others who are not proficient in manipulating the symbolic language we use to 'sense' – capture data about – our business environment, that is, numbers.

On the other side of the equation, our brains are very poor at other things, which are often unavoidable by-products of our strengths. For instance, the shape-spotting ability that helps us find fruit or catch sight of camouflaged animals makes us prone to seeing patterns where none exist – in clouds and in random data, for instance.

And there are some things that we are just really bad at – period. Most of us have brains that struggle with formal logic, or with very large or very small quantities. And all of us – including statisticians! – have a very poor intuitive grasp of probabilities beyond simple concepts like 'probably' or 'rarely'. Of course, we can learn how to get better at these things, but some of us will never master them. And even those of us who do become proficient find that this learning comes at a cost, because things that do not come naturally to our brains require more time and effort to process.

For information professionals in particular, it is important to keep in mind that – as far as our brains are concerned – *numbers are completely unnatural*. For example, 'primitive' hunter-gatherer tribes can count, but they don't have any concept of number beyond two – their numbering system is: 'one, two, many'. Symbolic numbering systems didn't really get going until the ancient Sumerians invented accounting (true!) and prior to the introduction of Arabic numerals into the West in the 13th century most of us didn't have the symbolic logic to enable us to manipulate numbers – if you don't believe me try multiplying VIII by MCIX. Amazingly, many mathematical concepts that we take for granted were invented even more recently – for example, there is no recorded use of the arithmetical mean before 1635. Virtually all mathematics before this time (in the West at least) was founded on geometry – a mathematical language based on shapes and relationships in space – which is not an accident.

Understanding how our brains process data is particularly important for information professionals because we cannot perceive the world that we are

---

[3]. This does not necessarily mean that sight is the most important sense. Blind people manage without sight, but it is unlikely anyone could survive without a sense of touch.

interested in directly – we can only access it through numbers, and we are not naturally endowed by nature with the ability to 'see' the world this way. This is why, wherever possible, it makes sense to translate the unnatural language of numerical symbols into one that we understand better – a visual language. This is critically important for communicating to an innumerate or time-constrained audience, but even seasoned analysts benefit from using a mode of representation that their brains have evolved to handle.

So, whether we are interpreting or communicating graphical representation is important, but it cannot solve every problem. We also need to compensate for our weaknesses by developing and using analytical tools, particularly where problems are more difficult to visualize or grasp intuitively – for example, when we have to make judgements that demand an understanding of probabilities, which is whenever we make inferences based on raw data.

The need to adapt our toolkit to compensate for the shortcomings in our brains is one reason why it is important to explicitly factor the brain into our thinking on the analysis and communication of performance.

But we should also be looking to exploit our neurological strengths, particularly since, for the first time in the history of business, we are faced with challenges of the sort that our brain has evolved to deal with – making judgements 'on the fly' while being bombarded with vast amounts of data. In a few short years we have gone from being data poor to being data rich, to the point that we now have too much – or at least we think we do.

I believe we think we have too much data because we are simply overwhelmed by it. And the reason we are overwhelmed is not just that there is lots of data, but that we have not yet worked out how to extract actionable insights from this super abundance of riches. Raw computing processing power has increased in line with (and has helped create) the explosion of data but our ability to exploit this data is constrained by our simplistic 20th-century mechanistic approaches to deploying this processing power.

This is where we should learn from nature since our brains are excellent at operating, making sense of and acting within an environment with a level of complexity and dynamism that is well beyond their ability to process. Our brains are encased in bone without any direct access to the world they are trying to understand. Just like the information professionals sitting in a fancy head office (no pun intended) the brain can only 'see' streams of sensory data, from which it has to work out what is 'out there' and what to do about it.

Human brains succeed, not because of their computational capacity, but because they have evolved ways of simplifying the problems they face. Evolution has equipped them with strategies that have helped them understand what data they can safely disregard, and to develop and validate 'good enough' theories of the world to guide our actions, without having to pause for thought.

The scale and the rate at which we perform these tricks is staggering.

Our bodies are bombarded with about 10^9 bits of data every second (that is 10 with nine noughts afterwards) of which all but 10^2 is filtered out before it reaches the brain – that's a ten-million-fold reduction. Even more impressive, all this happens below the level of consciousness while simultaneously monitoring the state of our body, moving around, talking and taking decisions ranging from what to eat for lunch to guiding a 2-tonne lump of metal along a narrow strip of asphalt at a speed much higher than any human being had ever experienced a mere century or so ago!

Wouldn't it be a good idea to work out how the brain does all of this and use some of its tricks to help us do a better job of making sense of our relatively simple business world? After all, if we can do all this using just the 1.5 kilogrammes of meat between our ears, what could we achieve now we have supercomputers that can perform calculations many millions of times faster. How difficult can it be?

This is what the pioneers of AI thought half a century ago, but progress in this field has been painfully slow. This is partly because they made the mistake of thinking that things that human beings could do easily were simple – but they aren't.

But they also struggled because they had the wrong idea of how the brain worked and so tried to solve brain-style problems using engineering techniques. They crunched lots of numbers in a systematic way, very quickly. But despite the formidable processing power of modern computers this approach didn't work because the complexity of the challenge is simply too great for the strategies they used.

It is important that we learn from the failures of the early AI researchers because we could easily make the same mistakes again in the era of Big Data. We mustn't think that if we throw enough data at a powerful enough computer running sophisticated enough algorithms somehow the right answer will come out in the end. Real-world complexity will always overwhelm simple strategies like this, even if the techniques and technologies used are highly sophisticated. And, because we have minor successes with AI – such as working out that 'people who bought this also bought…' – we shouldn't be fooled into thinking that we are on the way to solving the problem. In the context of the things we need to do to run a business, this kind of insight is stunningly trivial.

To be clear, I am not saying that Big Data or AI are unimportant – they are important, and they will undoubtedly transform our lives in many ways. Nor am I trying to devise an alternative approach to handling Big Data to those that many people much smarter than I around the world are working on. What I am saying is that the strategies we employ to help us make sense of and act in a complex and dynamic world, and for communicating our insights to brain-based life forms (like your colleagues – hopefully), should be squarely based upon an understanding of brain functioning, since it is the successful product of billions of years of research and development.

I am not saying that we need to become amateur neuroscientists. Some understanding of how the brain works its magic is helpful, but the most value will come from avoiding doing the stupid stuff. We need to respect the strengths and weaknesses of our own brains and stop treating other people's brains as if they were machines.

Performance Reporting: What is it and What Has it Got to Do With Brains?

Recent developments in our understanding of brain functioning are fascinating but, tempting as it is for a nerd like myself, this is not the place to explore these in detail. At this stage I will restrict myself to setting the context. And I don't think it is possible to grasp the significance of the 'magic' that the brain uses until we lay to rest our simplistic notions of how we incorrectly assume that it works.

HOW THE BRAIN DOESN'T WORK

Figure 2.2 shows the way we often assume that the brain works. According to a naïve model of brain processing we:

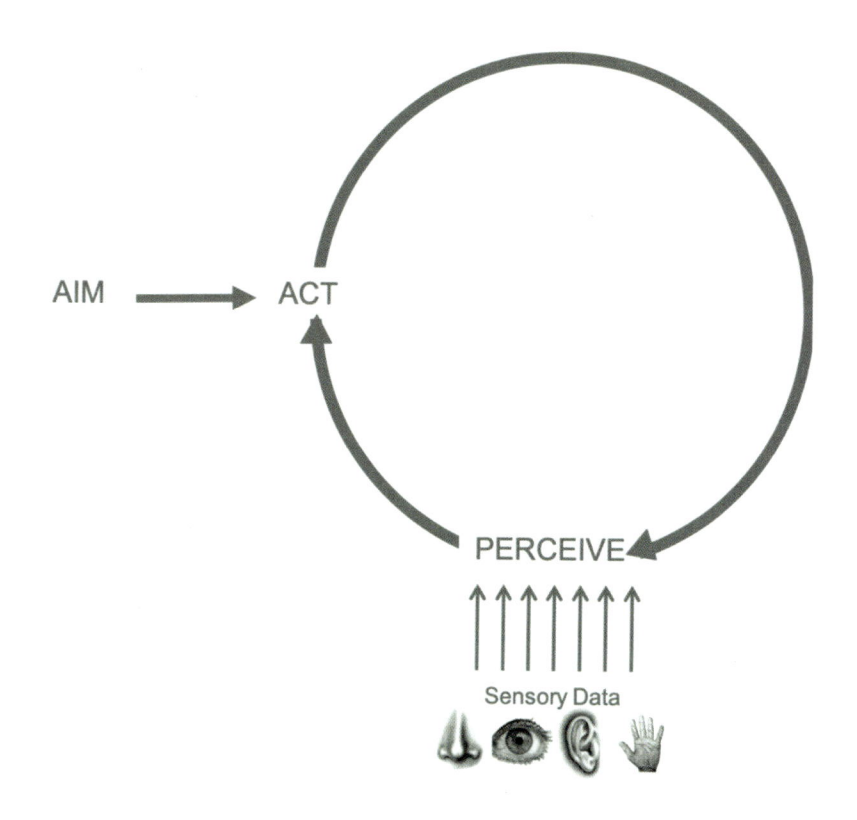

Figure 2.2:
A naïve model of brain processing

Intuitively, we assume that our perception of the world is based on what our senses detect, and that our actions flow from this and what we aim to achieve.

1. Collect data from our senses – eyes, ears, nose and touch receptors.
2. Construct an image of reality based on this data.
3. Based on this representation of reality and our aims (which we might express as a target) decide what we need to do to bring reality in line with our wishes.
4. Act.
5. Repeat the cycle.

This seems straightforward and familiar – it is basically the same approach we use to measure and 'manage' the performance of an organization.

Over the last couple of decades, however, cognitive scientists have come to realize that the brain doesn't work like this at all. We are not passive recipients of data that we then analyse in a structured way. As AI researchers have come to recognize, the sheer volume of data that needs to be processed and the time needed to do this before action can be taken means that it is virtually impossible to successfully navigate the world in this way. Our brain is not a passive recipient of sensory data. It makes sense of the world by selectively engaging in it. Perception and action are part of a whole, and both are driven by continuously updated assumptions about the nature of reality.

This, I believe, puts the work of information professionals in a different and bigger context. To use the awful business patois – we should stop regarding them as being part of the 'back office'. They should be very much front and centre.

HOW THE BRAIN ACTUALLY WORKS

The picture of brain functioning emerging is still incomplete but explains much of what has puzzled psychologists in the past. And the picture is simultaneously counter intuitive and familiar. Like that described in Figure 2.2, the process is circular, but the key – and very profound – difference is that it starts in a different place.

1. Any act of perception doesn't start with a blank slate – a mind free of preconceptions. We start with a belief about what we think is 'out there', what it is and what it means, and this provides us with a hypothesis of the world. This hypothesis (or perceptual model) of the world is informed by our context, our intentions, our instincts and what we have learned about the world.
2. Based on the predictions of our hypotheses we take action. In the very short term this action involves taking data samples from our environment. For instance, our assumption about 'what is out there' guides the rapid (about five times a second) movements of the eyes called 'saccades' that sample the environment.
3. The sampled data (and any other data from our sense organs that intrudes into our consciousness) is compared with the predictions of the perceptual model and we use this to update the model. If what our eyes tell us is consistent with what we expected to see, however, what we perceive is not what is actually out there – it is simply what we expected to be out there. What we think we see is not 'the world' as it really is. It is the world as our brains thinks it is. A model supported by evidence. A working hypothesis, not 'the truth'.
4. Over slightly longer periods, but in parallel, the action we take is consciously directed and purposeful, such as reaching out to pick an

object up. This action is driven by our goals and informed by our model of the world. And the process of acting and receiving feedback from our actions generates even more data, which can be tested against the predictions of the model. And in this way our models become richer, more robust and more reliable. We start out in life with a basic set of models, but we spend the rest of it refining, adapting and repurposing them to help us deal with the world as we experience it.

So, our perceptions of the world are not the result of passively collecting and sorting data, they are constructed based on our engagement with the world, which is informed by our preconceptions of it. Perception is the result of a fusion of our hypotheses of what is out there and sensory data – and all at an incredibly rapid rate.

'Just about every aspect of the passive forward-flowing model is false. We are not cognitive couch potatoes idly awaiting the next "input", so much as proactive predictavores—nature's own guessing machines forever trying to stay one step ahead by surfing the incoming waves of sensory stimulation'

From Andy Clark 'Surfing Uncertainty'

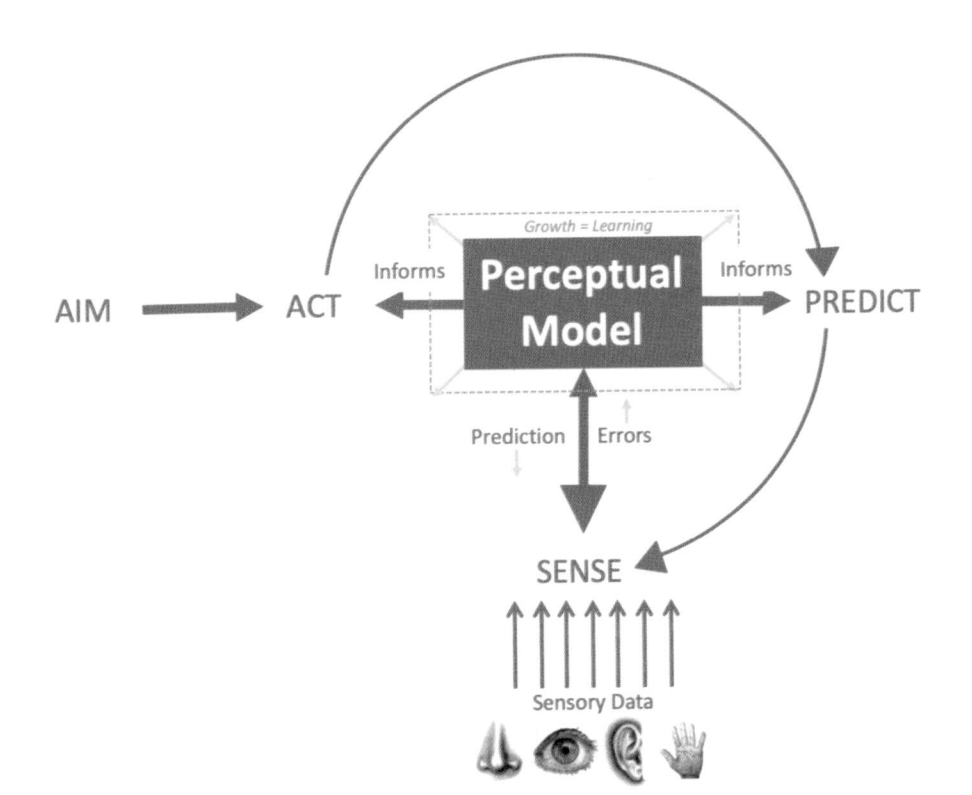

Figure 2.3:
A new view of brain processing

What we perceive is the result of an interplay between our preconceptions of the world, in the form of a generative perceptual model, and a process of data sampling driven by prior prediction errors of the model. We know that we have made sense of the world when the level of prediction errors is low. As we learn, our generative model of the world 'grows' and the level and strength of prediction errors (returning to update the model) declines. It takes a powerful error signal to change a well established model (belief).

What we think is a simple and straightforward act is in fact the end result of a subtle dance between our brain, our senses and the external world. We do not process data, we interact with the world to generate information, which we validate through our actions. If what happens is what we think is going to happen we take this to be the truth.

IT'S EASY TO SEE WHY

To get a sense of why the 'data processing' model of perception doesn't work, consider this scenario.

Somebody turns up at your office with a large bag. Inside are a million jigsaw pieces. She tips them out on your desk and tells you to work out what is going on and what she should do about it?

How would you go about this task?

You might want to start by throwing away all the irrelevant pieces. But how do you decide what is irrelevant if you don't know what you are looking for?

Probably you would start grouping together pieces with the same colour and hope that as you started to piece together several smaller jigsaws a pattern would emerge that would help you work out how the whole thing fitted together. And only when the whole thing comes together can you form a complete idea of what is going on and select what is most relevant.

This sounds stupid, but that is essentially what we are trying to do when we **process** data. Obviously, this is not something we can do manually so we simplify the problem by ignoring most of the data 'pieces' and focussing on just one small pile. Alternatively, we throw an algorithm at the pile and hope that somehow it will be able to assemble a picture – but since an algorithm doesn't have what we call common sense it might end up putting ladies with short haircuts on top of men's bodies and shorter people might be shown in the far distance rather than as part of a group. Also, even a high-powered algorithm will take hours to do this.

Alternatively, imagine that you know that the picture from which the jigsaw is made was taken on someone's birthday. They have just been blindfolded and led into a noisy room full of people who start singing when they enter the room. From these contextual details a reasonable hypothesis is that this is a birthday celebration and as a result you may predict that the room will contain a cake with lighted candles on a table.

All you need to do to provisionally validate the hypothesis is to pick up pieces of the jigsaw that look like they may be part of a table. These will not be pieces with edges because you are guessing that it will be in the centre of the room, and obviously there are a lot of pieces that are irrelevant - like ceilings, doors, carpets and so on.

If your samples confirm your hypothesis then you carry on and, based on this, you would call up a behavioural routine that helps you decide what to do. If you are the birthday girl or boy just smile and go to blow out the candles.

If the samples contain some disconfirming evidence, you might hesitate. For example, if the cake is very big - big enough to contain a human being - you might be very wary of going too close to it and want to take on some more data before deciding what to do.

This approach – guess and test – is much more like the way the brain works than the data-processing model and it's not difficult to see why. It is the ***only*** way to act in the presence of overwhelming amounts of data. So, when we are faced with a similar situation in the world of business, I believe that we should consciously apply a similar approach.

There are risks of course. Risks from having faulty hypotheses, sampling the wrong things and not giving the right weight to data that doesn't perfectly fit the prediction. But if you are aware of the risks it is possible to manage them.

Always bear in mind that there are many alternative hypotheses to explain what is happening. So, don't just look for confirmation of your prejudices. Capture data that could disconfirm your hypotheses or help you refine them, and give more weight to large prediction errors.

While the description of the process of perception might be difficult to square with our felt experiences it should not be entirely unfamiliar because it is essentially the same process that scientists follow to construct and test their theories of the world – the scientific method.

We think we see the world as it is, like a movie in our brain, but we don't. What we think we see is what our brain thinks is out there based on what it decides is useful for our purposes. Our internal perception of the world is a picture created by our brain stitched together from chunks of data using a pattern it has already created. Perception is simply a process of controlled hallucination.[4] As bizarre as this description sounds, it explains many phenomena that are otherwise puzzling, such as:

- Why you can't tickle yourself (your brain discounts sensations that it 'knows' are the result of own intentional actions).
- Why, when you look in a mirror, you don't see our eyes moving (we don't 'see' stuff that our brains know is irrelevant).
- Why you don't see the blind spot in your eye where the optical nerve meets the retina (the brain builds a picture of the world from its own guess supplemented by sampling from the eyes so there are no holes to fill in).
- Why the range of focussed vision for each eye saccade is only 2 or 3 degrees (about the size of your thumbnail at arm's length) but you see a complete picture – with no blurring – despite the fact that there are 'only' about five saccades per second. Our eyes don't generate our perceptions – they merely sample the world to check and update mentally generated images.
- Why you see continuous movement even though our eyes move in a discontinuous manner – as a series of jerky movements. Our brain generates the images – not our eyes. Try walking around a space using the video image from your phone camera and observe how isolating your brain from contextual data destabilizes your visual images.
- Why when you see famous optical illusions – such as those that can be seen

[4]. The theory of perception I have outlined in the last few pages is called 'Predictive Processing' or 'Coding'. At the back of the book you will find a number of recommended books if you want to learn more.

as a duck or a rabbit, or an old hag or young lady – you either see one thing or you see the other. Your brain 'chooses' for you based on what it believes is the most plausible context. You can hold two competing hypotheses in your brain, but you cannot actually 'see' both at the same time.
- Why illusionists manage to fool us even when we 'know' we are being fooled. They are experts at priming our mental models so that we fail to see something that is actually there – hidden in 'plain view'.

PERCEPTUAL BLINDNESS

Over the last few decades psychologists have uncovered many otherwise puzzling phenomena that are neatly explained by the 'predictive processing' model of brain functioning.

For example, 'change blindness' is where we fail to notice changes in what (without us knowing it) our brain decides are 'irrelevant details' of a situation - such as the clothes worn by a researcher conducting an experiment on the subject. Many readers will also be familiar with the video of an experiment that has gone viral where most viewers fail to spot a person in a gorilla suit moon dancing in the middle of a basketball game.[5]

Tantalizingly, some scientists speculate that it may also help understand and possibly treat certain mental conditions. Perhaps schizophrenics struggle to integrate real-world data with their preconceptions - in effect the mechanism that recognizes and acts upon prediction errors is somehow faulty. At the other extreme, autism may be associated with an inability to construct social models of the world. In effect, autistic people have data, but not the generative models to help them filter and organize it and to anticipate how other people will respond to them. In their world it is all trees and no wood.

At a practical level this demonstrates that we literally don't see what we don't expect to see. This is a powerful argument for scenario planning and risk assessment in organizations as it helps to prime our perceptions such that we are capable of detecting a wider range of phenomena. In this sense, the **process** of assessing risk and opening yourself up to a wider range of possibilities is more important than the output of the risk assessment.

[5.] Much of this work has been done by Daniel Simons and his colleagues at the University of Illinois. Go to http://www.simonslab.com/videos.html to view some of the movies that they have created which demonstrates these phenomena.

These examples demonstrate how the strategy employed by our brains carries some downsides, manifest as flaws in our processes of perception. But these are trivial compared to the massive benefits that this approach affords us. By simply sampling our environment, guided by models based on experience of similar environments, and using this feedback to rapidly update these models, we can be open to the enormous complexity and dynamism of the world without becoming overwhelmed by it. And because *action is part of the process of perception*, rather than being separate and sequential, we are not paralysed by analysis.

I believe this insight into the way that our brains enable us to make sense of and act in a world filled with data far beyond our ability to systematically process it is highly relevant to the situation that our organizations find themselves in today. It helps us to avoid drowning in irrelevant information generated by thoughtless large-scale data processing. And it will aid us to devise strategies and develop tools that will help us exploit the potential that Big Data holds.

So, instead of a funnel or a pyramid to represent the relationship between data and information, we should use a circle instead. And the circle should include us – people. Information and meaning do not exist independently of human beings. They are always embodied. As Nate Silver says 'The numbers have no way of speaking for themselves. We speak for them.'

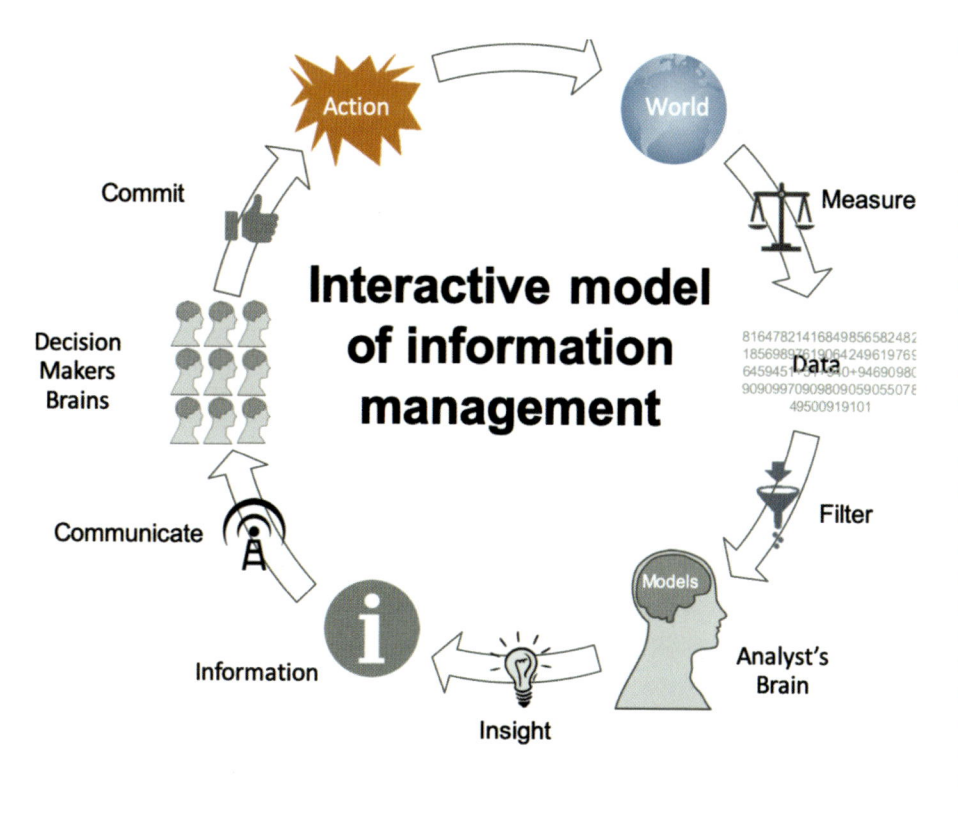

Figure 2.4:
An interactive model of information management

A more realistic model of how information is generated and consumed in an organization is circular rather than linear. Being circular it doesn't start anywhere but for convenience let's assume that it starts with us choosing what attributes of the world are relevant to us and how to measure them. This data is filtered by the analyst's own mental models – supplemented by methods and tools – and they attribute meaning to it. These insights are manifest as information, which is communicated to decision makers, who add their perspective to that of the analyst, which informs their actions, which in turn affects the world. On the next iteration the data reflects the impact of these interventions, and an important role of the analyst is to determine whether what decision makers expected to happen did happen. In other words, whether the working hypothesis or model that guided the action is robust.

SENSE MAKING

The study of how we make sense of complex, dynamic and ambiguous environments has a long history. You could argue that neuroscience joined this particular party quite late.

In an organizational context the most prominent contribution to the study of sense-making – the process of giving meaning to experience (i.e. data) – comes from Karl Weick who has written extensively on the subject over a 50-year academic career.

He identifies the key characteristics of sense making as:

- Identity and identification are central – who people think they are shapes how they interpret events.
- Retrospection provides the opportunity for sense-making: the point of retrospection in time affects what people notice.
- People enact the environments they face. As people speak, and build narrative accounts, it helps them understand what they think, organize their experiences and control and predict events.
- Sense-making is a social activity. Plausible stories are preserved, retained or shared and the audience for sense-making includes the speakers themselves.
- Sense-making is a continuous process whereby individuals simultaneously shape and react to the environments they face. By observing the consequences of their words and deeds they learn about their identities and the accuracy of their accounts.
- People extract cues from the context to help them decide on what information is relevant and what explanations are acceptable. Extracted cues provide points of reference for linking ideas. They become simple, familiar structures that are used to build a larger sense of what may be happening.
- Faced with overwhelming complexity, people favour plausibility over accuracy.

Like many ideas that originated in social science (I speak as someone with such a background) the language used to describe the phenomenon is florid and sometimes (deliberately) obscure but it is not difficult to see the strong parallels with the world that neuroscientists have uncovered.

More recently David Snowden, building on Weick's work, has defined the Cynefin framework, which posits different sense-making strategies based on the nature of the environment: simple, complicated, complex and chaotic. This could be interpreted as suggesting adopting different starting positions on the perceptual loop based on differing levels of confidence in starting hypotheses.

Figure 2.5:
The Cynefin model

The Cynefin model suggests that the nature of the environment determines the best problem-solving strategy to deploy. So, for example, 'Best Practice', thinking only work where the situation is well-defined (simple) and relevant precedents exist. At the other extreme chaotic environments, where no relevant pre-existing knowledge exits, can only be explored by acting first.

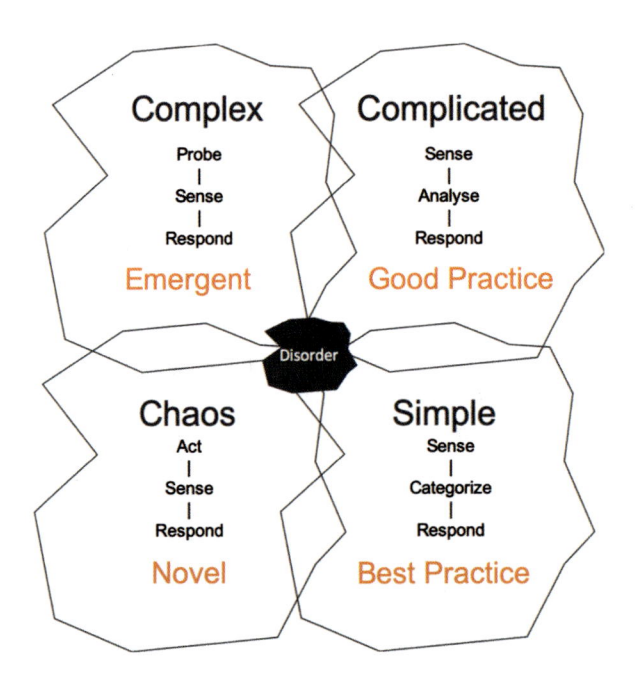

Performance Reporting: What is it and What Has it Got to Do With Brains?

Unsurprisingly, the process of making decisions in a complex, dynamic environment high in ambiguity is something that military thinkers have studied.

Everyone has heard of the phrase 'the fog of war' – an idea that dates back to the writings of Clausewitz in the mid-19th century. More recently (in the early 1960s) John Boyd conceived of the OODA loop based on his experiences as a US Airforce fighter pilot and this idea has influenced the military philosophy of our era.

The OODA acronym stands for:

Observe – collect data about reality

Orientate – make sense of it

Decide – commit

Act – take action that changes reality: thereby changing what you observe

The key idea is that by being able to make sense of reality and take action that changes that reality you can disorientate a slower thinking enemy and gain the upper hand in battle, thereby winning a conflict with minimum force. For Boyd, 'orientation' – making sense of the environment – was the most important part of the cycle.

While the picture that I have painted of the way that the brain operates may seem fanciful and irrelevant to the practical business of performance reporting, the fact that it resonates so strongly with other, independently derived theories of perception gives us confidence that the analogy is helpful.

There is one more scientific insight that is relevant to the subject of this book.

Everyone knows that the brain is divided into two hemispheres, linked by a neural super highway called the *corpus callosum* and some readers may have read that the two hemispheres appear to play different roles. In popular culture the right-hand side is often characterized as 'artistic', while the left is 'rational'. The reality is, however, much more subtle than this crude distinction suggests.

While there is some localization of certain brain functions – such as the language processing, which seems to be dominated by the left hemisphere – the two sides of the brain are virtually identical at a microscopic level.[6] The only other significant functional difference between the two hemispheres seems to be in the way they attend to the world – where we focus our limited cognitive resources.[7] And the fact that nature has preserved the massive redundancy in the bodily organ that is the most expensive to run suggests that this difference is highly significant.

The fact of the matter seems to be that we have two forms of attention, and that we need both to be effective.

The right-hand side of the brain looks at things holistically, paying attention to connections and patterns. It deals directly in real-world phenomena and 'navigates' by way of exemplars. Critically the right-hand side is stimulated by novelty and ambiguity and places phenomena in the context of time.

The left-hand side of the brain is more focussed and deals in abstractions such as categories.[8] So, whereas the right brain risks seeing everything as novel and new

6. Indeed, it is perfectly possible for children to grow to adulthood with only one hemisphere without them or anyone else being aware of it.

7. The neuroscientist David Eagleman writes: 'A good way to think about attention is as the brain's way of paring down the sheer volume of sensory input into something more manageable. You can then concentrate your resources on what's important (or at least perceived to be so on first blush) and ignore the rest. If processing capacity weren't limited, perhaps we wouldn't need attention at all—we'd be able to give the same amount of concentration to everything in our immediate environment, simultaneously.'

8. I am conscious of this when I am weeding in my garden. I find that I can only easily look for one kind of weed at a time – say crocuses, which create a nuisance. There might be other weeds, such as buttercups, in the same patch of ground but unless I consciously look for them, I don't see them. And since constantly switching from crocus to buttercup hunting is exhausting, I tend to stick to one type of weed at a time.

the left-hand side seeks to attribute phenomena to an existing category, and so is prone to confabulation to make the facts fit (which requires the right side to intervene to test the plausibility of these 'stories'). And in contrast to its partner it inhabits a more static world.

It is not that one side can see the wood but not the trees, or vice versa. The left-hand side would be able to tell you what species each tree belonged to and how they related to each other, but the right would see a wood populated by individual unique specimens.

The point here is not that one or the other perspective of the world is 'right'. What nature is teaching us is that we need both the context and the content to make sense of real-world data. So, when asked to draw a picture of a person people with left-hand side brain lesions can provide an accurate outline but no detail. While those with the opposite impairment can draw the limbs in great detail but have difficulty in working out how they attach to the body. We need both perspectives to navigate the world successfully.

We will touch on these neuroscientific insights as we work through the rest of the book, but for the moment let's summarize where we have got to on our journey of discovery into our brains.

WHY THIS IS IMPORTANT

While questions about the nature of reality and our ability to perceive it are fascinating, my motive for introducing brain functioning into this narrative is practical not philosophical. From this understanding we can learn a lot of lessons that are useful in the context of day-to-day business practice. These include:

- Our brains have great strengths that need to be better exploited to improve the ways we analyse data and communicate information.
- Our brains also have weaknesses. We need to be mindful of these to avoid being misled by them. We need tools and techniques to help us where we know that our natural capabilities are inadequate.
- To better exploit the super abundance of data that we now have access to we need to develop analytical strategies and tools based on an understanding of how the brain makes sense of potentially overwhelming quantities of complex and dynamic data. In particular, we need to appreciate that:

  o Data can have no meaning without context, and the context that you choose influences what data you collect and the meaning you attribute to it. Our preconceptions guide our conceptions. Choosing the right context – the right hypothesis to explore – based on an understanding of the situation and how information will be put to use is critical to generating useful insights.

o   Data is not processed, it is selected and used in order to test and improve the model of the world that is presented in performance reports. This means that data that 'doesn't make sense' or contradicts the received view should not automatically be treated as evidence of 'poor performance' but as a sign that the prevailing perception of reality should be questioned and perhaps altered.

These and other insights should guide our practical interaction with data and they paint a picture of the information professional as something more than a dry processor of data. The person at the interface between data and the consumers of information has a critical role. The way they work has a profound effect on how the business perceives reality and consequently on decisions that are made. They play a key role in determining what is relevant and what is not, and they direct attention to what is salient and attribute meaning to it. We call the product of this process 'information' and information underpins purposeful action.

It might seem fanciful but, if a business can be thought of as having the capability to think and act, then information professionals are, in a real sense, no less than guardians of the shared corporate consciousness.

The other insight that we get from understanding the process of perception and our knowledge of the role of the two brain hemispheres is that context is as important as content. We cannot make sense of the detail until we understand the 'big picture' in which it sits. To refer back to the jigsaw analogy, we need to make an educated guess at what the picture is before we can begin to work out what to do with the individual jigsaw pieces (data). This is the role this chapter plays in the book – it sets the context for the content that follows.

Let's get down to business, starting with the *process* of performance reporting.

WHAT IS THE PROCESS OF PERFORMANCE REPORTING?

I will start by referring back to the diagram of the interactive model of information management (see Figure 2.6).

Since I have defined performance as an expression of purpose let's use this as our jumping off point. Based on our understanding of purpose, we first choose to measure certain real-world variables and in doing so we create data.

Financial professionals have historically had a relatively easy time of this since transactional data (about sales and purchases) is captured for the purpose of producing accounts and can easily be repurposed for performance management. But, increasingly, non-financial data is rightly seen as at least as important to the process of managing a business. So, information professionals have to choose what additional non-financial variables should be managed and how to measure them.

Figure 2.6:
The interactive model of information management

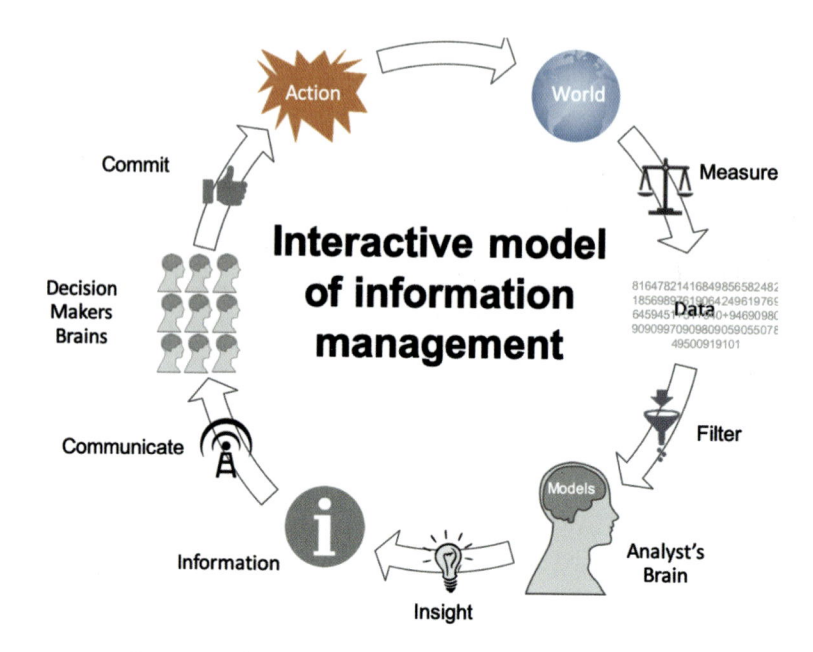

In principle, more data is a good thing because it creates the potential to create new insights, but data alone cannot do this because it is simply a statement of facts. Data has no meaning in itself. In order to create the conditions for purposeful action we have to extract meaning from data – to 'make sense' of it.

WHAT DO WE MEAN BY 'MEANING'?

Take a look at this picture:

Figure 2.7

What is it?

What it actually is is a series of black and white pixels ordered on a two-dimensional matrix (i.e. a piece of paper). Which is another way of saying it is data. And data has no meaning in itself - it has no information content on which we can frame our actions.

Now turn over the page and take a look at this image:

Performance Reporting: What is it and What Has it Got to Do With Brains?

Figure 2.8

It is obviously the same picture – it's just that we have converted white to yellow. But in doing so we now know what the pixels mean because it has triggered that part of the brain that 'recognizes' this pattern of data as a snake. We have attributed meaning to the data and in doing so we have created information.

And in this case 'meaning' carries with it not only a classification of the data as a recognizable pattern (in this case an object, but other patterns might be classified as an event) but also, most likely, a set of value judgements (most people regard snakes as 'bad', but a herpetologist might find it 'beautiful' or 'fascinating') and a repertoire of potential actions (i.e. 'run' or 'keep a safe distance' or 'pass me my snake catching kit'). Note that the judgements and the actions vary depending upon the purpose of the perceiver.

The same happens when we receive organizational data.

Before meaning is attributed to data, we are 'experientially blind', just as we were with the black and white picture, because our brains have not been able to attribute a conceptual category that we already have to the pattern of data. If we don't already have a conceptual category, or we are not sure, we build and test a hypothesis by seeking out (from a wider data set) or creating (through our actions) more data that will help us resolve the ambiguity.

The point here is that meaning doesn't exist in the data. It is something that is added to it by the observer based on his or her perspective and purpose. In our case, the information professional.

....

Extracting meaning from data involves selection. We have to identify what might *potentially* be meaningful from large and ever-expanding data sets that, by definition, will contain increasingly higher levels of meaningless data — not just useful stuff. In order to make progress we have to identify those data sets that are relevant to our purpose and then to filter out meaningless 'noise' to expose the potentially meaningful 'signal' buried within the data. This cannot be a purely mechanical process. To identify potentially meaningful signals, we need clarity about our purpose.

Think of this process as being like mining. First, we need to know what mineral we want to have extracted at the end of the process. Then identify the ore-bearing seams of rock. Having mined the rock we need to separate rubble from the nuggets that contain high concentrations of the mineral we want. Finally, we refine it.

Our nuggets of potentiality are refined to unlock the meaning buried within them. We make sense of these signals by working out what they mean in the context of the purpose of the organization – not in an abstract sense but in a way that could lead to action. Potentially actionable signals we call 'information'.

Perhaps the most important characteristic of good performance reporting is that it contains information rather than data, so we need to be really clear about the difference between the two. For something to qualify as information it must have the potential to 'inform action' as the word suggests. Data on its own does not. Data is the rock, information is the mineral bound within it, which only has value (meaning) in the context of the use we have for it.

In the context of performance reporting I will make a distinction between two types of information. First there is 'performance information'. By helping us work out whether performance is good or bad, getting better or getting worse, performance information helps us to dictate whether and where action is needed.

The primary purpose of performance reporting is to provide a context and thereby help to answer the question, 'Do I/we need to intervene?' In an ideal world the answer would be 'No', in which case performance reporting serves its purpose by stopping people taking action when none is required. Performance reporting is about creating what the military call 'situational awareness'.

Second there is 'diagnostic information' that helps us to determine what kind of actions might be appropriate by identifying the potential causal patterns. Here the focus of attention is narrow and more analytical in nature. Diagnostic information may form part of routine performance reports but if the problem (or opportunity) is not obvious it is likely that additional information will be required to determine the best course of action.

Finally, having made sense of data by converting it into meaningful information, to complete the process we need to convert the potential of information into reality by communicating it to those people that have the ability to act upon it.

Let me illustrate the process of performance reporting, and some of the challenges involved, by using an analogy from sport – an arena that is all about performance.

Imagine a weekend golfer; not a pro, but one who sprays the ball about quite a lot. And imagine that he (because it usually is) is playing an unknown (to you) golf course in unknown weather conditions, so (just like an information professional) the only way you can understand performance is through data.

You know the purpose of golf, which is to get the ball in a hole in as few shots as possible, so it is obvious what data needs to be collected to be able to measure performance – the number of shots taken per hole. This ultimately will yield performance information but to understand and improve performance you also need diagnostic information. So, you will also have to collect data on other variables, such as the length of drives or the number of putts on each green.

Having collected this data how would you set about making sense of the performance of our golfer?

For sure it would be dumb to use the score on a single hole, because we don't know how long the hole is, how difficult it is and the prevailing weather conditions, which can have a big systematic impact on scoring. Also, the score on a single hole is disproportionately affected by luck – good and bad. Perhaps the ball hit a divot and bounced into a bunker, or a tree stopped a wayward drive going out of bounds. Luck is all 'noise' and has to be discounted to properly assess performance.

So, we would need to analyse the scores for a number of consecutive holes and look for patterns that could help us answer the question, 'How good is this guy?' In business, as in our imaginary golf game, answering this question definitively 'in the moment' is not easy, at least with the data we have to hand, because we have no point of comparison, such as the performance of other golfers or a performance standard (such as the par for the hole). But if we track performance over time, with a big enough sample, it is possible to work out if performance is improving or deteriorating, which is a good start in deciding whether there is a need to intervene.

Unless there is no room for improvement, which is unlikely, performance information is essential. But to improve we need more than a simple assessment of the level and trend of performance; we need to identify patterns in a wider set of data to inform actions that will make things better. This is diagnostic information.

Having assembled our information – potentially actionable insights – we have to communicate this information in a way so that the golfer understands how well he is doing and what he needs to do differently to improve his performance.

In business communication usually involves reports containing symbolic information (numbers, works and shapes) but other media (such as video) might also be available to our golfer. And just like in business the ultimate decision maker (in this case the golfer) has access to other sources of information (such as personal experience) that will also inform the actions that they take.

Finally, the golfer acts upon this information, and in the process generates more data, which informs the next reporting cycle.

To summarize:

1. Business performance is an attribute of the dynamic pattern of behaviour that reflects the degree to which it is consistent with the organization's purpose.

2. Because we can't see an organization's behaviour we have to measure it.
3. The system we are attempting to measure is in constant flux, but we can only measure its attributes at a point in time. So, the process of understanding performance over time starts with measuring things at a point in time. These measurements we call data.
4. Any data point (a piece of data collected at a moment in time) is evidence, but it cannot tell us anything about performance in isolation from other data points, particularly since all data is infected by meaningless noise, which can obscure the signal.
5. The signals embedded in data have to be interpreted to create information – potentially actionable insights.
6. The role of performance reporting is to inform decision makers about the state of the whole system so they can determine whether intervention is required to improve performance and to direct focussed attention towards relevant variables or areas of the business.
7. To achieve this, performance reports contain:

    a. performance information where the variable is directly relevant to the purpose; and
    b. diagnostic information when it helps explain how performance can be improved.

So now we are in a position to answer the second question in the chapter title: 'what has this got to do with brains?' There are three ways in which adopting a cognitive stance to the performance reporting helps us:

1. It helps define a clear *purpose* of the process: to help create a shared organizational consciousness that facilitates rapid and coordinate action.
2. Understanding how the brain makes sense of its world when faced with huge amounts of dynamic and potentially ambiguous sensory data helps us define the *strategy* that information professionals need to adopt to fulfil their purpose: to iteratively and rapidly build hypotheses based on an appreciation of context and test them using data (content).
3. An appreciation of our brain's capabilities helps us to identify *methodologies and tools* that exploit its strengths and mitigate its weaknesses. Specifically:

    a. in *prospecting* for meaning we should exploit our brain's ability to spot patterns, particularly when data is presented graphically;
    b. in *validating* hypotheses we need to compensate for our brain's weaknesses and biases in making inferences, particularly when it involves assessing probabilities;
    c. we need to exploit the visual processing power of all of our brains to *communicate* insights quickly and faithfully.

Along the way we have also started to build a language that will help us to talk about the mechanics of the process of making sense of performance.

Variable	an attribute of a system that varies over time
Data	a set of measurements of variables: facts
Data point	the value of a variable at a point in time
Data series	a sequence of data points for a variable over time
Noise	meaningless patterns of data
Signal	potentially meaningful patterns in data
Information	potentially actionable insights

Having set the context, let's now tackle the content – the tools and methods that we should employ to make sense of the performance of organizations.

These methods I will share with you use conventional arithmetic that every reader will be comfortable with and simple statistics, but not in an unnatural or mechanistic way. They are tools that help us to make meaning out of data by amplifying and augmenting the capabilities that nature has endowed our brains with not by attempting to replace the human in the process or converting him or her to a number crunching drudge.

At the start of this chapter we identified three dimensions of performance: level, trend and variation. Chapters 3, 4 and 5 will address each one of these dimensions in turn, starting with methods to help us make sense of trend.

Learning	Reason
How to define 'performance'.	Performance is a measure of how well an organization is fulfilling its purpose, expressed as a pattern of behaviour of defined variables over a period of time. Since no two organizations, or parts of an organization, have exactly the same purpose the variables that need to be tracked will differ, but they will always include measures of viability, which are often financial.
Why it is difficult to assess the level of performance.	Given that the business world is dynamic, unpredictable and competitive in nature, it is difficult to determine in advance what an acceptable level of performance is.
Why an appreciation of trends is an important component of performance.	Since most organizations aim to survive in perpetuity, no single point in time measure can give a complete picture of performance. Trends provide the context for a meaningful assessment of performance.
How and why variation is relevant to measuring performance.	Variation is both an attribute of performance, since higher performing systems have lower variation, and the source of noise that needs to be filtered out to determine true level of performance.
What 'reporting' is and how it differs from analysis.	Reporting is the process of communicating information on a regular basis in a standardized format to a group of decision makers. Reporting is routine in content and timing whereas analysis is ad hoc.
What role performance reporting performs in organizations.	Performance reporting directs the attention of decision makers and helps them determine whether intervention is necessary.
What data is and how it differs from information.	Data is facts - a measure of the value of a variable with no inherent meaning - whereas information is something that has the potential to be acted upon because it has been given meaning.
How understanding the way that our brains work helps us do a better job.	To be effective the tools we use to help us make sense of data and to communicate information need to take account of how they interface with our brains and those of our audience.

Learning	Reason
Why our existing tools are deficient from a neurological perspective.	Traditional performance management tools fail to exploit the strengths of our brains, which are optimized to deal with images – shapes – rather than symbols. Also, they do not compensate for the brain's relatively poor ability to differentiate between signals and noise.
What lessons we can learn from the way our brains make sense of the world.	The strategy that our brains use to extract sense from potentially overwhelming amounts of data based on hypothesis formations and testing is one that we should adopt as our organizations are faced with exactly that same challenge. We should interact with data rather than process it. We also need to simultaneously attend to both the content and the context – the parts and the whole.
What implications the 'brain' model has for the role of information professionals.	By selecting what is relevant, directing the attention of the organization to what is important and communicating it widely to those who take action, information professionals act as guardians of an organization's consciousness – what and how it perceives.

chapter 3

Direction: Performance as Flow

> In which I will explain how adopting a dynamic perspective helps set the context to help frame meaningful explorations of performance and describe some simple techniques to help understand and present trend information and analyse causality and risk.

PAINTING THE BIG PICTURE

Alban William Houseago Phillips was born in 1914 to the wife of a dairy farmer from Te Runga near Dannevirke on the North Island of New Zealand. Before he finished school, he fled to Australia to escape his farming fate at an unpronounceable location and (unsurprisingly) adopted the name 'Bill'.

In Australia he had a variety of jobs including managing a cinema and hunting crocodiles (what else?) before moving to China, which he fled to escape the invading Japanese. After a trip across Soviet Russia on the trans-Siberian express he arrived in London and enrolled on an electrical engineering course.

But normality didn't last long for Phillips, because he was called up into the Royal Air Force (RAF) in 1938 and before long found himself in Singapore having to dodge the Japanese for a second time. The Japanese finally caught up with him when they overran Java. Phillips then spent the rest of the war in a concentration camp where he learned Chinese, built a secret radio in the heel of a shoe and an equally secret kettle linked up to the camp's electrical system that was used to make illegal cups of tea.

After the war Phillips returned to London to study sociology at London School of Economics (LSE) but, finding it boring, he quit that and transferred to the more exciting (!) economics course instead. Within 11 years he was a professor.

Little wonder that Phillips has been described as 'the Indiana Jones of economics'.

Phillips is perhaps best known for his work on the Philips curve, which describes the relationship between inflation and the level of employment in an economy. But perhaps his most innovative contribution to economics was a water-based analogue computer he built in 1948 in his landlady's garage in Croydon, in the suburbs of London while he was still a student, using parts from decommissioned Lancaster bombers.

Phillips was fascinated by the way national economies worked. And he recognized that to properly understand a complex interconnected system like the economy you needed more than the static records on expenditure and income – you needed to be able to trace how money flowed around the system.

The result of his efforts was the MONIAC: a 2-metre high physical model of the UK economy (Figure 3.0a). Coloured water sat in a tank representing the treasury at the top of the system and ran from there through a series of tubes in and out of other vessels representing government debt, household savings, national assets and so on. Changes in taxation and patterns of consumption was modelled by opening or closing valves and the impact was traced through the entire system. Originally built as an aid to teaching, Phillips discovered that it actually worked as an economic model with a tolerance of 2%. Hence, governments throughout the world, who did not yet have access to electronic computers, commissioned copies of the model. Although no one uses water anymore, the principles of using 'stocks and flows' to construct dynamic models of complex systems like economies, ecologies and climate are still used to this day.

In many ways, I think the challenges that we are faced with in trying to understand and communicate business performance are similar to those faced by Phillips in the 1940s.

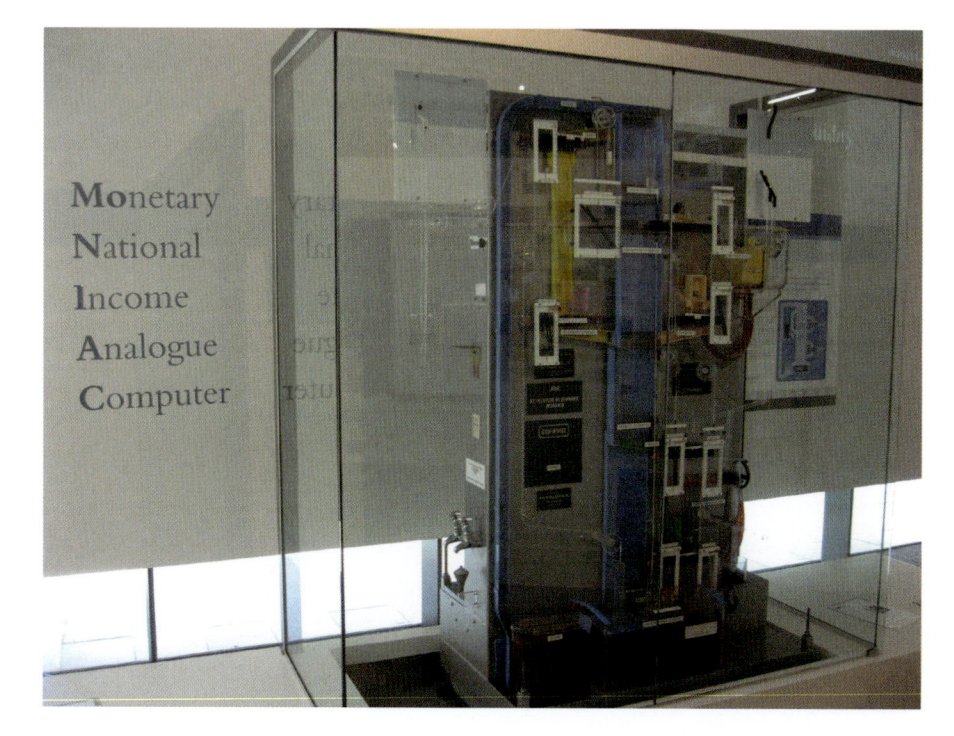

Figure 3.0
Bill Phillips and his MONIAC liquid computer

Direction: Performance as Flow

In Part 1 of this book I laid out my arguments for a transformation in the way that business performance is analysed and communicated.

Traditional static methods, based on single data points and comparison with arbitrary targets, fail us. They do not stand up to logical scrutiny, nor do they enable us to exploit the potential of IT or the nature and capability of our brains. Critically they strip away the context that we need to be able to make sense of the data – its relative position in a time sequence. So, a critical element of the transformation needed involves bringing a sense of business dynamics – the time dimension – back into performance reporting; a perspective that has been lost because of our narrow focus on single data points. Time is the context that we need in order to be able to help us make sense of what is happening, why and what needs to be done.

THE IMPORTANCE OF TEMPORAL CONTEXT

To illustrate the importance of placing data within the content of time, here are two data series.

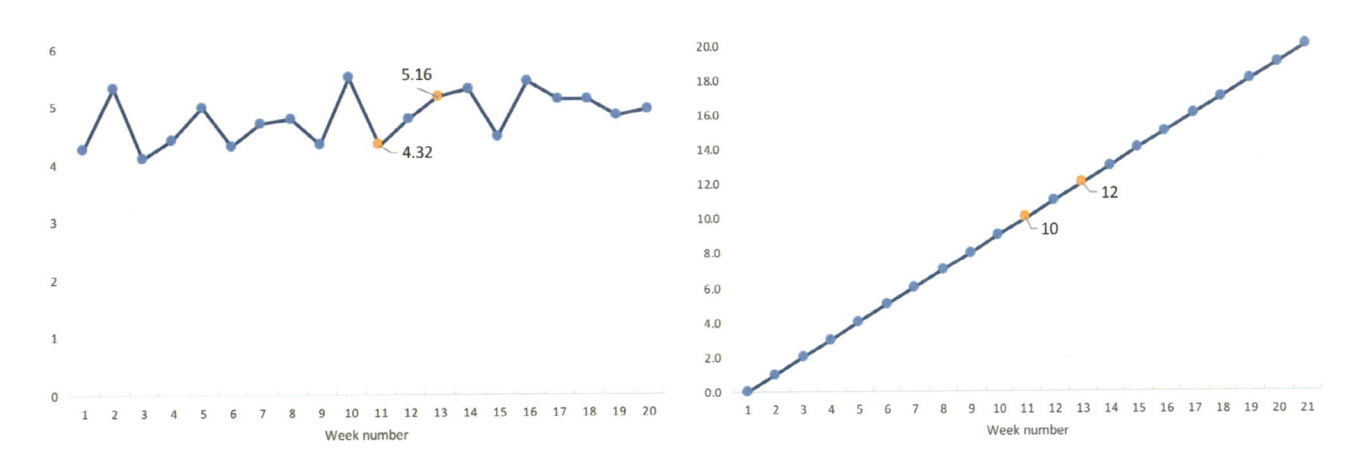

For both it is technically correct to say that week 13 is 20% up on week 11'. But this 'fact' means something very different depending on the context in which it sits.

Figure 3.1
Steady trend/noisy data series

Of course, it is easy for me to criticize. It is more difficult – and more important – to come up with practical ideas about how to do things better.

For me the word 'practical' means solutions that can be readily understood and put into practice by a reader as soon as they put this book down. Fancy software and mathematics have their place, but I will demonstrate how much can be achieved without their help using tools and techniques already at our disposal.

The critical change we need to make is in how we *think* about the process of making sense of performance. In a nutshell, we need to stop confusing data with information.

ORGANIZATIONS AS DYNAMIC SYSTEMS

In Chapter 2 I defined performance as a pattern of behaviour over time. Performance is a dynamic phenomenon. It is something that organizations do continuously rather than something that is trapped in a historic record. So, we need to measure performance trends.

At this point I'm guessing that some readers of this book are saying to themselves 'that's all very well, but there is no way that this will work because accountants have to work with discrete periods – book months, quarters and financial years'. I want to tackle the issue of accounting and how it works head on because before you can engage with potential solutions you need to be convinced that there are no barriers to change.

Contrary to what a lot of people – including many accountants – believe I think that financial people ought to be comfortable with dynamic concepts. The most important concept in accounting is the matching principle. Accountants manipulate the 'date stamp' on transactions to correct for the distorting effects of timing differences that make cash flow an unreliable measure of financial performance. Also, the most important skill that accountants acquire – double-entry bookkeeping – is based on measuring stocks and flows in a way that Bill Phillips would instantly recognize (see the 'Double-entry bookkeeping' box).

DOUBLE-ENTRY BOOKKEEPING

It transpires that the idea of measuring the flow of money using stocks and flows to understand the dynamic properties of an organization's behaviour predates Bill Phillip's MONIAC machine by at least 500 years. The measurement technique I am referring to is called double-entry bookkeeping and its use was first documented in 1494 when a Benedictine monk called Luca Pacioli described the 'Venetian Method' of accounting.[9]

In the Venetian Method the stocks are represented in the Balance Sheet - cash, assets inventory and so on - and the flows between them are recorded using a system of debits and credits to ensure that what leaves one balance sheet 'vessel' enters another. Flows in and out of the Profit and Loss reserves account are items we recognize in earnings statements - revenue and costs. Flows in and out of the cash account are called - for obvious reasons - cash flow (Figure 3.2).

So, double-entry bookkeeping is essentially a way of recording the dynamic properties of a business system. And the 'performance' that accountants are usually most interested in are changes in the contents of the profit and loss 'bath', which is the difference in the rate of flow in (revenue) and that of out (costs) of the bath. So, in seeking to understand performance, accountants need to be able to measure these flows and what influences the rate of flow.[10]

Given the dynamic foundations of accounting practice, how come accountants became part of the performance measurement problem? There are a number of reasons for this, the main one being a consequence of the difficulty of measuring flow directly, as I alluded to earlier.

---

9. Pacioli's description takes up only 27 pages in what was likely to have been the first mathematical treatise of the modern era in the West, although he was describing a practice that had been in use for probably many centuries. The term 'Benedictine Monk' doesn't do Pacioli justice since you had to be a cleric to teach in Renaissance universities. There is also a record of him being commissioned to provide consulting to an employee of the Duke of Milan – one Leonardo da Vinci – so he was a bit more of a whizz kid than the traditional descriptions make him sound.

10. It is not only accountants that model the behaviour of systems in this way. The 'stocks' and 'flows' concepts are the foundation of an approach known as 'Systems Dynamics', a movement founded by Jay Forrester at MIT in the 1950s. Systems Dynamic models are used to simulate complex interacting systems like economies, climate, ecosystems and disease spread, often producing counter intuitive results. To learn more refer to *Thinking in Systems* by Donella Meadow (2008).

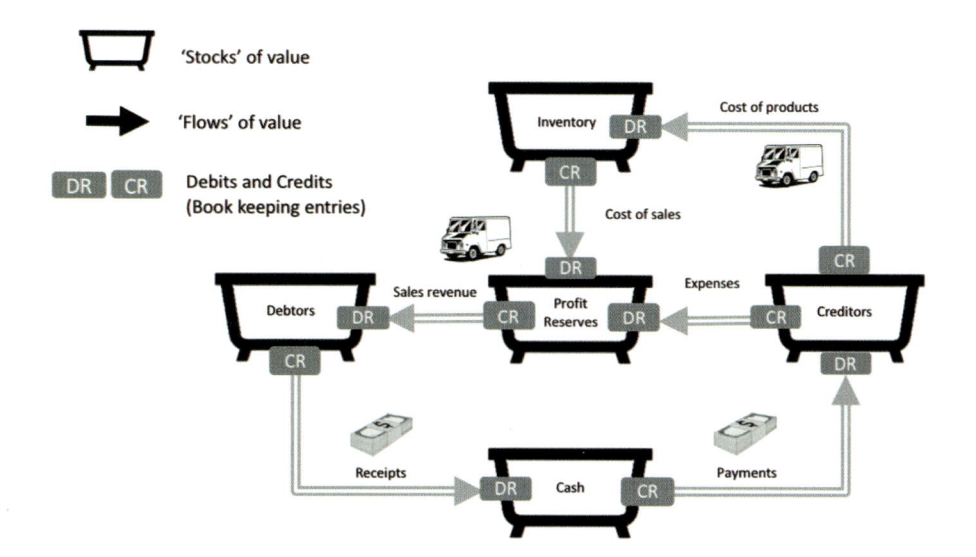

Direction: Performance as Flow

Figure 3.2:
Stocks and flows diagram

This chart shows how double-entry bookkeeping is simply a way of keeping track of the stocks and flows of value. Balance sheet accounts are stocks and a profit and loss account is simply a record of the flows in and out of the profit reserves Balance Sheet account, and so explains the change in level between any two points in time. Just like a good plumbing system using debits and credits ensures that there are no 'leaks' in the value system.

With a car, for example, speed is measured by counting the revolutions of a wheel, which can easily be done continuously, simply by counting. Unfortunately, there is no practical way of continuously measuring the financial performance of a business because inflows are always out of sync with outflows, so adjustments have to be made to ensure that performance measures are not distorted. As a result, flows have to be captured in batches by counting the flow over a defined period, usually a month, and adjusting for timing differences at the end. These adjustments are called either accruals or prepayments depending on the direction of the adjustment.

Referring back to our accounting flow model, this is equivalent to diverting the money pipe into a bucket that is then measuring its contents at the end of a period after having transferred some 'liquid' into the next bucket to balance timings out (Figure 3.3).

Figure 3.3:
Stocks and flows in buckets

Accounting periods are simply the mechanism that enables us to measure changes in this dynamic system. To properly understand what is going on, however, we need to recognize that what is important is the rate of flow, not the content of any set of buckets. And, of course, we need to ensure that the cash 'bath' doesn't run dry!

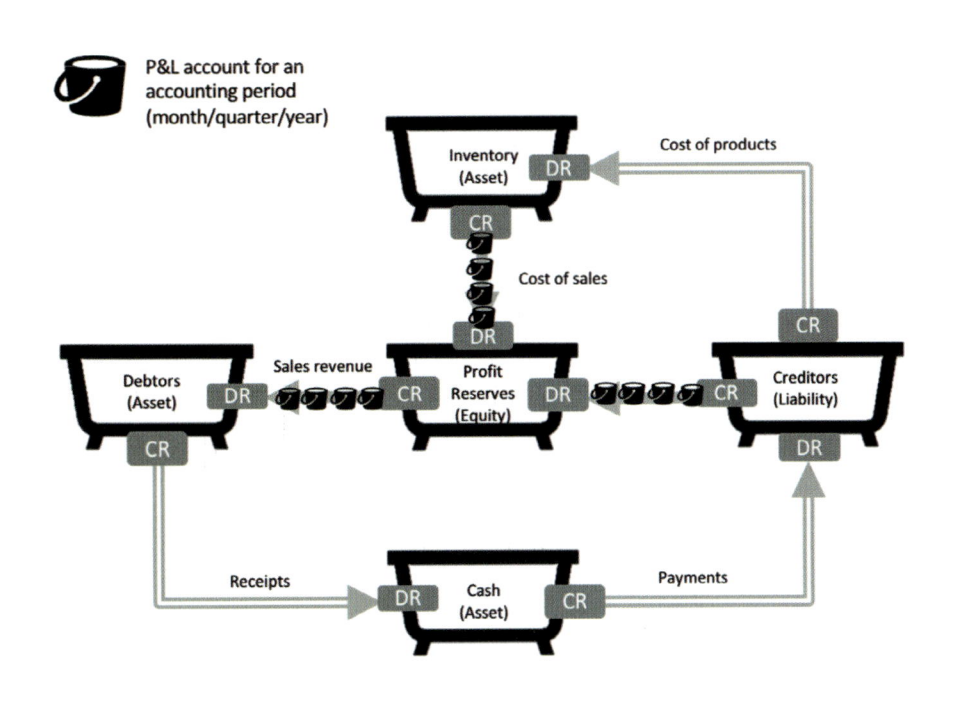

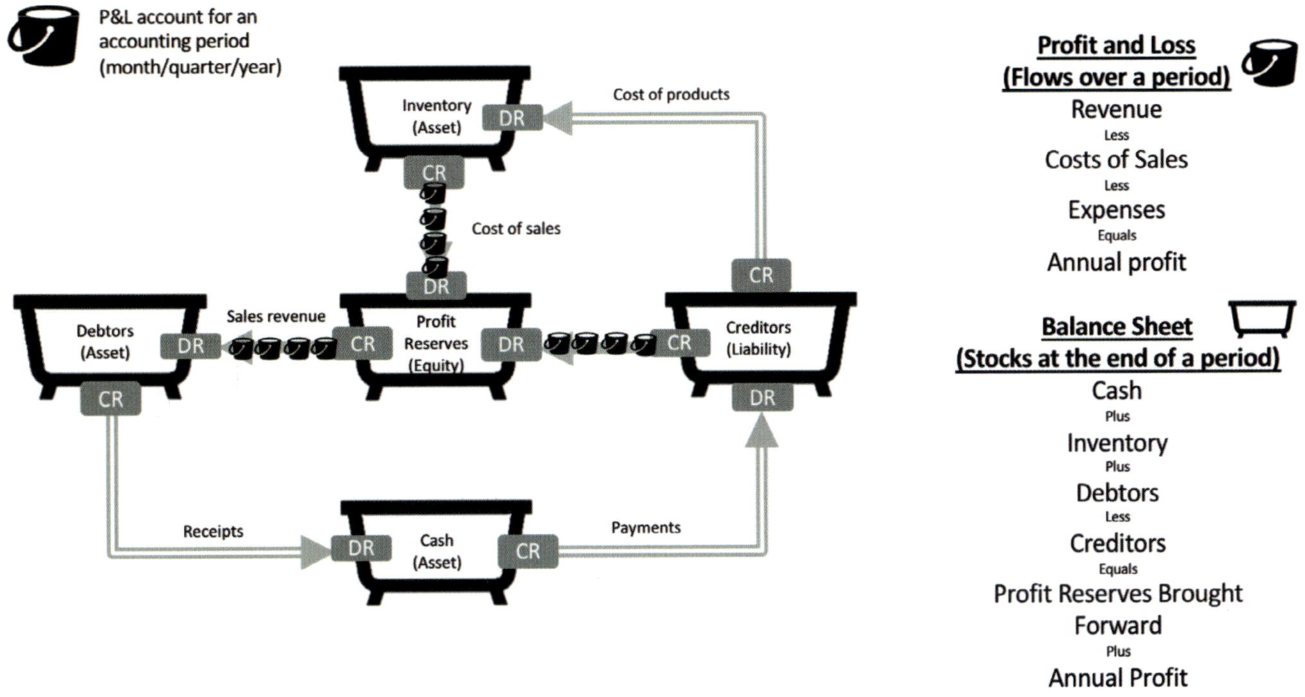

Profit and Loss
(Flows over a period)
Revenue
Less
Costs of Sales
Less
Expenses
Equals
Annual profit

Balance Sheet
(Stocks at the end of a period)
Cash
Plus
Inventory
Plus
Debtors
Less
Creditors
Equals
Profit Reserves Brought Forward
Plus
Annual Profit

This 'batchwise' approach has the merit of being more accurate than measuring flow directly (meteorologists would love to be able to count the wind by putting it into a bucket) but there is a risk that in 'bucketing up' reality like this **the quality of flow** is lost, particularly if very big annual buckets are used and the contents of previous buckets are ignored, as they often are in businesses that have a strong 'current year' focus.

The problem we accountants have is that we come to see performance being represented by the contents of each bucket rather than the buckets as being merely the means of measuring it. In effect, we focus on data – the measurement of quantity in periodic buckets – but ignore the information about the flow of money because we ignore the contents of a range of adjacent buckets.

How accountants lost the plot

Unfortunately, many finance people have lost the sense and the importance of time and movement. This is because we have become captive to our measurement frameworks (see the double-entry bookkeeping box) and the analytical techniques that rely upon them such as variance analysis that we discussed in Chapter 1. It is also because the internal processes of performance measurement have become subordinated to external reporting demands, in particular those anchored on the financial year and the quarter end, with negative consequences for our ability to make sense of data and communicate performance, as we shall see. We all know that the world doesn't end on the 31st December and begin again on the 1st January, but we cling to this myopic view of performance and, worse still, often force other parts of the business to wear the same straitjacket as ourselves.

THE CONVENTIONAL PERSPECTIVE

We will now explore these issues further at a practical level. Let's return to the traditional performance report I produced for my dummy company XYZ Ltd (Table 3.1) that you first saw in Chapter 1 (Table 1.4).

	Quarter 4				Year to Date				2017	
	Actual	Budget	Variance	v Last Year	Actual	Budget	Variance	v Last Year	Budget	v Last Year
Turnover	245	262	-16	-4%	944	970	-26	5%	989	5%
COS	131	139	8	3%	506	527	20	-4%	539	-7%
GP	114	123	-9	-4%	438	443	-6	5%	450	3%
Gross Margin %	47%	47%	0%	0%	46%	46%	1%	0%	45%	-1%
A&P	36	37	1	2%	141	141	-0	-2%	140	1%
Overheads	39	40	1	-5%	139	148	9	-4%	136	2%
Profit	38	46	-7	-14%	157	154	3	11%	174	11%

Table 3.1:
XYZ Ltd revenue variance analysis table

An example of how performance is traditionally analysed and presented.

I asked you to answer the following questions about the *level* of performance, and the *trend* in performance designed to help you decide whether there might be a need to intervene:

Direction: Performance as Flow

1. Is this good or bad performance?
2. Is it getting better or worse?

I followed this up with a question about variation in performance and one that directed your attention to a potential point of intervention.

3. Has anything significant just happened?
4. How credible is the budget for next year?

Remember how we found that it was difficult to provide answers with any conviction and how effortful it felt. Why was this?

There are a number of reasons.

First, as we discovered when we discussed variance analysis, the comparison of an actual value with an arbitrary target for a single period in isolation is not a reliable guide to performance. Neither can it tell us whether any actual value is typical of the performance of XYZ Ltd or in some way exceptional.

Second, two of the questions (Is this getting better or worse? and How credible is next year's budget?) require you to have a sense of the dynamics of this system. And because you were not provided with the contextual data – particularly data about the past – that you needed to be able to do this in a straightforward way you had to infer it from the scraps of evidence that were available and build a picture in your head (see the 'Why is it difficult to make sense of this table' box).

WHY IS IT DIFFICULT TO MAKE SENSE OF THIS TABLE?

To understand why it is so difficult to make sense of tables like this it is helpful to think a bit about what we are asking our brain to do. Here is the process that I would go through to attempt to answer these questions for just one variable (revenue).

| | Quarter 4 |||| Year to Date |||| 2017 ||
	Actual	Budget	Variance	v Last Year	Actual	Budget	Variance	vs Last Year	Budget	v Last Year
Turnover	245	262	-16	-4%	944	970	-26	5%	989	5%
COS	131	139	8	3%	506	527	20	-4%	539	-1%
GP	114	123	-9	-4%	438	443	-6	5%	450	3%
Gross Margin %	47%	47%	0%	0%	46%	46%	1%	0%	45%	-1%
A&P	36	37	1	2%	141	141	0	2%	140	1%
Overheads	39	40	1	-5%	139	148	9	-4%	136	2%
Profit	38	46	-7	-14%	157	154	3	11%	174	11%

Is performance good or bad?

1. revenue is below budget, but
2. it is above last year so...

...it is not clear whether this is good or bad

Figure 3.2:
Eye-tracking chart

This chart shows the six movements my eye needed to attempt to answer a set of simple questions.

Is performance getting better or worse?

3. revenue in quarter four is lower than last year, and
4. accounts for a significant chunk of the adverse variance for the year, but
5. more than 25% of the annual revenue was generated in the last quarter so...

...it is not clear whether actuals have declined, or the budget for last year's actuals was unrealistic or whether either the fourth quarter was an unrepresentative 'blip' or the business is highly seasonal and quarter four actually represents a downward trend in performance.

Has anything significant changed?

...it is not clear whether anything significantly changes since we have very limited visibility for what actually happened prior to quarter four.

How credible is the budget?

6. the budgeted growth is the same as the growth in the current year, however,
7. quarter four recorded less growth than the prior year so...

...there is conflicting evidence that makes it difficult to come to a conclusion.

In summary, it took seven different eye movements and a lot of speculative inferences, but I was unable to provide a definitive answer to any of these questions, despite having decades of experience of analysing information presented in this way. Looked at in this way it is difficult to argue that this is an effective way of communicating performance.

	Actual
Jan-15	78.3
Feb-15	66.7
Mar-15	57.4
Apr-15	71.7
May-15	65.4
Jun-15	63.5
Jul-15	82.7
Aug-15	79.1
Sep-15	83.2
Oct-15	89.6
Nov-15	81.4
Dec-15	80.7
Jan-16	81.1
Feb-16	73.8
Mar-16	72.6
Apr-16	89.9
May-16	67.8
Jun-16	71.6
Jul-16	82.3
Aug-16	78.5
Sep-16	81.2
Oct-16	91.6
Nov-16	76.7
Dec-16	76.8

Figure 3.3:
XYZ Ltd revenue by period

A data series presented in the form of a table. Note how difficult it is to infer trends when data is presented in this way, and how much space it consumes.

One reason for the lack of historic data is that it takes a lot of valuable space on the page to display the full data set. Figure 3.3, for example, is the time series data for just one variable in this report – revenue.

Clearly presenting information in this way takes up a lot of space, but is it any easier to answer the question, 'Is this getting better or worse?' And how about, 'How credible is next year's budget?' Not easy at all. The reason for this is to do with the way that our brain most naturally works, which doesn't involve the kind of mental gymnastics I describe in the 'Why is it difficult to make sense of this table?' box. This is perhaps the most important insight in this book and informs everything else in it, so pay attention!

To make sense of data and communicate it effectively we need to understand how we think, and to develop the ability to think about how we think and so better appreciate how other people think.

THINKING ABOUT THINKING

An important discovery of cognitive scientists is that human beings don't have just one way of thinking. 'Dual process' theory describes two modes of thinking – two different kinds of thinking process – which differ from each other in a number of important respects. Understanding how they differ, and their relative strengths and weakness, is critically important, both to the process of making sense of data and to communicating the meaning embedded within it.

The two types of thinking are called System 1 and System 2 thinking. In his book of the same name the Nobel Laureate Daniel Kahneman labels them 'thinking fast' and 'thinking slow' respectively, but speed is not the only way in which these two modes differ.

System 1 'fast'

This mode of thinking is evolutionarily very old – it has been with us for a very long time: perhaps before we could even be called humans. Think of it not as a thinking process with a series of steps but as a collection of logical shortcuts that help us make 'good enough' judgements quickly and with minimum effort. System 1 thinking is a set of decision-making rules of thumb (the technical term is 'heuristics'), because they are based on shortcuts, which are not only fast but also very frugal since they place limited demand on our mental resources.

For instance, System 1 processes provide us with astonishingly good pattern-recognition skills. So, we don't work out who someone is from their facial components – such as the colour of hair, the shape of the nose and so on, like in the game of 'Guess Who' – we recognize their face instantly from its overall pattern in a way that it is difficult for us to describe (or for a computer program to replicate). In particular, thanks to System 1, we are very good at detecting and acting upon movement, such as when we catch a ball.

It is easy to see why we have developed such extraordinary pattern-recognition capabilities. Being able to detect faces and quickly work out whether they are friendly, and to differentiate nourishing from harmful berries, confer a clear evolutionary advantage. And the skills we display in sporting activities that depend on tracking the trajectory of an object are simply hunting skills that have been repurposed. Also, as we discussed in Chapter 2, encountering the world armed with a hypothesis of 'what is out there' based on experience is a much more efficient strategy than having to work everything out from scratch by sorting through the enormous volume of sensory data that continuously bombards us.

Although many of these heuristics are hard wired in our genes, most are capable of being modified by experience. We can enhance existing conceptual abilities by practice, or we can learn new ones. For example, a new System 1 heuristic might be 'my partner always freaks out when I…' (you can probably easily fill this one in yourself).

Anyone who masters a skill, such as driving a car or playing a musical instrument has done so by laying down a complex set of thinking rules and embedding them in their System 1 routines. But the good news is that whatever their levels of sophistication System 1 heuristics are fast and frugal. You don't have to think about what is going on because they largely operate below our level of consciousness. As a result, we have the misleading impression that what we are doing is simple and easy – when it isn't. The sense of effortlessness is entirely down to the fact that we are using pre-programmed neural circuitry, rather than creating 'new code'.

But there are downsides to relying on System 1, which is what Kahneman explores in his book. Because System 1 processes largely operate below the level of consciousness, we can experience them as 'simple' and 'right' even when they are complex and wrong. So, we can be very mistaken and not be aware of it, which is how illusionists make their living and Kahneman earned his Nobel Prize.

Only by spotting when we may be wrong, which might be reflected in a very mild feeling of discomfort or confusion that we normally suppress or ignore, can we avoid making mistakes now, and similar ones in the future[11]. When this happens what we need to do is to refer the matter to System 2 – a process we call 'paying attention'. Ironically then, we can get better at thinking by being more aware of our feelings.

11. It might be helpful to refer back to the cognitive model I described in Chapter 2 and think of this discomfort being associated with a high level of prediction errors.

FEELING AND SEEING

The cognitive scientist Antonio Damasio argues that from the perspective of our brain, trapped inside its bony shell, there is no conceptual difference between the sensations detected by, say, our eyes and those of our internal organs. They are both sources of sensory data that informs the process by which our brain perceives the world.

Different patterns of bodily sensations are as relevant as visual, auditory or olfactory patterns and like them can be used to inform the model that enables us to perceive and

Direction: Performance as Flow

act. Equally they might be the source of dissonance – the sense that something doesn't (or does) feel right.

In this way, Damasio's 'Sensory Marker Hypothesis' provides a scientific rational for what we call 'gut feeling'.

System 2 'slow'

System 2 thinking is evolutionarily more modern and, unlike System 1, this kind of thinking is usually available to our consciousness. Also, unlike System 1, System 2 thinking is effortful and slow. We literally pay for its attention by increasing our brain's consumption of energy (glucose). Also, our speed of thought is constrained by the capacity of our working memory, which is very small – typically only seven 'chunks' of data (plus or minus two) at any one time. Ironically, given how puny it is, we normally think of our System 2 thinking when we are asked about our intelligence!

Although they operate differently, System 2 and System 1 can both get it wrong, albeit in varying ways. System 1 fails by making false assumptions (hidden hypotheses) about the world. System 2 errors are the result of ignorance, a shortage of mental horsepower or errors of reasoning.

Relating this back to what we learned about brain functioning in Chapter 2 we can conceive of System 1 as the source of the generative model (hypothesis) that primes our perception. System 2 thinking is what we use when we discover that we don't have an 'off the shelf' model that squares with the evidence of our senses.[12]

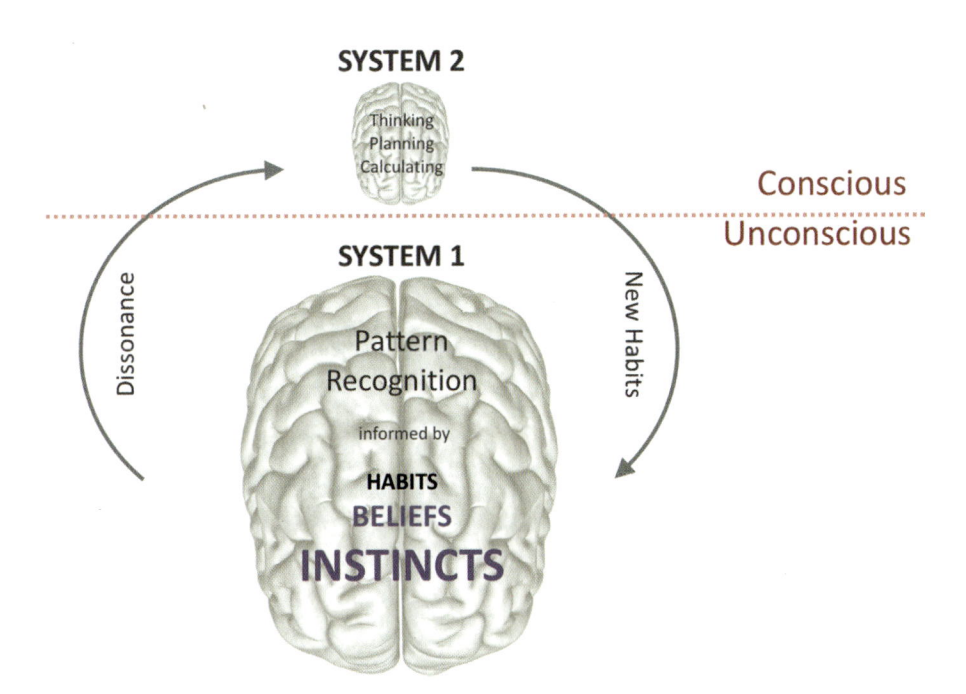

12. Despite having different origins Dual Processing theory is entirely consistent with the model of brain processing I described in Chapter 2 (usually called 'Predictive Processing' or 'Predictive Coding'), which provides an overarching theory. I use it here because many readers will already be familiar with it and it is conceptually easier to grasp.

Figure 3.4:
Two brain picture

This chart illustrates the nature of the relationship between System 1 and System 2 thinking. Sensory data is filtered through System 1, which may act 'without reference' to System 2. Only when there is a discrepancy between the situation that is perceived and the models of the world (which might exist as habits or beliefs) used by System 1 is System 2 enlisted. This might result in learning, and so change the models used by System 1. Note that they do not physically exist as separate system in the brain.

Why is it important to understand this?

It is important because in attempting to make sense of the world of organizational performance and communicate it to others we need to consciously exploit the strengths of the two different styles of thinking and avoid their weaknesses. To do this we need to develop an awareness of our different patterns of thought type and when they are in play. We need to be able to think about thinking. The fancy word for the ability to be aware of the process of thinking is 'metacognition' but I prefer the Buddhist term 'mindfulness' because it describes what it feels like to be aware of what is going on in our mind, and many people will have had experience of the practice inside and outside of a business context.

By developing mindfulness and becoming more aware of how we assimilate and process sensory data we develop the capability to exercise choice. We can choose how we interpret and attribute meaning to data rather than responding to it in a thoughtless manner. And we can decide how to communicate meaning so that our audience receive a high-fidelity message. One of the aims of this book is to help you develop mindfulness to enable you to make better choices and so be more effective in how you analyse and present statistical information. This is summarized in Figure 3.4.

Figure 3.5 shows a list of the different characteristics of the two modes of thought:

Figure 3.4: Characteristics of the two modes of thought

Cognitive Processes

System 1 (Fast)	System 2 (Slow)
Unconscious	Conscious
Automatic	Requires attention
Fast	Slow
Easy	Effortful
Involuntary	Invoked
Innate or learned patterns	Created associations
Not necessarily 'right' (cognitive bias)	Not necessarily 'right' (faulty reasoning)

Let's return to the practical example I introduced earlier to help us understand some of the implications of approaching our work with an appreciation of brain functioning.

We know that our System 1 brains are good at spotting patterns visually and particularly sensitive to movement, but in Table 3.2 I presented a data time series as a set of abstract symbols (numbers) in a column, which only System 2 can access. Trying to make sense of this data series felt like very hard work, because it was. As you scanned the numbers your brain will have been consuming glucose at a high rate, leaving you feeling tired after a few moments.

Now let's look at Figure 3.6, which shows the same data presented in a graphical form that is more easily accessed by System 1.

Direction: Performance as Flow

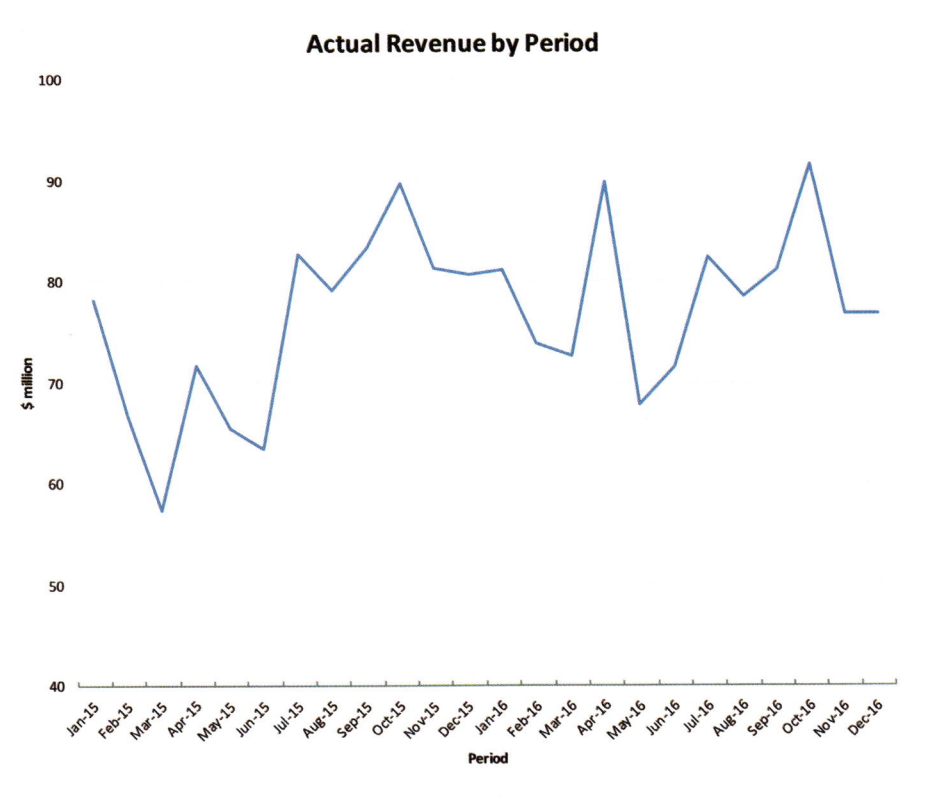

Actual Revenue by Period

[Chart showing $ million on y-axis (40-100) vs Period (Jan-15 to Dec-16) on x-axis, with a line fluctuating primarily between 55 and 95]

Figure 3.5:
A data series presented in a chart

This data series is the same as that contained in Table 3.3 and appears to show a difference between the level of sales before and after period 6.

Notice how quickly and easily your brain assimilates data presented in this way. Also, I'm betting that you quickly realized that your slow System 2 analysis failed to pick up features that are obvious when we look at the data graphically – like the sense we have of an upward trend after the first few periods and the subsequent plateau, and perhaps outliers in March and October 2016. And maybe some of the things that you originally 'noticed' now don't seem so clear. Remember, our aim is not just to make things easier for analysts who work all day every day with data; what this teaches us about the communication of statistical information is even more relevant for the lay people who are routinely assaulted with indigestible tables of data by analysts.

In summary

Organizations, whether they are economies or businesses, are dynamic systems and performance can only be properly understood and managed with information that has a historical perspective. Although data about performance is necessarily captured numerically as a series of snapshots, we need to find ways to communicate performance in a way that is readily accessible to our brains, which evolution has tuned to easily assimilate visual information, particularly when it represents movement. The challenge for information professionals is to align the processes they use to interpret and communicate information with the way that our brains work – so that it looks and feels easy without creating false impressions or compromising analytical rigour.

Earlier I compared individual data points with snapshots, like frames in a movie. They are 'true representations' of reality – facts – but the meaning that we can extract from each individual one is limited because we cannot see movement –

we have to infer the behaviour of the system. Even when a data series is presented visually in a graph like the one in Figure 3.5, the picture is blurred by noise it contains. In simple terms, the way that the individual data points 'bounce around' makes it difficult to spot the true trend and easy to be misled into seeing one that isn't there.

How can we create a clearer dynamic picture of our organizations using the 'snapshot' data we routinely capture?

THE DYNAMIC PERSPECTIVE − SIMPLE AVERAGES

Let's use another analogy to understand how we can use data to get a dynamic perspective on performance.

Imagine that a driver of a car has knocked over a pedestrian and we need to understand how the accident happened.

In assessing the culpability of the driver for the accident knowing their position at a point in time (a data point) is not enough. We need to know:

1. the speed at which the driver was travelling (an average),
2. whether they were accelerating or decelerating (the change in average) and
3. whether the acceleration or deceleration was gradual or rapid just preceding the accident (the rate of change in the average).

Only with this information can we get a sense of the driver's contribution to the accident.[13] If a driver was already travelling quickly and had just sped up, they would be more culpable than one who was travelling slowly and had just hit the brakes.

In our everyday life we use these kinds of measures to explain behaviour and assess performance without realizing it (because our System 1 thinking processes are subconscious). Take the example of a sailor on a single-handed transatlantic journey. We need to know their position in space, of course, but our judgement about how well they are doing is based on their rate of progress over the most recent period and on how well that compares with previous periods. If the sailor is in a race, we will compare this with the progress of fellow competitors since, although many people have sailed the Atlantic before, the weather conditions are always different, and they are in a competition. We therefore 'know', without thinking, that comparison with a predetermined target is unhelpful.

While our intuitive System 1 brain 'knows' it is wrong to do this, our professional System 2 mind suppresses this knowledge when we are at work, so we end up using techniques (like comparisons with arbitrary targets) that we would not use in our private life in the mistaken impression that they are more 'correct'.

We will return to the issue of targets later. Let's focus for the moment on how best to measure what is actually going on.

[13]. Isaac Newton had the same problem when he was trying to understand the movement of planets. He had to invent differential calculus to model their behaviour. Fortunately, we can get by with simpler methods.

Direction: Performance as Flow

I have argued that to understand the dynamics of performance we need to measure the rate of change, and this involves calculating an average. But there is more than one way of calculating an average. Which one should we use?

Finance folk, struggling in their self-imposed financial year straitjackets, often use a year to date average like the one shown in Table 3.5.

	Period 1	Period 2	Period 3	Period 4	Period 5
Actual	250	100	120	110	115
Year to Date Average	250	175	157	145	139

Table 3.5:
Year to date average

Here a year to date average is calculated using the value for the current and all prior periods.

Using year to date averages doesn't make any sense, because the average after one month isn't an average, and after two periods the average isn't very representative. And as you progress through the year the number of periods over which the average is calculated increases, so the change in the average will tend to become less extreme, but this reflects the change in sample size (the denominator in the equation), not necessarily a change in performance. It also means that averages made at different points in time cannot be compared, so we cannot use them to understand the dynamics of performance.

One answer to this problem is to use a rolling (or moving) average where the sample size remains constant. The example in Table 3.6 uses a four-period moving average. Because the sample size is constant this better reflects performance and moving averages calculated at different points in time can be compared to give us a sense of how performance is changing.

	Period 1	Period 2	Period 3	Period 4	Period 5
Actual	250	100	120	110	115
Year to Date Average	250	175	157	145	139
P4 Moving Average				145	
P5 Moving Average					111

Table 3.6:
A four-period moving average

Here an average is calculated using the current and the previous three periods.

Clearly, a rolling average is a better measure of performance than the 'to date' average, but it has another weakness, which you may have spotted.

In the example in Table 3.6 we can see that the moving average changed significantly between period 4 and period 5. But this is nothing to do with a change in the measures between these two points in time, in fact you will notice that the actual increased between periods 4 and 5 while the average went down. The reason the average moved in the way that it did was because period 1 fell out of the moving period range. So, we recorded a change in the average not because of something that has just happened, but because of something that happened a while ago (five periods ago in this case). This means that moving averages are a less than perfect measure of current performance.

SMOOTHED AVERAGES

Statisticians, being clever people, noticed the problem with moving averages some time ago and invented a different sort of average to get around it. This is called a 'smoothed average' and it comes pretty close to the top of my list of 'things I wished I had known when I had a proper job'.

Smoothed averages are a simple technique with many uses. For example, the most commonly used forecasting techniques are based on analysing time series using smoothed averages, because they provide a reliable measure of the current state of a system – and consequently provide a good basis for a forecast going forward. But, surprisingly given their obvious attractions, smoothing techniques are little used outside forecasting, which is a failing I hope this book helps to remedy. Although the technique is simple, it can be a struggle to understand them at first, so I will take it slowly.

Although we don't normally think about them this way, averages work by giving each data point in a series an equal weighting. Because all the weightings add up to 1, the sum of these calculations provides an average of the data series. For example, in Table 3.7 every period in a four-period rolling average is assigned a weight of 0.25 (because 1 divided by 4 is 0.25).

Table 3.7:
Four-period average with weightings

A simple moving average assigns the same weight to every period within the defined range.

	Period 1	Period 2	Period 3	Period 4	Period 5
Actual	250	100	120	110	115
Year to Date Average	250	175	157	145	139
P4 Moving Average				145	
P5 Moving Average					111
P4 Weighting	0.25	0.25	0.25	0.25	
P5 Weighting		0.25	0.25	0.25	0.25

As we have seen, because every period within a range attracts an equal weight a period towards the beginning of a range has the same level of influence on the average as the most recent period. But it is obvious that something that happened recently is more representative of the current state of a system than something that happened a long time ago. Ideally then, you would assign a higher weighting to the more recent past, compared to the distant past. This is what smoothed averages do, as shown in Table 3.8.

Direction: Performance as Flow

	Period 1	Period 2	Period 3	Period 4	Period 5
Actual	250	100	120	110	115
P4 Smoothed Average				113	
P5 Smoothed Average					107
P4 Weightings	0.063	0.125	0.250	0.500	
P5 Weightings	0.031	0.063	0.125	0.250	0.500
Smoothing Parameter (alpha)	0.5				

Table 3.8:
Smoothed average

A smoothed average gives a greater weight to the values for more recent periods. The weighting decays exponentially, because the same smoothing parameter is applied to values that decline in a non-linear way. Hence why this technique is sometimes called exponential smoothing.

As you can see, in the example in Table 3.8 the last period is given a weighting of 0.5, and the period before that a weighting of 0.25 (0.5 x 0.5) and then 0.125 (0.5 x 0.5 x 0.5) and so on. This procedure means that the weighting declines exponentially, with the cumulative sum of the weights getting closer and closer to 1 the further back we go in history. This is why this technique is called an *exponentially* smoothed average.

This technique is a very powerful tool in helping us to make sense of data, particularly if it is very volatile or 'noisy'. The outcome also appeals to our (System 1) intuitive sense of what is going on. It 'looks right' to the eye even if the observer doesn't understand how the numbers were calculated. For example, the chart in Figure 3.6 analyses margins in XYZ Ltd. Because of the level of noise in the data, this pattern is difficult to pick up from the raw numbers for each period, even when they are plotted graphically, but the smoothed average very clearly shows a clear downward trend over most of the period that looks like it may have reversed in period 15. Moreover, without this smoothed trend to guide their eyes it is likely that any two people would have 'seen' different things in the data and so come to different conclusions and taken different actions.

Figure 3.6 illustrates the power of smoothed averages to summarize data and demonstrates how presenting it in this way mobilizes our System 1 brain. Thus, it becomes easier to understand and interpret the data and makes us less prone to 'detecting' patterns that aren't there, in the way we can 'see', say, animal shapes in clouds. Put simply, when data is presented graphically in this way, we don't have to *infer* performance *from* data – we can *see* it *in* the data. And once we are clear that what is actually happening – in this case the apparent reverse in a declining trend – we can refer the problems of 'Why?' and 'What should be done?' to our analytical System 2 brain. Presenting and analysing data in this way matches the relative strengths and weaknesses of the two types of thinking and this is a theme that I will return to time and time again. But, before we get to the end of this book, I hope your metacognitive powers (i.e. mindfulness) will have developed to the point that I don't need to keep pointing it out.

Smoothed averages are very useful, but you need to be aware of a couple of technical issues before you can use them in anger.

Figure 3.6:
XYZ Ltd margins with smoothed average

Note that each point on the smoothed average line represents the average value at that point in time. The angle of the line represents the rate of change and changes in the angle changes in the rate of change. Note how the smoothed average declines until about period 15 when it reverses – a fact that would not be immediately obvious from an examination of individual period values.

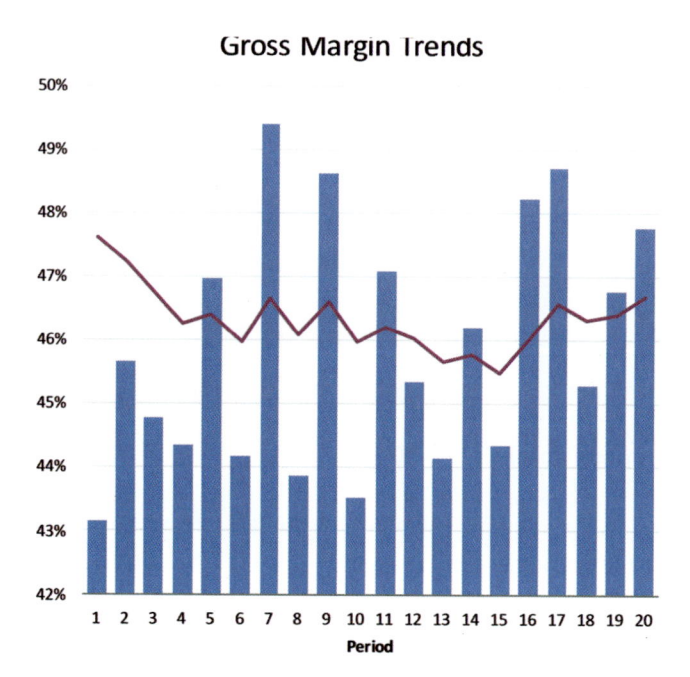

First, the results you get depend on the factor you use to weight the periods. This factor is called the 'smoothing constant' and is sometimes just abbreviated to the Greek symbol for alpha (∂). I chose an alpha of 0.5 to illustrate the principle in Table 3.3 because it made it easy to demonstrate the principle, but in Figure 3.6 I used 0.2. There is no correct alpha to choose, just in the same way that there is no correct range to choose for normal rolling averages; it is a choice. I used 0.2 because 0.5 would have made the average overly sensitive to the most recent values. If the data you are looking at is even more volatile than this you might choose a smaller alpha value.

This problem of what value to use as the smoothing constant also provides an opportunity, however, because you can use different alpha values to bring out different trends, as we will see later. For example, a factor of 0.3 produces an average that is more representative of the short-term trend than one using 0.2 (the medium-term trend) and 0.1 (the longer-term trend). Later in this chapter I will demonstrate how this feature can be used to do something very useful.

The second 'technical' issue is that any exponential series like the one I used earlier (0.5, 0.25, 0.125…) declines towards zero but never reaches it *exactly*, meaning that the sum of the weightings is never exactly 1. The good news is that every data point, no matter how old, makes a contribution to the average but at a diminishing rate. There is a downside, however, because the sum of the series never equals 1 exactly the average is always understated. This is not a problem in practice if the alpha used is large or the data series is long enough. If not, I recommend that the first period in a series be allocated the 'left over' or residual weighting so that the sum of the weightings always equals 1. This means that with very short data series the first period can have an undue influence on the average (as shown in Table 3.7), so care needs to be taken when interpreting smoothed average values when the data series is not very long.

Weightings by Period (alpha = 0.2)

	By Period	Cumulative	Residual
P0	0.200	0.200	0.800
P-1	0.160	0.360	0.640
P-2	0.128	0.488	0.512
P-3	0.102	0.590	0.410
P-4	0.082	0.672	0.328
P-5	0.066	0.738	0.262
P-6	0.052	0.790	0.210
P-7	0.042	0.832	0.168
P-8	0.034	0.866	0.134
P-9	0.027	0.893	0.107
P-10	0.021	0.914	0.086

Table 3.9: Showing impact of early periods on smoothed values

In this example for a data series comprised of 11 values, the 'oldest' data point (P-10) has a weighting of 0.107, made up of a weighting of 0.021 for the period and a residual 'unused' weighting of 0.086. This is probably not enough to skew the average, but if the sample size is smaller the residual weighting attributed to the first period increases, thereby increasing the risk that the overall average could be distorted by an abnormal value in that period. So, in this example, P-7 has a greater impact (0.210) on the smoothed average than the most recent period (0.2) because of the impact of the residual value.

In practice, I always use an alpha of 0.2 unless there is an obvious reason not to, and I ignore the smoothed average for the first four periods because after this point the undue influence of the first data point will have 'washed through' the numbers.[14] Follow this advice and as analysts you will find smoothed averages to be a reliable and trusty friend, capable of guiding you through all manner of tangled data jungles.

Finally, I want to touch on the practical issue of how to efficiently calculate smoothed averages. For the purposes of illustration, I will demonstrate this technique by taking the value for every period and applying a different factor to each one. This approach is very clumsy but there is a shortcut method that makes it very easy to implement in a spreadsheet as only two numbers are required.

First, weight the last data point by the chosen alpha (e.g. 0.2). Then multiply the prior period's smoothed average by the 'unused' weighting (i.e. 1 less 0.2 = 0.8). Finally, add the two numbers together. Once you have calculated the first smoothed average the rest is easy – you can copy/paste the formula and use it for all subsequent periods, as shown in Table 3.10.

Smoothed averages are a very useful and powerful approach to understanding trends but sometimes trends can be hidden or distorted if there are strong seasonal patterns in the data – something that affects financial data in commercial organizations – in which case a different way of averaging may be more appropriate.

14. Unless the value for the first period is abnormally large or small, in which case it is permissible to adjust it, for example, by using a simple average of the first few periods so that its impact is not distorting. This practice is known as 'initialization'.

SEASONALITY

Seasonality is a word used by statisticians to describe any repetitive pattern in a data series. This could literally be related to seasons of the year – for example, ice cream sales are higher in summer than in winter – but repetitive patterns are often not weather related, for instance those due to public holidays like Christmas

Period By Period Method (Period 8 only)

CALCULATIONS

Period	Value	Period Weight	Smoothed Period Value
1	5	=1-SUM(F9:F15)	=+E8*F8
2	2	=+F10*0.8	=+E9*F9
3	7	=+F11*0.8	=+E10*F10
4	12	=+F12*0.8	=+E11*F11
5	5	=+F13*0.8	=+E12*F12
6	6	=+F14*0.8	=+E13*F13
7	8	=+F15*0.8	=+E14*F14
8	12	0.2	=+E15*F15
		Period 8	=+SUM(G8:G15)

RESULT

1		0.2097152	1.048576
2		0.0524288	0.1048576
3		0.065536	0.458752
4		0.08192	0.98304
5		0.1024	0.512
6		0.128	0.768
7		0.16	1.28
8		0.2	2.4
		Period 8	7.5552256

Continuous Method (all Periods)

CALCULATIONS

Period	Value	Smoothed Period Average
1	5	=+L8
2	2	=+(L9*0.2)+(M8*0.8)
3	7	=+(L10*0.2)+(M9*0.8)
4	12	=+(L11*0.2)+(M10*0.8)
5	5	=+(L12*0.2)+(M11*0.8)
6	6	=+(L13*0.2)+(M12*0.8)
7	8	=+(L14*0.2)+(M13*0.8)
8	12	=+(L15*0.2)+(M14*0.8)

RESULTS

1		5
2		4.4
3		4.92
4		6.336
5		6.0688
6		6.05504
7		6.444032
8		7.5552256

Table 3.10:
Shortcut way of calculating smoothed values

Calculating a smoothed average from scratch every period is very laborious. Instead, simply weight the current period by the alpha (here 0.2) and the previous period's smoothed average by the residual (1-alpha, i.e. 0.8) to achieve the same result with minimal effort.

and New Year. And there is almost always pronounced seasonality at a daily level because people's patterns of behaviour differ at weekends.

Wherever there is significant seasonality the smoothed averages can be distorted. Smoothing will supress noise in the data but instead of seeing a simple straight-line trend, for instance, the average will fluctuate in a regular way. This might be what we want to show if we are using smoothed averages to detect seasonality in a noisy data series. But if we are trying to track subtle longer-terms trends, we may find that seasonal fluctuations swamp the analysis. For example, raw financial data such as sales and profit are almost always highly seasonal, even if the products that are sold are not, because of the impact of major public holidays like Christmas, and unless we adjust for this we might get a distorted impression of performance.

These aforementioned examples exhibit what I call 'natural seasonality' but analysts of financial performance often have to deal with 'induced seasonality'; repetitive patterns brought about by the way that the business is managed, rather than the environment in which it operates.

For example, Figure 3.7 illustrates the pattern of sales, by month, for a major subsidiary of a large multinational company.

The quarterly spikes in revenue we see in Figure 3.7 are nothing to do with the business environment. They are purely the result of the business manipulating its practices to hit its quarterly revenue targets. It does this by encouraging customers to buy more at quarter end, thereby pulling forward sales that would have naturally fallen in the first month of the subsequent quarter. This is why we see a spike in sales at the end of one quarter (as indicated by the red dots) followed by a dip at the beginning of the next. This is an example of performance being distorted by the mechanisms used to manage performance that ironically end up making it more difficult to measure. This perverse behaviour is what happens when we attempt to control a continuous dynamic system using discontinuous periodic processes.

Direction: Performance as Flow

Average Weekly Sales (by month)

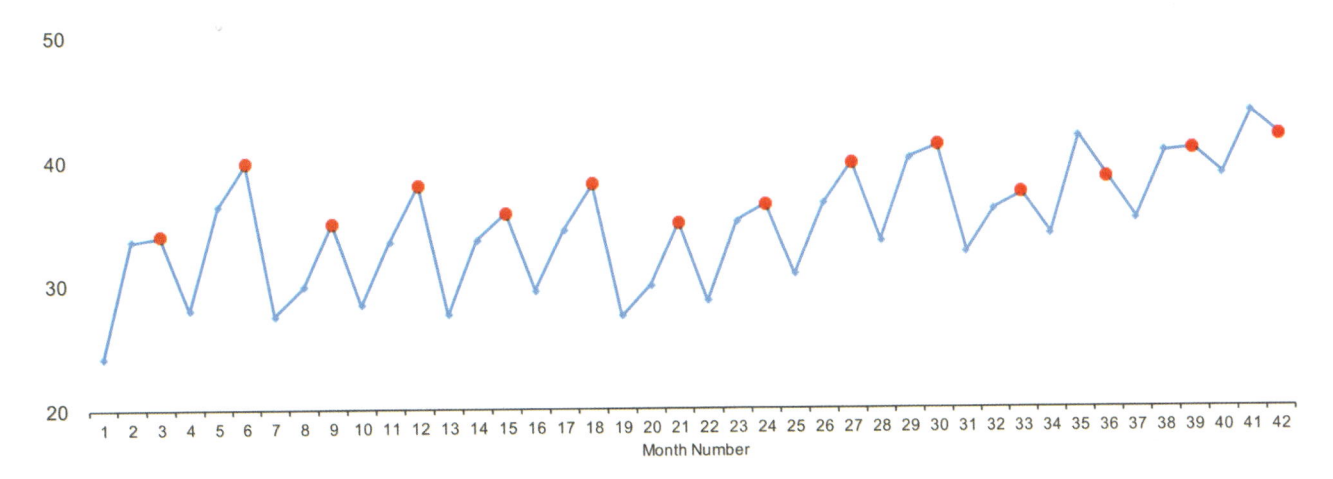

This is more than an arcane technical issue of concern only to financial analysts. But we can see this pattern of behaviour at a much larger scale, manifest in a way that costs businesses millions and seriously misleads investors, not just the managers of businesses.

For example, Figure 3.8 gives the patterns of sales and sales discounts for a large US business listed on the Dow Jones index, shown in a way that even managers of the business would not normally see.

In this example, after a period of steady but declining sales, which created unrest amongst investors, the business set more aggressive quarterly targets and rewarded managers handsomely when they hit them. This they did, not by improving performance, but by manipulating it.

We can see that in 2017 sales started to exhibit a clear pattern of quarterly peaking. The fact that the level of sales discounts follows the same pattern tells us that this has been achieved by the business giving customers incentives to buy

Figure 3.7:
Extreme quarterly seasonality

Here the blue lines represent monthly sales and the red dot indicates the final month in the quarter. It shows a consistent pattern of quarter end peaking over 11 quarters, which is broken in the last four. This is the result of improvements made to the business planning and performance reporting processes.

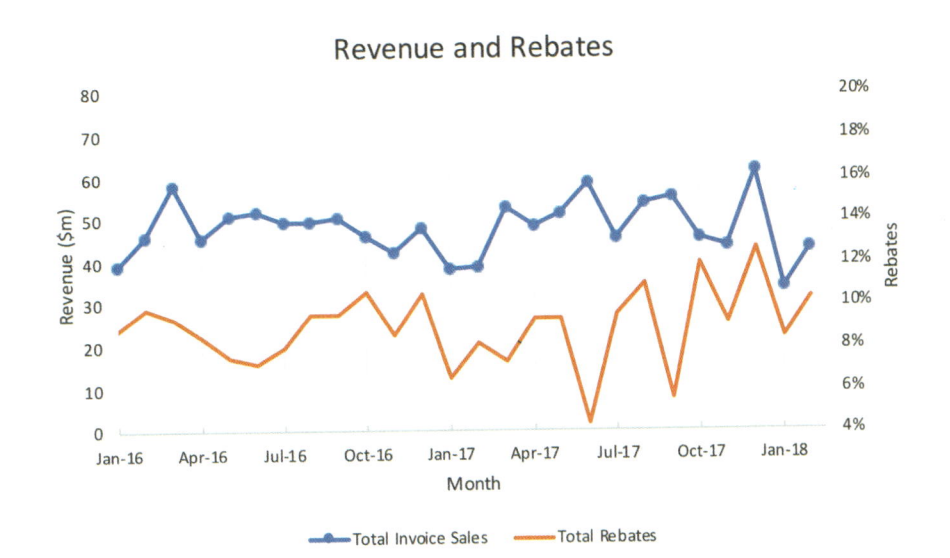

Revenue and Rebates

Figure 3.8:
Chart showing seasonality

Note how sales (blue line) exhibit a clear quarterly peaking from 2011 onwards and how this is associated with increased volatility in the level of rebates given to customers. Not a coincidence!

early and hold the company's products in stock in order to present a flattering picture of performance. The end result is that many millions of dollars have been spent purely for cosmetic effect as part of a conscious effort to mislead investors – and all because performance has been measured in the wrong way.

There are a number of things that appal me about this. The waste of money, and the short-sighted mentality. Like gamblers doubling up to recoup losses, once it takes hold this pattern of behaviour is difficult to give up but impossible to sustain, and it usually ends in tears. But the puritan in me is most angered by the cynical effort to deceive. It is tolerated because it is seen as 'part of the game', particularly where the quarterly earnings cycle is an important feature of business life. And all this waste, stupidity and deception is an entirely avoidable consequence of the way that business performance is measured and managed.

A good performance measure therefore needs to see through seasonality and any attempt to distort reality. Smoothed averages are powerful, but they are less well equipped to analyse trends in highly seasonal data of the sort that many financial performance analysts work with.

In my experience, MATs are the most powerful tool for measuring and analysing trends in financial performance, particularly at the high level at which they are normally reported and analysed. The technique is simple to understand and straightforward to apply but has an uncanny way of uncovering patterns in performance that otherwise would lie hidden.

MOVING TOTALS

MATs measure the aggregate number (for sales, costs, profits and so on) over a moving 12-month (or 52 week) period as shown in Table 3.11.

Table 3.11:
How to calculate MATs

A MAT is the sum of the values for the last 12 months, so once a year the MAT will be the same as the value for a financial year.

Moving Annual Total		
Dec-20	Jan-21	Feb-21
Jan-20		
Feb-20	Feb-20	
Mar-20	Mar-20	Mar-20
Apr-20	Apr-20	Apr-20
May-20	May-20	May-20
Jun-20	Jun-20	Jun-20
Jul-20	Jul-20	Jul-20
Aug-20	Aug-20	Aug-20
Sep-20	Sep-20	Sep-20
Oct-20	Oct-20	Oct-20
Nov-20	Nov-20	Nov-20
Dec-20	Dec-20	Dec-20
	Jan-21	Jan-21
		Feb-21
SUM	SUM	SUM

Direction: Performance as Flow

The benefit of using a rolling annual period for financial data is that all 'within year' cyclical patterns – natural or otherwise – are eliminated. As a result, any movement in the number is a much more faithful representation of reality. Also, using a relatively large sample size has the additional benefit of dampening the noise that can distort averages calculated using shorter data ranges. But I advocate using MATs rather than moving annual *averages* as it is easier for the brain to assimilate and interpret in this form because sales or profit figures for a financial year are more likely to be already embedded as a reference point in our System 1 brain.

So, MATs plotted on a graph work on a number of different levels. The graph measures performance in a way that filters out noise and the impact of seasonality, including conscious efforts to mislead. It also exploits our System 1 brain in that it is visual, it taps into our bias towards movement and it references numbers that we use as a mental anchor.

The chart in Figure 3.9, which uses the same revenue data for XYZ Ltd that I presented in Table 3.1 earlier that we find so difficult to interpret, illustrates this perfectly.

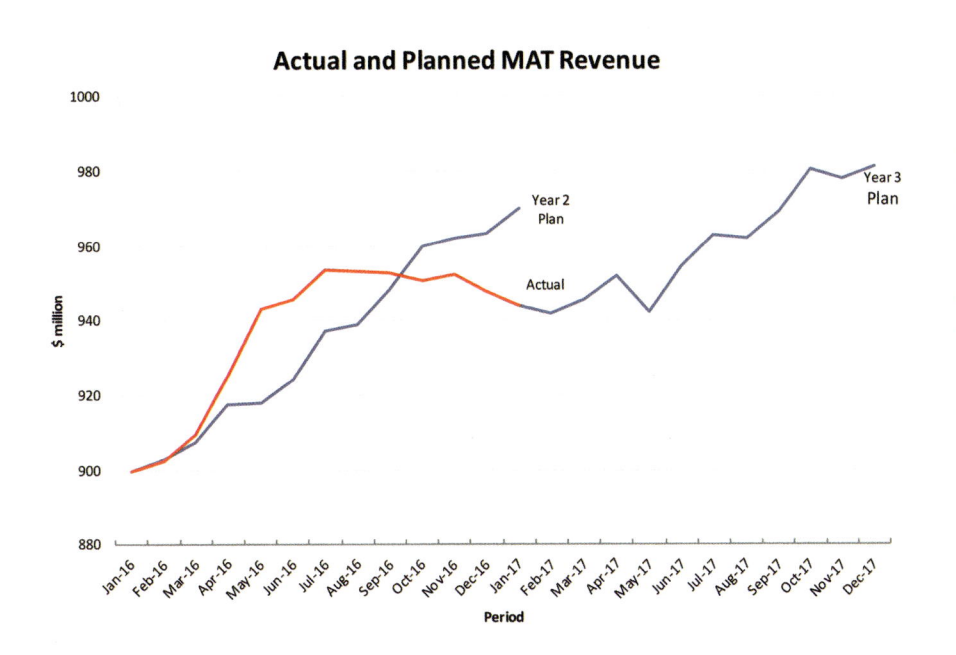

Actual and Planned MAT Revenue

Figure 3.9:
XYZ Ltd revenue MATs

Note how MATs when plotted on a line chart clearly expose patterns in performance. Here we can see clearly how, after experiencing exceptional level of growth, actual values have 'stalled' falling below the plan in August 2016 and how, after a plateau, it is assumed that revenues will start growing strongly again in March 2017 – at about the same rate of growth assumed in the plan for the previous period.

Looking at Figure 3.8 it is clear that actual sales (red line) grow nicely until June 2016 when it flattens out. Because I have also plotted the budget numbers on this graph (blue line) we can see that sales were ahead of the budget until September but that it ended the year behind. It is also clear that after a period where sales flat line the budget for 2017 assumes that they start growing again, which begs the question 'Why?'

Analysing and presenting information in this way enables us to easily answer the questions that we struggled with earlier when the data was presented in a tabular format:

- Is performance good?
- Is it getting better or worse?
- Has anything significantly changed?
- How credible is next year's budget?

And while some of these patterns were discernible in the graph using individual data points (Figure 3.6) using a MAT removes all potential confusion and reveals more insights.

In my experience, one of the key advantages of this approach is that, because it presents information in a way that accesses the System 1 processes that we share by virtue of our common evolution, there is relatively little ambiguity and scope for alternative interpretation of the data. Everyone looking at this chart will tend to 'see' the same thing.

This point was brought home to me when, as the leader of a global performance management project in Unilever, I visited a business unit that was in most ways a beacon of enlightened management. To break the ice at our first meeting I asked my two contacts there, 'How is the business doing?' Their answers shocked me, because they told completely different stories despite them being responsible for producing the numbers. But then I showed them the MAT chart that I had prepared earlier, and their confusion and embarrassment disappeared in a flash. 'That's right, April was lousy because of x, but then y happened…', they told me – and so on. Simply as a result of presenting data that they were familiar with in an accessible way the stories that had been so different had suddenly become the same!

This experience brought home to me how effective this technique is for exposing what is really going on. But it also got me thinking.

How many of the arguments I had witnessed over the years in business teams about what should be done were really the result of everyone in the room seeing different things in the same set of numbers? I had always assumed that I was seeing differences of opinion, but were they really differences of perception? My guess is a lot, maybe even most, of these debates were simply the result of information being presented in the wrong way.

THE ARGUMENT FOR DYNAMIC MEASURES

Before we explore other ways to apply these techniques, let me take stock of the arguments for using dynamic measures more extensively in performance analysis:

Direction: Performance as Flow

1. Performance is active not static
When we talk about the performance of a car, we refer to measures of speed and acceleration not the distance travelled in an arbitrary period of time compared to an arbitrary target. The principle of performance as a measure of the rate of flow of value also applies to business performance. Since flow cannot be measured directly, we need to infer it by calculating a moving average of measures of the value of transactions between points of time and avoid becoming overly fixated on snapshot measures and their associated conventions of financial quarters and years. The values for individual periods enable us to track patterns of behaviour over time and not have limited usefulness in themselves.

2. Averages dampen distortions
Every measurement is unavoidably infected by noise – random perturbations that distort the signal and so make it difficult to assess the 'true' underlying performance. Measuring the flow of value using averages dampens this noise. By choosing the right method to calculate moving averages we can also suppress non-random perturbations of the signal associated with seasonality or data manipulation that creates a false impression of performance. Think of averages as helping to 'boil off' unwanted noise, to leave a distillate with a high concentration of information. Also, using averages to dampen noise that would otherwise distract the human brain means that it is easier to faithfully communicate information particularly when it is presented in a graphical format.

3. Measuring performance dynamically reduces the reliance on arbitrary targets
Pairwise comparison of actuals against target for single periods is an unreliable way of assessing performance because most targets are arbitrary, and actuals are always infected by noise. Flow-based measures of performance not only dampen noise but also go some way to reducing the reliance on traditional targets. While it is difficult to establish the 'correct' target value of a variable, the desired direction of movement is almost always obvious. For example, all other things being equal, increasing revenue is better than declining revenue and reducing costs better than increasing costs. By focussing more on movement and less on individual data points we not only make it easier to establish the true level of performance, but we can also easily assess whether the trend is positive or negative, thereby reducing our reliance on targets as the only measure of good. We will return to this thought in Chapter 4 when we tackle the issue of target setting in more depth.

4. It is easy on our brain
Our way of apprehending the world relies heavily on visual input and nature has tuned our senses to be especially sensitive to shape and movement. Presenting dynamic information graphically directly accesses these brain circuits, meaning that we find it easy to understand and communicate performance in this way.

5. It sets the context
Finally, by presenting the big picture in a simple way, having removed the ambiguity introduced by noise in the data, the right context is set for further analysis and constructive debate about 'what this means' for the organization.

As I write these conclusions seem so obvious and self-evidently right that I almost feel embarrassed. But for most of my professional career I was as conventional as the next person, churning out dense tables of variances. My epiphany came when I recognized that part of the reason why I had been so attached to traditional approaches to the analysis and presentation of information was that, although these were simple to produce, the end result looked complex and sophisticated, which made me look clever and management more reliant on me.

The confidence that comes with experience has helped me let go of my intellectual conceit and insecurity (at least a little!). But my real breakthrough was the realization that because something *looks* simple it doesn't mean that it is easy to create. It is often easier to make things obscure and difficult to understand than to make them simple and straightforward. The genius of Apple is that they have made complex technology so easy to use that no manual is required. Any idiot could make a smartphone difficult to use.

These are powerful arguments for making more use of trend-based measures than has been done in the past, but there are more. There are at least two other ways in which we can use a dynamic perspective to hijack the neural circuits that have evolved in nature in order to help us understand performance better.

Firstly, when we are trying to understand causality in the world we often compare the movement of two things in time to help us uncover causality – what has led to what. Secondly, to predict the future state of a variable we observe the direction and rate of movement. And there are ways we can use the simple techniques that I have already introduced to exploit these capabilities and hence provide us with a range of simple but powerful tools to analyse performance.

OTHER APPLICATION OF MATS

MATs provide a powerful method for eliciting the patterns in data and help us to communicate performance particularly when the data is very noisy or distorted by seasonality. By helping to paint the big picture MATs set the context for more in-depth enquiry. But they are more than a descriptive tool for presenting performance information – they can also be used as a diagnostic tool to help answer deeper performance management questions.

For example, you might wish to understand what is driving the trends in performance that the MATs have exposed. Using year on year analysis in combination with MATs helps answer these 'why' type questions. Let me explain how.

Direction: Performance as Flow

Why?

The movement in the MAT number from one period to the next is the result of the difference between the actual value of the period that has just dropped out of the date range and the one that has just been added to it, as shown in Table 3.12.

Moving Annual Total			Change in MAT	
Dec-20	Jan-21	Feb-21	Dec-Jan	Jan-Feb
Jan-20			less Jan-20	less
Feb-20	Feb-20			Feb-20
Mar-20	Mar-20	Mar-20		
Apr-20	Apr-20	Apr-20		
May-20	May-20	May-20		
Jun-20	Jun-20	Jun-20		
Jul-20	Jul-20	Jul-20		
Aug-20	Aug-20	Aug-20		
Sep-20	Sep-20	Sep-20		
Oct-20	Oct-20	Oct-20		
Nov-20	Nov-20	Nov-20		
Dec-20	Dec-20	Dec-20	add	
	Jan-21	Jan-21	Jan-21	add
		Feb-21		Feb-21
SUM	SUM	SUM	SUM	SUM

Table 3.12:
Why MATs change

Each month the oldest value drops out of the range to be replaced by the most recent month. Changes in the MAT from one month to the next therefore represent the difference in the value for the same month from one year to the next.

So, for example, the difference between the MATs for the 12 months to December 2016 and the period to January 2017 is explained by the difference between the value for the month of January 2016, which has dropped out of the range, and January 2017, which has replaced it. Knowing the difference between these two numbers doesn't tell you anything that you don't know already, but by breaking down the difference into its constituent parts you can gain an understanding of what is driving the movement in MAT. Was the difference the result of a change in the sales of product A, B or C, for example?

For any single pair of MATs this difference may simply reflect noise in the data. But if a pattern emerges when you analyse the differences over time – for example, if the same products were responsible for the revenue increase every period – then we can safely conclude that it was this that was driving the change in MAT.

This kind of year on year analysis works best when it is presented as a stacked bar chart in combination with the MAT graph, as the analysis of profit for XYZ Ltd in Figure 3.10 shows.

The chart in Figure 3.10 clearly shows that the increase in the MAT profit in the first four months of 2016 was the result of an increase in gross profit (GP) but also a reduction in advertising spend (A&P).

This approach helps us to gain a better understanding of *what* is driving the change in a variable such as revenue or profit. This is a start on the road to enlightenment, but we can't yet answer the question of *why?* Decision makers need

Figure 3.10:
MATs and stacked bar charts

The profit MAT is represented by the blue line and is plotted against the secondary axis. The elements of the P&L account that explain its movement are shown on the stacked bar charts. Improvement is above the X axis and the grey line shows the net improvement/deterioration in year on year performance.

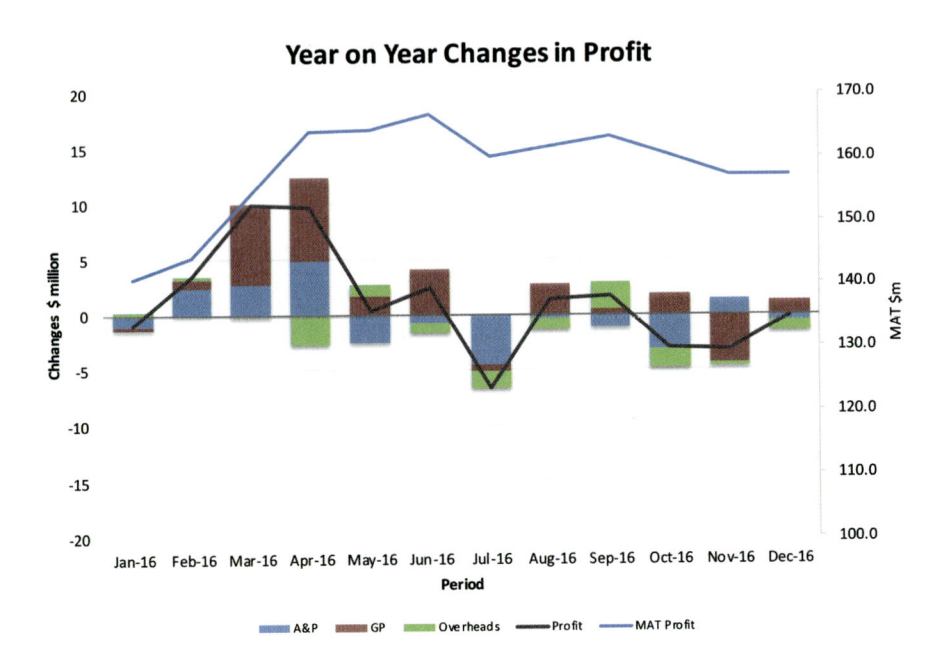

to understand what is causing the changes to be able to make the interventions in the system that will maintain or change a trend. If sales of product X are the primary reason why a MAT revenue line is declining, for example, they need to know what levers to pull to arrest this trend. To do this they need to have some understanding of the correlations *between* variables, and MATs can also be used to help answer this question.

What is driving change?

Statisticians typically use regression analysis to help understand what is causing what. This will give a precise answer, but we can achieve much the same end in a simpler way by showing graphically how a pair of MATs move with respect to each other. If two variables are causally linked then we would expect the dependant variable to move after a change in the independent (causal) variable. If this is what we see, it would not only support our hypothesis but also give us a sense of the lag between cause and effect.

For example, I might want to understand how the level of advertising impacts sales. It is easier to compare movements of two variables if they have a common scale so, in the example in Figure 3.11, I have indexed the revenue MAT for XYZ Ltd and advertising and promotional (A&P) MAT to 100 at the beginning of the period.

On the left-hand side of the chart in Figure 3.11 we can see that revenue growth seems to flatten off around period 7, some four periods after the level of advertising dropped. This suggests that the plateau in revenue that we saw in the revenue MAT in Figure 3.8 is related to the cuts in advertising that were made in periods 4 and 5 that boosted profits in the short term, but perhaps at the expense of their growth over the longer term.

On the right-hand side of the chart I have plotted the budget MATs for revenue and advertising to help me evaluate future plans. The budget assumes

Direction: Performance as Flow

Revenue and A&P MAT Trends (P1 = 100)

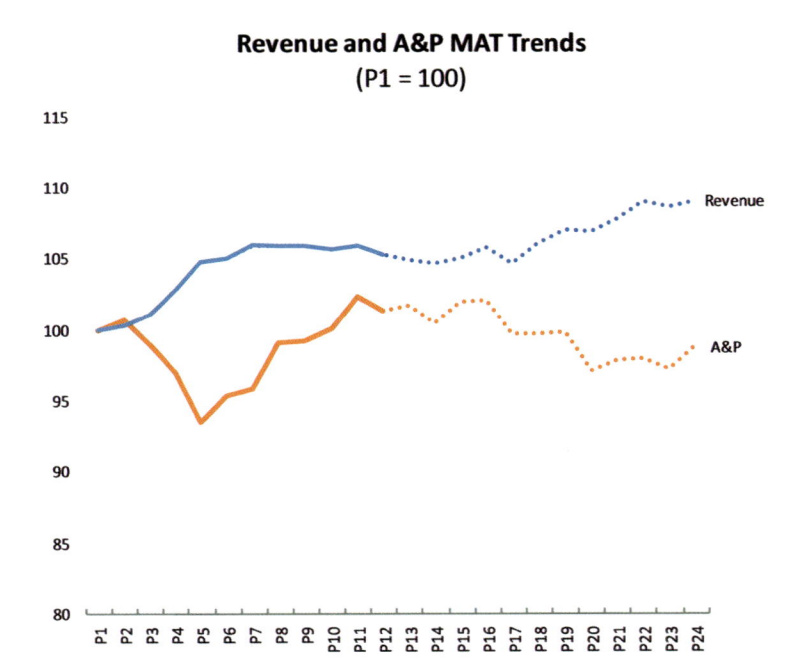

Figure 3.11
Indexed A&P and revenue MATs

In this chart the revenue and A&P MATs have been indexed to 100 at the beginning of the period so that the relative changes in their values can be easily compared. It looks like the reduction in investment between period 3 and period 5 could be responsible for the flattening off of revenue from period 5 to the end of the year. It is also clear that the level of revenue and A&P in the planned period are moving in opposite directions, which – if there is meant to be a causal relationship between the two – suggests that the revenue plan is optimistic.

that after a period of stagnation sales growth will resume in about period 17. But this increase in revenue is associated with a further decline in advertising. In the light of what we have learned about the casual relationship between the two variables in the past this seems implausible. Based on this we can conclude that this revenue projection looks very optimistic indeed.

What this approach lacks in comparison to the precision of a regression analysis it more than makes up for in simplicity of use and interpretation. So simple that even the most numerically-challenged business person can make sense of it. When performance information is presented in a way that is dense and confusing it is easy for myths to grow about 'what is happening to business performance', which can be very debilitating, particularly if it is used to bolster the prejudices of different factions in the business. I find that this kind of technique is a powerful 'myth-busting' tool, which can help the whole business to work with a consistent narrative driven by facts rather than by distorted or self-interested interpretations of reality.

Assessing risk

We have already seen how MATs can help us make sense of what has happened in the past, but also shed some light on the credibility of aspirations for the future. Used in combination with smoothed averages, however, we can quantify the level of risk in plans in a simple and structured way.

As we have seen when we compared actual MAT trends for XYZ Ltd with budgeted revenue, we can get a good sense of how credible future projections are by simple visual inspection. If a forecast shows a break in the historic pattern of performance, we need a convincing explanation if we are to be persuaded that it is not just wishful thinking.

Ideally, we would like to be able to assess the risk (or opportunity) more scientifically, but this requires us to be able to precisely measure the deviation

Table 3.13:
Use of different alphas on revenue MATs

Using different alpha values for weighting changes in a MAT enables us to put a value to short-, medium- and long-term trends since higher alpha values attribute a higher weighting to more recent periods.

from the historic trend. This might sound straightforward but in practice it isn't because trends are rarely stable over a prolonged period of time. Do we put a straight line through the last three years, MATs, for example, based on the assumption that everything that has happened since has been perturbations around a long-term trend, or do we extrapolate from the last six months based on the assumption that it represents the 'new normal'?

This is where smoothed averages can help us.

As we have seen, in calculating a smoothed average we have to choose a smoothing parameter to use. A larger 'alpha' such as 0.3 will give more weight to recent periods than a smaller 'alpha' such as 0.1. We can use this feature of smoothed averages to help us produce multiple future scenarios that we can use to measure the credibility of plans and the risk attached to them in a replicable way. To do this, rather than applying smoothing to individual data points in a series, we apply the technique to differing weights to *changes* in values – in this case changes in the MAT from period to period – to create a series of estimates of the trend.

	Actuals					Projection		
	Period 1	Period 2	Period 3	Period 4	Period 5	Period 6	Period 7	Period 8
Moving Annual Total	250	100	120	110	115			
Change	-100	-150	20	-10	5			
Weightings (alpha 0.3)	0.07	0.10	0.15	0.21	0.30			
Weightings (alpha 0.2)	0.08	0.10	0.13	0.16	0.20			
Weightings (alpha 0.1)	0.07	0.07	0.08	0.09	0.10			
Short Term Trend (alpha 0.3)					-6			
Medium Term Trend (alpha 0.2)					-9			
Long Term Trend (alpha 0.1)					-11			
Projected MAT - short term						109	103	97
Projected MAT - medium term						106	96	87
Projected MAT - long term						104	94	83

In Table 3.13 you can see that, since the MAT is trending upwards, the smoothed average created using an alpha of 0.3 (+7 per period – biased to the short-term trend) is higher than that using 0.2 or 0.1 as the alpha (+5 and +3 respectively) as they reflect longer-term trends.

The next step is to take these different smoothed averages for changes to the trend and apply them to the historic MATs to create a range of possible outcomes (the projected triangle is sometimes called 'windsock' for obvious reasons) that can then be compared to the plan. In Figure 3.12 I have used the revenue data for XYZ Ltd.

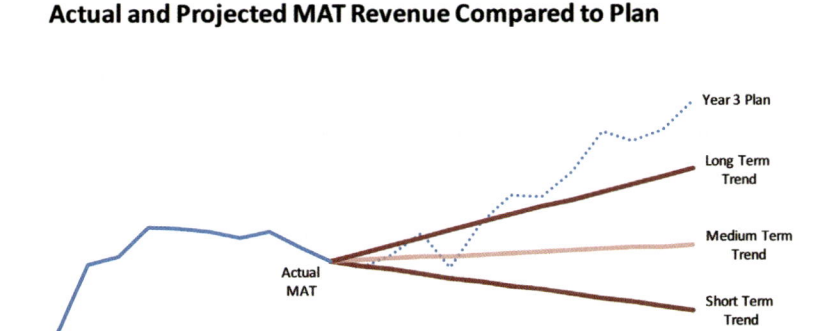

Direction: Performance as Flow

Actual and Projected MAT Revenue Compared to Plan

Figure 3.12:
Risk windsock

Extrapolating from an actual MAT using differing assessments of historic trends as shown in Table 3.8 creates a framework that enables us to easily assess the credibility of plans. Here the windsock shape defines a range of possible future values, which are consistent with past trends. Anything outside this range assumes that something will fundamentally change in the system, and so carry a higher risk.

Here we can see that the plan lies outside the range of projected trends from July 2017 onwards, and that by the end of the year the gap between the planned and projected revenue (the size of the downside risk) is between $20 million and $60 million.

The benefit of using this approach is that it is no longer a matter of opinion that the plan for the coming year relies on a significant change in the pattern of performance – the analysis conclusively demonstrates that the budgeted trend is inconsistent with anything that has gone before. Also, we are able to quantify the level of risk and, if we are unconvinced by the arguments presented in support of the plan, either change it or put in place contingency plans that help us manage the downside risks if they materialize.

While it is useful to have a technique like this that helps us identify overly optimistic (or pessimistic) forecasts, it would be even better if we could help people produce more effective plans in the first place. Research has demonstrated that the surest way to improve forecasts is to provide evidence about the reliability of past forecasts – feedback – and encourage people to improve the process they use for producing them.

MATs can help us here as well. The chart in Figure 3.13 plots the MAT over a one-year period showing the budget and all the profit forecasts made. As is clear, all those except the forecast made in December were poor predictors of actual performance (as shown by the blue line).

What has happened here is that the budget assumed steady profit growth and subsequent quarterly forecasts (PFs) only slowly recognized the reality that profit was, in fact, slowly declining. The tendency to 'anchor' on a target, even when it is demonstrably wrong, and only adjust slowly to the emerging reality is a phenomenon that many readers of this book will recognize and is endemic in budgeting cultures where change is an unwelcome visitor. Anchoring like this is one of the cognitive biases that helped win Daniel Kahneman his Nobel Prize.

Figure 3.13:
Fishbone diagram for MATs

By comparing planned to actual MATs persistent patterns of over or under forecasting are made visible. Here it is clear that the budget and the two subsequent forecasts were over optimistic, anticipating an uplift that did not materialize.

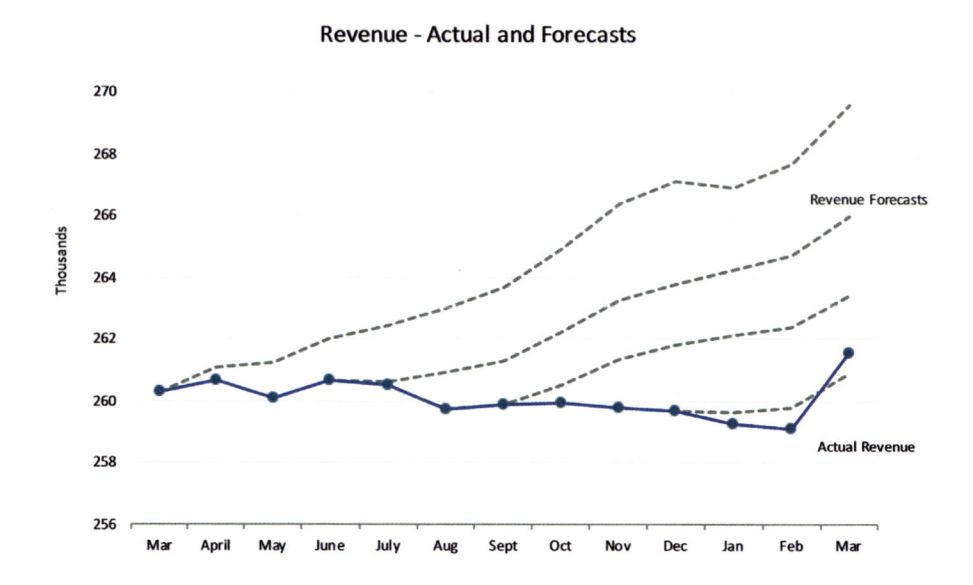

This simple graphical device can help to avoid this problem by keeping everyone anchored in data rather than wishful thinking.

This concludes the chapter on how to use trend-based measures to provide a richer picture of performance and to promote the deeper understanding that is a prerequisite to meaningful analysis and debate.

But for the purposes of explanation, I have been forced to use simplified examples that don't do justice to the ability of these approaches to help make sense of complex and dynamic business scenarios.

To correct this imbalance, I will finish with an example of how I used these techniques to understand performance in a business I was closely involved in a number of years ago.

A REAL-LIFE EXAMPLE

This example of the use of MAT in practice is based on a national business unit in a major multinational fast-moving consumer goods (FMCG) business. Every year, the business unit is set a profit target (budget) by the parent company. More often than not the business is able to 'deliver' on its profit target – usually achieved by cutting discretionary A&P (expenditure). But there is an equal amount of pressure to grow revenue (sales) at a faster rate than the market, which has historically proven to be much more difficult, partly because (it is assumed) this is driven by A&P spend.

This is typical of the tricky practical performance management problem that many businesses struggle with.

Let us start trying to make sense of performance by taking a look at the turnover numbers for the business, by profit category over a four-year period displayed in a conventional tabular format (Table 3.14).

Direction: Performance as Flow

2010

	Q1	Q2	Q3	Q4	Year
Product A	€ 109,302	€ 103,699	€ 108,334	€ 112,017	€ 433,351
Product B	€ 59,956	€ 49,705	€ 46,821	€ 73,135	€ 229,618
Product C	€ 104,951	€ 105,405	€ 124,184	€ 127,078	€ 461,618
Products D	€ 25,433	€ 19,900	€ 21,749	€ 28,826	€ 95,908
Product E	€ 1,578	€ 4,702	€ 1,028	€ 1,425	€ 8,732
Total	€ 299,630	€ 278,706	€ 300,231	€ 341,259	€ 1,219,827

2011

	Q1	Change	Q2	Change	Q3	Change	Q4	Change	Year	Change
Product A	€ 101,677	-7%	€ 117,846	14%	€ 129,289	19%	€ 130,283	16%	€ 479,095	11%
Product B	€ 59,604	-1%	€ 44,801	-10%	€ 48,882	4%	€ 76,540	5%	€ 229,826	0%
Product C	€ 117,570	12%	€ 89,807	-15%	€ 101,227	-18%	€ 111,234	-12%	€ 419,838	-9%
Products D	€ 26,640	5%	€ 20,106	1%	€ 19,959	-8%	€ 30,048	4%	€ 96,752	1%
Product E	€ 796	-50%	€ 1,969	-58%	€ 1,830	78%	€ 1,470	3%	€ 6,065	-31%
Total	€ 305,786	2%	€ 272,777	-2%	€ 299,702	0%	€ 348,365	2%	€ 1,226,631	1%

2012

	Q1	Change	Q2	Change	Q3	Change	Q4	Change	Year	Change
Product A	€ 101,152	-1%	€ 108,565	-8%	€ 107,749	-17%	€ 112,961	-13%	€ 430,427	-10%
Product B	€ 61,009	2%	€ 56,514	26%	€ 54,475	11%	€ 76,547	0%	€ 248,545	8%
Product C	€ 98,850	-16%	€ 98,750	10%	€ 97,044	-4%	€ 99,139	-11%	€ 393,782	-6%
Products D	€ 23,631	-11%	€ 21,110	5%	€ 21,049	5%	€ 27,924	-7%	€ 93,715	-3%
Product E	€ 1,276	60%	€ 2,298	17%	€ 3,055	67%	€ 565	-62%	€ 7,195	19%
Total	€ 284,906	-7%	€ 285,178	5%	€ 280,555	-6%	€ 316,811	-9%	€ 1,167,451	-5%

2013

	Q1	Change	Q2	Change	Q3	Change	Q4	Change	Year	Change
Product A	€ 95,106	-6%	€ 102,948	-5%	€ 104,343	-3%	€ 119,867	6%	€ 422,265	-2%
Product B	€ 62,202	2%	€ 56,532	0%	€ 59,034	8%	€ 75,878	-1%	€ 253,646	2%
Product C	€ 110,155	11%	€ 103,063	4%	€ 95,288	-2%	€ 112,169	13%	€ 420,675	7%
Products D	€ 23,867	1%	€ 22,132	5%	€ 20,077	-5%	€ 28,002	0%	€ 94,078	0%
Product E	€ -	-100%	€ -	-100%	€ -	-100%	€ -	-100%	€ -	-100%
Total	€ 291,527	2%	€ 284,883	0%	€ 278,965	-1%	€ 336,208	6%	€ 1,191,584	2%

2014

	Q1	Change	Q2	Change	Q3	Change	Q4	Change	Year	Change
Product A	€ 112,899	19%	€ 103,144	0%	€ 108,941	4%	€ 115,819	-3%	€ 440,802	4%
Product B	€ 65,435	5%	€ 59,710	6%	€ 64,059	9%	€ 83,400	10%	€ 272,604	7%
Product C	€ 121,703	10%	€ 118,118	15%	€ 116,138	22%	€ 122,361	9%	€ 478,320	14%
Products D	€ 25,791	8%	€ 23,073	4%	€ 21,291	6%	€ 28,655	2%	€ 98,810	5%
Product E	€ -		€ -		€ -		€ -		€ -	
Total	€ 326,071	12%	€ 301,383	6%	€ 288,508	3%	€ 359,274	7%	€ 1,275,237	7%

For all the reasons we have already discussed, it is very difficult to extract any meaning from data presented in this way. The 'big picture' is completely obscured, and, in its absence, it is easy to see how managers could be driven to micromanagement and obsession with irrelevant detail when this is all they have.

Let's look at the same revenue data presented graphically in a time series.

Figure 3.14 is a little easier to interpret than the tables. What is clear is that there was a period of volatility beginning in mid-2010, which subsided after about a year. Also, if you look carefully, this appears to be followed by a period of gradual growth, across all the product categories, but it is difficult to be sure because of the scale used to produce the graph and noise in the data.

Table 3.14:
Conventional table

This chart shows actual revenue by quarter (compared to the prior year) over a five-year period. Presented in this way, it is difficult to make sense of what is going on.

Figure 3.14:
Simple graph

It is difficult to draw out patterns from the simple run chart, which shows revenue in total and by product by month over the same five-year period.

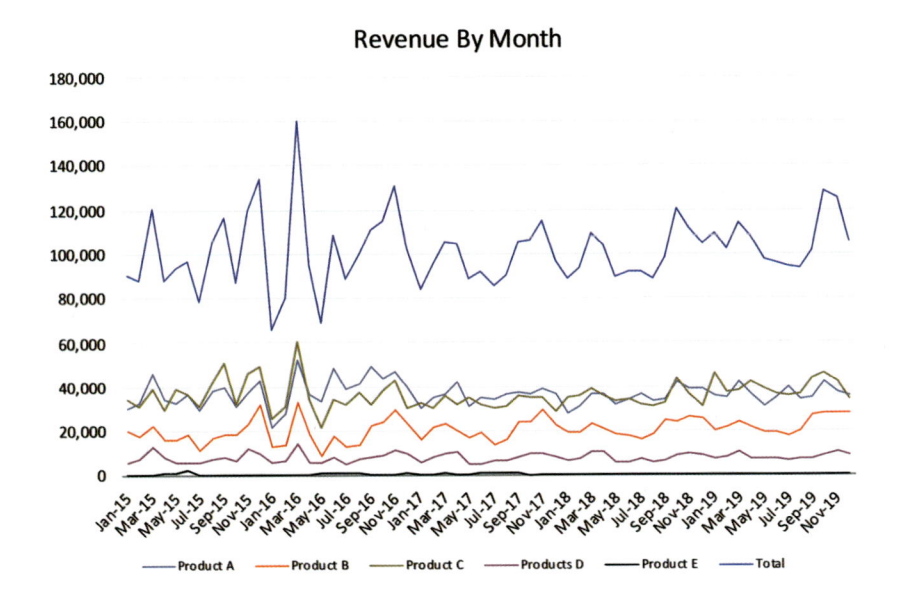

Let's now look at the same data using a MAT for the total revenue and year on year changes in sales for product categories.

What emerges is a stunningly clear picture (Figure 3.15).

Figure 3.15:
Drivers of revenue growth

The same data used in Figure 3.12 has been used to calculate a MAT (blue line, using the secondary axis). Year on year changes in product revenue are plotted using stacked bars. Displayed in this way the changes in the pattern of behaviour in this system become clear.

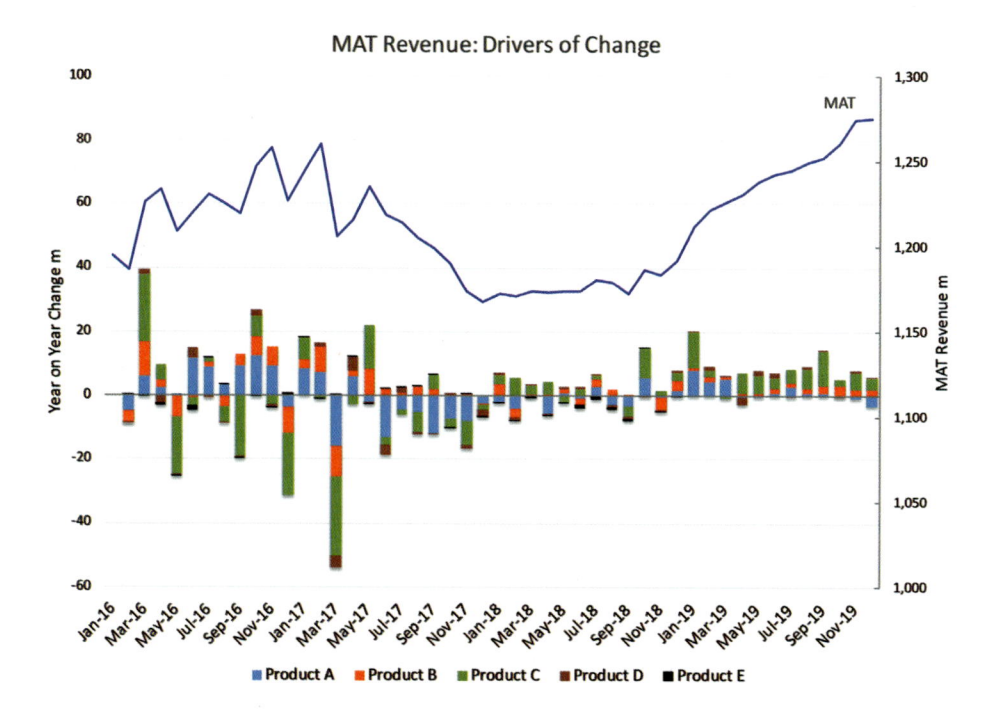

If we look at the total revenue line first, we can clearly see the volatility that we noted in the simple run chart, but after March 2012 the period to period volatility completely disappears. If we look at the bar charts in Figure 3.14 we see that this volatility is replicated at the product category level. In particular, product C (green) swings wildly between year on year growth and decline.

But after this period of volatility we see something that wasn't evident from either of the first two charts. The revenue line starts to decline, but it reverses at the beginning of 2013 after which we see gradual and then accelerating growth.

When we use MATs to plot trends it is discontinuities like the one that we see here that interest us most. What has happened to bring about this change? And what do we need to do to maintain or perhaps even improve this positive trend?

The character of the year on year changes, as represented by the bars in Figure 3.15, also changes around the inflexion point in the revenue line. The wild gyrations stop and are replaced by a pattern of steady growth across all categories.

This much is clear from just looking at the numbers. With some contextual knowledge of what was going on in the business at the time we can begin to better understand why.

In the period up to mid-2012, faced with the pressure to grow the business the board increasingly intervened in an attempt to hit self-imposed monthly revenue targets. They did this, not by increasing the appeal or the value of the products to the customer, but by aggressively promoting them. Unfortunately, rather than increasing overall sales this simply encouraged existing customers to buy ahead, which means that sales were higher in the period in which the promotion was run but lower in the next one, hence the volatility we see in demand. Because product C was the biggest seller, this is where the majority of this futile activity was focussed.

This costly and disruptive way of working couldn't continue, and the chairman was replaced in mid-2012. His first act was to stop this misdirected aggressive promotional activity, but as it was not replaced by anything else in the short term the sales began to nose dive, albeit in a graceful manner!

In January 2013, however, a new way of working was introduced, and the impact was almost instantaneous, as the MAT graph reveals.

Instead of trying to 'hit the number' and sticking to budgets that were allocated at the time that the budget was struck, the business spent money on marketing activity based on the quality of the ideas that the board were presented with by the marketing teams. As a result of focussing on doing the right thing rather than trying to hit a number the business soon found itself beating all the targets set!

So, by presenting information in the right way a clear and compelling story begins to emerge, but we are not quite finished.

In this FMCG business, the conventional wisdom is that the level of marketing spend has a simple and direct impact on sales. And sure enough, as sales grew the amount of money available to spend on marketing grew as well, because the company could spend more and still hit its profit target. As a result, some outsiders (based in head office) thought the improved performance was a

Figure 3.16:
The relationship between advertising spend and revenue growth

The MATs for revenue (red line) and the relative level of A&P spend (blue) are not tightly correlated in the way that management assume. The surge in revenue form the end of 2013 is not related to an increase in spend, although there is some suggestion that the dip in spend towards the end of 2015 and 2018 might have some impact on the easing off in growth. This requires further investigation, as does the reason for the oscillation in spend levels for management to get a better understanding of how their business actually works.

15. I have left this example at the point that we move from (routine) performance reporting into (ad hoc) analysis. If I were to take the next step, I would select data to test my hypothesis as to why we see the change in pattern in Figure 3.16. Is it because the mix of spend has shifted from promotions (such as price discounts that have a short-term impact) to advertising, which operates at a longer lag? If so, I might want to test another hypothesis: that precisely because reducing advertising doesn't have an obvious and immediate negative impact, management might have been misled into thinking that doing so was a painless way of managing profit delivery to help 'hit' the year end profit target. This demonstrates how well crafted performance reports help us create and test precise hypotheses and so uncover subtle insights into performance.

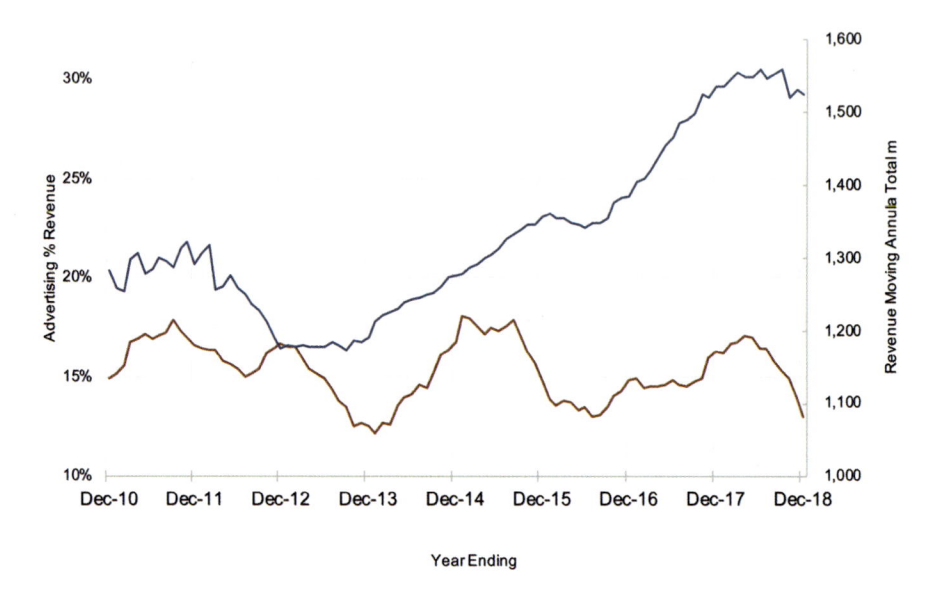

straightforward consequence of spending more, rather than the result of a change in the way that the business worked – *how* the money was spent.

A comparison of revenue growth with the level of advertising spend destroys the simple 'spend more, get more' narrative of the corporate centre.

Although the level of spend increased, in percentage terms the level of spend did not rise over this period. What we see instead is a strange cyclical pattern in the level of spend as Figure 3.16 shows.

The way that growth stalls in 2016 and towards the end of the period might be related to a dip in advertising spend, but the initial period of growth was associated with a *reduction* in the level of spend. So, while it looks like there is some kind of relationship between the level of spend and revenue growth, it is obvious that the relationship is not as clear and as straightforward as the 'official' narrative would have us believe. In Figure 3.16 we dive into this issue further still by comparing the change in revenue with the change in A&P, which clearly shows clear cyclical patterns in both, but for reasons that are not immediately obvious.

Note how, from 2013 onwards, changes in Gross Profit and A&P are out of sync. Why has this changed?

The fact that this description ends with an unanswered question is OK in my book. Performance reporting does not and should not aspire to giving management all the answers – a simple story tied up with a neat bow. Instead it sets the right context and helps to direct the attention of decision makers to the really important questions, stopping them wasting time, money and energy doing the wrong things.[15]

I will return to the dangerous myth of corporate 'storytelling' later.

Direction: Performance as Flow

Relationship between Revenue, A&P and Gross Profit (MAT)

Figure 3.17:
Showing the relationship between changes in A&P and Gross Profit

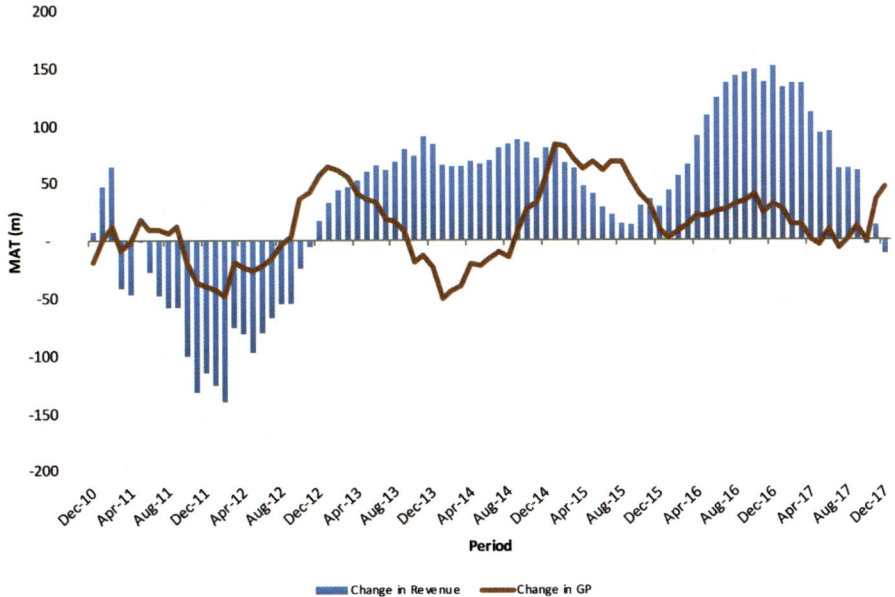

SUMMARY

In this chapter I demonstrated how you can use simple techniques such as smoothed averages and moving totals to help better understand trends – the dynamics of performance that often got lost when we focus exclusively on 'this period's' results, particularly in an environment dominated by the financial year perspective.

I am aware that to many people who are steeped in the use of numeric targets to measure performance and the sense of precision that variance analysis creates this approach might appear 'unscientific' and somehow unprofessional. But I believe the apparent rigour and sophistication of conventional variance analysis is an illusion. Because of the arbitrary nature of most targets, the noise inherent in any measure of reality and the absence of the context needed to make sound judgements, the results are often no more than a fantasy story dressed in sober clothing.

Understanding trends in important business variables gives us a perspective of performance that is more faithful to the purpose of the organization and, as a by-product, has the benefit of supressing noise that would otherwise cloud our view. And it also reduces our reliance on arbitrary targets as a way of making judgements about performance.

Just as important, particularly when this information is presented graphically, it keys into our brain's sensory system in a very direct way, which is why the results often appear to be childishly simple. Understanding and communication are easier, quicker and more effective but, most importantly, free from the ambiguity associated with traditional approaches that purport to provide definitive answers.

A dynamic perspective also enables us to go beyond description. It helps us access insights into causality by exposing the relationship between movements in variables. Also, understanding the direction of travel of the business provides us with clues about the future and helps us quantify and assess the risk inherent in plans and forecasts.

It is clear then, why the brain latches onto dynamic patterns so easily. Dynamic data provides a rich and highly concentrated diet of information – actionable insights – and sets the right context for properly targeted deeper analysis. I believe information professionals need to get over any misplaced sense of professional pride associated with traditional variance analysis and other 'sophisticated' forms of mathematical procedure. They – we – need to accept that simpler 'common-sense' approaches to analysing data have much greater explanatory power and ability to communicate insights than we appreciate.

For those of you worried that the demise of variance analysis means that you will no longer be able to impress colleagues with your mastery of its arcane arithmetical processes there is some consolation. Simple trend analysis is not the answer to everything.

The approaches I have shared in this chapter work best at 'high level' using aggregated data covering an extended period of time. They help us to see the big picture – to set the context – which gives us a sound platform for more detailed enquiry, that is, hypothesis generation and testing.

But, unfortunately, trend analysis isn't the 'magic bullet' that solves all our performance reporting problems. For example, because trends change slowly, they cannot help us make sense of a single piece of data like 'this period's results'. If we only use these techniques there is a risk that we will be able to elegantly describe what has happened after the event, when it is too late to do anything about it.

At the root of this problem is the fact that the simple visual analysis of graphs is a very clumsy way of interrogating the lower-level, disaggregated data we need to detect the weak signals that could be a precursor of a change or a symptom of a deeply buried issue that trend analysis is too insensitive to detect. Low-level data is also infected by much higher levels of noise, which can make the results misleading – over relatively short runs even completely random data can generate what may easily be mistaken for meaningful patterns. So we can't rely on our brain's inherited visual pattern recognizing skills. We need to be able to make sound statistical inferences – something that our brain has not been programmed to do by evolution. Finally, the sheer volume of data in modern sophisticated organizations will overwhelm the relatively simple analytical approaches described in this chapter as easily as it does traditional variance analysis.

To exploit the rich reserves of data that most businesses now capture we need new ways to help us filter the wheat from the chaff, so we can focus time and attention on the limited subset of the data where the nuggets of useful insight lie. This is the subject of Chapter 4.

Direction: Performance as Flow

Learning	Reason
Why it is important to measure the dynamics of organizational performance.	Trends help us to assess the sustainability performance measured at a point in time, reduce reliance on fixed targets and supress noise and facilitate graphical representation of data, which makes it easier for everyone to make sense of what is going on. By painting a picture of the whole they set the right context for more detailed enquiry into the parts.
How accountants lost the plot.	Accountants have confused the means they use to capture data about an organization – typically monthly data points – with information about performance, which requires more than a single period perspective. Also, the fixation with financial quarters and years further frustrates attempts to understand trends.
How tables of numbers fail as a means to communicate patterns of performance.	Tables usually present too little detail to infer patterns and make it difficult to assimilate data because they use a language foreign to our brains (numbers) that is tricky to translate to the graphical language that our brains are most comfortable with.
Why information professionals/analysts need to understand the difference between thinking fast and thinking slow.	Unconscious System 1 thinking processes are fast and frugal and help us make sense of the complex and natural environment in which humans evolved with little effort. System 2 is slower and requires conscious effort but is capable of being explicitly logical. We need to get better at exploiting the power of System 1 processes to improve our ability to make sense of the complex world that organizations now inhabit.
How averages help us make sense of trends.	Averages dampen the noise in individual data points and so help us better detect trends and changes in trends.
Why cumulative and rolling averages are deficient as a means of measuring trends.	The results of cumulative averages cannot be used to assess trends as the sample size is variable. Also, cumulative averages are often too sensitive to single data points at the beginning of a sequence, as are rolling averages.
How smoothed averages are calculated and why they are effective.	Smoothed averages weight the value of recent data points more than older ones and so present a stable picture of the current state of a variable. They are a powerful way to make sense of very noisy data series.
Why MATs are a powerful tool for making sense of performance.	MATs dampen noise and the impact of seasonal impacts with an annual cycle (or less) and exploit the fact that we are mentally primed to think of the value of many performance variables as annual sums.
How MATs can be used to understand causality and risk.	When plotted visually we can assess causality by looking at the behaviour of MATs for different variables. Extrapolating MAT trends helps us to determine the credibility of forecasts or plans.

chapter 4

Uncertainty and Predictability: Big Data and the Weak Signal

> In which I explain how variation is an important attribute of performance and why we need to understand it to be able to make meaningful inferences from data. I also describe some simple tools that help information professionals effectively engage with it.

SIGNALS, NOISE AND THE MANAGEMENT OF VARIATION

In Chapter 3 you learned how to use averages and moving totals to provide a sense of the dynamics of performance; the behaviour of an organization across time.

Through a better understanding of where an organization has come from – the story behind its performance – we have a sense of where it might be heading to: if things do not change, which of course they will.

This change might be positive change that we would like to encourage and exploit, or it may be negative change that we want to mitigate or halt. Ultimately these changes will be manifest as a break in the trend we have exposed but it will take time for these high-level analyses to detect discontinuities and we often cannot afford to wait, whether the change is positive or negative.

So, an understanding of trends and patterns of performance helps set the context for the routine analysis and reporting of performance, but we cannot use it to make sense of any individual data point, which is the challenge we have at the end of every period when the next batch of data arrives. The problem of using short data sequences to make sense of what is going on is that these days most businesses have large quantities of it, and all of it is infected by noise.

Faced with such a torrent of highly variable data how can we use the real-time sensory capabilities we now have to make meaningful judgements about performance and direct the attention of decision makers to the things that matter before it is too late?

I have made numerous references to 'noise' up to now without offering more than a superficial explanation of the term. So, let's start this chapter by getting clear about what the word means and why it is important.

What is noise?

Noise is another one of those words that we are so familiar with that we can fool ourselves into thinking that we all know what it means.

I have often made this mistake, and this was brought home to me after I had listened to a presentation at a conference sponsored by a large multinational software company. I commented to my colleague who worked for the sponsoring company that the analysis we had just seen was flawed because it didn't take account of noise in the data that had been used.

'What is noise?' he asked.

This response floored me.

It had never occurred to me that other people – especially bright people like my friend – would not know what I thought I knew. Because I had never given it much thought myself, I wasn't able to answer his question – and that made *me* feel stupid.

In the moment he wanted me to give him an example of noise, but I couldn't. Only later, on reflection, did I realize that the reason I couldn't was that noise isn't a *thing* – it is a *pattern*.

I'm not going to make the mistake of assuming that everyone sees the world as I do again, so before we go any further, I need to make sure that you and I share an understanding of noise and why it is important.

Data analysis is a relatively new phenomenon in organizations, but astronomers have been trying to make sense of the movements of stars and planets for millennia. However, only in the 19th century did they get the tools to measure the heavens with great precision. And when they did, they encountered a problem.

The great mathematician Carl Friedrich Gauss was the first to notice that the position of planets always differed, no matter how diligently he did his observations. In the context of what 19th-century planetary scientists were trying to achieve the noise that infected his measurements was relatively small. And because Gauss found that these 'errors' could be described mathematically astronomers were able to work round the difficulty.

Soon after, people who aspired to apply the same rigour to understanding earthly phenomena (social scientists, as we now call them) discovered that noise also infected their measurements, and because human affairs are much more complex than those of planets, these errors were on a much bigger and problematic scale.

One of the first to seriously grapple with this problem was Francis Galton, a 19th-century gentleman scientist who, like many of his ilk, didn't have to work for a living and indulged in a passion for discovery.

Uncertainty and Predictability: Big Data and the Weak Signal

As you may be able to tell from the eyebrow ridge in portraits of Galton, he was related to Charles Darwin, another gentleman scientist of the Victorian era. But, whereas his cousin focussed all his energy on one big idea – the evolution of species – and in so doing changed the course of history, Galton flitted around making relatively minor discoveries in a number of areas some of which have been in their own way very influential.[16] In particular, Galton has earned the sobriquet of 'the father of statistics' as the result of work he did trying to solve a problem he had with the work of his more famous relative – the inheritance of physical characteristics.

Galton was particularly fascinated by the work of Adolphe Quetelet, a Belgian astronomer and sociologist (not a combination that you will find today) who became famous in his own lifetime for discovering that the incidence of many social phenomena such as height, weight, crime, suicide and marriage all followed the same distribution around a mean value – the classic bell shape we now call the 'normal' distribution. This was a great surprise because it was exactly the same distribution that Gauss had observed when he was measuring the position of the moon some decades earlier. What really shocked people, however, was that Quetelet's discovery seemed to invalidate the notion of free will, but without affirming the existence of God because, as Einstein said years later, 'God doesn't play dice'.

But Galton was not shocked – instead he was curious.

The problem that piqued his curiosity was this. If, as Darwin had proposed, characteristics such as height were passed down by some, as yet unknown, mechanism from parent to child, and given that married couples tended to be of similar stature, why was the world not inhabited by giants and pygmies? Why, instead, did we find the smooth curves of Gauss's distribution around a single arithmetical mean? Good question.

With his cousin's reputation on the line, Galton set to work.

To explore this problem Galton built a device that has come to be called a Galton Board. It consists of a wooden tray that looks a bit like a game of bagatelle. It has a funnel at the top into which small balls are loaded. And below the funnel are a series of pins nailed into the board in a regular pattern with the first pin located exactly beneath the funnel. At the bottom are a set of bins that collect the balls when they fall to the bottom, usually having hit a number of pins along the way.

Galton discovered that after a large number of balls had passed through this device their distribution in the bins at the bottom assumed the shape of a normal distribution as shown in Figure 4.2.

This is when Galton had his brainwave.

He, like everyone else had assumed that heredity was deterministic, probably the result of some mixing process. To put it simply, people had thought that if a 6-foot man mated with a woman who was 5 foot 10 inches tall their offspring would be 5 foot 11. But what if the process was not purely deterministic?[17] What if random factors – equivalent to the nails of the Galton machine – interfered with the inheritance of characteristics like height?

16. Unfortunately, one idea in particular (Eugenics – selective breeding of human beings to eliminate undesirable traits) became very influential in interwar Germany.

Figure 4.1:
Francis Galton (probably from around 1850)

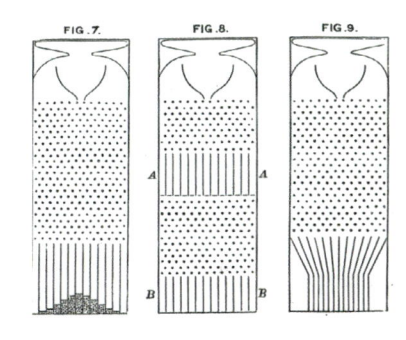

Figure 4.2:
Normal distribution in a Galton Board

This image (as drawn by Galton himself) shows the normal distribution of the balls in their 'bins' after they have travelled from the funnel at the top of the device through the 'nail field' in the centre.

17. Victorians couldn't use the word probabilistic because they hadn't yet discovered statistics!

If this were the case, very tall or very small people might be like balls in a bin towards the tail of the normal distribution. In other words, their position (height) wouldn't (just) be a reflection of heritable characteristics. It would simply be the result of chance variation around a stable mean. Another ball drawn from the same population (i.e. their child) would be unlikely to fall into the same bucket – it could fall into any bucket – but it is highly probable that they would be closer to the average of the distribution than their parents if they were from an extreme.

This was how Galton came to discover the phenomenon we now call 'reversion to the mean' – that is, the recorded average value of any process will gravitate towards the mean of the total population as more measurements are made.

This might seem blindingly obvious, but the consequences of this insight are liable to catch us out whenever we try to make inferences from limited data – such as the new data points that information professionals receive at the end of every period.[18]

For example, if you criticize someone for a negative variance in one period and subsequently observe that his or her performance 'improves' you might believe that it is the result of your intervention. But maybe this 'result' is just down to chance and there is no causal link between your criticism and the outcome. Perhaps both the negative and subsequent positive variance are simply manifestations of noise in a stable process and the performance improvement is just the consequence of the simple statistical tendency to revert to the mean, and your intervention had no effect at all.

The root of the problem (and many others like it when it comes to interpreting data) is this: the assumption that a single measure captures the 'truth' about an object. The 'truth' – if such a thing exists – is often heavily disguised by noise, and a failure to recognize this fact explains many failures in reasoning and practice.

What Galton discovered was that the height of a single individual doesn't tell us anything about the genetic capacity for tallness because it is impacted by innumerable other factors that are inherently unknowable, which we have to assume are random. So, the concept of tallness cannot be understood using simple arithmetic – we need to take account of probabilities – which is how Galton came to become known as the father of statistics.

The Galton Board illustrates the challenge we *always* face in interpreting real-life data, whether we know it or not. The position of the exit of the funnel at the top of the device represents the signal – the truth that we are trying to uncover. Each of the nails represents something that distorts the signal – in other words, a source of noise. The bins at the bottom represent a data point.

In real life we can't see the funnel (the source of the signal) – we only see the bucket into which the balls fall, which we record as a piece of data. Any individual ball is a data point. Just by looking at a single data point we can't tell where the funnel is located, and it makes no sense to say that any single ball is 'the

18. This is yet another example of the cognitive biases that Kahneman observed, which helped him win the Nobel Prize. He saw it in the training of Israeli fighter pilots whose bad performance always 'improved' when they were criticized and who 'became complacent' after they had performed well. At least according to their instructors!

signal' or is 'noise'. We can only infer what is signal and what is noise by analysing the results of many balls falling through the machine. This is what I meant when I said earlier that noise isn't a thing, it is a pattern – it is the spread of values around the signal, which in the case of a Galton Board is a stable mean because the funnel is fixed in place.

ANOTHER WAY OF THINKING ABOUT NOISE

The Galton Board is a very simple abstract example. In real life, distinguishing noise from signals is much more difficult, but unsurprisingly, given how it affects all our existence, it is something that our brain can (often) do incredibly well, below our level of consciousness. It is only when we think about it that we have problems!

For example, imagine that you are in a busy bar talking to a friend. Because most of the people around you are talking at the same time it is hard to hear what she is saying. Put another way, it is difficult to pick up the signal (her words) because of the distorting and distracting effect of the noise (other people's words). In this case, as in any data-processing challenge, the noise is not meaningless in itself, after all your conversation is distracting noise to someone else. Noise is the word that we give to any data that is irrelevant to our purpose. It therefore does not carry information about the thing that we are interested in - the signal - so before we can extract any meaning, we need to filter it out.

Evolution has provided us with the tools to deal with verbal and visual noise. Unfortunately, it has not equipped us with the ability to deal with noise expressed in symbolic form, so we need to find tools to fill in the blind spot in our capabilities.

Hence, we can now answer the question, 'What is noise?'

Noise is any data that is irrelevant to our purpose, and that is as a result 'meaningless' in our context. All data is infected by noise to a greater or lesser extent, so to make sense of data we need to be able to identify the likely contribution of noise – the qualities of a data set that we can safely discount – in order to expose the potentially meaningful signal.

The fact that we cannot make sense of a single data point because there is always a spread of data values around the mean shouldn't come as a big surprise, after all it is the principle upon which insurance works. While every car accident is unique and has a specific identifiable cause, on average the rate at which car accidents occur has a predictable pattern (noise) around a predictable average (signal). Insurers base their premiums on the average and in this way protect us against a large loss if we are unlucky enough to fall in the wrong part of the distribution. Despite this I sometimes find that people (particularly those who analyse performance for a living) have difficulty accepting that individual pieces of data have limited meaning.

Discovering that what you have been doing for a living is pointless has that effect on people.

NEWS AND NOISE

For another example of our tendency to attribute meaning to single data points listen to the report on stock markets or currency movement that tends to come at the end of news bulletins. 'Today on Wall Street the Dow Jones index was down 12 points on news of the Justice Department's intention to launch an enquiry into blah blah blah'. Since the index has never been the same for two consecutive days the fact that it moved up or down really isn't news, and there is absolutely no way anyone can determine the impact that any particular event had on the buying or selling decisions of thousands of people (and a similarly large number of machines doing automatic trading). But the urge to treat any and every change as significant, and our brain's need for a coherent story to back it up, is so overwhelming that we cannot help ourselves – even when we know that it makes no sense at all.

Nassim Taleb nicely illustrates this search for causality in his *Black Swan* book. On the day of Saddam Hussein's capture in his hiding place in Iraq bond prices initially rose. Investors were apparently seeking safer assets that morning, and the Bloomberg News service flashed this headline: U.S. TREASURIES RISE; HUSSEIN CAPTURE MAY NOT CURB TERRORISM. Half an hour later, bond prices fell back and the revised headline read: U.S. TREASURIES FALL; HUSSEIN CAPTURE BOOSTS ALLURE OF RISKY ASSETS.

I will return to the subject of 'storytelling' and how it can be so dangerous in Chapter 7.

If you are struggling to grasp the implication of the fact that all data is 'infected by noise', try this quick experiment that I often run at workshops.

In the first part of the exercise I ask participants to find the stopwatch function on their smartphones. I then ask them to start the watch, then close their eyes and then try and stop the clock at exactly 10 seconds. After noting the results they then repeat the exercise nine further times.

I created this deliberately stupidly simple task because it should be easy to target and assess performance, and, because of the lack of 'moving parts', there should be relatively little noise compared to the real world.

Based on your own experience of counting in your head, what do you think would constitute good performance? And what level of variance would be worthy of explanation and perhaps coded amber or red on a RAG chart – 5%? 10%?

Figure 4.3 gives an example of the results for one participant from a recent workshop.

As you can see there was a lot of variability in the results, despite it being a very simple exercise involving nothing more than counting up to ten in one's head.

How would you go about assessing the performance of this participant?

You clearly wouldn't form a judgement based on a single data point – it makes no sense to say that she performed well on the first attempt but then got worse, worse still then even better before getting better again. We know that there

Uncertainty and Predictability: Big Data and the Weak Signal

Variance from Target

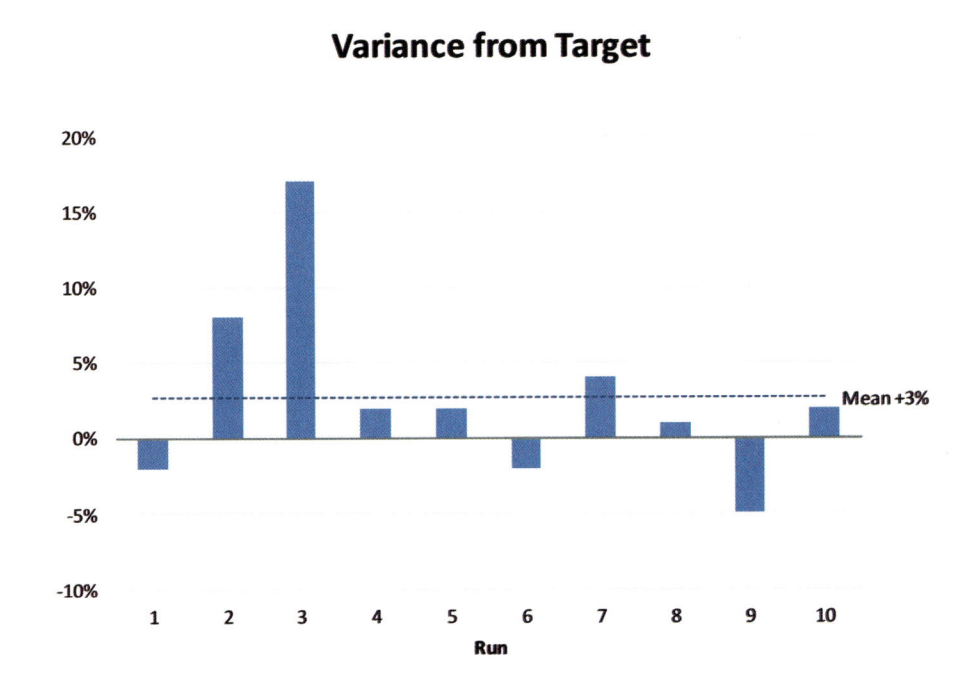

Figure 4.3:
Individual example from stopwatch game

The vertical scale shows the difference between each timed exercise and the target of 10 seconds, expressed as a percentage. The horizontal scale records the result of each of the ten trials.

were all sorts of minor things that affected what happened on each run, from failing to hit the stop button properly to stray thoughts or background noises that distracted her for a split second. Most people rightly conclude that to judge performance we need to measure the average error, which in this case is 0.27 or roughly 3%.

Because we know how these numbers were generated and I have given them to you in one go rather than in sequence, it is clear that the variation from one period to another represents nothing more than a person's inability to perfectly replicate a set of actions.

Imagine instead that these numbers measured, say, the cost of an activity over a ten-month period rather than the results of a simple counting exercise. What conclusions might you be tempted to draw? Does this represent good or bad performance? And if this data was revealed to you in a sequence – one month at a time – what data points would you treat as significant and which would you dismiss as just noise? My guess is that periods 2 and 3 would be highlighted as exceptional, and subsequent periods as evidence of 'things being brought back under control'. Yet we know that this is not the case. It is all 'just noise'. There's no story here folks – just move on.

But this is just one data series with a small number of data points. In real life we have to make sense of many data series at the same time – perhaps, with the advent of Big Data, there might be many thousands. Looking at the results from all 21 participants in the workshop (Figure 4.4) gives us some sense of the additional challenges this presents.

Figure 4.4:
Results from population playing stopwatch game

Here the vertical scale shows the variance from target in terms of seconds. The blue dots show the average difference and the bars the range between the highest and lowest value recorded by each participant.

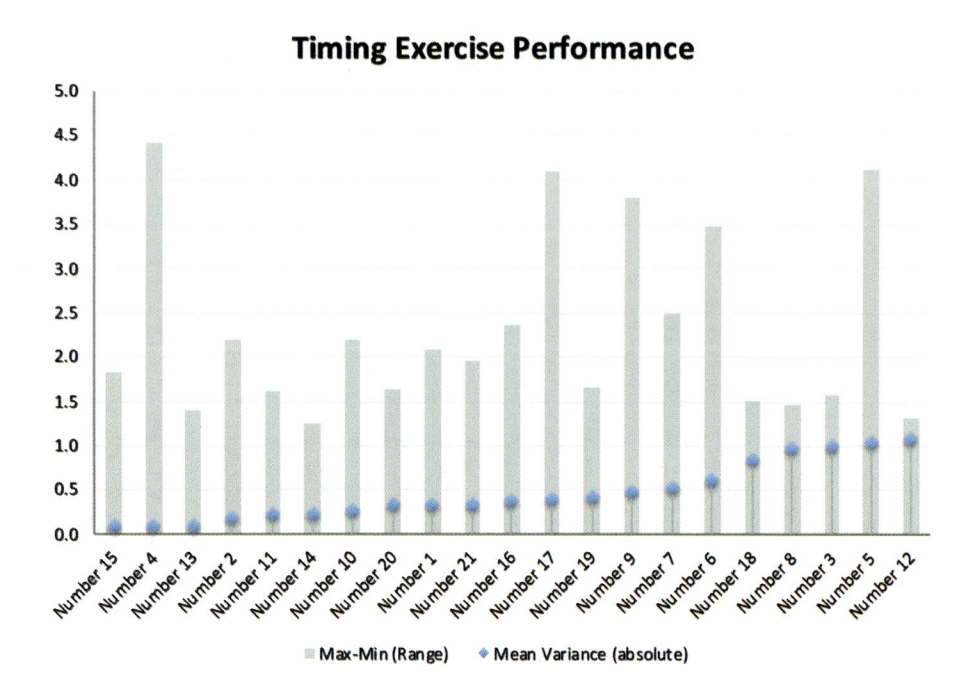

Timing Exercise Performance

■ Max-Min (Range)   ♦ Mean Variance (absolute)

How would you judge who performed well or performed badly based on the data in Figure 4.4? Even with this very simple exercise there is clearly a lot of noise, so how easy would it be to spot an exceptional data point or an improvement or deterioration in the level of performance? Also, to assess performance, should we only take account of the average level or should we factor the range of results into our assessment? In other words, how do we determine who has performed better – participant 4 who has a low average but a large range or participant 18 whose average was higher but had a lower range?

By now it should be clear that, even in a very simple situation like this, there are a number of factors that need to be taken into account when assessing relative performance and simple arithmetic alone does not give us a rational basis on which to base judgements.

This simple example demonstrates a couple of important things.

There are always minor variations in the output of any process, even the most simple and repetitive task. Therefore, it is simply not possible to make sense of performance using a single data point. We are unable to determine what is the performance signal and what is the noise. To be able to make such a judgement we have to look at a data series. We need to look at the average value and the average level of deviation around it.

This much is obvious; the second learning is less so but just as important. We are used to thinking about performance in terms of a level – in this case the average value. But there is a second dimension to performance – the spread of values around the mean – what statisticians call variation – has to be factored into our judgement.

If we ran this little game twice and came up with exactly the same mean value both times but the spread of individual values for the second run was half of that from the first, we would have no hesitation in saying that we had improved. But

Uncertainty and Predictability: Big Data and the Weak Signal

in our professional life we rarely factor the level of variation around the mean into our performance analysis processes, partly because we do not have the tools to measure it.

So, we need to slightly amend our definition of performance, as follows:

Performance is a measure of the extent to which the purpose of an organization is being *consistently* fulfilled.

Therefore, understanding noise is critically important to information professionals for two reasons. First, we need to take into account when we seek to make inferences – extract meaning from data. Second, noise – or variation – is an important attribute of performance itself.

We will return to the issue of variation as a key dimension of performance later. First, let's continue to explore the theme of differentiating signals from noise, starting with our brain's perspective of this challenge.

OUR BRAINS AND NOISE

Thus far I have painted our System 1 brain as a bit of a hero. In many ways it is smarter than the System 2 brain that we normally credit as being the source of our intelligence. System 1 handles enormous volumes of sensory data, and crunches through it at a staggering speed using parallel processing techniques that boggle the minds of computer scientists and all sorts of clever shortcuts, always on the lookout for significant patterns. It is logical for us to make use of this power wherever possible to help make sense of data and to communicate meaning. And we have already seen how our unconscious System 1 brain helps us distinguish signal from noise in situations that are biologically familiar to us, such as picking out words spoken in a noisy environment.

But our System 1 brain can make horrible mistakes when it is confronted with a challenge that it hasn't evolved to deal with.

Take toast for example.

In Figure 4.5 you have just seen a picture of a piece of toast. You know that it is toast and that the patterns on it are the random result of the toasting process. But that doesn't stop your brain also seeing the face of Michael Jackson in it. And even if you didn't see it at first, now I have told you about Michael Jackson you will never be able to look at this piece of toast and *not* see his face.

This shows that our pattern-seeking System 1 brain is so powerful that it is capable of detecting patterns that aren't there – things that are simply random – and that we know, intellectually, are random. But once our System 1 brain is activated in this way it is extremely difficult to overrule it; it requires an act of will.[19]

From an evolutionary perspective this makes a lot of sense. The world in which our brain grew up was long on threats but short on structured data. Overreacting to noise (such as shapes in the undergrowth) had huge survival upsides and relatively few downsides. But, fast forward a few million years and the equation has been reversed.[20]

Figure 4.5:
Face in toast image

19. The medical term for our ability to see meaningful patterns in noise is called apophenia, a term that was originally coined to describe the delusions associated with the onset of schizophrenia – which, as we have already speculated, may be partly the result of the suppression of prediction errors. It has subsequently been applied more widely to describe other defects of reasoning, such as the gambler's fallacies. The tendency to see faces in randomness has a specific name – pareidolia. Faces are one of the first patterns that babies learn to recognize, so pareidolia is almost certainly a phenomenon that is deeply embedded in our heritable neural circuitry.

20. Leonard Mlodinow, author of *The Drunkard's Walk,* thinks that our obsession with patterns is also related to another fundamental need: 'because if events are random, we are not in control, and if we are in control of events, they are not random. There is therefore a fundamental clash between our need to feel we are in control and our ability to recognize randomness. That clash is one of the principal reasons we misinterpret random events'.

Compared to our ancestors there are relatively few threats to our survival but there is an unimaginably greater amount of data relating to situations that have never ever arisen in our shared evolutionary history. As a result, there is a much greater chance of being misled by our instincts and it is much more difficult to spot that we are being misled. Ultimately the absence or otherwise of a man-eating tiger in the undergrowth is easy to detect, but spotting (and owning up to) a mistake in analysing a complex business situation is much more difficult. Also, the consequences of getting it wrong are probably bigger than we realize.

By overreacting to randomness at best we have wasted time and energy. Moreover, just like with the toast, once you have 'recognized' a pattern it is difficult to unrecognize it, so at worst we will be much slower to react to real threats and opportunities because we will not 'see' them. Worse still, if we react to noise, by our actions we inject more noise into a noisy world, making it even more difficult to spot the signal.

So, System 1 is in trouble. Surely System 2 can help out here.

Unfortunately, System 2 struggles with randomness as well, albeit in a different way, as these questions illustrate:

1. What are the odds of a fair coin flip coming up with three heads in a row?
2. What are the chances of getting eight heads in a row?

Unless you are a professional statistician you will probably struggle to answer these questions at all. But even if you know how to answer them it will have taken some time to calculate the answer despite it being a very simple and straightforward example of probabilistic logic.

Again, the reason for our brain's shortcomings in dealing with this kind of logical problem makes sense from an evolutionary point of view. For most of the existence of our species, a useful answer and response to the question 'Is there a man-eating tiger in that bush?' would take one of three forms:

1. definitely yes (run),
2. probably (run just in case) or
3. probably not (carry on picking those berries but keep an eye open just in case).

Precisely calculating the probability to three decimal places was not a useful skill for our Mesolithic ancestors. And a measure of just how little it mattered even in our more recent history is that the great Greek, Hindu or Arabic mathematicians paid no attention to the subject of probability. Only when some 16th-century mathematicians started to subsidize their paltry income by gambling on cards was the problem recognized at all.

But the challenge of dealing with probabilities in business is much more complex than most games of chance, as we shall discover.

Uncertainty and Predictability: Big Data and the Weak Signal

THE CHALLENGE OF NOISE IN REAL LIFE

The probability of occurrence of an event can be represented by the distribution of values (data points) around an average of a set of data points. And we assume that the central point of the distribution is the signal and the spread of the distribution represents noise. One of the biggest challenges that statisticians face is that many real-life phenomena do not produce nicely-behaved normal distributions that Quetelet and Galton thought were ubiquitous.

For example, if the average value of a variable is close to zero, or if there is some upper or lower limit on what can be achieved, we often find skewed distributions, and if we are measuring infrequent events it will follow a skewed Poisson distribution.[21] And many processes in nature have distributions that look 'normal' at first glance but have 'fat tails', which means that extreme outcomes are *much* more likely to occur than we might expect – as many bankers found out to their, but mainly our, cost in 2008.[22]

[21] The Poisson distribution is the discrete probability distribution of the number of events occurring in a given time period, given the average number of times the event occurs over that time period: named after French mathematician Siméon Denis Poisson.

[22] Nicholas Nassim Taleb has popularised the impact of 'fat tailed' distributions, which he described as 'Black Swan' events - things that cannot be contemplated as being possible until they happen.

[23] You can try for yourself using any of the simulations that you will find on the web such as the one here:

https://ww2.odu.edu/eneukrug

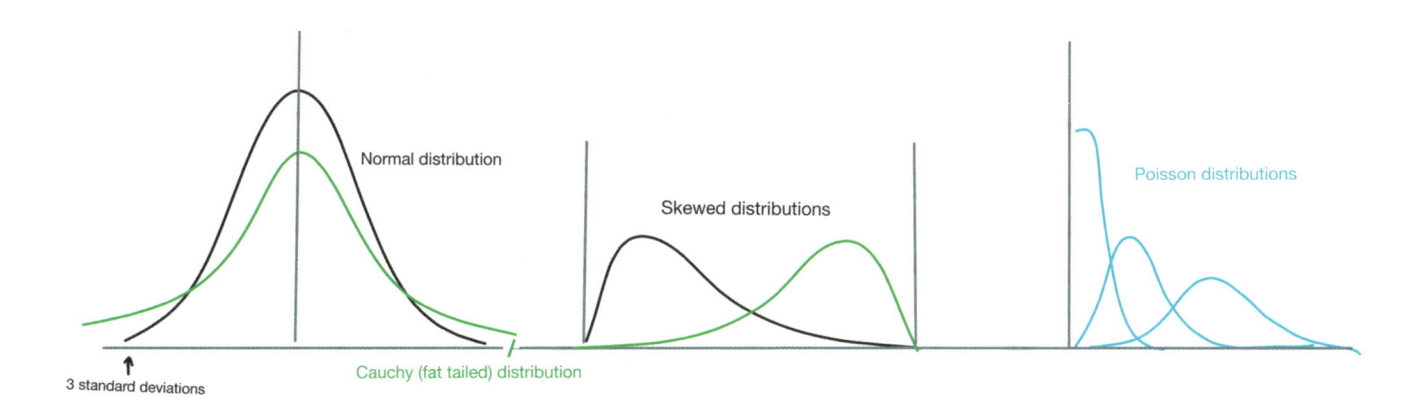

For a quiet life, statisticians often assume that noise adopts a normal distribution, and for our very practical purposes of trying to get a handle on what noise is here this is usually a reasonable approach to take. But even with a run of the mill normal distribution, separating the chaff of noise from the wheat of the signal can be tricky. I will illustrate this with the help of a Galton Board simulation I created in Excel.[23]

First, even when we *know* that the distribution of noise in a data series is Gaussian (as it is here) we do not know how much noise there is in there, and if we don't know how much noise is there it makes the task of separating signal from noise much more difficult. The amount of noise affects the 'flatness' of the bell curve distribution and it is measured by the standard deviation (SD), until we have collected a large enough sample. But estimating this is difficult without a big sample, and we might only get one data point a month as the simulation demonstrates.

In Figure 4.7 there are a series of histograms showing the distribution of simulated balls (data points) across 15 bins. The first shows the distribution of 12 balls; the equivalent of a year's worth of monthly data. The second shows the first 24 data points and the third 36. Even in year 3 it is not clear that we are looking

Figure 4.6:
Some common probability distributions

A normal distribution is symmetrical as is a Cauchy distribution, but because it has 'fat tails' extreme events are many more times likely to happen, as the banking industry discovered in 2008. Distributions are often skewed, however, when there is a constraint on the behaviour of a system (e.g. it is not possible to have negative sales!) and infrequent events always follow a skewed Poisson distribution. In real life it is often difficult to determine what kind of distribution is most relevant.

at typically a normal distribution. It is not until we have 50 or so data points that we can be reasonably confident that we know the shape of the distribution. So, with any less data it is difficult to assess the level of noise, and consequently interpreting data is problematic.

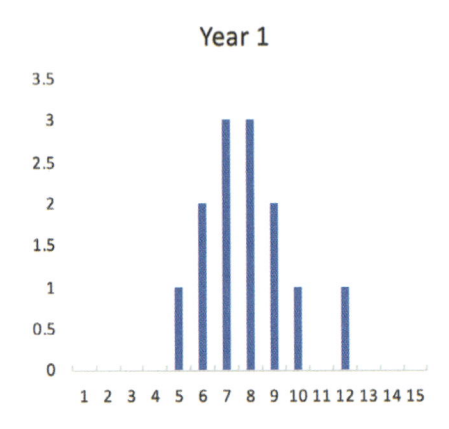

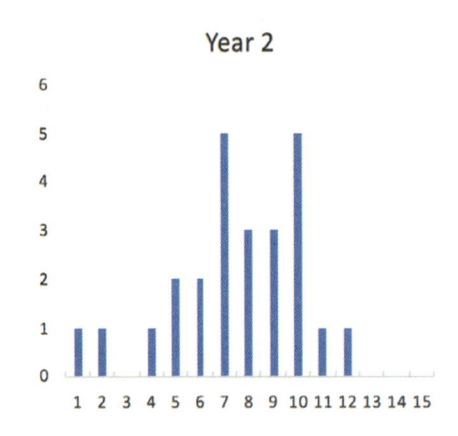

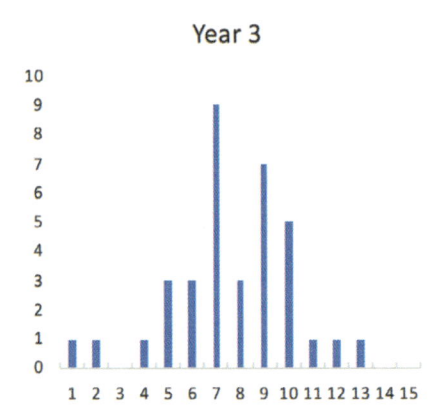

Figure 4.7:
Simulations with small samples

Here the bars represent cumulative distributions - the number of balls in each virtual bucket or trap at different times. Even with a sample of 36 (years 1-3) we do not see a perfect normal distribution shape emerging.

What makes it even more difficult to spot our signal is that we receive data about our business 'one ball at a time', we can't wait for four years before making a decision. But if we 'decide' too soon based on a small sample a random sequence can look like a pattern – even to an arithmetical algorithm – so we run the risk of intervening when we should not or making the wrong decision.

For example, in Figure 4.8 there are three graphs drawn using the output from a simulated Galton Board with 15 bins. The results are plotted in the order in which they arrive – as if they represented data collected over three years. When we fit a simple trend line to each 'year's' data we can be misled into thinking that things are changing when we know that they are not because the signal (the position of the simulated funnel) is stable.

Figure 4.8:
Run charts with small samples

The green dotted line is the signal because the funnel was placed above trap number 8. This doesn't move but, as you can see, the sequence in which the simulated balls arrive makes it look like there is a downward trend in the first year made up of the first 12 balls. This impression is 'confirmed' by Excel when we fit a trend line to the data. And while the second year is 'flat' - in line with what we know the true signal to be - in year 3 we 'see' growth. Not only is our eye fooled into thinking there is a trend in this data; the trend-fitting algorithm is fooled as well.

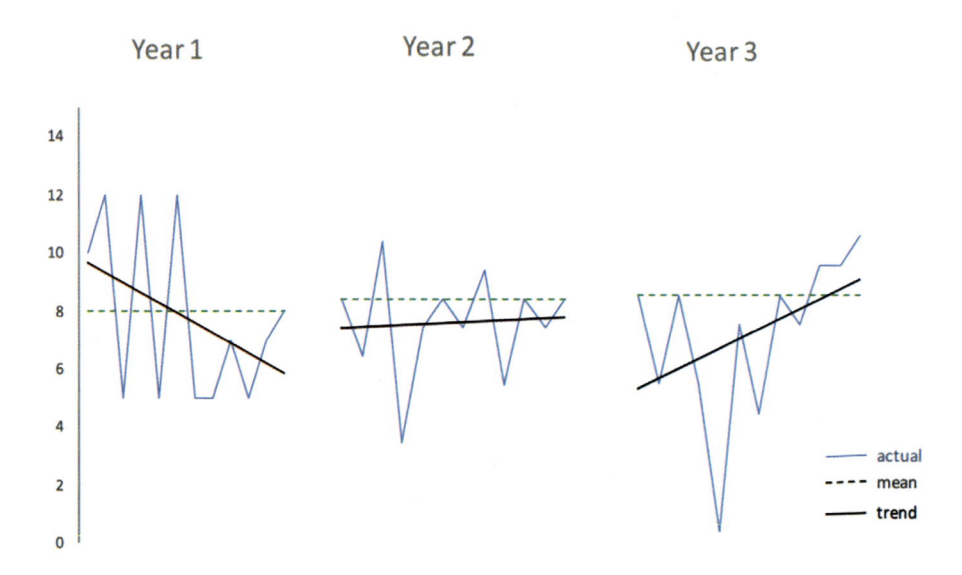

So, we can see that even a very simple simulation produces data that can easily be misinterpreted using our common-sense pattern-seeking mental algorithms.

In real life, our job is even more challenging because we have no way of knowing in advance whether the level of noise in any data set is small or large in comparison with the strength of the signal. We don't know how many 'nails' there are that interfere with the signal.

Worse, in real life we cannot assume that the signal is fixed in the way that the Galton Board funnel is. In fact, the only reason that we are interested in measuring performance at all is because it isn't likely to be stable – or it is and we don't want it to be!

A signal could assume the form of a steady linear upward or downward line. It could be curved (exponential). Or it might be seasonal (cyclical). And the signal may also change behaviour, either temporarily (producing 'spikes' or outliers) or permanently ('breaks' or 'discontinuities') – which, whether it is in a positive or negative direction, is always significant for decision makers.

Faced with the difficulty of separating an unknown pattern of signals from an unknown amount of noise it is not surprising that most people shy away from the challenge of trying to make sense of the huge data sets that their businesses now diligently harvest. It is simply too difficult to extract meaning from many hundreds of data series that may display a wide range of behaviour using traditional arithmetical techniques like totals or simple averages.

But closing your eyes to the problem doesn't make it go away. Clearly it is wasteful to ignore this data resource because we will be missing out on valuable insights. However, the alternative of using common sense to interpret it is risky, but also impractical given the volume of data.

It is clear. Our brains need help.

THE SOLUTION

So, we cannot trust our intuition, and we cannot trust simple arithmetic. What is the solution?

When working with data infected by noise, we need to think in terms of probabilities, and use statistical tools not simple arithmetic. In short, we need to understand something about the process of statistical inference.

The mere mention of the word 'statistics' is guaranteed to scare many people forced to learn about it at school or as part of their professional qualification. This is mainly because the way it is traditionally taught is heavily biased towards theory and precision, often using examples far removed from practical everyday experience.

The good news is that I have discovered that the vast majority of what performance analysts need to know about statistics in practice is easy to understand and use, not least because we only have one type of problem – making sense out of time series data. Also, unlike academics, we are not in search of 'the truth' in a strict scientific sense of the word. We just need enough understanding to quickly do the right thing, most of the time, so we can cut some technical corners that might appal the purists and still make much better decisions than we would using simple arithmetic. I'm looking for 'good enough', rather than 'correct'.

In the end our decision still may be to do nothing but, if after analysing the situation statistically, that is what we decide, it is much better than doing nothing by ignoring data because our inaction is based on evidence. And better still than taking action without good evidence; acting when we should be sitting on our hands is not just wasteful, it usually makes things worse.

Put simply, our challenge is to detect signals in a noisy data series. There are two ways to do this. The first involves analysing the *sequence* in which data arrives, the second the *size* of the data values.

SEQUENCE

Let's first look at a simple way to detect signals by looking at the sequence of data from a probabilistic perspective.

What are the chances of flipping a coin and getting eight heads or eight tails in a row? And at what point should you become suspicious that the coin you are using is 'bent' – that it has either two heads or two tails rather than one of each?

This is the same problem we face whenever we analyse a sequence of numbers. The values have gone up or gone down for the last x periods. What is the chance that the sequence of numbers is evidence of a trend in the data rather than the outcome of chance process like the balls falling into the traps of the Galton Board?

We struggle to answer this question because our brains have not evolved to tackle them. If we had evolved in an environment where our survival depended on our ability to make precise probabilistic judgements, I am sure that our System 1 brain would have been genetically primed so that we regarded this as 'easy' because the logic behind the answer is very straightforward.

Table 4.1:
Flips and probabilities

This table shows the chances of getting all heads or all tails from a given number of flips of a fair coin. Note that it is always possible to get such a sequence however many times you flip, but the odds become vanishingly small as the sequence extends. Note also that the chance of getting either a head or a tail on the next flip is always 50% as the coin has no memory of what has gone before (this is related to the idea of 'the gambler's fallacy').[24]

[24]. Although statisticians like to work with percentages there is evidence that our brains find it easier to deal with probabilities expressed in terms of odds i.e. one in 256 rather than 0.4%.

Coin Flips	Chances of: All Heads or All Tails	Probability
1	1:1	100.0%
2	1:2	50.0%
3	1:4	25.0%
4	1:8	12.5%
5	1:16	6.3%
6	1:32	3.1%
7	1:64	1.6%
8	1:128	0.8%
9	1:256	0.4%
10	1:512	0.2%

Uncertainty and Predictability: Big Data and the Weak Signal

The chances of getting either a head or a tail on one toss of a fair coin are – obviously – 100%. The chance of getting either another head or another tail on the second throw is half of this since whenever you flip the coin there is a 50% chance of getting a head and a 50% chance of getting a tail. And on the third throw the chance is reduced by a further 50%, and so on. Proceeding in this way it is easy to calculate the probability of any number of heads or tails in sequence, as shown in Table 4.1.

Obviously, you cannot commit Table 4.1 to memory, and I wouldn't expect you to perform the mental arithmetic every time that you face this kind of problem. Instead, I recommend that you prime your System 1 brain using a simple heuristic (rule of thumb) that goes like this. 'Ten–Four' is how I remember that there is roughly a 10% chance of seeing the same binary outcome (heads or tails, up or down) four times in a row. 'Five–Five' is how I remember that there is roughly a 5% chance of five in a row. By using these rules, you can compensate to some degree for the fact that we have not been genetically well primed to deal with probabilities.

Taking a step back from the technicalities, there are two profound conclusions that we can draw from this simple example.

First, whenever there is any degree of chance involved, *it is impossible to make a useful judgement from a single data point by the direction of movement alone.*

Our coin will either land on heads or tails, just in the same way that any new value will always either be higher or lower than the last one. The fact that the second value is higher or lower has absolutely no significance at all – it's a 50:50 call.

But too often in everyday life as well as business we believe that any and every change is significant and that every difference in a number signifies a difference in the world. This is partly because traditional techniques do not provide us with the ability to make probabilistic judgements but also because we can always discover something that we think has 'caused' a value to move. So, if revenue is higher this month than last, we will always be able to point to, say, a customer who has bought more than normal. In that way we fool ourselves into thinking that the value of the data point is significant when it might not be.[25]

It may be factually correct to point out that there is something different in the value of a variable between two periods, but it is a mistake to think that this is an explanation, because it isn't. The logic is tautological, because it is rather like saying we won a football match *because* we scored a goal – we wouldn't have won the match if we hadn't! Unless we get lucky, all we have done is identified a contribution to a random change in a variable. If the change is indeed just random a commentary on the results referring to the upswing in sales for customer x is the numerical equivalent of seeing the face of Elvis in a cloud.

How does that make you feel about variance analysis now?

The second conclusion is that *we can never be absolutely 100% sure of anything.* Whenever there is randomness involved in a process there is always a chance that the result might simply be due to 'luck'. Any judgement we make could be

25. We come across this phenomenon all the time in the media. For example, how many times have you heard that the stock price for Company X or Y has changed because of… (insert supposed cause)? The reality is that the commentator has no idea whether the change was random or not. She is simply providing a story to satisfy our brain's need for coherence – it doesn't like loose ends. And the thing is that *there will always be something* that could conceivably have caused the movement, so the commentator cannot fail, which is what makes this approach so pernicious – and why we are more inclined to listen to good storytellers than scientists.

wrong. But we cannot avoid making decisions, so we have to be sure that we are prepared to accept the level of risk of getting it wrong in the context of the consequences of making a mistake.

Those consequences will differ depending on the kind of decision that we are making, as well as the degree of confidence we have in our evidence. For example, if a country is on high alert for terrorism, the police are most concerned about missing the signs of an imminent attack and so are likely to make an arrest based only on suspicion, accepting that there is perhaps a 1 in 10 chance of arresting an innocent person, because the consequences of missing a terrorist attack will be catastrophic. Before someone is charged, however, the probability of being wrong needs to be smaller – perhaps 1 in 20. And, because it involves someone being deprived of their liberty, a successful conviction requires that there should be proof 'beyond all reasonable doubt' – so the chance of a 'false positive' might be 1 in 100 or even higher.

The medical profession faces dilemmas like this all the time – breast screening for cancer is the classic case. No test is foolproof so they have to balance the probability of missing a problem (a false negative), with obvious negative consequences, against the chance of detecting a problem when none exists (a false positive), which might lead to expensive and potentially dangerous unnecessary treatment.

Let's now apply this logic to a business scenario. Just as with coin flips, if we have four monthly data points in a row moving in the same direction, there is a 1 in 8 chance of us being wrong if we interpret this as a trend. So, if we used this as our criterion, on average we would expect one or two false alarms (false positives) on average in a year. Five data points in a row would reduce this risk to 1 in 16, meaning the chance of us being wrong is about 5%, but we would have to accept that if there is a problem (or opportunity) we will be slower to react to it.

The more observant readers might have noticed something troubling in this simple description of the process of how to form scientifically robust judgements purely based on sequences in data.

If we need at least four consecutive data points before we can make a judgement about trends with any degree of confidence, that means we have to wait at least four months before we can take action – or a year if we only measure a variable every quarter. If we are running a business this is far too slow. So, does this mean that we have to jump before we have statistical confidence that we are right, and just hope for the best?

Fortunately, we do not have to base decision-making on what – from the probabilistic perspective – might be little better than a guess. The reason for this is that we will almost always have information from other sources that we take into account when we are assessing the probability of an event. In legal parlance, incorporating evidence from other independent sources increases the 'weight' of evidence, dramatically reducing the probability of false positives that we would calculate based on a single data source.

For instance, in our coin tossing example, if we used a coin from our own pocket, we would need perhaps thousands of consecutive heads before we believed

Uncertainty and Predictability: Big Data and the Weak Signal

that we have got a two-headed coin, because we know from our past experience that this is likely to be a very rare occurrence.

If, on the other hand, we conducted the coin-tossing trial with a magician or a guy with a stall on a street corner our judgement would be very different because we have no information about the probability of the coins that they are using to factor into our judgement. We might start with an open mind or by being very suspicious, which would change the way that we interpreted the evidence we got from each coin toss.

This is why it is extremely important to use other sources of data that are independent of our primary source to help us make sense of what is going on.

If you are interested in exploring this idea more deeply read on, otherwise skip the rest of this section for the moment.

BAYESIAN LOGIC

There are two different fields of statistics that have different approaches to the challenge of analysing evidence.

The first is called 'frequentist' because it is based on calculating the odds of something happening by chance by counting the frequency with which something **has occurred**. This is the method I used in the coin toss example. It is possible to combine the frequencies from two different distributions (e.g. the frequency of coin tosses and the frequency of dishonest people on street corners) but in practice this is often difficult. This is because you need to have data on both things and you also need to know whether the data sources are independent – that is, whether one is causally related to the other, and if so how strongly. If I was to flip two coins, I know that one doesn't influence the other, and that the result of one coin flip doesn't influence the next one. But complete independence like this is very rare in the real world and where it doesn't exist it is often difficult to determine the strength of the relationships and calculate the combined probabilities.

The second approach allows you to combine evidence from multiple sources, even if some of the evidence is based on judgement. Also, we can use it to calculate – and update – the probability of a hypothesis being true when data arrives in a haphazard or messy way. So, rather than counting the chances of an event based on a set of data collected in a rigorous way we can calculate the plausibility of an event based on a combination of limited and potentially unreliable data and prior knowledge.

This approach is called Bayesian statistics after the 18th-century English clergyman who first came up with the idea (as a way of assessing the probability that there is a God). For many years this method was deeply unfashionable and – in the eyes of frequentists – discredited because it uses 'subjective' inputs (i.e. inputs not derived from frequentist methods!).

Today it lies at the heart of many of the machine-learning algorithms that are used for spam filters, voice recognition systems and self-driving cars because it works well in real-world situations. After all, in everyday life, it is rare that we have no previous experience on which we can draw.

It is extremely unlikely that you will ever use Bayesian statistics in anger but it is helpful to get a sense of how it works because it may help sharpen your intuitions. Indeed, scientists believe that our brains use something like a Bayesian process to make sense of incoming data, which is why (superficially at least) it sounds like simple common sense.

Bayes' theorem says that the probability of a hypothesis being true (e.g. that a coin is unbiased or that there is an upward trend in the data) is the product of the likelihood of the evidence and your probability of your prior belief (e.g. that the coin is likely to be unbiased or that there is a trend in the data) - which could be based on independent data (e.g. an industry survey) or on a hunch (e.g. about the character of the person who gave you the coin).

The neat thing about the process is that the output of one round (the probability after evidence has been assessed) becomes the input into the next (the prior belief) so the plausibility of the hypothesis is continuously updated as new evidence comes in, ultimately converging on the 'truth'.

Let's see how this works using the coin toss example. I will reference this in italics to the formula at the end. First, let's determine the prior probability (*PA*).

Let's assume that we have drawn the coin we are going to use from an urn that has 80 unbiased coins and 20 biased coins (two heads or two tails). The probability of our prior belief (that the coin is unbiased) is therefore 0.8.

Now we need to generate some evidence.

We flip the coin twice, which gives us some evidence we can use. If the coin lands twice on heads (or tails) there is a probability of 0.5 (50%) that this is a false negative result - that the coin really is unbiased but that it happened to fall on the same side by chance (*P(A|B)*).

We now need to assess the probability of this evidence.

As we have seen, if the coin is unbiased there is a 50% chance of it landing by chance on the same side. And we originally assessed the chances of the coin being 80%. So, the combined probability of getting two heads (or tails) when the coin is unbiased is 0.5 x 0.8 = 0.4.

But the coin might have landed twice on the same side because it *is* biased. To start with we assessed that there is only a 20% chance of the coin being biased. But if it is biased there is a 100% chance of it landing on heads (or tails) twice. In other words, there is zero chance of a false positive result. So, the combined probability is 0.2 x 1.0 = 0.2.

So, we are now able to calculate the probability of the coin landing on the same face twice whether or not it is unbiased - it is the sum of the two combined probabilities: 0.4 + 0.2 = 0.6. This is the probability of the evidence (*P|B*).

So, we can now calculate the likelihood of seeing this evidence if our hypothesis (of an unbiased coin) is true.

It is 0.5 (the probability of a false negative) divided by 0.6 (the probability of the evidence) = 0.83.

But there is one more step because we can't ignore our prior belief.

Originally, we thought that there was an 80% chance of the coin being unbiased. This now needs to be updated with our new evidence. To do this we simply combine the probability attached to our prior belief and the likelihood of the evidence: 0.8 x 0.83 = 0.66.

So, we initially thought that the probability of our coin being unbiased was 80%, but based on this new evidence it has now fallen to 66%. And this new probability of our belief now feeds into the next round of evidence gathering (flipping). If we got the same result

Uncertainty and Predictability: Big Data and the Weak Signal

next time round the probability of our unbiased belief (technically this is called the posterior probability) *P(A|B)* would fall to 0.5, and in the subsequent round to 0.33, and so on. But it only takes one flip to land on the opposite face to send this shooting up to 1.0 (100% confidence) since this kind of evidence will **only** be seen when the coin is unbiased.

Phew!

So, you can see that the procedure may sound a bit convoluted - at least when it is described in this way - but given a moment's thought you can see how well this resonates with the way that we make judgements in real life.

For instance, in real life we would not start by drawing a coin at random from an urn that enables us to quantitatively assess prior probabilities. We might begin by making a judgement about the trustworthiness of the person providing the coin, but mathematically this would work perfectly well. It's just that the speed at which you calculate the 'correct' probability will vary depending on the accuracy of your initial judgement.

Just like in real life, we need more evidence to overturn a strongly held view, and less to confirm it, than when our initial assessment is more balanced. Which is exactly what we need for practical performance analysis purposes - sound initial judgement based on an understanding of the business and its environment supported by a rigorous method for assessing evidence.

Frequentist statisticians view this process as a thoroughly bad thing and argue that the **only** way you can get valid inferences is from observed frequencies in the data.

However, in the real world we hardly ever start with a blank slate and things never stand still for long enough for us to be sure that we are measuring the same thing over and over again when we estimate frequencies. Therefore, the intellectual tide is moving in favour of Bayesians, at least for real-world rather than experimental applications.

So, the message is this. It is important that you are able to evaluate evidence based on probabilities, but try not to use this in a naïve way. Always look for independent sources of evidence - a context - that will help you to quickly refine your judgement.

Bayes' theorem - the formula:

$$P(A|B) = \frac{P(B|A) \times PA}{PB}$$

Where

$P(A|B)$ = posterior probability of the hypothesis (A) given the evidence (B)
$P(B|A)$ = probability of seeing the evidence (B) if the hypothesis (A) is true
PB = probability of seeing the evidence whether or not A is true
PA = prior probability of the hypothesis (A) being true

Ultimately then, other than a basic requirement that rational decisions should be based on evidence there is no right answer. The level of statistical confidence you need before you commit to a judgement or an action is a choice based upon a balance between the risk of false positives and false negatives and the cost attached to each outcome.

At a practical level, the problem that businesses now have is that they have large quantities of noisy Big Data that they don't have the time to analyse in detail. Consequently, they either ignore this source of insights or jump to conclusions without sufficient evidence. Given the waste of investigating false alarms, when we set out to 'mine' large data sets I would suggest that the statistical bar for flagging up potential signals be set very high – perhaps the equivalent of eight values in a row since this means that the chance of a false alarm is less than 1 in 100.

So, we now have a very simple statistical procedure that doesn't require anything more than the ability to count to help us identify a small number of significant events in very large data sets. These are the 'ten–four' or 'five–five' rules.

Sequences are one way to distinguish between signals and noise, but this approach has some weaknesses. Specifically, one stray data point can break a sequence and also no account is taken of the size of the difference from one data point to the next. Obviously, the bigger the difference between one value and the rest the more confidence we should have that something significant has happened that cannot be attributed to noise. For example, in a large and stable market a change in the level of sales of 1% may be significant, but in a very small volatile market the difference between every consecutive data point is likely greater than this, purely because the level of noise in the market place is higher – so maybe something closer to 10% would be a better criterion. But how do we decide exactly what size of difference is significant in any given situation?

SIZE

To solve this problem, we need a statistical method that enables us to set thresholds that help us identify what data we can safely ignore based on the size of changes to values, not just their sequence. This is particularly valuable wherever we have very noisy data sets where there is a high risk of false positives. Fortunately, there is a simple but very robust technique that has been extensively used by businesses for nearly 100 years, but which many of you will never have come across. It is called 'control charting'.

CONTROL CHARTS

At this point I think I owe you, the reader, an apology. You probably already knew that making sense of numbers, particularly the overwhelming flood of detailed data, can be a tricky business. So, you might resent me having just spent a dozen pages and wasting 10 minutes of your life to remind you of the fact! The reason why I took the time is to demonstrate how easy it is to draw the wrong conclusions even when you might normally feel very confident. In this context

Figure 4.9:
Walter Shewhart

Uncertainty and Predictability: Big Data and the Weak Signal

– being perhaps for the first time aware of how flaky traditional techniques and your own intuitions are – I hope you will fully appreciate the usefulness, power and profundity of the approach that I will now introduce.

The gentleman we have to thank for it is pictured in Figure 4.9.

His name was Walter Shewhart, and in 1918 he started work at Western Electric's Hawthorne works charged with improving the quality of the components used in the early telephone handsets. He had a problem that we recognize – lots of highly variable data but a limited ability to make sense of it. But, being a clever fellow, by 1924 he had developed an analytical approach that has become the corner stone of the modern quality management practice, and which is still in active use across the world today.

Shewhart realized that, even in a controlled environment like a manufacturing plant, every measurement that was made will be infected by noise – he called it 'variation'. As a result, he saw that in order to determine whether you have a problem or not you need to be able to estimate the level of noise in real time so that you only act when something occurs that is unlikely to be the result of a noise infection, because if you react to noise as if it were a signal (i.e. in response to a false positive) it makes matters worse. His other stunning insight was that he also realized that the existence of noise was itself a problem and that by progressively tracking down and eliminating the causes of variation – using a process we now call 'continuous improvement' – he could improve the quality of the product *and* make it easier to spot problems in the future.

Figure 4.10 shows what a Shewhart control chart looks like.

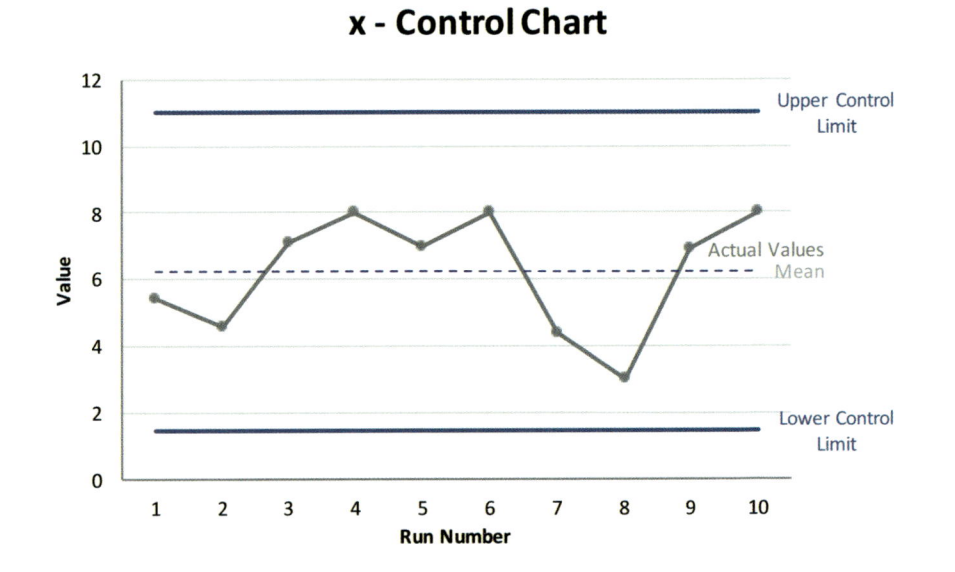

Figure 4.10:
A control chart

A control chart plots actual values and then constructs three lines around them. Firstly, the arithmetical mean of the sequence, and then two control limits spaced equidistant from the mean and set based on a statistical analysis of the period to period movement of the actuals.

The actual data is shown by the line in the centre of the chart along with its mean value (the signal). The two parallel lines either side of the mean are the upper and lower control limits, which are set based on the level of variation observed in the data. The range between the upper and lower control limit represents noise; what Shewhart called 'common cause variation'. In other words, 'normal stuff' that is associated with the way that the current system works.

Together, the mean and the range are the 'voice of the process', what we would call its performance. If a data point falls outside of the range, it is unlikely to be due to noise and so is worthwhile investigating. The name he gave to abnormal events like this is 'special cause variation'.

In Shewhart's view, the job of management is therefore to:

1. ensure that the mean of the process is in line with customer requirements,
2. investigate and eliminate the special cause variation and
3. work over time to reduce the level of common cause variation.

Shewhart realized that in the presence of noise it is not possible to ever be totally right because absolute certainty is unattainable. The wisest course of action is therefore to avoid making the wrong kinds of mistakes. As we have already discussed, there are two kinds of mistakes that you can make:

1. Type 1 mistakes are those that produce false positives because you react to noise in data (e.g. arresting an innocent person).
2. Type 2 mistakes produce false negatives, where you fail to react to a signal in the data (e.g. failing to arrest a guilty person).

Unfortunately, without the aid of tools like control charts we often make *both* kinds of mistakes. Under the control of our pattern-seeking System 1 brains we are very prone to seeing things that don't exist in noisy data series – that is, a Type 1 error. And when we ignore large volumes of data because we don't have the ability or the time to make sense of it, we make Type 2 mistakes by default.

Shewhart decided that in a high-volume production environment his main concern was to avoid making Type 1 errors. As a result, he set the control limits at a level that contained over 99% of the variation so that if any data point fell outside this range, he could be very confident that 'something was going on'. Given the huge amount of data that we now have it makes sense for information professionals to adopt the same strategy. As well as limiting the number of false positives, setting the control limits widely (at the level of three SDs) has the additional benefit of making the technique insensitive to the shape of the probability distribution and so safe to use in a wide range of scenarios.

In the data rich environment that we now inhabit there is clearly a place for statistical filters like the one that Shewhart devised. We need algorithms that help us to focus our time and unique problem-solving skills on the small number of things that require further investigation by helping us to identify the large number of things that we can safely ignore. Despite the advent of computers and the development of sophisticated analytical techniques, it has proved difficult to beat the control charts Shewhart invented nearly a century

Uncertainty and Predictability: Big Data and the Weak Signal

ago. And because they were invented before the computer era control charts are simple to create and easy to interpret and have proven to be reliable and robust over decades of use.

I will now demonstrate how to set up a classic control chart. While I have tried to avoid technicalities in this book, it is important to devote some time to them here in order to demonstrate how simple this technique is, illustrate how it could be applied and give you enough knowledge to be able to try it out for yourself. I won't be able to make you an expert, however, so if you are interested in learning more about the topic, I will point you in the direction of other sources.

SETTING UP A CONTROL CHART

To start with you need a data series like the one shown in Table 4.2.

Although it is not essential, to start with I recommend that you first plot the data graphically on a run chart. This gives you a better feel for the data and makes it easier to understand how the technique works.

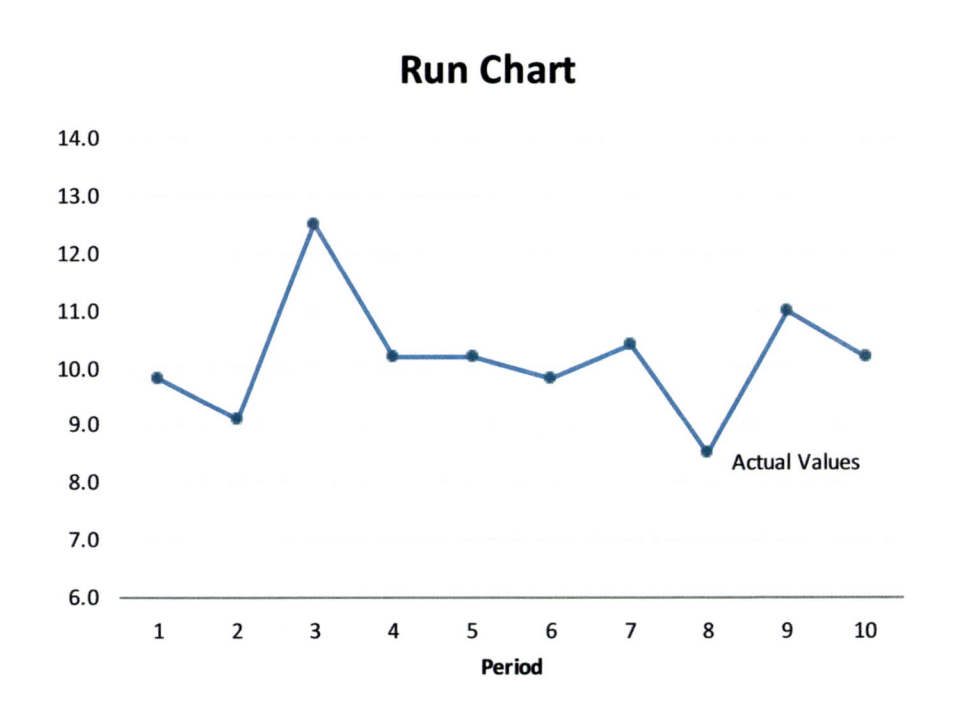

Run Chart

Table 4.2:
Sample data series

All that is required to construct a control chart is a sequence of measurements of a process over time.

Period	Values
1	9.8
2	10.8
3	11.7
4	10.2
5	10.2
6	9.8
7	10.4
8	10.1
9	9.5
10	10.2
Average	**10.3**

Figure 4.11:
Data series plotted on a run chart

Let us assume that our interest is to determine whether any of these data points in Figure 4.11 represents special cause variation; something unusual that warrants further investigation and should not be ignored. The first step involves calculating the level of common cause variation (noise) – anything that isn't noise must be a signal of some sort. The control chart assumes that it is noise that causes the data to 'bounce around' so we need to measure this 'bouncing', which we do by calculating the average moving range (AMR) – which is the average difference between every two consecutive data points, as shown in Table 4.3.

Table 4.3:
The calculation of AMR

Third, the AMR should be calculated. Note that there are only nine moving average values in a sequence of ten data points.

Period	Values	Moving Range	Formula
1	9.8		
2	10.8	1.0	abs(P2-P1)
3	11.7	0.9	abs(P3-P2)
4	10.2	1.5	abs(P4-P3)
5	10.2	0.0	abs(P5-P4)
6	9.8	0.4	abs(P6-P5)
7	10.4	0.6	abs(P7-P6)
8	10.1	0.3	abs(P8-P7)
9	9.5	0.6	abs(P9-P8)
10	10.2	0.7	abs(P10-P9)
Average	10.3	0.7	

Since there is a statistical relationship between the AMR and the SD of a date series, and we know what proportion of events fall within any given SD of the mean, we can now calculate where the upper and lower control limits (UCL and LCL) should be positioned. To do this we simply multiply the AMR by 2.66 (the equivalent of 3 SD). Since in this case the mean is 10.2 and our AMR is 1.4, the control limits should be set at 13.9 (10.2 + (1.4 x 2.66)) and 6.4 (10.2 − (1.4 x 2.66)).

The end result looks like the chart in Figure 4.12. Simple!

Figure 4.12:
Final control chart

Finally, having calculated the positions of the control limits plot them on the chart and use them to monitor subsequent values of the process.[26]

26. Note: this control chart could also have been constructed using the values of the variance from the target (10), as shown in Figure 4.16. The results (where the control limits are placed) are the same.

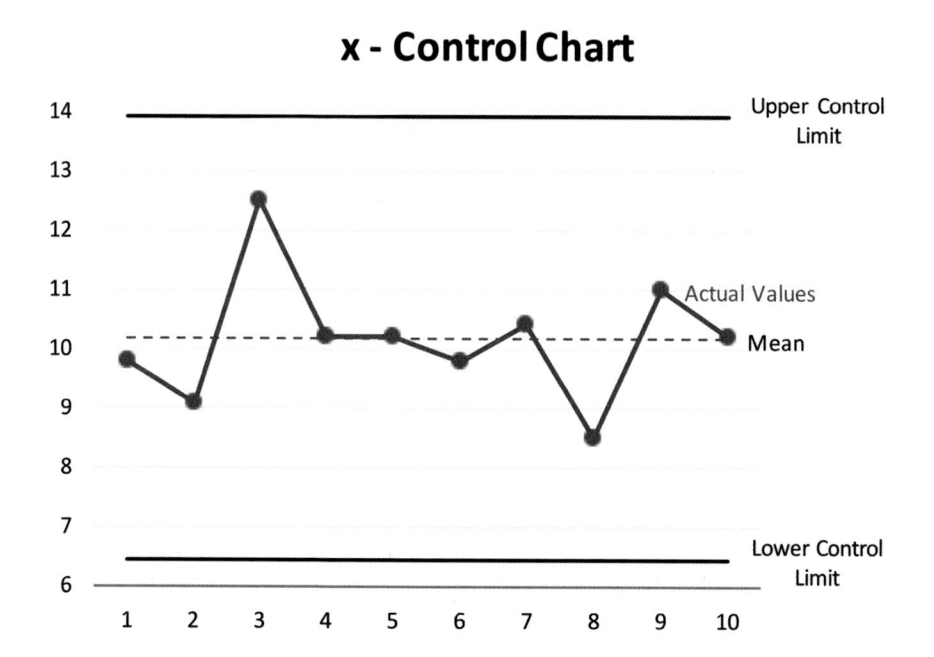

Uncertainty and Predictability: Big Data and the Weak Signal

What this tells us about the pattern of data in this series is that we do not have strong enough evidence to suggest that what we see is anything other than noise, so we should not take action. There are no detectable deviations from the norm, no changes in the trend, no nothing – so we can safely ignore what is going on – for the moment!

Once we have set up a control chart like this, we keep the control limits in place. At some point it is likely that data will arrive that the control chart identifies as 'exceptional'. After investigation we may decide it is a one-off event that warrants no more than a mention in a report, but it might be that we have detected a significant change in performance – perhaps the mean has shifted, or the level of common cause variation has changed. In this case we need to recalculate the control limits and work out what it means for our business.

The chart I have shown you is known as an 'X-bar' chart (because it is based on the mean of a data set) and it is usually accompanied by what is known as an MR chart, so-called because it uses control limits based on the moving ranges we have already calculated. Using the two in combination gives the approach extra power because the MR chart is more sensitive to a single data point than the X-bar chart. The MR control limits are positioned at 3.27 of the AMR so in our example the combined X-MR chart now looks like Figure 4.13.

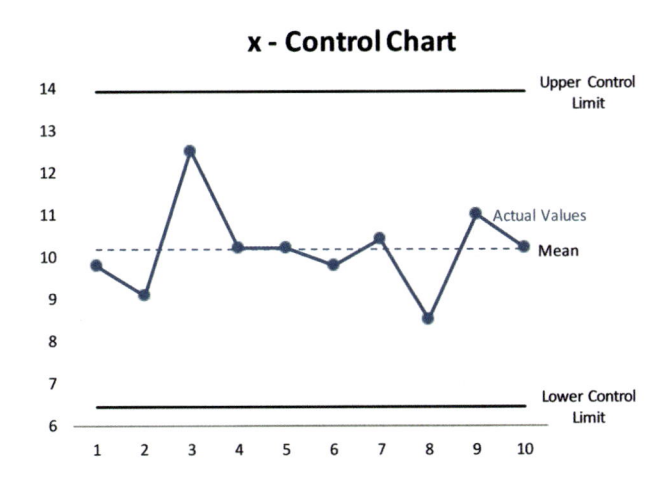

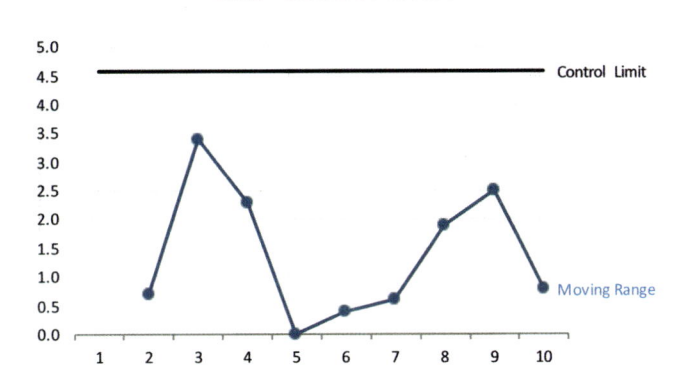

Figure 4.13:
Combined X-MR chart

Using a conventional (X-bar) chart in combination with an MR (moving range) chart gives extra diagnostic power.

INTERPRETING CONTROL CHARTS

Control charts can be used in a number of ways to detect potentially significant events. According to the acknowledged authority in this area, Don Wheeler of the University of Tennessee, there are three main rules:[27]

1. **Points outside the limits**. A *single point* outside the limits of the X-bar or MR chart. This should be interpreted as an indication of a special cause with a *dominant effect*.
2. **Runs about the centre line**. *Eight or more successive data points* either side of the mean on the X-bar chart. This is an indication of a *weak but sustained effect*.
3. **Runs near the limits**. *Three out of four successive data points* outside the *inner 75%* of the upper or lower range on the X-bar chart. This is a manifestation of a *moderate but sustained effect*.

The literature around this topic sometimes uses different terminology or differs in emphasis but the fundamental approach is simple, robust and is still going strong. There are other statistical techniques that may perform marginally better than the classic control chart in some circumstances and variations of the basic approach are needed for dealing with count data (such as the number of occurrences), for example. But for basic business performance analysis it is not worthwhile looking further afield.

In particular, ignore approaches that use the statistical textbook approach to calculating SD or limits other than the ones that Shewhart recommended. Shewhart's method has been tried and tested and does not rely on any assumptions about the nature of the data used to calculate the control limits. Crucially, it also recognizes that the order in which values arrive is important and so it is suited to analysing time series, whereas the traditional approach to calculating SD was designed to analyse populations. For example, as you can see in Figure 4.14, using the traditional (frequentist) approach these two time series have the same SD but very different ones using Shewhart's method.

---

27. Wheeler has written many excellent books and articles that would reward a read. For the newcomer to the topic I recommend his 2002 book *Understanding Variation* and a visit to the SPC Press website.

Figure 4.14:
Two time series with the same SD (using the traditional methodology)

Because the traditional method of calculating an SD is based on the deviation for the average of a population these two data series have the same SD. Because Shewhart's method is based on the period to period movement, it recognizes what is obvious from visual inspection: that the data series on the right is much more volatile.

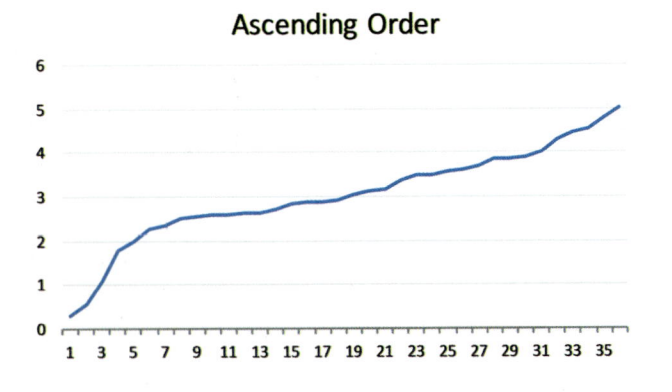

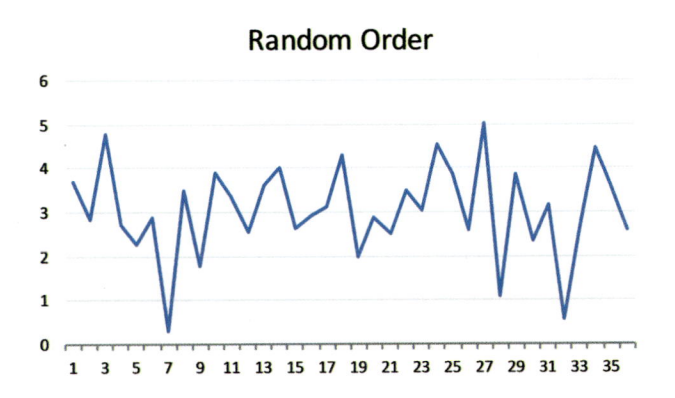

Uncertainty and Predictability: Big Data and the Weak Signal

CONTROL CHARTS IN FINANCE

Hopefully this has given you sufficient confidence to start experimenting with control charts for yourself, but before you do that you need to be aware of a number of issues that can trip up a novice, as I discovered for myself when I first found out about control charts over a decade ago.

Setting control limits

Some text books say that you need 32 or more data points from a stable system before you can set control limits. If you only have monthly data this is often not feasible, but fortunately Don Wheeler is much more pragmatic. Wheeler takes the view that a 'roughly right' control chart is better than none – the important thing is to get started. Providing that you have six or so data points from an unchanged process and without an obvious extreme value that is enough to set up a control chart.[28]

The detection rules will alert you if it turnsout that your first attempt to set control limits were too crude, and you can recalculate them using the additional data you have collected. When we are using control charts, we mustn't lose sight of the fact that we are not seeking the 'truth' – we are merely aiming to do a 'good enough' job of filtering out noise. When we have done this, we can use our judgement and contextual knowledge to determine what, if any, sense can be made of what is left.

Resetting control limits

When an alarm has been triggered, you may need to reset the control limits to reflect the new state of the process but remember to base them on the whole period subsequent to the change, not from when the change was detected, as this will be several periods later. For example, in Figure 4.15 we see the control chart applied to the revenue data for XYZ Ltd where we detected a change in the level of revenue using the 'runs around the centre line rule'. But, in February 2016, when an alarm was triggered and I recalculated the limits, I did so from the first data point in the sequence, which was August 2015.

---

[28]. And if there is an obvious extreme value then it is permissible to ignore it when calculating control limits.

Figure 4.15:
XYZ Ltd – resetting control limits

Here control limits were reset from August 2015 to reflect a change in the behaviour of the system that was detected in January 2016.

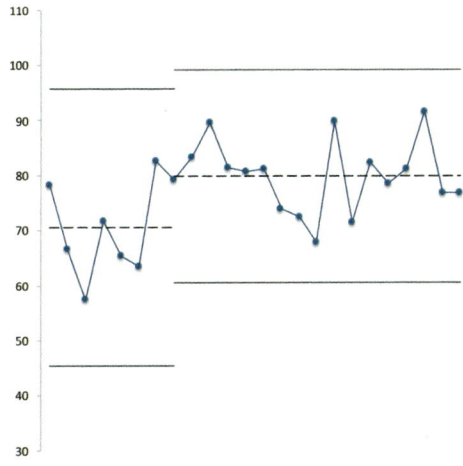

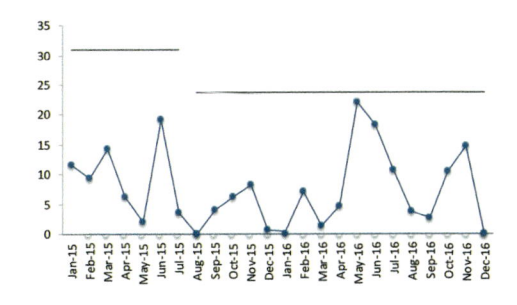

Drifting processes and seasonality

Another potential problem arises from the fact that there is a critical difference between the context in which control charts were originally used and that we face when we are trying to understand performance. In a process environment we can safely assume that the underlying signal (i.e. the mean of the data set) is stationary, because manufacturing processes are designed to produce a consistent output.

We can make no such assumptions about business performance data; indeed, it is highly likely to exhibit trends (i.e. be a drifting process) or seasonal patterns. While this doesn't stop us using standard control charts it makes them less useful as these distorting effects will render them less sensitive to other changes.

But there are ways around this, however. For example, you can set control limits around a trend line rather than a stable mean, or you could build a control chart using year on year variances (to eliminate the impact of seasonality rather than individual data points). Segmenting data in this way is a good strategy to employ whenever you have data that has a predictable cyclical pattern as it ensures that you are comparing 'apples with apples'.

(Dis)aggregated data

When I started experimenting with control charts with financial performance data, I found that their limits were 'too wide' – I never detected any special causes. As a result, I rather prematurely concluded that they 'didn't work' with my financial data, without understanding why.

Part of my problem was that, because I hadn't yet shaken off the 'variance analysis' mindset, I found it difficult to accept that most of the data I had was noise. I mistakenly thought that if my reports failed to show that 'something had happened' I wasn't doing my job properly. I now realize that most of the time when I commented on a variance, for example, I was wasting everyone's time by inventing a story to explain noise – events that hadn't occurred. But there was another reason for my unreasonably wide control limits, which means that you need to be more careful in applying this technique than I was.

Control charts work best with very detailed disaggregated data, where there are relatively few 'forces' at work driving the numbers. Finance folk like myself, however, are more used to analysing aggregated data, for a whole business or a major part of it. Unfortunately, aggregated data contains the impact of many different factors, and collectively their impact can cause the control limits to 'explode' so that they are too wide to detect anything other than the most major (obvious) changes, which are probably easy to see by eye.

So, the bad news is that we cannot simply replace our conventional analytical tools with control charts. But the good news is that the trend-based measures I shared in Chapter 3 already have this type of analysis covered. However, we do not currently have any way of analysing the enormous amounts of disaggregated data that we now collect, which is where control charts come into their own. Control charts help us find needles in the data haystack, because once aggregated data is

Uncertainty and Predictability: Big Data and the Weak Signal

disaggregated into individual data streams the signature of the signal becomes more legible and the control charts more sensitive to changes in it.

But using control charts to screen individual data streams does mean that we need to use scores – hundreds perhaps thousands of them – to provide us with the coverage we need. This is why it may be necessary to use specialized software that is built to filter a large number of data series in the background and only to raise an alarm when something happens that demands our attention. It is not a coincidence that this way of dealing with large amounts of noisy data mirrors the way that our brains work. The vast majority of data that assails our senses is 'ignored' because it falls within predictable ranges. Only when a large or unusual signal breaches a threshold and a nerve synapse fires is our brain 'told' about the sensory data, at which point the signal is potentially available to our System 1 or System 2 processes. If the signal to the conscious brain is large enough it can take the form of 'ouch' or a rush of the pleasure hormone, dopamine. In business we call this 'exception reporting', which sounds less exciting but serves the same purpose – it tells us to pay attention.

Earlier in this chapter I described a workshop exercise where participants used stopwatches to study the impact of noise on measuring the performance of a process. Applying control charts to this data illustrates the value of using control charts as statistical filters because it confirms what we knew to be the case – that all the observed variation is simply the result of noise.

Figure 4.16 shows the result of the analysis of the data for the highlighted individual (figure 43).

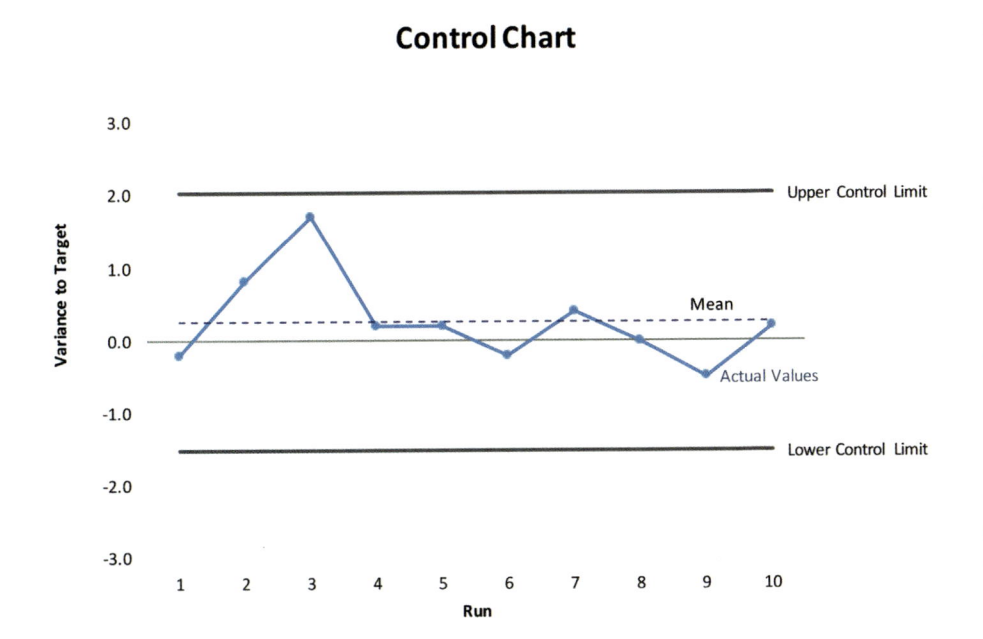

Control Chart

Figure 4.16:
Population stopwatch data with CC limits

Here a bar with a drop line shows the difference between the calculated control limits on the control charts. This means that 99.7% of values should fall within this range provided that nothing abnormal occurs and the process remains stable. Note how the control limits are wider than the arithmetical range of values in all but one case (number 17) but by varying amounts. This is a further illustration of the danger of relying on arithmetical measures to make probabilistic judgements. We tend to set them too narrowly.

What happened when we applied control charts to the results for all the other participants?

Figure 4.17:
Individual stopwatch example

As we can see, none of the data points breach either the upper or lower control limits, so we can say with confidence that there is no evidence for anything of any significance in this data series. We can safely assume that all the variation we see is just noise – the results of this person sometimes doing better, sometimes worse, for no reason that we can identify. Had we instead intuitively set the limits of acceptable variation at, say, 5% (0.5 seconds) we would have treated the values in periods 2 and 3 as being significant, and perhaps everything that happened subsequently as evidence of improvement or as part of an improving trend. But we would have been wrong.

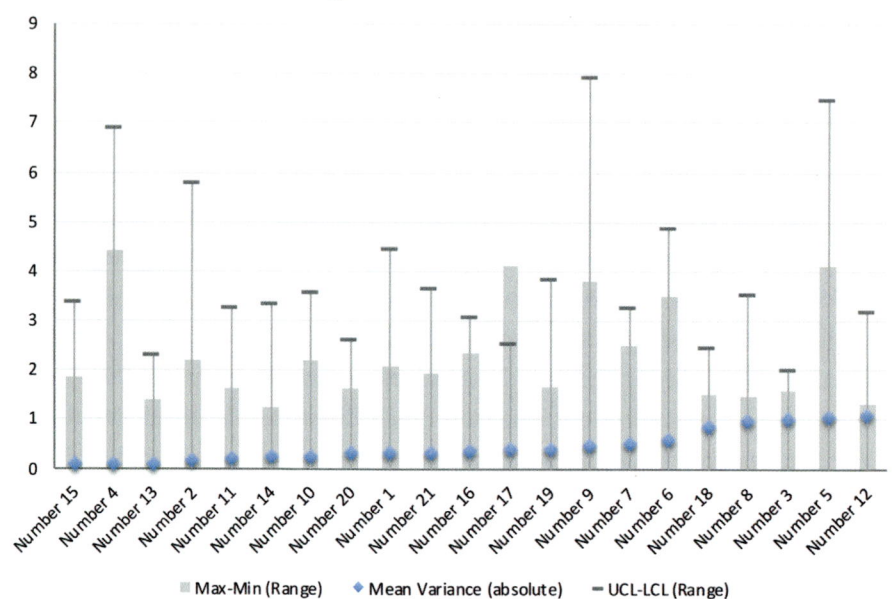

Timing Exercise Performance

■ Max-Min (Range)　♦ Mean Variance (absolute)　— UCL-LCL (Range)

In the chart in Figure 4.17, the calculated control limits for participants are shown as drop bars. Note how in all but one case the control limits are wider than the observed range of measurements (light grey bars) because the use of the moving range to measure variation results in the data 'setting its own control parameters'. The fact that this technique automatically reflects differences or changes in the level of volatility in a data series is one of its great strengths. Every participant gets control limits that reflect the nature of their own process rather than having an arbitrary target imposed on them, and the target alters to reflect changes in their performance. It is also clear that while the average level of performance does not vary enormously, the consistency – as measured by the control limits – does; a fact that is never captured by conventional performance analysis.

But the acid test is: does this technique help us make sense of the data we generated in this small-scale simulation of a real-life business scenario?

The difference to the conclusions we might have drawn using normal common-sense methods is dramatic. Had we taken +/– 5% as our guide to determining a significant deviation rather than using statistically derived control limits, we would have been driven to investigate 119 of the 210 of these data points. In other words, over 50% of the trials would have required explanation! Even using +/– 10% would have generated 50 alarms. But only three out of 210 data points fell outside the statistically calculated control limits and all of these came right at the beginning or the end of the exercise and so can probably be attributed to experimental design rather than evidence of a significant event or change in performance.

In summary, by using control charts methodology we avoid having to investigate (and potentially react to) false positives alarms that comprise 25% to 50% of the entire data set. The vast majority of the data can be safely ignored.

Uncertainty and Predictability: Big Data and the Weak Signal

The potential savings in terms of time, effort and the consequences of taking action when we should do nothing are potentially enormous. Instead, we can focus our attention on real issues as and when they arise – the signals that would otherwise be obscured by noise.

If we are in the business of looking for issues that require explanation or intervention, we would need to understand what caused the three statistically significant 'alarms'. Is it 'special cause variation' that signifies a process (performance) issue or is it a data problem? It is easy to see how something like this could be of value to people other than performance analysts. For example, it could provide financial managers with an audit capability, helping them detect unusual transactions or patterns of behaviour.

But if we are concerned with improving performance, we might be more interested in common cause variation – as measured by the range of the control limits – which varies enormously between the participants, and which we have already identified as a crucial, but often neglected, dimension of performance.

Thus far in this chapter we have dealt with variation and its impact on our ability to make inferences from noisy data. Let's now turn our attention to variation and performance.

CONTROL CHARTS: RISK AND PERFORMANCE

Control charts are robust and versatile tools, and like a Swiss army knife they have many applications other than the one I have described. For example, we can use control limits to assess risk since we can expect that 85% of all future values will fall within the inner 50% of the control limit range. Being able to measure 'normal risk' – something that is not possible using traditional arithmetical techniques – is important, but I sometimes feel that we (and I'm thinking about financial people in particular) tend to accept risk as a 'given'; something that we need to acknowledge but we can't change. And I think by taking this passive approach we might be missing a trick.

We know that predictability of performance is valued by investors and to managers predictability is sign that a business is under control. And, as consumers, we know that the variation in the performance of a process or a product – how reliable it is – is as important to us than the average level of performance – perhaps more so. MacDonald's might not be the best quality food you have ever tasted but it is consistent, so we continue to go there. But we would soon stop going to a restaurant whose quality of offering from visit to visit varied between a Michelin star and a MacDonald's arch.

So, predictability (as measured by the level of variation) is an important component of performance. Yet it is something that we do not routinely measure and the idea that it is something that can be managed never enters our heads. Indeed, as we have seen, the practice of 'hitting the numbers' that is an accepted part of conventional performance management practice can increase the volatility of returns and so actually degrade performance, if we accept this broader definition of the term.

I would therefore argue that the most important application for control charting is in the area where it was first applied – in the world of process improvement. Here managing variation (by reducing the span of the control limits) is at least as important as the position of its mean level of performance.

This is why I believe that it is important that performance analysts need an appreciation of how control charts can be used to improve performance, not just measure it. Indeed, there is a good case for using control charts as the tool for measuring all non-financial KPIs like those in the BSCs, since they present a much more faithful (I'm tempted to use the word 'balanced' here!) picture of the performance of business processes as they are experienced by the customer than conventional target-based metrics.

CONTROL CHARTS AND CONTINUOUS IMPROVEMENT

I will use a practical example to illustrate how control charts can be used to improve the performance of process.

The example I will use relates to a branch of a sandwich and wrap bar company called Troncho's. This branch is located in a business district of a major city and specializes in creating bespoke lunchtime meals for office workers. Uniquely, Troncho's actively encourages its staff to build a relationship with 'their own' customers, unlike its competitors who employ low-paid staff who stay only until they can get a better job. By understanding customers' tastes and habits and building a better relationship with them they aim to promote loyalty and so command a price premium in a crowded market where it is otherwise difficult to differentiate an offering.

But there are downsides to the approach that Troncho's has adopted. They discovered that by allowing customers to 'create' their own meals and encouraging interaction between staff and customers, the ordering process was slow, and the bespoke nature of the meals created logistical problems in the meal assembly area. As a result, queues often built up, and this threatened to undermine the goodwill that the business has generated. What management found particularly puzzling is that these queues sometimes even appeared in quiet periods when the (average) capacity of the shop (i.e. the number of people on duty) matched the average level of demand.

To solve this problem, the company called in a performance management consultant. She started by studying the flow of work in the shop to help form a hypothesis of what might be causing the problem. To test her hunch, she collected data on the number of people coming to the bar in each 5-minute period between 9 am and 12 noon, before the lunchtime rush. She also measured how many meals were produced in each period (the capacity) and the length of time that customers had to wait for their meal. She then plotted the data on the control charts shown in Figure 4.18.

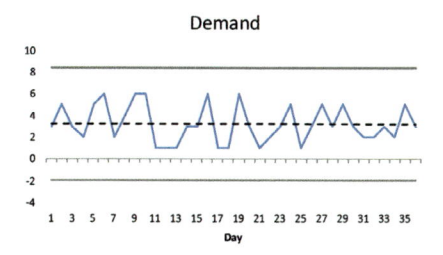

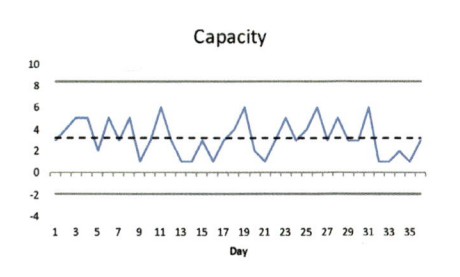

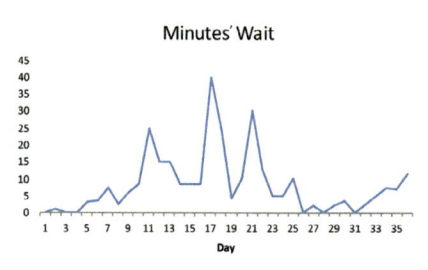

Uncertainty and Predictability: Big Data and the Weak Signal

Figure 4.18:
Troncho's process control charts – and the results

These control charts confirm the perception of management – that while demand and capacity vary around a stable average within predictable limits wait times periodically 'explode' to unacceptable levels.

This exercise confirmed that the waiting times were often completely unacceptable (over 40 minutes) and that this happened despite the fact that on average the level of demand and the capacity were in balance – roughly 3.5 meals in every 5-minute period. It was also clear that the long waiting time could not be attributed to any specific event (special cause variation) – because the level of demand and the capacity were both well within the control limits at all times. The fact that sometimes customers didn't have to wait any time at all made matters worse. The inconsistency in the speed of the service was a source of major frustration for their customers who had short break times.

One other puzzling thing in these numbers is that both the demand and the capacity always fell in the range of 1 to 6 in every 5-minute period. What could account for this?

The reason why the numbers are so regular is that Troncho's doesn't exist. It is a simulation I created using a pair of dice – one to simulate the demand the other to simulate the capacity. Using a simulation makes it easy for me to illustrate the importance of variation in managing the performance of processes – and the irrelevance of average values. In this case, we can see how even when there are no 'exceptional events' we cannot guarantee consistent, acceptable performance by simply managing averages. And setting targets will not change the outcome because the poor performance of this work system is entirely the result of the interaction of variation in demand and variation in capacity.

This problem is nothing to do with the performance of individuals and cannot be solved by targeting average outcomes. It is the result of the way that the system is designed, and must be solved by working on the system, not the people.

In 'real life' how might you expect a 'normal' performance management consultant to tackle a problem like this?

The most obvious response would be to increase the capacity so that the process is better able to absorb the variation in demand. Let's assume we do this by installing iPad terminals so that customers don't block the order station when they can't make up their minds. Installing extra capacity that will be unused for a period of time is costly, but it would be surprising if this didn't improve matters. I simulated the impact of this by adding 0.5 to the value got from the 'capacity die' to increase throughput by 14%. Figure 4.19 shows what happened to waiting times.

Figure 4.19:
Control charts with increased capacity

Adding extra capacity reduces wait times, which peak at around 20–30 minutes compared to over 40 minutes before.

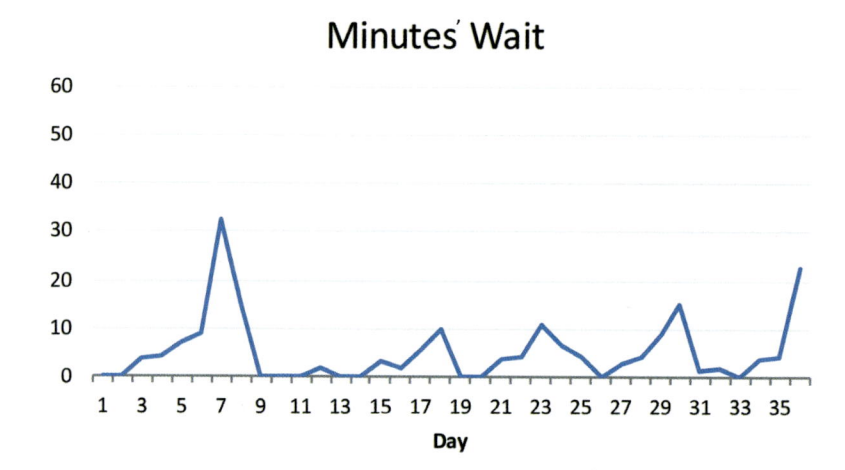

Minutes' Wait

You would expect that this shows some improvement, but we still see many waiting times of over 10 minutes, which if you only have a lunch break of 20 minutes is still a problem. Management at Troncho's believes that 5 minutes is the longest length of time a customer should have to wait for a tailormade meal, and we are still some way outside this limit. What should they do now? Should they employ more staff (add extra capacity) who might spend most of their shift waiting for something to do, or is there another solution?

The key to cracking this problem is recognizing that the length of time that any customer has to wait is the result of the interaction between the random variation of demand and the random variation in the capacity. The long waiting times come about when there is a spike in the demand that corresponds with a dip in capacity. This creates a backlog of orders that takes time to work through the system and it is this backlog that creates the unacceptably long waiting times. Reducing variation doesn't stop spikes and dips, but it will minimize their impact, and backlogs will be smaller and disperse more quickly. This is a big win from a customer perspective, simply reducing variation in the process lessens the variability in service *and* the average length of time that she or he has to wait!

Reducing variation is an extremely effective process improvement strategy in this case and many others. How might it be possible to reduce variation?

It is difficult to do anything about the variation in demand (except by turning people away!) but it is possible to reduce the variation in the capacity if we understand what is causing it. In this case it could be the result of how the preparation area is laid out – whether servers' paths cross a lot or if they have to wait to get access to ingredients because the making process isn't properly scheduled. As this is something that is likely to be relatively easy and cheap because it simply involves changing the layout of the preparation area, let's assume that this is what they do. I have simulated this by treating any value of my 'capacity' die in the range of 1 to 3 as 3 and anything larger I treat as 4, so while the average capacity is unchanged, the level of variation is reduced. The results are shown in Figure 4.20.

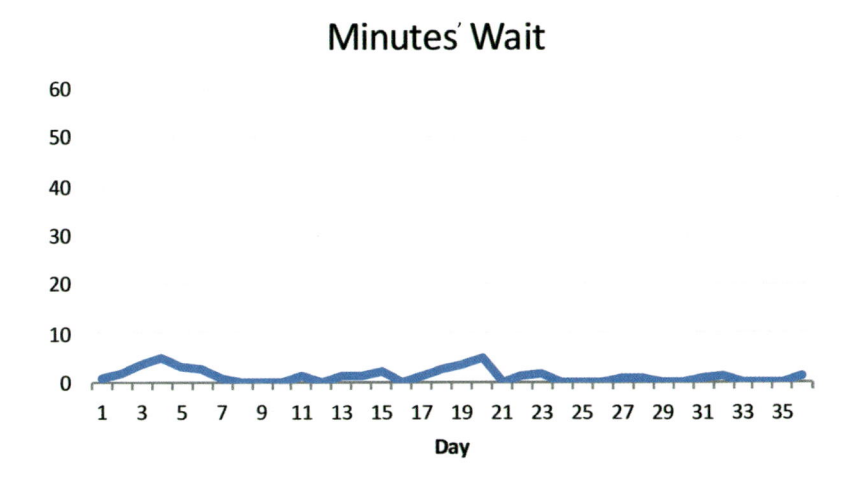

Uncertainty and Predictability: Big Data and the Weak Signal

Minutes' Wait

[Chart showing minutes' wait over days 1-35, with values mostly near 0 and small peaks around days 3, 19-20]

Figure 4.20:
Result of reducing variation

Simply reducing variation in the capacity has a significant impact on wait times even if the average capacity is unchanged.

As you can see, the results are significantly better. There are no 5-minute periods where the wait exceeds 5 minutes. But the biggest improvement is in the consistency of performance – the reliability of the service, which is the major issue for Troncho's customers.

So, a relatively cheap and easy to execute change to a process that makes no difference to the average time spent preparing meals has an enormous impact on the speed and consistency – the quality – of the service offered to customers. This shows what a radical difference bringing variation into our thinking about management can make – as the folk behind the 'Lean Revolution' have been preaching for years.

Getting back to Troncho's, I have made some big claims on the back of a limited data set, so let's simulate the impact of running a series of trials with different configurations over an extended period taking into account both average and maximum waiting times (Figure 4.21).

Figure 4.21:
Simulation over time with multiple configurations

These charts show how increasing the capacity (Process A) and reducing the variation (Process B) impact the customer experience over a number of days. Reducing variation has a particularly big impact on the maximum wait time, which, from a customer perspective, is probably a more important statistic than the average.

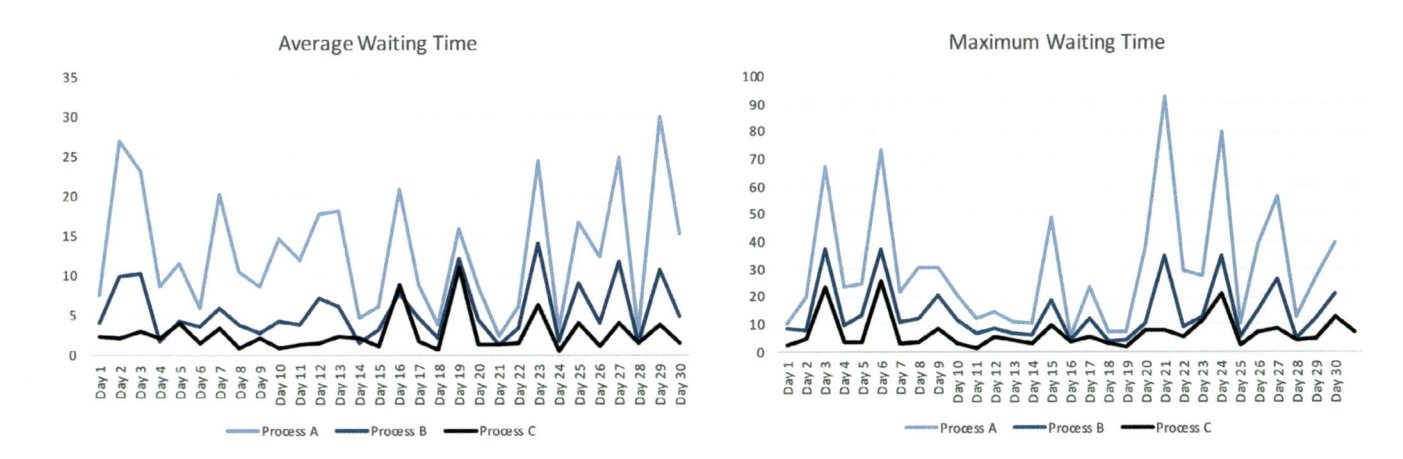

[Two charts: "Average Waiting Time" and "Maximum Waiting Time" over Day 1 to Day 30, showing Process A, Process B, and Process C]

In this simulation, investing in iPads to increase the capacity by a small amount (15%) reduces both the average and maximum waiting times by 50% – a big reduction. But dampening the variation in capacity (the noise in the process), which might not require any investment at all, improved things by the same amount, a further 50%.

Contrast the process of continuous improvement using control charts with what might happen if we were to use traditional 'target-based' measures to 'drive' improvement. (I don't think it is accidental that the verbs used in conventional performance management patois imply the use of force!)

Using traditional 'carrot and stick' management head office might impose a new waiting time target such as 'no customer should wait more than 5 minutes'. And to make sure that it gets the attention of the branch manager they may attach a bonus to achieving the target. Investing in iPads is out of the question because they are not in the budget, so the manager has to find other ways of achieving hitting her numbers. Perhaps customers with complex orders might be encouraged to change their behaviour by putting them in their own 'slow lane' – which runs counter to the strategy of the business. Or if the queue has become too long customers might be asked to come back later, which of course isn't counted as waiting time!

We see performance measures being 'gamed' like this all the time particularly in public sector organizations because, in the absence of competition as a motivator of change, they are particularly reliant on arbitrarily imposed fixed targets. For example, employing a triage nurse to assess patients as they arrive in casualty 'reduces' the measured waiting time because it counts as 'having seen a member of the medical staff' even though he or she hasn't actually done anything to make the patient better.

Although these kinds of practices help the manager make her customer service numbers in the short term, this doesn't feel like good service from a customer's perspective, so they go elsewhere. Before long we find that the manager is 'let go' when performance slips away over the longer term. 'It's sad but that is what happens if you don't *perform*', is what you hear people saying. Right?

Comparing a single data point to a target, as we do in traditional variance analysis, is easy. So, it is not difficult to see the attraction of this approach to an analyst or a manager far removed from the action and with many other things to worry about. But this 'hit the numbers' approach not only often fails to improve performance; it often makes things worse.

This is why Walter Shewhart and those that followed him believed that targets are a dangerous way of measuring and managing the performance of processes. In assessing the performance of an organization targets are (almost) inevitably arbitrary and as a consequence they are usually too high or too low and rarely – like Goldilocks's porridge – just right. If they are too lax, they stifle improvement, but if they are unrealistically stretching people can do things that have negative unintended consequences in trying to force output back to a number. It also is possible for any one product or batch of products to hit or miss a fixed-point target entirely by chance.

So, according to their detractors, using targets produces misleading information, locks in costs and doesn't reflect the wishes of customers who don't make their judgement about product quality, or their purchasing decisions, based on the producer's production specifications. Other than that, targets are great!

As a result, the process improvement community believe targets are evil.

But we know that targets are a ubiquitous feature of corporate life. Without them we can't control performance – so goes conventional wisdom.

Who is right? And is it possible for the two to coexist in one organization?

This is the topic we will address in Chapter 5.

SUMMARY

In this chapter you have learned something about noise and randomness; concepts that are widely recognized but often improperly understood. You will now recognize the importance of variation and the risks of making simplistic judgements about performance when it is ignored, as it is when we use single data points, for example. Moreover, it is clear that the level of variation is a critical dimension of performance that is routinely ignored, partly because it is easier to measure and make sense of averages and totals.

You have also been introduced to control charts and shown how they enable us to measure variation, identify outliers and spot changes in performance levels in a rigorous fashion. Specifically, they have a big role to play in helping to filter the vast amounts of data that most modern businesses capture but which is routinely ignored because they don't have the capability to analyse it. Control charts can be used to alert us to the 'special cause variation' that might be a signal that something significant has happened and so help trigger and focus management's attention on something that would otherwise have lain buried.

Additionally, you have learned how to use control charts to help improve processes in a way that is not possible using conventional techniques like point targets and simple averages. I believe that adding this to our armoury makes us as information professionals better equipped to meaningfully analyse non-financial performance metrics and partner those charged with running business processes. Crucially, in the example we worked through, it was clear that the traditional approach of setting improvement targets and 'holding people accountable' for performance, doesn't work because the problem lay in the system and the way it was designed, not the people who worked in it.

Finally, I hope that working through the examples in this chapter has helped build up your brain's System 1 'statistical muscles'. Our genetic makeup does not equip us with the intuitive ability to make sense of noise and randomness. But with awareness, knowledge and the help of a few mental crutches we can learn when we need help and so avoid making the kind of naïve errors that we are so prone to.

In our efforts to measure and manage noisy data series, moving from a position of unconscious incompetence to conscious incompetence represents a major step forward!

It is said that we are living in an age of surprises when many of the things we took to be obvious or 'settled' are denied or called into question.

One of the most troublesome features that has raised its head in political discourse is the idea described by the US President's press spokesman as 'alternative facts'.

But even when the facts are not in dispute, we have the POTUS confidently describing a situation as 'really bad' when I – and I naïvely assume, the rest of the sane world – think it is pretty good.

This experience has forced rationalists like me to question how we decide what is a fact and what is not, and how we set about attributing valency to it – that is, deciding whether it is good or bad.

I had something of a similar feeling as I wrote the early drafts of this book, which started its life focussed exclusively on the challenge of measurement. I soon realized that perhaps the most important question that performance analysts were required to answer was, 'How well have we performed?'. In other words, is it good or bad?

In practice we have two problems with answering this question.

First, the tool that we typically use – a comparison of a single data point – is a lousy measurement tool. It doesn't capture two critical dimensions of performance – trend and variation – or provide us with the ability to determine whether differences represent a signal or are the result of random noise.

In addition to the measurement problem there are more fundamental issues associated with the process of setting targets. In the dynamic and uncertain world that organizations inhabit it is simply not possible to determine in advance what constitutes good performance for any single variable. Also, most organizations are so complex and interdependent that to assess their performance we need to take account of many variables, which are unlikely to be in the same state of 'wellness' at the same time.

So, it is obvious that crude variance analysis doesn't work. But common sense suggests that to assess the level of performance we need to compare actual data with a meaningful benchmark. What other ways are there to do this? It is clearly more difficult than it sounds, and we know how easy it is to get it wrong and drive dysfunctional behaviour. This has led some people to take the radical position that targets are inherently evil and unnecessary.

As I was writing this book it became clear that I couldn't avoid the issue of target setting. Measurement is important but meaning can only be derived by comparing a measurement with something else. These are deep and murky waters, where we have to confront one of the most deeply held beliefs of traditional management practice: that targets are indispensable tools without which businesses would fail because of their inability to manage performance. So let's take a deep breath and dive in.

Uncertainty and Predictability: Big Data and the Weak Signal

Learning	Reason
What noise is.	Noise is that part of any data that is irrelevant for the purpose for which measurements are made.
Why noise is important.	Noise is an unavoidable feature of any and every process, including the process of measurement itself, and its existence means that making inferences based on data is more challenging. In addition, the level of noise - variation - in a process is itself a feature of its performance.
What qualities of noise make it inherently difficult to deal with in a performance reporting context?	It is difficult to determine the level of noise, particularly as we don't have a population we can analyse because we receive the data in a sequence. We also cannot assume that the data is normally distributed or that the underlying signal is stationary.
Why human beings struggle to deal with noise in assessing organizational performance.	Our brains are prone to perceive and fix on patterns in noisy data that don't exist, and they are very poor at making probabilistic judgements. Furthermore, the tools that we traditionally use are arithmetical rather than statistical.
What we need to take into account when we are making statistical inferences based on data.	We can never be sure of being right, so we need to be able to assess the probability that the data we see confirms or disproves our hypothesis and the consequences of getting it being wrong, as this affects the burden of proof we should apply.
How to increase the level of confidence when making probabilistic inferences.	Use evidence from multiple independent sources.
How to use patterns to detect a change in the signal in a noisy data series.	We can use sequences to allow us to assess the statistical likelihood of a given repeating pattern. Four in a row has a roughly 10% chance of being the product of an entirely random process, for instance.
How to use data values to detect a change in the signal in a noisy data series.	Control charts enable us to determine where to place confidence limits on a simple run chart, thereby enabling us to make probabilistic judgements based on the value of individual data points.
Why understanding the level of variation in a data series is important for measuring and managing performance.	The level of variation, as measured by confidence levels, provides a scientific grounding for exception reporting and enables us to measure risk. Reducing variation is a measure of an important dimension of performance and also suggests how it can be improved.

chapter 5

Level: What Does 'Good' Look Like?

> In which I describe a method to enable performance to be tracked dynamically, taking account of noise, and explore the nature of targets, how they can be set and whether they are required at all.

There is an old adage that even a broken watch is right twice a day. For younger readers brought up in the digital age this refers to the fact that if a watch stops at say, 3 o'clock, it will be correct twice in any 24-hour period.

The adage describes how it is possible to be right by dumb luck and persistence. But it also illustrates how a watch fails in its purpose, because we need it to tell the right time all of the time.

So it should be with performance – we need to know 'how fast' we are going at all times, not just at certain times of the year. Back in the stone age, before Copernicus demonstrated that the change of the seasons had nothing to do with what we did on earth, there was a good reason for our ancestors to perform rituals and sacrifices at what they believed were propitious times, like the winter solstice. One would hope that we might have kicked the habit by now, but we are still deeply wedded to the annual cycle and pay too little attention to what goes on in between year ends.

Compared to a mechanical watch, the problem we have with measuring the performance of an organization is that we do not have a valid external definition of 'good' against which to compare. In addition, the system we are measuring is not stable – it sometimes runs fast and sometimes slow – and it is infected by noise, which means that any single measurement is inherently unreliable.

Let's put the tricky 'comparator' problem to one side for the moment and start our journey with the more tractable measurement challenge. I will set the context by recapping what we have discovered thus far.

In Chapter 3 we discovered the power of using trend-based approaches to measure the output of a business system. This tells us about the *direction* of performance. But also, particularly when information is presented graphically, this perspective on performance is intuitively easy to interpret because it keys directly into our brain's pre-existing visual pattern-recognition circuitry. Crucially, we also know whether performance is improving or not – we can distinguish between 'good' and 'bad' in a very general way by using past values as a comparator.

This is all well and good, but without an external comparator – a target, benchmark or guide – we cannot determine just how good (or bad) performance is. We don't know whether the *level* of performance is acceptable.

Typically, organizations use 'point' (i.e. single value) targets fixed in time to help make judgements about the level of performance but we have also seen how difficult it is to estimate what good looks like in the future given the inherent uncertainty of the world. We have also seen how they can drive dysfunctional behaviour, such as period-end peaking because of the pressure to 'hit the number', and in so doing undermine the purpose of the performance management system. Clearly it would be very useful to find some way to unambiguously measure performance in a dynamic way, against a moving (perhaps rate-based) target, because it makes it much more difficult to 'game' the measurement system.

In Chapter 4 we saw how noise is an unavoidable fact of life. This affects the *predictability* of performance, which is important in its own right, but it also affects our ability to measure the direction and level of performance. This means that any meaningful analysis of performance requires us to take account of probabilities. Because of noise (and variation – the way noise manifests itself in our measurements) we can never have direct access to the 'truth', just degrees of confidence in the evidence. So, it is clear that the way we compare actual performance to a target needs to be probabilistic. Simple arithmetic can't do this job for us, we need statistics.

To summarize, in order to measure how well we are performing we need a statistically-based method to enable us to assess actual outputs compared to a moving target or benchmark. Ideally this method should be simple to administer and easy to interpret. Fortunately, such a tool exists and has been successfully applied in another field of performance measurement for many years. It is called a 'tracking signal'.

TRACKING PERFORMANCE

The clue to what a tracking signal does is in the title; it tracks the difference – over time – between a measure of reality and a comparator and raises an alarm when the difference goes beyond statistically defined limits. As a result, we know just how confident we can be in our assessment of performance, unlike when we use traditional variance analysis where the 'significance' of any difference is entirely a matter of personal opinion. So, it works a bit like a control chart, except that it is anchored on an external frame of reference (a target) rather than the measured mean of the process.

Level: What Does 'Good' Look Like?

The beauty of this approach is that the comparator (i.e. the 'target') doesn't need to be fixed; it can vary. Hence, it can be a rate of change (such as growth), for example – or it can be another moving measure, like a forecast for the period.

It works by taking account of the average difference between a target and actual over a period of time rather than a single point in time and triggers an alarm when the statistically defined limits are breached. The method I will now describe has been in use for half a century, so it is robust. Even better, it relies on a simple technique that you have already been introduced to – the smoothed average.

Before I get technical, let me explain the concept behind the tracking signal with a simple example of the principle behind the technique.

Here is a series of differences over four periods between an actual value of a variable, such as revenue, and a comparator. The sign represents whether the actual was above or below the target.

$$+4, -4, +4, -4$$

The average net difference (taking account of the sign) between the target and actual is the sum of these four values: zero. The average *absolute* difference between the two (i.e. ignoring the sign) is 4. The tracking score that we use to determine whether there is a systematic deviation between the actual and the comparator is the ratio of these two numbers, which in this case is 0/4 – in other words zero. An answer of zero means that on average the actual is tracking the target perfectly, and we can conclude that the individual differences for each period are likely to be just noise.[29]

But what happens if the actual is not tracking the target? For example, let's assume that all the values in the aforementioned sequence are positive rather than being an equal mix of positive and negative. In this case the tracking score will be 4/4, that is, +1.0. If all the differences were negative the score will be –4/4, that is, –1.0.

Now let's see what happens when the actual is still off target but in a less extreme way. If there are three positive differences and only one negative the tracking score will be (12–4/4) = 2/4 = +0.5.

It should now be clear that the tracking score reflects how far adrift the actual is from the target. If the actual is way above target the tracking score is +1.0, if it is way below it is –1.0. If it is bang on target (on average) the tracking score will usually be exactly zero. In practice, however, the tracking score will be somewhere between these three extremes and the value of the score will reflect how close the actual tracks the targets and in what direction: high side or low side.

The tracking score enables us to determine how close performance is to the target. And recalculating the score every period using a moving average will allow us to track performance continuously over time.

Tracking signals also enable us to do three things that simply are not possible with conventional approaches to measuring performance.

---

29. Statisticians would describe this differently. They would say that we have no evidence that the difference is *not* noise. This is technically more correct but double negatives scramble the brain, so I have avoided this correct but convoluted expression.

1. We can track performance against a moving target. For example, we can assess actual revenue against a targeted rate of growth – where the target for period 2 was based on the actual for period 1. Because the tracking signal works on analysing differences it doesn't matter whether the actual target value is fixed or not.
2. We can eliminate the distorting effect of period-end peaking (and the possibility of manipulating perceptions of performance in this way). Because the difference used by the tracking signal is an average over time, is doesn't matter much whether something was booked in period 1 or period 2 – both are taken into account. Any kind of timing difference 'comes out in the wash'.
3. We can automatically adjust for scale. If one simply looked at an average of net differences over a period of time the result could be unduly influenced by a large value in one period, which may be an outlier that is unrepresentative of normal performance. But because the tracking signal uses the absolute value as the denominator in the equation, single large values do not distort the tracking score.

The method I have described here is deliberately crude, but the 'production ready' tracking signal differs in only one respect: both the net and gross difference are calculated using a smoothed rather than a simple moving average.

As we discovered in Chapter 3, weighting the recent past more than the distant past makes the tracking score more representative of current performance. Also, using smoothed values enables us to set 'control limits' based on statistical criteria (i.e. using limits that take account of the impact of noise), which can then be used to trigger alarms.

Table 5.1 gives the control limits for smoothed averages calculated using a smoothing parameter ('alpha') of 0.2.

So, if you have a tracking score of plus or minus 0.92 then there is a less than 1 in 100 (1%) chance of a false positive signal (Type 1 error). As there is very little chance of registering an 'off track' performance purely by chance this is very strong evidence of performance having deviated from target.

But a tracking score of 0.54 means that there is a 1 in 5 (20%) chance of a false positive. This still constitutes evidence, but of a weaker sort, which should make you wary of acting upon it, or (if you can't wait) trigger a search for more evidence from other independent sources.

What control limits should we use?

When I use the tracking signal, I usually set my lower warning signal at a confidence level of 90%. This means that on average, when I use monthly data, I will generate a false 'warning' signal roughly once a year (a 1 in 10 chance). At this level, I have some evidence of a signal (in this case a deviation from my target – good or bad). It isn't overwhelming, but it is worth the effort of investigating.

The higher limit I set at 95% confidence. Since the chance of a false positive signal is only 1 in 20, I'm inclined to treat this as strong evidence of a problem

Tracking Score	Confidence Level
0.92	99%
0.81	98%
0.74	95%
0.66	90%
0.54	80%

Table 5.1:
Control limits for smoothed averages

Level: What Does 'Good' Look Like?

(with either the actual or the target) unless I find evidence to the contrary (such as a large exceptional value). My thinking is that at 90% confidence level the burden on the analyst is to find evidence that would support the assertion that there is an issue. But at 95% the burden of proof is reversed – you need to explain why you think there *isn't* a problem (or opportunity).

Figure 5.1 provides some fully worked up examples for XYZ Ltd, showing how the tracking score is calculated and how it is used to track performance and generate alarms.

The first example uses single period values and a static target.

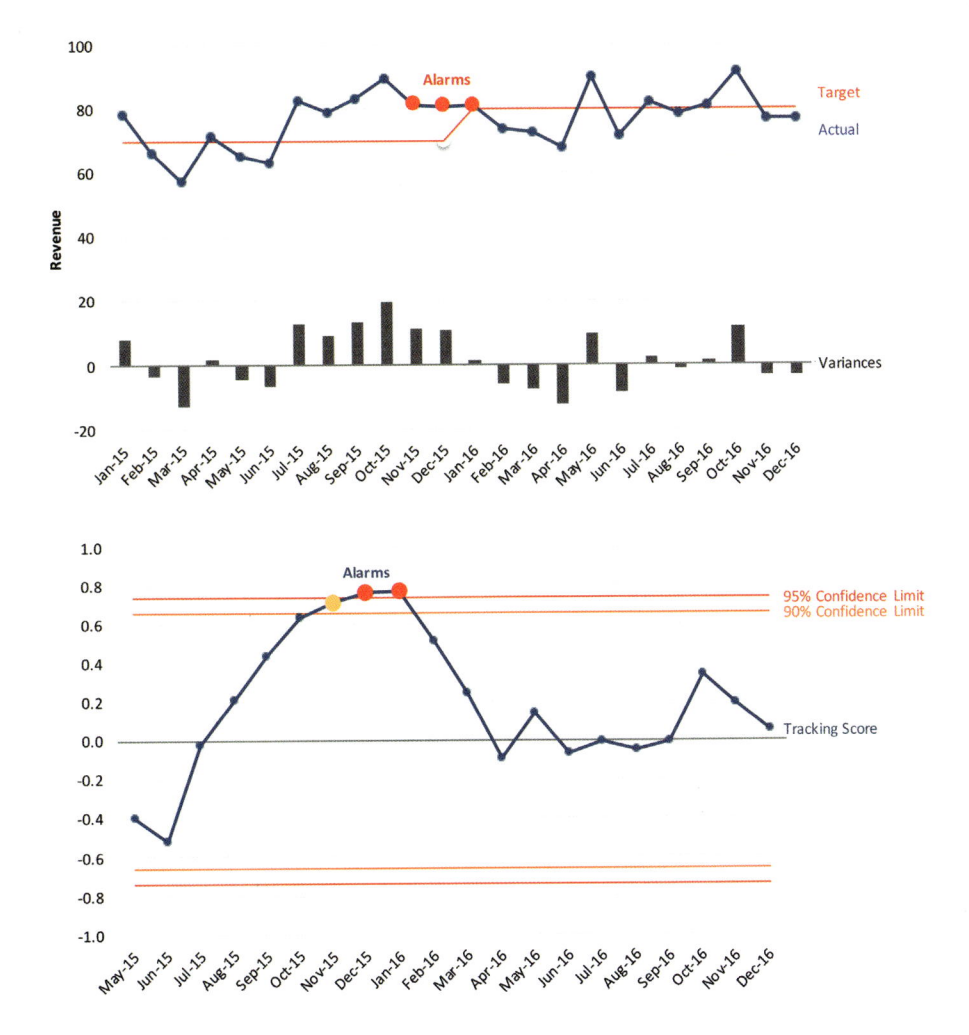

Figure 5.1:
XYZ Ltd revenue tracking signal with static target

The lines in the uppermost chart shows the actual value by month, the target and the difference between the two is represented by the grey bars. The lower chart shows the tracking score, which, when breached, generates a signal and – in this case – triggers a target reset.

As you can see, a target of 75 per month has been set for this variable and a positive 'warning' amber alarm (based on the 90% confidence limit) has been generated in period 10, followed by two further red 'take action' alarms in subsequent months. In response, the target has been increased to 80 and as the level of performance is now in line with the target (as evidenced by the tracking signal hovering around zero) the alarm 'switches itself off'.

The second example, in Figure 5.2a, uses a MAT and a rate-based target.

Figure 5.2:
Tracking signal with a moving target

The tracking signal methodology works equally well with a moving target.

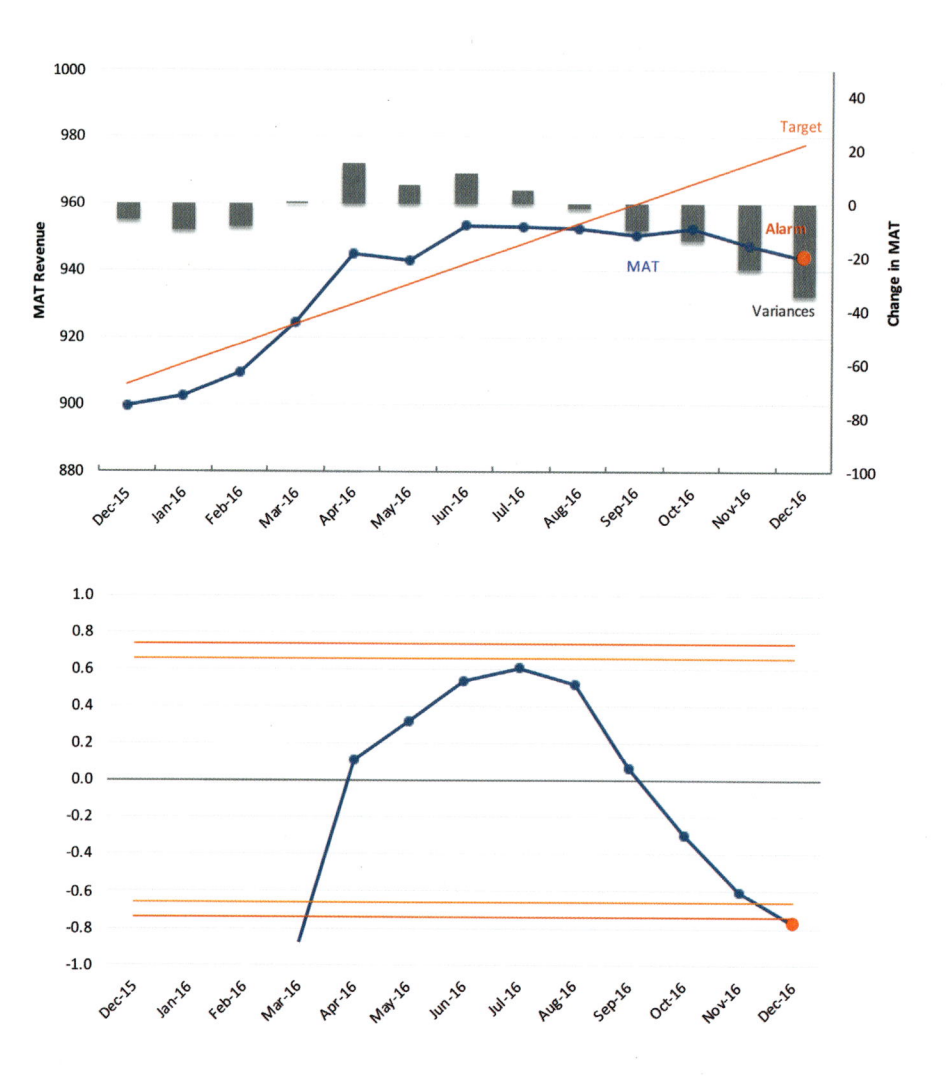

Here the target is expressed as a rate of growth. In fact, in this example, I set the growth rate based on historic levels, so any deviation from this rate signals an improvement or deterioration in performance. In this case, after performance tending upwards around periods 18 and 19 (but not sufficient to trigger any kind of alarm) it deteriorates to a point where a negative alarm is triggered in period 24.

Used in this way a tracking signal has multiple uses. For example:

- It allows us to move away from fixed period-end targets by providing us with a methodology to continuously assess performance.
- It enables us to regulate the performance of the business continuously, since targets can be changed as and when required rather than as part of an annual set piece exercise.
- It removes the ability (and the incentive) to game the performance measurement system by trying to 'hit' a number.
- By using past trends as a comparator, you can track performance without the need for an external derived (and often arbitrary) target.

- It can be used to track many aspects of performance. For example, you can track independent variables (drivers) as well as dependant variables and it can be used to provide feedback on the reliability of forecasts (where the forecast is the target).
- It supports exception reporting by providing a scientifically robust approach to support traffic light style visualization methods. For example, any value above the 95% confidence level can be assigned the colour red, whereas anything between 90% and 95% is amber.

In summary, the tracking signal provides us with a simple, statistically-robust and flexible tool for the continuous monitoring of the dynamic performance of a business that doesn't rely on fixed annual targets or variance analysis. It is particularly well suited to analysing high-level trend-based measures of the sort I outlined in Chapter 3, which are not amenable to control chart-based statistical methods.

For me, the tracking signal is another technique that comes fairly close to the top of my list of things that I wished I had known about when I had a proper job. It enables us to measure performance continuously, taking into account the level of statistical confidence we can have given the level of noise in the system.

So, the tracking signal is a distinct advance on traditional period-end target-based systems, but it shares one major shortcoming. It assumes that the comparator we use – the target – is valid. In other words, it does not address the major challenge that we have when we are attempting to make sound judgements about the level of performance, which is where I will now turn.

WE NEED TO TALK ABOUT TARGETS

So, there is a way in which we can track performance against a moving target in a manner that takes account of the noise that is inherent in any system of measurement.

But having a mechanism to track actual outcomes against a comparator (a target or a goal) doesn't address the big problems. How do we decide what to track and how do we determine the 'right' level of performance? Referring back to our watch analogy, we do not have a definitive source of 'good' to refer to. Even worse, unlike a watch, organizations are so complex that we need to track performance using multiple measures in order to assess the performance of the whole. How many comparators (different targets) should we have? Is more better, or worse? And how do we assess overall performance when different measures appear to be telling us different things?

This is central to the challenge we have in making sense of performance, so we cannot duck it.

And it is not just a technical problem. It goes right to the heart of management, as we have all learned to our cost over the last few years.

The financial sector has become something of a laboratory for studying the impact of financial management practices, playing the same role as laboratory rats, albeit with more serious consequences for all of us – whether we are customers, shareholders or tax payers.

In the period since the (2008) financial crisis, the regulator has fined UK banks over £7 billion for the misleading selling of a range of financial products to consumers and small businesses, ranging from protection against loss of valuables and identity fraud, through payment protection insurance (PPI) and exotic interest rate swaps. In addition, the banks have been made to pay back over £20 billion to customers in respect of PPI alone; equivalent to over £1,000 for every household in the country. And this is on top of the other huge fines they have paid to authorities around the world for manipulating benchmarks and facilitating money laundering.

How did this happen? Was it that banks employ bad people? I'm sure that there are a few in there, as there are in all walks of life, but I'm also sure that they are outnumbered by ordinary, decent people. Often, what happened is put down to 'culture'. But what exactly does that mean? And where did it come from?

The more recent example of Wells Fargo bank in the US is particularly instructive.

For those of you that are not familiar with this case, a huge scandal blew up in 2016 when the bank admitted to firing over 5,300 staff in the previous five years for unethical practices. These included opening up around 2 million phantom accounts for existing customers and transferring their money without their permission. The number of employees Wells Fargo dismissed would make up the sixteenth largest bank in the US.

The bank was clear where the blame lay (cue the 'few bad apples' excuse).

A spokesman said: 'Instances where we provided a customer with a product that they did not request are totally counter to our culture and our values'. Testifying to a senate committee the (ex) CEO was clear that 'the 5,300 were dishonest, and that is not part of our culture'.

No less than the Director of the Center for Ethics at the American College of Financial Services echoed this line: 'this was a systematic attempt to meet production goals through the misappropriation of customer funds (which is corporate speak for paying bonuses for hitting a target)…this is a cultural issue and it needs a cultural fix' (as reported in 'Fake Accounts cast cloud over Wells Fargo culture' *Financial Times* 9th September 2016).

Clearly doing bad things is evidence of a bad culture, but does the culture cause the bad practice or is it the other way around? Put another way, is culture what you say it is or is it what you do? If you focus attention on hitting targets that are not consistent with treating your customers well, is it a surprise that this is what happens?

This is my take on the matter.

It's not 'the culture' that creates the bad behaviour, nor is it deviant behaviour that can be eradicated by dismissing people who are caught doing bad things.

What happened here, and which happens to some degree in most organizations, is that the choices that people make about what to target, how to compare actual output to the target and how to interpret and respond to the difference help create the culture – which is nothing more or less than the set of behaviours an organization demonstrates by its actions. In this case, employees who hit their targets got rewarded, those who behaved badly and got found out were fired along with the people who tried to blow the whistle on them.

What does that tell you about the *real* corporate culture in Wells Fargo? To me it says, 'Do what you have to do to hit the numbers, but if you get found out or embarrass us (the bosses) by telling the truth, expect to get fired'.

We started this journey by describing performance as the degree to which observed behaviour fulfils the purpose of the organization. These examples show how a target can become the de facto purpose of the organization. In other words, the means become the end. Clearly, setting the right targets in the correct way is critical if we want to get the right kind of performance. As a well-known systems guru said, 'The purpose of an organization is what it does'.

But how do we 'set the right targets'?

Perhaps this is the wrong question, at least to start with.

In Chapter 2, one of two major problems with traditional variance analysis that I described was the arbitrary nature of most targets: they are often little more than an out of date guess. Even if we have a measurement system that can deal with noise, like the tracking signal, any comparison between an actual and a target is likely to present a distorted picture of performance. Arguably, trend measures alone enable us to answer many of the most basic questions about performance – such as 'Are things getting better or worse?' – without the need for targets.

In Chapter 4 I demonstrated how control charts can be used to filter out noise and so determine what, if anything, has changed, hence eliminating the need for targets to be set.

So, if targets are arbitrary and drive dysfunctional behaviour, and if we are clear about our purposes and have ways of making sense of what is going on that don't require targets in the traditional sense of the word, perhaps we should be asking a much more fundamental question. *Do we need targets at all?* And if we ultimately decide we can't live without them, can we avoid some or all of these problems or do we just have to suffer them in the interests of the greater good?

To most people schooled (like myself) in traditional management practice, the answer is obvious. Targets are critically important to the process of controlling an organization, measuring performance and holding employees accountable for their contribution to it.

End of debate.

'Good targets', we are told, have to be SMART: Specific, Measurable, Attainable, Relevant and Time bound. This mantra is not new, but in the last few decades we have seen an increase in the profile and use of targets as a means to measure and manage performance in both the public and private sectors. 'Accountability' is the watchword of modern management. And to most people being accountable means hitting targets, and financial incentives are essential tools in motivating people to comply with them.

Advocates of these traditional practices argue that dysfunctional behaviour, of the sort that is normally manifested in artificial peaking at period ends (rather than banking fraud) is just an unavoidable and relatively harmless by-product of an otherwise necessary and benign practice. After all, everybody knows how the game is played, they say with a wink.

But is what we have seen in the financial sector extreme and isolated examples of targets used in a reckless or thoughtless manner or do they reflect something fundamentally wrong with the whole process. Do they help to improve performance at all, or do they make it worse?

The pernicious nature of targets or quotas is certainly the view held by the revered gurus of the quality movement. The most well-known, W. Edwards Deming, is famously quoted as saying that 'people with targets and jobs that are dependent on them meeting them will probably meet the targets even if they have to destroy the enterprise to do it'. Sound familiar?

Perhaps Deming was guilty of hyperbole, but targets can be responsible for much more subtle and pervasive damage. 'Management by numerical goal is an attempt to manage without the knowledge of what to do' is another famous Deming aphorism. In other words, one of the attractive features of target setting to many managers (not to mention politicians and other leaders) is that it creates a sense that they can get the desired results without having to understand anything about what needs to be done to achieve them. And if anything goes disastrously wrong, you can deny all knowledge or claim that any miscreants are acting contrary to the 'culture' you profess to promote – as we saw with Wells Fargo.

But this notion of 'remote control' management – the whole idea that businesses can be run by generalists who (like torturers) know what buttons to press to get what they want – is a dangerous illusion. I illustrated this in Chapter 4 using a thought experiment that showed how fixed targets and simplistic performance measures drove poor performance outcomes in the fictional Troncho's sandwich and wrap bar. Setting targets for waiting times while simultaneously constraining the ability to invest in the process forced the manager of the shop to do things that were stupid in the context of the strategy and detrimental long-term health of the business. She would certainly have been aware of this, but those administering the process from their ivory head office tower would probably not have been. Their belief in the efficacy of 'tough love' – shape up or ship out – would be left unshaken.

This fictitious case demonstrated how conventional target-setting practice, far from improving performance, can actually make it worse. This happens when the objective of the exercise becomes to hit as many of the targets as possible, rather than improve service to customers or financial performance. The means have become the ends. And hitting the number becomes the de facto purpose of the organization.

Level: What Does 'Good' Look Like?

Also, it illustrates how setting more targets makes it more difficult for those being asked to improve to make the changes required because their freedom to act is constrained by the need to 'hit' more numbers. It's not just actual targets themselves that are an issue, the number of targets and how they are expressed is also part of the problem.

Let's illustrate the subtlety of the target-setting process and its role in shaping performance using an example from the world of sport, specifically English football (soccer). Like business, football is a team game and shares an obsession with motivation and, more recently, with measuring many aspects of performance, so it provides a good model of the challenge of target setting in organizations.

For the benefit of readers not familiar with football, this is what you need to know.

- A soccer team is made up of 11 players, each of whom has a defined role, just like the employees in a business organization. This might involve scoring goals (attackers), stopping the opposition from scoring goals (the goal keeper), blocking the path to goal (defenders) or acting as a link between attack and defence (midfielders).
- Within each of these groups individual players may have specific additional duties but everyone is expected to contribute to the team whenever they can. So, when necessary, an attacker might take on some defensive duties or vice versa, if the situation demands it.
- The English Premier League has 20 clubs who compete to win the league and avoid relegation (three teams per season). The position of each team in the league table is determined by the number of points that they accumulate based on a system of 3 points for a win and 1 for a draw.

What kinds of targets – if any – should be used to measure the performance of a team and motivate its players?

Clearly, the league position is the most appropriate measure of performance since the ultimate goal is to win. Over a season each team plays every other, so performance is truly comparable. The position in the table is an example of what is called a relative target because the goal of every team (e.g. winning the league, or avoiding relegation depending on your ambitions) is defined in relation to the performance of its peers.

In a system like this what would happen if a team used a fixed quota of points as a target instead of the relative target of the league position? Perhaps they could phase it over the year – maybe by quarter of the season like businesses often do?

The reason why a fixed 'point in time' target does not make sense is that, although there is a relationship between the number of points and performance, the number of points is not a perfect predictor of the league position – which is, as we have agreed, the ultimate goal.

Since the inception of the Premier League in 1992, a club has won the league with as little as 75 points and has failed to do so with 89. At the other extreme,

30. In the jargon this is known as a 'proximate goal'. Imagine that you are trapped on a mountain in the fog. Your ultimate goal is to get back to base but as you can't see it you choose a proximate goal, such as 'move downhill'. This promotes the right kind of action but it must never take precedence over the ultimate goal, particularly if you find yourself on the edge of a cliff!

a club has survived relegation with 34 points, but another suffered the drop with as many as 42. So, while it might make sense for a team that has ambition merely to survive to have the rough aim of securing 40 points over a season, this is no guarantee of survival and so should never be *the* target. It is simply a rule of thumb that helps guide performance in a way that is consistent with the purpose of the organization.[30]

In the same way, having an ambition to achieve 10 points in the first quarter of the season might be a good performance milestone but it would make a poor target since, in the first quarter, simply by chance, your team might have had easy matches against struggling teams weakened through injury. Even at the end of the season when the league position is known, when assessing performance fans and commentators will take notice of contextual factors like the length of the injury list, how well the team performed in other competitions or whether the final league position was an improvement on the previous year. Performance evaluation is never a purely numerical context-free exercise.

In summary, the only true measure of performance is relative performance made by comparing the output (numbers of points achieved) to an equivalent organization facing the same conditions. Other metrics can be used as a guide, but they should only be used as a proxy for the real aim, or to achieve a subordinate purpose (e.g. to improve an aspect of performance such as their defensive record), not as *the* goal.

When it comes to measuring and motivating individual members of the football team things get even trickier.

Some attributes of individual performance have always been measured, such as the number of goals scored by each player, but these days many other things are quantified as well, such as the number of passes or tackles made, how many were successful and the distance each player runs in a game.

Clearly there is a relationship between each of these things and the performance of the team. In business parlance we might call them performance drivers, KPIs or perhaps leading indicators. You would always like your strikers to score more goals, and the more ground your midfielders cover in the game the better – all other things being equal.

But, in a complex system like football, all other things are never equal, which means that performance on one measure does not automatically translate to performance on another. For example, in order to win matches the team needs to be in control of the football. However, in the 2015/6 season Leicester City won the Premier League despite having fewer touches of the ball than any other team in the competition.

What would happen if – as is often the case in business – a football manager decides his or her players should be given targets on each of these measures in order to 'manage' their performance. After all, it makes sense that if every individual achieves their targets, then the team as a whole will achieve its goal – right?

If the answer to this rhetorical question isn't already obvious to you, imagine what would happen if a full-back (whose job involves sprinting up and down

Level: What Does 'Good' Look Like?

the edge of the pitch to support both attack and defence) discovered that he or she was 600 metres short of the '3 miles per game' target 5 minutes before the end of the game. The likelihood is that the player would spend the rest of the game running up and down the touchline irrespective of what was happening – particularly if he or she was incentivized to hit his or her target! And what about the midfielder who made easy passes all the time to fulfil his or her quota of 'successfully completed' passes or a striker that achieved his or her annual quota of 20 goals halfway through the season? Would fans be happy if that player stopped trying to score any more goals? Finally, imagine what would happen if the main striker was on a bonus for each goal scored? Would this increase the performance of the team or would teammates be jealous and stop helping their team mate?[31] And in all of these cases how could we decide in advance what the right target for each measure should be?

The clear message is that context is critical when it comes to assessing performance or determining the right thing to do, particularly in a complex and uncertain environment. Excessive focus on targets crowds out context. Hitting the target becomes the purpose rather than an aid to achieving the purpose – the means become the end. Targets have become a substitute for judgement, not an aid to it.

In the context of football, it is easy to see how the automatic application of fixed targets to measures would promote stupid and suboptimal behaviour. And comparing the actual performance to individual targets provides us with very little useful information about their contribution to the performance of the whole. And yet, in business, the practice of attaching an arbitrary comparator to almost every dimension of a business that can be measured – including every employee (and especially the leader!) – is treated as an essential ritual[32] and lauded as 'best practice'.

So, targets can be misleading and damaging. But does that mean that we can dispense with them altogether? If there were no quantitative reference points at all for a football team and no constraints placed upon the actions of its players, we can be fairly sure that performance would suffer. 'Targets', in some sense of the word, are essential. What is the right thing to do?

The answer to the question – 'Do we need targets?' – is not at all obvious. To me, it is clear that we need to think more deeply about targets and target setting. The simple exchange of opinions between people on opposite sides of the argument will not help us resolve this problem.

A good place to start in our quest for an answer involves addressing the fundamental question. 'What is a target?'

31. When I used this example at a conference I was speaking at in Brazil, the translator told me that this has actually happened in the team he supported. Nobody passed the ball to the striker!

32. A famous systems thinker, Russell Ackoff, explicitly made this point in a famous article 'The Corporate Rain Dance' (*Wharton Magazine*) where he suggested that like a rain dance much of corporate planning (and budgeting) served merely as a ritual because it had no discernible influence on the weather. But like rituals it perseveres because people are scared of what might happen if they don't perform it and the blame that will be attached to anyone who has the courage to challenge orthodoxy. Instead we focus on improving the dancing.

WHAT IS A TARGET?

'Target' is one of those words that is used so liberally we seldom stop to consider what we mean when we use it. My guess is that if ten people in a room were asked to define it they would come up with ten different answers and many of the definitions would vary, depending on the context.

Let's first take a step back and think about performance measures.

A performance measure is a value of a variable that we believe to be relevant to the health and success of an organization. This could be an input 'flow' variable (e.g. cost, time taken), an output 'flow' variable (e.g. revenue or customer service) or a 'stock' variable (e.g. cash, inventory or creditors). It might also include KPIs, which may be non-financial measure or a compound metric such as cost expressed as a percentage of income, or the number of days stock cover.

The way I see it is that, by definition, *if a performance measure captures something important – how well an organization is fulfilling its purpose – we must care what the value of that measure is.* We cannot be indifferent. At the most basic level we have to know whether, all other things being equal, bigger values are better than smaller values or less variation is better than more variation. We must have a hope or aspiration for the values of a variable.

Following this line of logic, a target is therefore a measurable expression of this aspiration and must take one of a limited number of forms: 'exactly', 'more than', 'less than' or 'between'. And it should be anchored at a point in time or be continuous over a time range (Figure 5.3).

Figure 5.3:
Some examples of performance variables and how they are 'targeted'

A target implies some kind of constraint on the value of a variable – but this can take many forms.

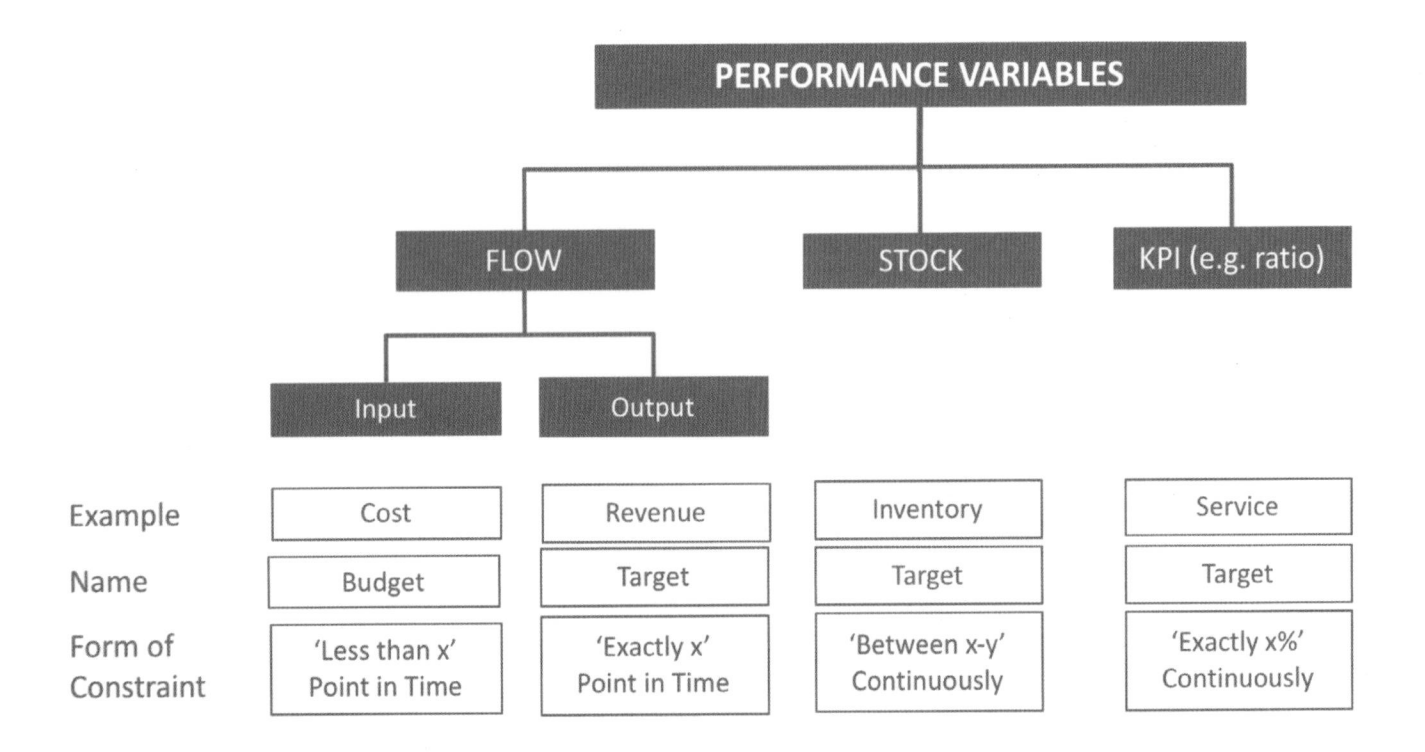

```
                        PERFORMANCE VARIABLES
                        /        |          \
                     FLOW      STOCK      KPI (e.g. ratio)
                    /    \
                Input    Output
```

Example	Cost	Revenue	Inventory	Service
Name	Budget	Target	Target	Target
Form of Constraint	'Less than x' Point in Time	'Exactly x' Point in Time	'Between x-y' Continuously	'Exactly x%' Continuously

Although any kind of performance variable may be constrained, the word target is usually used to describe how output variables (performance) are constrained at a point in time. The term 'budget' is most often used to describe a constraint applied to an input variable, like cost, within a financial year. But whatever the term used, these comparators all have the same purpose, to constrain or influence behaviour by acting as a reference point for the value of a variable.

I want you to note at this point that a target doesn't need to be an exact value, even though it is usually expressed in this way. It might even be expressed as an exact value but interpreted in such a way that it is clear that it is not treated as an exact value.

For example, if I give my son a budget of £50 to buy new football boots, he knows that I mean that he shouldn't spend much more than £50, not that he has to spend £50 exactly. Similarly, if a business delivered a profit of £99.6 million but had an aspiration of £100 million, most people would accept performance being 'on target', even though a range was not explicitly specified.

It is not even necessary to express a target in quantitative terms. For example, in the world of continuous improvement where opprobrium is heaped upon the idea of targets, there is a clear expectation that the value of the variable being worked on must be higher (or lower) than the value of a same variable in the past. Although it is not written down there is clearly a target in the sense that there is a measurable aspiration that guides behaviour and enables people to determine whether what has happened is 'good' or 'bad'.

So, what we see is that different words are used to describe things that serve the same purpose, and sometimes the same word is used to describe things with different purposes. To avoid confusion and the negative connotations often associated with the 't' word, I will use the word 'goal' rather than 'target', to describe any form of constraint applied to a variable or comparator used to guide behaviour and assess performance.

In summary, a goal is a desired value of a variable used to constrain or guide behaviour. *A conventional fixed target is simply one form that a goal can take, but not the only one.*[33]

Now we have a working definition, and some understanding of the range of ways that goals can be specified, let's return to the original question. What is a good use of goals? How do we decide when, where and how to use them?

I believe that this is one of the most important questions for management, precisely because most people think that they know the answer and act accordingly, when they really don't. It is not a trivial or simple matter. It is a subtle, complex and important question, which sits right at the heart of the practice of management. For that reason, I urge you not to skim read the next few pages.

No sleeping at the back of the class. Pay attention!

WHAT KINDS OF GOALS ARE THERE?

Since we are not completely indifferent to what happens in the future, we need to have an idea of what 'good' and 'bad' looks like. So, you require some reference point or comparator in order to be able to manage at all. The question is what form should this expression of an aspiration take?

33. For me, the difference between a goal and a target is that the latter is 'harder' because its role is more prescriptive (constraining) and less indicative (guiding).

Figure 5.3:
Alternative ways of specifying a goal

Goals typically have at least five different dimensions. SMART targets (shown in grey) represent one of a number of potential forms that a goal can take.

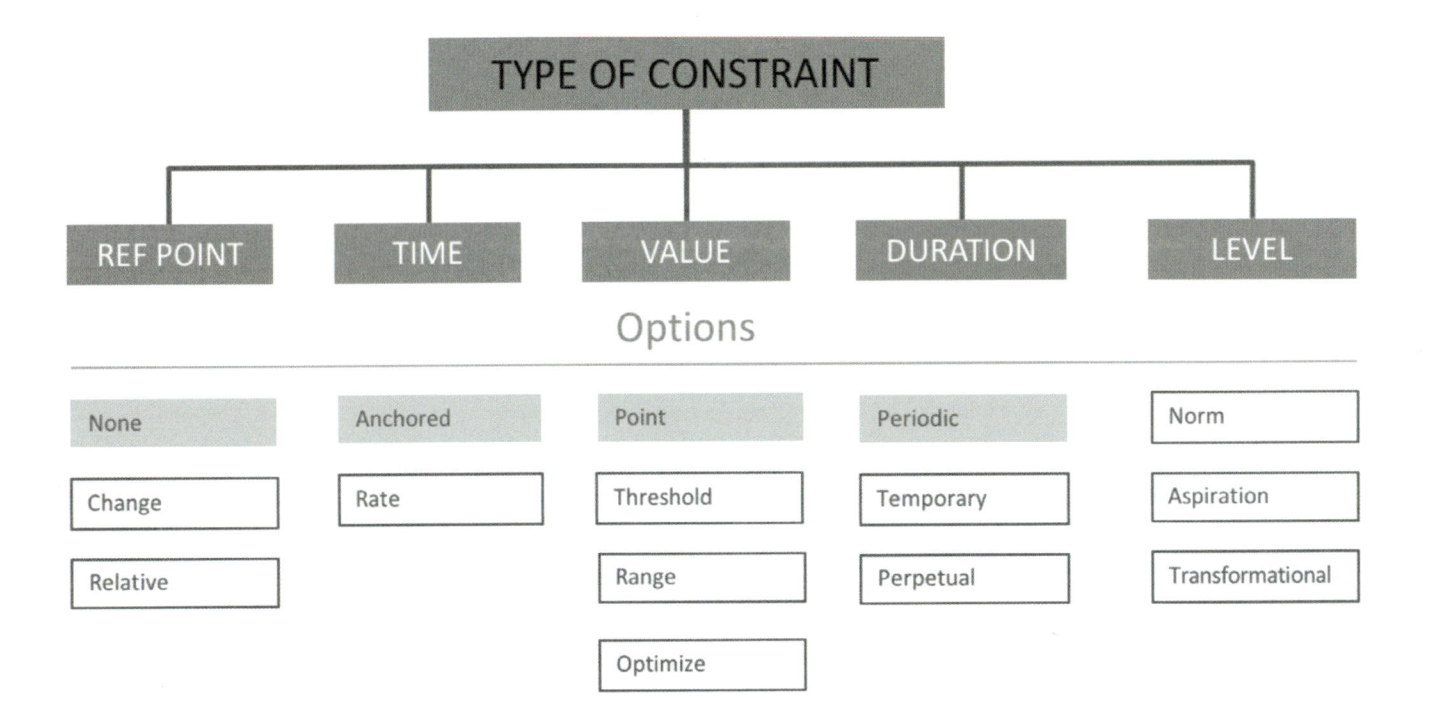

The word target triggers a very specific set of thoughts, since most of us have been brainwashed into thinking that targets have to be SMART. In practice this often means fixed 'period-end' targets of the sort that I have criticized in this book.

If a goal doesn't meet any of the SMART criteria, we are led to believe that is a bad target – a deformed monstrosity that will bring calumny down on our heads.

But as we have seen, 'hitting the number' is no guarantee of performance and doing so may actually make matters worse. SMART targets can distort the activity of an organization, prevent well-intentioned employees from making sensible trade-offs between competing objectives – in the long-term interests of the business and its customers – and promote dysfunctional and unethical practices. Even if you recognize that they are the root cause of problems it is difficult to change things because SMART targets are cemented in place. We have no alternative to traditional variance analysis, which demands the specificity and lack of ambiguity that they provide.

Over the last two chapters I have introduced you to techniques that allow you to measure, track and analyse performance without the need for SMART targets. Having been liberated from this straitjacket, we now need to think about whether and where we should use explicit goals, how they should be expressed and how the difference between the actual outcome and the aspiration should be interpreted and acted upon. Once we remove our SMART blinkers, we find that we have a lot to choose from, as Figure 5.4 shows.

```
                    TYPE OF CONSTRAINT
        ┌──────────┬──────────┬──────────┬──────────┐
    REF POINT    TIME      VALUE    DURATION     LEVEL

                        Options

    None       Anchored    Point     Periodic     Norm
    Change       Rate      Threshold  Temporary   Aspiration
    Relative               Range      Perpetual   Transformational
                           Optimize
```

Let's explore the range of possibilities and draw out some lessons about how best to deploy them.

Reference point

Conventional SMART targets have no external reference point: they are either imposed by or negotiated with someone higher up in the organizational hierarchy. Either way the result is an arbitrary value; which begs the important question of what is the 'right' level?

The future is unpredictable because it has never happened before. As a result, there is no firm evidential basis on which to determine, in advance, what represents good performance. For example, although the Atlantic has been crossed millions of times before, a sailor in a transatlantic race can only judge his or her performance against that of other competitors in the same race facing the same weather and sea conditions. A Formula 1 racing car engineer can only judge the performance of their car with reference to other teams and this cannot be predicted in advance of the new season. And in business the performance of an organization is ultimately judged (by shareholders at least) against that of its peers – which also cannot be predicted.

This is really important because one of the myths of traditional management practices such as variance analysis is that it eliminates or reduces the need for judgement. This is rubbish. The act of setting a target is usually highly judgemental. The mechanistic process of variance analysis creates the illusion of objectivity because the highly subjective process of target setting was conducted many months previously as part of an opaque budgeting process. What is worse, the targets that are used are usually bad targets because they are always out of date and often set as part of a highly politicized process.

The impossibility of specifying in advance what 'good' looks like is the simple argument for setting targets relative to the performance of peers. It is the only process for defined goals that is relatively free from subjectivity and is so compelling that some organizations like Handelsbanken, the largest bank in Sweden, embed this principle right through their performance management system. The bank as a whole has one simple goal – to consistently beat the average return on equity of its peer banks. And within Handelsbanken the performance of individual branches is measured by their cost to income ratio relative to their internal peers. In this way the target is always set at the 'right level' because the average performance always reflects achievable performance in the prevailing economic conditions. Also, performance is continuously driven upwards without the targets ever being changed because no one wants to be below average.

This seductively simple idea is not always easy to follow in practice, however.

It may be impossible to define sensible internal or external peer groups and, in the case of the latter, getting hold of comparable performance information can be difficult. In these circumstances using targets based on a rate of change (i.e. relative to the past) might provide a workable alternative to a 'pure' relative target since it is not as dependent on having reliable up-to-date information on peer group performance. A reasonable understanding of long-term trends in a business or industry might allow us to set aspirations at the right level.[34] So, a

34. In some industries or sectors it is possible to source data from organizations, such as AQPC and Hackett, whose business is to collect data for benchmarking purposes.

35. The Quality folks like to think that they don't have targets, but in a sense they do. By advocating 'continuous improvement', the 'target' they are shooting for is their own past performance. The big difference from other forms of target is that it does not come from outside the process or system. This reinforces the point that you cannot make sense of data without a comparator. The challenge is to find the right one.

rough sense of historic trends might be sufficient to set a rate-based target for reducing costs at say 3% year on year (i.e. improving relative to the past). Or holding the KPI for administrative costs below the industry norm of 5% of revenue could be another good (relative target) alternative to a fixed (absolute) annual budget.[35]

Time

Traditionally goals are anchored in a point in time and expressed in absolute terms, for example, 'profit should be $1 million in the year to December'. But, while it is convenient to set goals in this way, this isn't aligned with one important part of the purpose of all businesses, which is to survive – to remain viable by continuously generating profits. At best the year end number is a *proximate goal* and, as we have seen, when it is treated as the *ultimate goal* trouble soon follows. Attempts to hit a period-end number can disguise the true level of performance and destabilize a business by inducing volatility (period-end peaking). Worse, people do things that are at variance with the ultimate purpose and espoused ethics of the business.

Arguably, it would be better to express the goal as a (continuous) rate of change. This would also make manipulating the system to 'hit the number' impossible to sustain. And, as a result, performance data will be more reliable, and more effort focussed on managing the business rather than managing the numbers. Tools like the tracking signal can be used to monitor performance against a moving target.

Value

Conventionally, goals are expressed as an exact value (a 'point' target). But the ubiquity of noise in any system means that it is highly improbable that we would ever hit a number exactly without manipulating the system – which is another reason why period-end peaking is an endemic in many publicly quoted companies.

Also, expressing a goal in such precise terms may not reflect the behaviour we might want to encourage. For example, if we set a revenue goal of £100 million, we usually don't want people to stop if they can sell more; just as if we set a cost budget of £100 million, we don't want to spend all the money if we don't need to. But because goals are set in such a crude manner, this is exactly what often happens.

There are many other ways in which you can set goals to more accurately reflect the objectives of the business that are less likely to generate dysfunctional behaviour.

For example, rather than using a 'point target', an objective could be stated as 'more than' or 'less than' or 'between'. For example, it is very important for the human body to maintain equilibrium, which it achieves by controlling variables within ranges. Body temperature is targeted at 36.1°c to 37.2°c, but our heart rate is allowed to fluctuate more widely, generally between 60 and 100 bpm in normal conditions, and often very much wider. In the same way, organizational stability is a prerequisite for measured rational decision-making in business. So, rather than setting a point target for customer service, for example, it would be much more sensible to set a range since higher or lower levels of performance are costly – but in different ways.

This last point illustrates that goals for individual variables should never be set in isolation. For example, for the reason referred to earlier, it would make sense to set a customer service target as a range, but to optimize cost within that constraint – in other words, cost should be 'as low as possible' or 'lower than last period' with no minimum value.

Duration

Another benefit of expressing a goal as a rate or in relative terms is that it doesn't need to be reset every period, thereby eliminating the bureaucracy and disruption associated with the annual process. Dispensing with annual process also means that it is possible to change goals at any time within the year, thereby enhancing agility. Goals can additionally be expressed as milestones, which lapse when an objective has been achieved rather than at a defined date. For example, it might make sense to constrain the amount spent on a project or activity over its life cycle, which may span a year end, rather than bundling it with other projects in an annual budget. Similarly, if an improvement goal is achieved early, goals should be immediately reset rather than waiting for the annual target-setting exercise.

Level

Finally, goals can be pitched at different levels. There can be 'stretch' targets that are difficult to achieve, in which case failing to meet them should be interpreted as an incentive to try harder rather than as a failure. Or goals can be set at the minimum acceptable level, hence a shortfall would have a very different meaning. Or they could be norms that help orientate or guide behaviour, in which case it might not be appropriate to use them to analyse performance at all. And it is possible for one variable to have multiple targets representing different levels of achievement like the bronze, silver and gold medals awarded at the Olympic Games, all of which represent success but at different levels of achievement.

A SYSTEM OF TARGETS

So, there are many ways of setting goals for specific variables, and it is nuts to restrict ourselves to one method. When choosing how to frame an objective it is important to bear in mind what behaviour you are seeking to encourage and remain mindful that all formulations have a dark side as well – that is, a potential to drive dysfunctional behaviour.

Also, if a goal is used to assess and make sense of performance, we should not fall into the trap of using the simplistic formulae of variance analysis whereby any deviation is automatically labelled good or bad. The nature of the goal and how it was set needs also to be taken into account. *Assessing performance always – and unavoidably – involves judgement.* Goals provide the framework that help us make sound judgements.[36]

So far, however, we have only looked at how to set goals for addressed individual variables. In practice organizations have many, many, important variables, many of which are non-financial or difficult to measure. In order to assess the performance of the whole organization in a balanced way they all need some frame of reference. Furthermore, the way they collectively shape behaviour is arguably more important than the way that any individual target is expressed. We need to see goals as part of an interconnected system – a set of goals. And this system has become increasingly complex and difficult to administer as the practice of setting SMART targets at increasingly granular levels has become 'de rigueur' in contemporary performance management practice.

Because conventional fixed targets have come to be seen as the only way to measure and manage performance, it is not surprising that there has been a corresponding increase in their number. This often leads to a targeting 'arms race' where different interest groups compete to have 'their' targets and, even better, embed them in personal performance plans and bonus systems, for example.

One of the arguments for conventional targets is their relative simplicity and role as tools to focus and coordinate activity. But as targets proliferate and the system becomes more complex these 'benefits' soon evaporate. There are other, less obvious, downsides associated with this proliferation, however.

As we have seen, goals constrain behaviour and single point targets are a very unforgiving form of constraint. They effectively insist that the value of this variable has to be brought back to 'x' – exactly. And the more constraints an organization has the less flexibility it has, particularly when variables are independent – since changing or constraining any one variable can have an impact on many others.

Sometimes this effect is clear, direct and short term. Constraining costs so that there are fewer people available to answer the growing number of calls in a customer service centre will increase backlogs and reduce customer satisfaction, for example. And imposing targets on the numbers of calls to be answered in a defined period will only increase the number of dissatisfied customers and lead to more calls in the future (so-called 'failure demand'). But more often the negative impact of poor goal setting is hidden, indirect and operates at a lag. As a result, the collective impact of goals can distort behaviour in ways that are difficult to understand and even harder to anticipate.

In practice, the untrammelled proliferation of targets in many organizations, promoted in the name of improving performance and making it more predictable, makes it impossible to meet all the targets that have been set. This is because of systemic interdependencies and the limited time and attention of staff.

Employees have two options if they are faced with a complex and confusing set of demands expressed in the form of large numbers of mutually incompatible fixed targets.

---

[36]. Using the word 'judgement' makes this sound like an explicit, rational process, but in the human body holistic balanced judgements about our current state are synthesized into something that we call 'feelings' if Antonio Damasio's somatic marker hypothesis is correct. He came to the recognition of the importance of feelings after he observed patients who had lost their ability to sense their bodies after an illness and who were utterly incapable of making a decision without the directional steer that emotions provided. Provided, of course, that they are evidence based, we need to acknowledge the role that feelings can play in business judgements. From the perspective of our brains, which are the only part of the body that has no sensory apparatus of its own, there is no inherent difference between emotions, perception and cognition.

First, they can prioritize their goals – perhaps focussing on achieving just one at the expense of the others. The likelihood is that they will chose the one that is clearer, most visible and easy to achieve, particularly if it has a reward attached – which might not be the one you want them to focus on. Often, as Wells Fargo discovered, things that may actually be more important to the business in the longer term, such as ethical behaviour or acting with your customer's best interests at heart, can be neglected particularly if they are less visible to the business.

The second option is to game the system. This often involves negotiating targets that are easier to achieve or manipulating the system to make it look like they have achieved their goal (e.g. by 'pushing' sales at period end) or in extreme cases falsifying data.

What can we do to avoid this situation?

The most important stratagem is restraint. We should consciously limit the number of goals that are set, perhaps in conjunction with a 'one in, one out' policy to help maintain a consistent, manageable number of targets. Reducing the number of goals forces a business to explicitly consider its priorities at that point in time and acts as a brake on the targets arms race.

Another approach would be to 'loosen' goals by using ranges rather than fixed points to frame targets. But a more sophisticated way of guiding behaviour is to use differentiated 'goal sets'.

One way of doing this is to build a hierarchy of goals, whereby the achievement of the high-level 'ultimate' goal takes precedence over second level 'approximate' goals or lower-level KPIs that serve merely as guidelines.[37] This doesn't mean that 'lower order' goals are somehow 'bad'. If you don't know which road to take to reach your destination, 'keep heading north' is a very useful lower order goal. The point is that proximate goals or guidelines shouldn't substitute for the ultimate goal.[38] So 'hitting' your sales target should not override more important, higher order goals such as 'remain profitable' or 'safeguard the bank's reputation with customers'.

Differentiated goal sets are used by the military to guide the action of individual fighting units. The defined mission and the rules of engagement for an operation both constrain the system, but in different ways. The mission gives direction and defines success. The 'rules of engagement' set out the boundaries of action. Defining what a soldier cannot do gives them freedom to act within those parameters.[39]

In a business context, for example, a growth business might define its goals as 'maximizing revenue' (mission) while 'maintaining margin' (rules of engagement). Whereas a mature business that is being 'milked' could be asked to 'maximize cash generation' (mission) while 'restricting volume decline'.

[37]. Bjarte Bogsnes, a friend and colleague from the Beyond Budgeting community, likes to stress the importance of the word 'indicator' in the acronym KPI. He argues that numbers should not determine what is treated as 'good' or 'bad' – the evaluation of performance always involves judgement to some degree. Measures (and goals attached to them) can never be more than indicative.

[38]. In his book *Obliquity* John Kay (2010) argues that in complex organizations operating in an inherently uncertain environment, where you can never know for certain what is the right route to take, it is unhelpful to focus on the ultimate goal since there is rarely a simple and straightforward means to achieve it. Instead, we should use a series of temporary proximate goals that we can be confident that will move us in the right direction. Since we do not have a map of the territory, we have to navigate by compass and be prepared to change course as and when threats or opportunities present themselves.

[39]. This form of control can be traced back to von Moltke's work in the Prussian staff college in the 1860s. *Aufstragstaktic*, as it was called, lay behind German military success up to and including the Second World War and now, as 'Mission Control' is a central tenant of Western military philosophy.

DIFFERENTIATED GOALS IN PRACTICE – AND IN THEORY

I found differentiated targets to be an extremely effective way of shaping and guiding business performance when I was in charge of strategy for a large consumer goods business.

The reason it worked, I believe, is that the way that performance was measured and judged was aligned with the stated strategy for different business units. In effect, it articulated the unique role of each business unit within the context of the overarching purpose of the whole organization and so brought a consistency and clarity of approach that would not have been possible if we had continued to manage the business by judging its performance against scores of fixed targets derived from a budget.

Our thinking was informed by the ideas behind the linear programming optimization technique, which involves optimizing the value of a variable (the objective) given a set of restrictions (constraints). In the aforementioned example 'maximize revenue' is the objective, subject to first meeting a constraint, which might be 'maintain margin', for example. Although no mathematics was involved in the process of setting targets or running the business, what we learned from the technique helped us do a better job in two ways. First, it is only possible to maximize one variable at a time, and this forced us to be clear about our definition of the strategy. Second, we knew that increasing the number of constraints would lead to a reduction in the value of the optimized variable, so this forced us to limit the number of variables that we targeted. In effect it forced us to think about targets from a systemic standpoint.

Setting goals involves defining what variable is to be optimized and what variables are to be constrained, and how. One way of looking at this is to treat the job of running the business as a problem-solving exercise. And mathematics tells us that the way that a problem is defined has a big impact on how difficult it is to solve.

For example, it tells us that it is only possible to optimize one variable at a time. You cannot optimize two or three. However, in business we usually do not define the variable that we want to optimize because targets are regularly expressed as single numbers – 'this much, and no more or no less' rather than 'maximize' or 'minimize'. As a consequence, we may stop looking before an optimum solution has been found – we sub-optimize. Another possibility is that individuals may choose to optimize a variable of their choosing – perhaps the one that maximizes their bonus, which may not be in the interest of the organization as a whole.

Mathematics also teaches us that the more constraints there are, and the more tightly they are defined, the more difficult it is to find a solution. Indeed, it may be that a problem with many defined constraints cannot be solved at all. In a business context, I suspect this means that it is usually technically impossible to hit all the targets that have been set – and what is really a target-setting problem is treated as a performance failure.

As a result, mathematicians often deal with optimization problems by relaxing the constraints on the grounds that a 'good enough' solution identified quickly is better than a perfect solution that takes a long time to find. This resonates with my warnings about the dangers of setting too many, too tightly defined targets.

Finally, mathematicians often talk about 'fitness landscapes', which their algorithms need to explore to find a solution. The hills of fitness landscapes are good solutions and the highest hill is the optimum solution. One of the most effective ways of solving problems is called 'gradient ascent'. This is where you follow the 'slope' of the fitness landscape (i.e. trend in the optimized variable) until you can climb no further, at which point you stop.

In the language of business, we call this continuous improvement.

And if you can't get any further up the 'improvement hill', you either stay there or jump in the hope that you will land on a bigger mountain. Mathematicians do this by introducing random values into their equations. In business we make these leaps by being creative and through innovation.

Finding that there is a scientific rationale for an approach that feels intuitively right is always reassuring.[40]

40. I cover the theory behind creating feasible 'goal sets' in the companion book *The Little Book of Beyond Budgeting* (2017), in the section on Ashby's Law of Requisite Variety.

TARGETS AND MOTIVATION

Although it is not within the scope of this book, I can't leave the subject of goals without touching on the topic of motivation.

In this chapter – and in the book generally – I have focussed on the rational case against conventional practices. Specifically, I have argued that fixed, time-bound targets are a lousy way to guide decision-making in a complex organizational system operating in a dynamic and uncertain environment.

But, for many people the primary role of a target is not as much to *guide* behaviour as it is to *encourage* the right sort of behaviour. They believe that targets are necessary to motivate people to perform, particularly when they are tied to financial incentives.

The field of human motivation is huge – much bigger than I can do justice to in this book. But because impact of goals on motivation is perceived to be so important, it's not something we can ignore altogether.

The 'common-sense' view is based on the simple argument that human beings respond to punishments and rewards – a view that also underpins classical economic theory, which assumes that we are all hyper rational 'utility maximizing agents'.

If this is what you believe, it certainly makes the job of management easy.

You just set the 'right' targets, add the 'right' amount of financial incentive and let everyone get on with things. This is certainly the way that virtually every CEO of public listed companies is managed, so it is unsurprising that this approach permeates every corner of most organizational life. And the 'carrot and stick' model also dominated behavioural psychology in the middle decades of the 20th century when BF Skinner and his acolytes sought to model human behaviour using mazes, pigeons and a combination of bird seed and electric shocks, although this is unlikely to work with most CEOs I know.

By now I hope you agree that it is impossible to set the 'right targets'. But even if it were, is this simple stimulus–response model an accurate description of the way that human beings behave? Are we capable of being controlled like machines?

Academic research suggests that conventional goal setting can work when it is applied to simple well-defined tasks. And unsurprisingly we do respond to monetary incentives, especially when we haven't got any money to start with. But these findings need to be highly qualified, since even when the tasks are very simple and easy to define, people respond best when they set their own targets and have control over how they perform them.

And tying money to targets is a one-way street. Like an addictive drug, you have to increase the dose to maintain the effect, and removing it triggers a 'cold turkey' experience where all the short-term gains – and some more – are wiped out.

Modern organizations have very few simple tasks of the sort that I have described. Most of them have already been automated. And most people working in these organizations do not come to work just to put food on the table. Their needs are much more complex. They have climbed Maslow's hierarchy of needs and are looking for something more than the satisfaction of their physiological requirements.

Research points to three key drivers of motivation:

- **Autonomy** – Human beings perform best when they feel they have some choice over what they do, when they do it and how they do it. Remove autonomy and the best that you can hope for is compliance, and the carrot and stick might be the only way you get *any* movement.
- **Mastery** – Peak performance is a 'flow' experience, where the difficulty of the task matches the level of skill of the 'performers'. In these circumstances, the reward is the sense of achievement itself. Setting the bar too high generates stress and burnout. But set the bar too low and there is no sense of challenge to motivate people, and as soon as you attach rewards to targets any remaining potential for fulfilment is extinguished. Chore has completely displaced challenge. To engender the motivation that flows from mastery, the best sorts of goals are those that we strive towards but never quite achieve. The kind where the kick comes from getting better rather than 'hitting the number'.
- **Purpose** – I have spoken already about how meaning flows from an understanding of the purpose of the organization. Well, the same principle applies to us as human beings. We work best when we believe that our work has meaning, and that comes from an understanding of how it is aligned to something bigger than ourselves that is inherently worthwhile.

Over the last few decades it has become clear that human motivation cannot be reduced to a simple stimulus–response model, but economists and business people have not caught up with the findings of behavioural science. They are still trapped in a mental model based on simple mechanical principles.

This is another reason why we need to take a completely fresh look at the role of goals in management and how targets are used to try and achieve them.

Read Daniel Pink's book – *Drive* – for an overview of research on the topic of motivation.

TARGETS AND PERFORMANCE REPORTING

I warned you earlier that this chapter might take us down some underexplored paths, and by now you might be feeling a little disorientated.

'What has goal setting got to do with performance reporting?', you might be thinking. Let's loop back to the definitions we started this chapter with to answer this question.

Goals are the measurable expression of the purpose of an organization. They help us to work out what things we need to measure, out of the potentially infinite number of things that we could measure. And they guide and constrain behaviour and serve as a reference point to helps us determine to what extent that the purpose has been fulfilled – how the organization is performing. To achieve these objectives, goals need to be defined in a way that help promote the right behaviour and – here is the important bit – any *deviations from goals need to be interpreted in a way that informs good decisions*. In other words, information professionals need to be able to attribute meaning to the difference between outcomes and stated aspirations.

The traditional model of performance analysis, on the other hand, requires relatively little thought. Variances between actuals and targets are easily calculated and labelled as good or bad, and the role of management is equally straightforward – eradicate bad variances. Analysts need to do little more than state the 'facts' and perhaps spin a story that offers a plausible explanation of why things happened – overlooking the uncomfortable reality that the variance could be attributed to the arbitrary nature of the target-setting process or random noise infecting the measured outcomes.

The way I see it is that in the future information professionals will face greater technical challenges because they need to master techniques that require more skill than being able to subtract one number from another. They will also face non-technical challenges of a higher order, since they will be required to make judgements about what the results *mean*, based on an appreciation of the business, its purpose, strategy and interactions with the environment in which it operates.

All this makes the role of an information professional more demanding. But also much, much more important.

DO WE NEED TARGETS? (ONE MORE TIME)

I will conclude this chapter by returning to the question that I posed a few pages ago. 'Do we need targets at all?' It should be clear by now that, while it is a simple question, the answer is not straightforward.

At its simplest a goal sets a boundary: a limit on acceptable variation of variables. These boundaries help guide decision-making, coordinate actions, constrain or encourage behaviour as well as acting as a reference point for assessing and interpreting performance. Organizations need boundaries, because without them they would not be organized. So, goals are necessary, but they are not inherently good or bad – it depends on how they are applied. Like any tool they can be used to do good or misused and cause damage.

Over recent years we have seen an increase in the use of 'hard' targets in business, partly because we have more data than ever before but also because they simplify the complex task of management, reducing it to a simple arithmetical operation. But the price of simplification has resulted in a simplistic approach to complex problems that has done enormous harm. I believe the way that goals have been used lies at the heart of many of the problems that plague businesses, particularly those that are too big to manage using informal networks and bonds.

Today we have too many arbitrary targets that are too tightly specified and locked into inflexible and bureaucratic planning processes. And the differences between targets and actuals are usually interpreted (and acted upon) in crude mechanistic ways. Good? 'Here's a pat on the back'. Bad? 'Change or else'. 'Just sort it – I don't want to know the details'. The grip that traditional target setting has on the corporate imagination means those things that cannot be easily measured and so cannot be targeted are neglected. And by linking incentives to those things that can be targeted they become the primary focus of management attention, often distorting collective behaviour in grotesque ways.

So, what has this got to do with performance reporting?

There is an old adage that goes: if the only tool that you have got is a hammer everything looks like a nail. I believe that the crude and limited manner in which we traditionally measure and analyse 'performance' has contributed to the rise of target-based management, and this needs to change.

A friend recently described to me a conversation he had with his boss following a new report on forecast error. Like many measures, forecast error is highly sensitive to context – particularly the level of volatility in the demand being forecast – so it is not straightforward to make sense of the numbers.

Boss: 'Thanks for the report – but I need a target for this'.
Friend: 'That doesn't make any sense'.
Boss: 'I know. But I need a target'.

Conversations like this take place all the time in every kind of organization. We know that what we currently do doesn't make sense, but we carry on doing it anyway because we don't have the wit or the courage to do anything different.

We must do better.

We need to focus less on points in time and more on trends. We must acknowledge the existence of noise. We have to adopt a statistical perspective on data and stop treating the simple arithmetical difference between two numbers as being potentially meaningful. We need to question the assumptions upon which goals are based and adopt a more sceptical stance rather than treating them as 'God given' and unquestionable. We need to include in our scope things that are not or cannot be targeted. We need to look at goals 'in the round', taking into account how they relate to and interact with each other. And we should help fight the corporate vice of setting targets to 'drive' performance, since there is a good chance that it will have exactly the opposite effect to that intended.

Put simply, goals should be an aid to judgement, not a substitute for it.

The fact of the matter is that the future is too uncertain to be able to define in advance what we need to do to succeed, and what that success looks like. All goal setting should be seen as no more than a necessary attempt to shape and guide the actions of the organization as it gropes its way forward. Simple mechanistic ways of targeting and measuring performance simply do not work in this environment.

We need the capability to generate more nuanced, thoughtful and useful evaluations of the state of organizational affairs. And we should acknowledge and reward the importance of sound judgement based on a rational assessment of evidence.

We don't need more SMART targets to help measure and manage performance. We just need to use targets in a smarter way.

Learning	Reason
How to continuously track actual performance against a moving target.	Using a tracking signal based on the ratio of the (smoothed) average net and absolute errors enables information professionals to determine the degree of confidence that the actual results are in line with a comparator, which need not be a fixed number.
What benefits accrue from the ability to continuously track performance.	The main benefits are that targets can be reset whenever necessary and not before. Performance cannot be 'gamed' around period ends and confidence limits enable performance to be scientifically categorized.
How targets shape organizational culture.	Culture is a product of what people perceive they are rewarded and punished for, which is powerfully influenced by the behaviour of senior management in setting targets, judging performance against and the system of incentives around targets.
How conventional fixed targets can make things worse.	Hitting 'local' targets can encourage people to do the wrong things – sub-optimizing the system – and make it more difficult to do what they know to be right, particularly when there are very many of them.
How we define a goal.	A goal is the desired value placed on any variable that is used to constrain or guide behaviour.
What points of reference goals could have.	Goals can be based on past performance of an organization (change goals) to the performance of peers (relative goals) or they can simply be based on judgement with no external point of reference.
How goals might be expressed with reference to time.	Goals can be anchored on a point in time or expressed as a rate of change over time.
What different ways there are for expressing the desired value of a variable.	A goal can be expressed as a single point value, a range, a minimum or maximum (threshold) or as a value to be optimized.
When a goal can be changed.	Goals can be perpetual, temporary or periodic.
What kind of aspiration the desired value of a goal represents.	A goal can represent a norm, a realistic aspiration or be set at a level that would require exceptional performance.

Level: What Does 'Good' Look Like?

Learning	Reason
How different goals relate to each other.	Organizational behaviour is shaped by a range of goals. The relative importance or purpose of differing goals may be specified in the form of a hierarchy or by default individuals may be left to make these judgements for themselves.
What role goals play in motivation.	Goals have been shown to motivate behaviour when the task in hand and individual needs are simple, for example, the requirement to provide the means to live. Research suggests that, once basic needs have been met, motivation comes not from hitting targets but from autonomy (the freedom to choose), mastery (the challenge associated with accomplishing a complex task) and the sense of work serving some higher purpose.
What role goals play in organizational performance.	Goals help shape and guide the collective behaviour of an organization as it navigates an uncertain world as well as acting as a point of reference to help direct attention to those things that are of potential significance for the survival and future prosperity of the organization. This requires a sophisticated and subtle approach to goal setting.

summary of part 2

What Have We Learned So Far?

> In which we reprise the argument for better tools in the service of a biologically inspired model of an organization and discuss how technology can and cannot help.

We have reached the half way point in this book. Thus far we have tackled the challenge of making sense of data. And I have introduced you to a new way of thinking about the process and some techniques to help you do a better job than you can with traditional variance analysis.

Before we move from the topic of 'sense' to that of 'present' where we tackle the communication of meaning, let's take a moment to reflect on what we have learned and perhaps speculate about what implications might be for the future. One of the few things we can be sure of is that technological advances of the last decade that have transformed our ability to capture and analyse data over the last few years will only accelerate.

The traditional methods of measuring and analysing data, which are now nearly a century old, rely almost exclusively on the simple arithmetical comparison of an actual and a target. This approach has the merit of being simple to understand and superficially it has an aura of rigour, but this is an illusion. It does not and cannot measure performance in a reliable way. As a result, decision makers are misled, and it promotes dysfunctional organizational behaviour.

This is because:

1. Single data points are infected by an unknown amount of noise and so are not a reliable measure of the true state of a system when taken in isolation.
2. Targets are always arbitrary to some extent and so only loosely related to the purpose of an organization.

Consequently, the difference between these two values at any one time is often meaningless. We therefore need to be highly circumspect in interpreting and acting upon the results.

Unfortunately, often this is not the case. The mechanistic approach of target–measure seems to offer a way of imposing order and direction in a complex and dynamic world, but it is a mirage. It is not simple; it is simplistic. It produces a distorted image of reality and so drives the wrong behaviours. Furthermore, all the benefits of this apparent simplicity fall to those who administer the system because it is easy to produce the numbers. It is the end user – the customer of the performance measurement process – who has to try and reconcile the often-irreconcilable demands of the market and the performance management system and suffer the consequences. Their difficulties are compounded by the stilted and ambiguous fashion in which information is presented – thin slices of the world served up in tables of numbers is an unnatural food for our brains, which have not evolved to consume them.

The current tools of the trade of information professionals are simply not fit for purpose. But this is not just because they are technically deficient – which they are. It is because they are a product of an impoverished way of thinking about organizations and the role of people within them.

Organizations are not machines operating in a controlled environment. And people are not cogs, whose role is simply to manage compliance to a predetermined plan. Organizations are complex, they operate in a fundamentally unpredictable environment and for them to succeed people need to exercise judgement in a rational way – to make sense of performance, make appropriate interventions and to provide guidance and leadership. To do this they need to shed their mechanistic mindsets and think holistically and organically.

And they need better tools.

The best kind of tools – the ones we need – do two things. They effectively accomplish the specific purpose for which they were designed and can do so efficiently because they are a good fit with our physiology. They feel like a natural extension of our bodies or our brains.

Think of a nutcracker. It fits neatly into the human hand and helps us extract nuts from their shells – usually undamaged. The combination of functionality and fit to a human being makes this a good tool. In contrast, traditional tools for analysing performance are like large rocks. They *can* be used to crack open data 'nuts', but they are difficult to use and often destroy the information held by the shell in the process.

The scale of data-processing challenges we now face amplifies the flaws of our current toolset. Target setting is not a process that can be automated. Most of the additional data we collect is noise, which we don't have the capability to filter out. Consequently, it is even more difficult to make sense of variances than is always has been.

As a result, most of the Big Data we now have is ignored because we do not have the capability to make sense of it. At the same time, there is more demand than ever before for our limited attention because of the march of Big Data across our personal, social mindscape. We are in desperate need of simpler and more direct ways of engaging our brains if we are to stand any chance of assimilating and making sense of performance information.

In Part 2 I set out an alternative approach to making sense of performance data so as to direct the attention of decision makers to those issues that may require an intervention – and away from those that can safely be ignored.

This involves analysing trend through time rather than focussing exclusively on arbitrary points in time such as financial year ends. The primary purpose of performance reporting is to determine the extent to which an organization, or part of one, is meeting its purpose. To do this we need to identify those variables that are germane to its purpose and continuously monitor the level and movement in the level of these critical variables in the context of the organization's need to survive and thrive.

There are many other benefits from shifting from a 'hit the number' to a trend-based approach. Averaging measures over time has the effect of dampening down noise that would otherwise muddy the performance waters. Particularly if it is used in conjunction with rate-based or relative goals, the need for periodic large-scale target-setting exercises is reduced and the ability to manipulate outcomes to hit period-end 'point' targets eliminated.

Most importantly, presenting dynamic information graphically, rather than in the tabular form associated with traditional variance analysis, keys into the brain's most powerful System 1 apparatus, which has been primed by evolution to pick up shapes and patterns and, especially, movement. Also, extrapolating trend information also helps us to predict future outcomes and correlations in trends unearth causal connections. Dynamic data is a very rich source of information, which is probably why our brains have grown to favour it.

The secondary role of performance reporting is to expose those otherwise hidden events or patterns of behaviour in variables that have a bearing on the future state of the system and its ability to achieve its purpose. In other words, to stimulate and guide interventions. In today's world of business this requires vast reserves of data to be prospected, mined and refined in order to unearth nuggets of diagnostic data. To succeed, you need to know where to look, based on a hypothesis of where the ore-bearing seams lie. Trend-based information sets a context that helps to prime our brain and frame the hypotheses that guide our enquiries. But you need to be able to sort through mounds of noisy data 'rubble' and focus on the nuggets that contain potentially actionable signals. Finally, the excavated ore needs to be refined by extracting and distilling meaning, so that the knowledge it holds can be safely acted upon.

This task cannot be completely delegated to a machine because a machine does not have the contextual knowledge of the organization, its purpose and how it works, required to guide the process and attribute meaning to the results. But we do need help to be able to tell the difference between noise and potentially meaningful signals because our System 1 brains are poorly equipped for this job.

It has a bias towards pattern seeking that evolved in data sparse environments and struggles to adjust to one where we are overwhelmed with sensory stimulation. As a result, we have a chronic tendency to 'see' things that aren't there. To compensate for this deficiency in our mental software we need to learn to think probabilistically and use tools and techniques that help filter out the vast majority of data that is simply meaningless noise. We need help to work out what it is safe to ignore, so that our capacity constrained System 2 brain can focus its attention on the right things.

Today we are all part of a huge experiment, in both a personal and professional capacity. For most of our existence, humans have received data directly from our senses and mostly processed it subconsciously. Evolution has programmed us to respond to this sensory data in very particular ways that are often not 'logical' in the strict sense of the word. Systematically captured, symbolically recorded data is mainly a phenomenon of the last century or so. And, until very recently, there was so little of it and it was so highly structured that we could process it in simple, well-defined ways. But the world is changing dramatically and rapidly. We now have so much data, from so many different sources, that our traditional procedures cannot be tamed. If we want to retain control, we need to change the way that we handle data. Instead of trying to *process* data in a mechanical way we need to *interact* with it.

We cannot put 'raw data' into one end of a mechanical process and hope somehow that in time something meaningful will emerge at the other end. Instead, nature has taught us that we need to start with hypotheses and continuously refine or reject them through an iterative process of questioning and acting – updating our understanding of the world as we engage with it.

What I am arguing for is a scientific approach to making sense of data. Science starts, not with a mindless trawl through mountains of data, but with an idea. A very specific form of idea – a hypothesis – informed by an understanding of context and by curiosity. Hypothesis creation is a creative act, of the sort that our System 1 brains excel in. But once a hypothesis is formed, System 2 kicks in, because the only way that we can distinguish between reality and a hallucination is rigorous logical testing against the world data. Some of the data needed to test and refine our hypotheses may already have been captured, but ultimately the only way that we will ever discover what we know is by taking action in the real world and observing what happens.

This is the scientific method, but it is also the way that our brains use sensory data to make sense of the world. As I've already said, I don't think this is a coincidence. This iterative process of hypothesis creation and testing is probably the only viable way of extracting meaning from a complex environment, which is why our brains have evolved in the way that they have.

To some readers, this cognitively inspired approach to making sense of business performance might sound idealistic or impractical. But I hope that over the last few chapters more readers will have been convinced that changing the way that we go about making sense of data is important and within the compass of most information practitioners – and with minimal investment. After all, a lot of what I have described is just 'common sense' because it is the way we conduct ourselves outside work. We just need to learn to do it in a different context, on a larger scale and in a professional and disciplined way. Although specialized software will undoubtedly help, everything I have described so far can be put into practice quickly, easily and cheaply with the tools that everyone has on their laptop. And although there are some statistics in the mix, there is nothing that should intimidate any numerically literate business person.

HOW TECHNOLOGY CAN HELP – AND WHY IT ISN'T *THE* SOLUTION

My sense is that the main thing we can learn from our brains is how to go about the process of making sense of the world. Technology can provide our brains with tools – prostheses that can amplify our strengths and compensate for our weakness. But some tech companies are making big investment bets on machine-learning technology using strategies, explicitly modelled on the functioning of our brains, with the stated aim of replacing human beings.

It is a sign of the pace at which technology is advancing that the conversation has moved from Big Data to Machine Learning in the time it has taken for me to write this book. Is 'cognitive computing' the precursor of a revolution in the ways that we use data in business that will lay waste to the jobs of millions of knowledge workers? Or is it another false dawn for AI? It is risky to make predictions as it is very early days for this kind of technology, but we cannot take our leave of the topic of sense-making without saying something about where AI is heading, particularly as most software vendors in the 'performance management' space feel obliged to include this as part of their offering.

If we put aside for one moment the question of how much of this capability is real and how much is hype, I think there are good reasons to be sceptical of the claims for AI. The reason for this is because we misunderstand what we mean by intelligence, and how computers can acquire it.

AI is the term originally coined to describe attempts some decades ago to equip computers with intelligence by coding them with decision-making rules. What software engineers soon discovered is that even the most apparently simple 'real-world' process, like recognizing an image, is far too complex to program in a conventional manner.

The recent revival of interest in this area is driven by the development of new mathematical approaches and the ease of access to large-scale computing platforms in the 'Cloud', which have enabled computers to by-pass the programming bottleneck by 'learning' for themselves.

But for so-called Machine Learning to work you need two things.

First, there has to be massive amounts of training data, which means that the learning environment needs to be well defined and for there to be enormous amounts of data available for the machine to be able to build its models. So, machines can master games like chess or Go or learn how to drive cars because the problem can be easily specified, and large quantities of data can either be captured (from cameras in cars) or generated (by a computer playing hundreds of thousands of games against itself).

But even when data is available the learning algorithms often need help – for example, they need to be shown over and over again images of plastic bags blowing in the wind and running dogs by human instructors before they can learn to tell the difference between them. Human beings, on the other hand, are excellent at generalizing knowledge (about how 'living things move' and 'the likelihood of plastic bags being blown about in this place and at this time'), which means that we can learn (some things at least) much more quickly and with much less – sometimes no – experience of a particular situation.

Also, most real-world performance management situations are complex, ambiguous, difficult to specify and if they have ever happened before there will almost certainly be little relevant data available to train a computer.

Second, the goal also needs to be capable of being specified clearly.

This is easy and obvious when it comes to games, but even in a well-defined real-world domain like driving a car this is surprisingly difficult. For example, telling a self-driving car to get you to the airport 'as quickly as possible' requires it not only to calculate the fastest route but also to make lots of sophisticated trade-off decisions between speed and safety, for instance. Look what happens in businesses when people believe that the only thing that matters is 'hitting the number' to get a sense of how 'good judgement' requires the ability to make sophisticated trade-off decisions between competing objectives.

And anyone who has a so-called 'smart speaker' in their home will soon come to appreciate how 'understanding' involves so much more than the ability to recognize the content of speech.

For example, I recently returned to my empty house to find, to my horror, my speaker playing Neil Diamond's greatest hits. I have no doubt that the speaker had heard noises that were a good approximation to the words 'Alexa, play Neil Diamond'. The fact that it is capable of recognizing commands in a natural language is an astonishing technological accomplishment, but this was a mistake that human beings with our puny brains would never make.

Why?

1. We know that human beings do not make zero noise for 24 hours and then request music to played – before going quiet again. At the very least we would expect to hear doors opening and closing and the sound of someone moving around.
2. We can recognize the voices of people we know live in the house.
3. Everyone who knows the most likely person to be in the house (me) knows that I would never ask for a Neil Diamond track.

What this demonstrates is how much our understanding of the world depends on a deep and subtle appreciation of context. Our hidden 'knowledge about the world' and what to expect helps us to distinguish effortlessly between what is normal (and so can be ignored) and what looks odd and so needs further investigation. We only have to see how difficult social situations are for people on the autistic spectrum to appreciate how important it is to have an intuitive sense of 'what to expect' in a particular unique situation when we engage with the world.

So it is with AI.

Although the processes by which the machines learn are enormously sophisticated, just like variance analysis they still rely on being able to specify (by being told or by learning with reinforcement) what 'normal' or 'good' looks like in advance. It takes the wet biological computer between our ears with the ability to make inferences from a wide range of sensory information and experientially derived 'theories of the world' to deal with novelty.

We can't delegate the task of making sense of the world to a machine. As Pedro Domingo says in his book *The Master Algorithm: How the Quest for the Ultimate Learning Machine Will Remake Our World*, our 'job in a world of intelligent machines is to keep making sure they do what you want, both at the input (setting the goals) and at the output (checking that you got what you asked for). If you don't, somebody else will.'

There is no doubt that Machine Learning will transform our world in ways that are impossible to predict right now. But in my view, they are unlikely to take over any process that is at all complex, any time soon.

Personally, I am lining up with the futurist Roy Amara who has argued that we tend to overestimate the effect of technology in the short run but underestimate it over the longer term. I think that the future will be very different, but perhaps not in the way that we currently assume. Ultimately, only time will tell.

There is one area of performance management where the future has already arrived in the form of software where an appreciation of the way that the brain works has been assimilated into the technology used to deliver information. What has come to be called 'data visualization' has made great strides over the last decade. Often this software is labelled 'data analytics' or 'BI', which conveys an aura of sophistication, but in practice it primarily aims to facilitate the process of generating visualization of data so that our brains can more easily assimilate it.

We need help to assimilate data to help make sense of data – what is called 'data discovery' in the jargon. But I believe data visualization has an equally important role to play in communicating these insights to the wider organization. Here I'm not talking about sophisticated graphical presentations of the sort that require specialized software and graphical design skills. My concern is with using this technology to facilitate what we now understand about our brain to design the interface between information professionals and their audience – what appears on a piece of paper or on a screen.

I'm as excited as the next person when I see a sexy new way of presenting data, but my sense is that this is less significant than the changes that have been made to the way that data is presented that we don't ever notice. Techniques that help us communicate information quickly, intuitively and with the maximum of fidelity, that is, without the intended message getting lost, overlooked or distorted. And I believe that these principles, which are a practical application of the science of perception, can and should be applied to all forms of performance reporting, even when we are just using 'old fashioned' paper.

Part 2 of this book has been about how to make sense. Part 3 is dedicated to explaining how best to *present* the insights once they have been uncovered. Clearly there is a strong link between the two. There is little point in uncovering insights if you are unable to communicate them effectively. But the connection is more profound than is immediately obvious.

As we discovered when we explored the idea of sense-making, I believe the key to successful communication involves understanding, respecting and exploiting the capabilities of our brain, particularly the power of our unconscious System 1 brain, which has been overlooked and undervalued for too long.

What Have We Learned So Far?

Learning	Reasons
How technology can enhance performance reporting.	Software tools can be used to amplify and exploit our brain's strengths and compensate for its weaknesses. The best ones are those that feel like a natural extension of ourselves.
Why Machine Learning will not replace human beings in the performance reporting process.	A machine can only 'learn' by direct experience in a situation where the goal and the boundaries of the system are well defined, often only with the help of human 'trainers'. Most situations that performance reporters are in are in some way unique, requiring an understanding of context and ability to assimilate data from many sources to be able to generalize from similar but unrelated situations in the past - skills that machines have not acquired.
Why 'insight' is not enough.	To perform their role, information professionals need to be able to communicate their insights, efficiently and effectively. Data visualization tools have a big role to play, provided we have the knowledge to exploit their capabilities.

part 3
Present:
The Art of Communicating by Visual Means

present

/ˈprɛz(ə)nt/
adjective

1. existing or occurring now

verb

2. show or offer (something) for others to scrutinize or consider

chapter 6

Communicating by Visual Means

> In which I explain how the brain interprets visual stimuli and how this underpins visual literacy. I also describe a process to help design reports that communicate performance more efficiently and effectively.

GRAPHICAL GRAMMAR

As I started to write this chapter of the book a news bulletin on the BBC caught my eye.

It said that California's Department of Motor Vehicles was due to meet to discuss a road accident involving a bus. 'At the time of the collision the car responsible for the accident was travelling at less than 2 mph, and the bus was travelling at about 15 mph. at the time of contact', according to the BBC. In mitigation the writers of the report argued that 'the car's movements were made more complex by the presence of sandbags on the road'.

Apart from the fact that the driver must have been pretty useless, your other thought might have been that it was a very slow news day for this to be broadcast on the BBC national news. The reason that it did was the author of the report was Google and the perpetrator of the accident was one of its driverless cars.

The newsreader could barely contain a smirk when he read out the last part of the news item:

> Google said it had now refined its self-driving algorithm: 'from now on, our cars will more deeply understand that buses (and other large vehicles) are less likely to yield to us than other types of vehicles'.

1. He writes: 'Encoded in the large, highly evolved sensory and motor portions of the human brain is a billion years of experience about the nature of the world and how to survive in it. The deliberate process we call reasoning is, I believe, the thinnest veneer of human thought, effective only because it is supported by this much older and much more powerful, though usually unconscious, sensorimotor knowledge. We are all prodigious Olympians in perceptual and motor areas, so good that we make the difficult look easy. Abstract thought, though, is a new trick, perhaps less than 100 thousand years old. We have not yet mastered it. It is not all that intrinsically difficult; it just seems so when we do it.'

Why was the newsreader so smug?

In Part 2 of this book I talked a lot about the limitations of our brains, and in particular our inability to understand even the simplest statistics without help. This story is an insight into the flip side of this narrative. While in some respects our brains are puny and rather pathetic, they do have a remarkable ability to process and make sense of visual information that dwarfs the collective efforts of some of the smartest coders on the planet who struggle to reach the proficiency of a baby.

Hence the snigger.

AI researchers have a name for this: it is called Moravec's paradox.[1]

So, we have this phenomenal ability. Great!

The problem is most of us in business roles don't know how to use it.

Let me illustrate what I mean. How do you react to this?

Ok - so the first part of this this book is about making sense of **data** in other words extracting **meening** and now this bit of the book starts with meening that has **no value** in itself and takles the proccess of how to transfer this meening to other people something we call **Communnication** and since we have already seen that making sense of data relys heavily upon **Visual Techniques** so should come as **no surprice** that Communnication similarly uses **Visual Devises** to achieve its ends!!!

I'm sure that you managed to make sense of this passage but only with some conscious effort. In particular, it is a struggle to work out where the full stops and other punctuation marks should have been and ignore the spelling mistakes and random emphasis in the text.

Some people are less tolerant of this kind of thing than I am. I once had a boss who was normally extremely polite and mild mannered but who could be guaranteed to react to misfunctioning written English like this in an almost comically extreme way. I know because I can sometimes be a careless writer. A single spelling mistake on a page, one that I wouldn't even notice, would trigger a stress reaction – blushing and sweating – that would render him incapable of reading the page until the mistake was corrected. Another of my friends has to walk out of a restaurant if they spot a grammatical error on a menu. And although I am much less fussy, even I would never employ anyone whose CV was written as badly.

The reason for our intolerance of poor written English is that we have all been taught to write 'correctly'.

But what does 'correct' mean?

It means understanding the meaning of words (semantics), how they are spelt, how they are organized (syntax) and how to use punctuation. Collectively these represent 'good grammar' and are a prerequisite for effective communication of meaning in writing – one of the two symbolic languages we are all taught (the other being numbers).

Now take a look at Figure 6.1.

Communicating by Visual Means

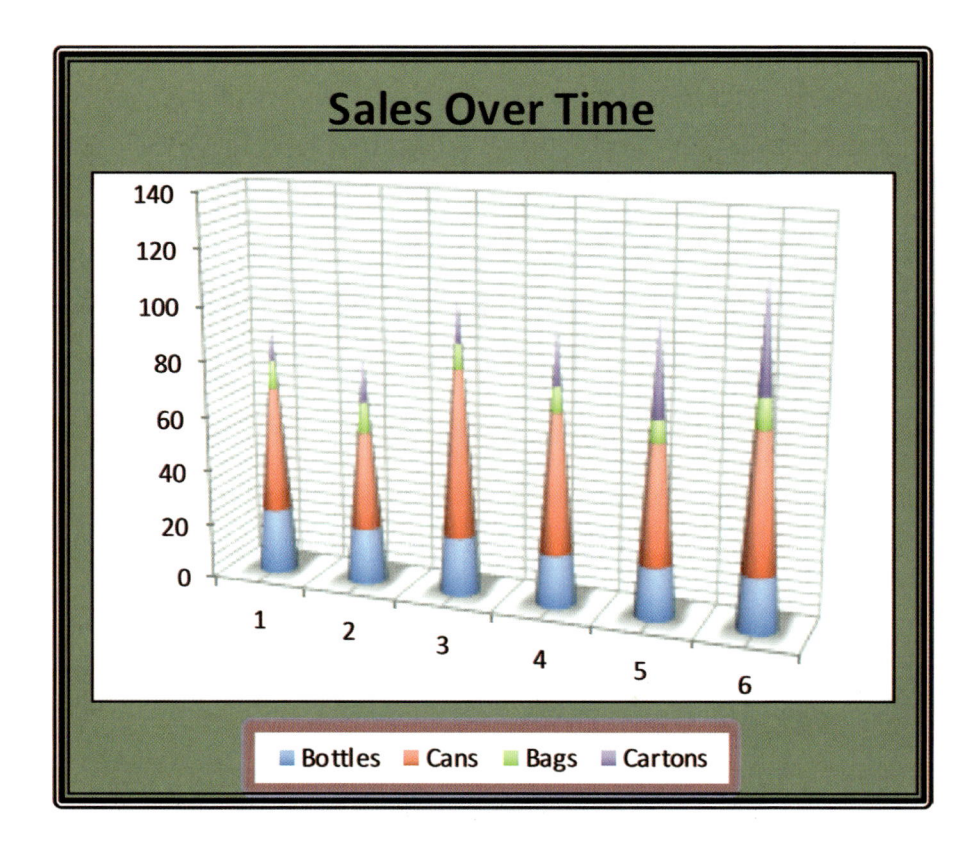

Figure 6.1:
Example of poor graphic design

This is an example of the sort used by Edward Tufte, the original guru in the field of the visual display of quantitative information and it illustrates what happens when people are not taught how to communicate well in a visual medium.

I'm sure that most of you will have an uncomfortable feeling that it doesn't 'look good' but, unlike the earlier sample text, few of you will be able to identify the specific 'mistakes' I made and so wouldn't be able to correct them.

The brutal truth is that, whereas everyone knows the rules of written communication, most people have very low standards of visual literacy, particularly in communicating quantitative information. Worse still, some of these people do this for a living!

This deficiency isn't a problem in many walks of life. Lawyers don't need to be worried about their lack of visual literacy. But information professionals will find it a crippling handicap.

If you are one of those people who struggles with graphs and charts, there is no need to feel guilty or inadequate. It's not your fault. The reason why you don't know is that you have never been taught or shown how. Which, when you consider what a large part of your job is concerned with communicating quantitative information, is shocking.

If you are thinking 'This is not for me' or 'I'm no good at art', I can reassure you. I have no artistic flair at all. My aim in Part 3 is not to turn you into some kind of Picasso, it is merely to raise your awareness of some of the most basic skills of visual presentation – the equivalent of punctuation and spelling – in a way that will enable you to quickly improve your ability to *communicate meaning*, almost overnight.

I've written this book, but you will have realized by now that I'm unlikely to win any literary awards for it. I don't need to be *that* good. I just need to be able to string sentences together in a way that you, the reader, can easily understand with minimal effort. So it is with visual communication. Basic literacy is good enough.

It is therefore with good reason (and not before time) that data visualization has become a 'hot topic' in business. It's great to be able to create presentations that are beautiful and eye-catching but I'm not concerned with aesthetics for their own sake. In my book, elegance always takes second place to the practical need to transfer knowledge.

Authors like Stephen Few have written graceful and insightful books on the topic and many software vendors boast of data visualization capabilities, but I'm not setting out to compete with these guys. If, after reading this book, you look Few's or Tufte's work up I will regard that as a win, as it means that you have come to recognize and value these skills.

My simple aim is to provide you with enough knowledge to enable you to critique and improve your own work using the tools that you already have at your disposal (such as Excel and PowerPoint), and in the process make you a more effective and well-rounded professional and a better-informed customer and buyer of software.

I think the comparison between written and visual literacy is a telling one, but there is one key difference between symbolic and graphical communication.

Although Noam Chomsky has argued that there is a common 'deep structure' in all languages, most of the surface structure of written or spoken language – spelling, punctuation and so on – is the product of agreed conventions that differ significantly between linguistic communities. Visual literacy, on the other hand, is less the result of societal norms than of how every human brain processes visual data in every culture and walk of life.

As a result, mastering how to communicate effectively using visualizations doesn't involve learning a set of arbitrary rules, such as whether the word 'pants' refers to over or undergarments, or when to use a semicolon rather than a full stop. Instead, it requires some appreciation of how brains process visual stimuli – your own and those of your audience. And as we discovered when we tackled analytical reasoning in Part 2, most of the struggles we have with traditional methods can be traced back to the operation of (System 1) mental processes that normally operate below the level of consciousness.

But once we understand what is going on – exactly how our brain processes visual information – it is a simple matter to redesign our methods to communicate complex and subtle concepts in a way that feels effortless to the audience! The result of sharing this knowledge is, I hope, not a prescriptive 'style book' but a heightened awareness – mindfulness – of how to communicate meaning effectively, in a way that exploits the processing power that nature has endowed us with.

COMMUNICATION

In Part 2 we tackled the issue of how to make sense of data by extracting meaning. Now we will set about understanding how to communicate this meaning effectively making extensive use of graphical methods. Together these two elements will help you better *Present Sense*. Both are founded on an understanding of how our brains interact with the world.

Over the last few paragraphs I have used words like 'data', 'information' and 'communication'. Because these words are part of everyday speech, you may have thought that you understood me, but in this book they have a precise meaning – and if you and I do not have a shared understanding of terms it is likely that I may have failed to communicate *my* meaning. As an author I am in the communication business and one of the prerequisites of effective communication – the transfer of meaning – is that the sender and the recipient have the same understanding of words, since words are the tools that I use to encode my message. As you and I cannot clarify my meaning, high-fidelity communication is only possible if you can decode what I have encoded using words.

Let's start with the word 'data'.

Data simply means 'facts' and, in the context of performance measurement, normally these are facts expressed in the form of numbers. These numbers record the value of a variable captured according to a defined measurement system. When these values are captured in sequence over time, they make up a data series.

Data itself has no meaning. Meaning is *read into* data by identifying patterns that are relevant to the purpose of the organization and its continued viability. And to be able to identify patterns we first need to structure or 'codify' it.[2] This is done using 'metadata'. **Metadata is data about data**, used to organize the data into categories, hierarchies and so on.

Meaning is extracted from codified data and expressed as 'information'. **Information is actionable insights**. The word itself confirms this: 'inform', 'a(c)tion'.

I think the distinction between data and information is critically important because we often use the word information very loosely to mean a collection of facts – like those that populate traditional variance analysis, for example. Facts themselves – data – are not information. For something like a number to be capable of being meaningful we need to know how it relates to other numbers, and this meaning must have the potential to be translated into action – to be capable of leading to a decision to do (or not do) something – before we can call it information.

Collecting and codifying data and extracting information from it is important, but it does not in itself create any benefit for the organization. To generate value, information has to be diffused – communicated to others – and it needs to be acted upon.

Information theorist Max Boisot called this four-step process the Social Learning Cycle:

2. One definition of Big Data is: data that has high volume, variety, velocity and variability, and the greater the variety and variability the more difficult it is to codify. For our purposes, however, we will put so-called 'unstructured data' to one side as it (currently) does not play a significant role in performance analysis, at least as yet.

1. Encode data.
2. Abstract information.
3. Communicate information.
4. Act on information.

Steps 1 and 2 create value potential, but this potential is only realized in steps 3 and 4. Thus far, we have focussed on step 2, how to extract meaning from encoded data. We will now turn to step 3, communication, which is simply the word we give to the process of transferring information between brains.

Many information professionals – myself in a previous life included – often act as if their job is done once they have finished analysing the data, and that if their audience doesn't 'get it' it is somehow their own fault. In my head – I am ashamed to admit – I branded them as 'stupid'.

This view is wrong, and it is arrogant. Communicating insights is just as important as generating them. If we fail to communicate what we have learned personally to people capable of acting on these insights, we have not added any value. I now realize that when I pumped out 'raw spreadsheets' or simple tables and called them 'reports', without any thought about how they were going to be consumed, I was only doing half a job.

We wouldn't give someone a pile of nuts and bolts and call it a car, so why do we think our spreadsheet calculations comprises a report?

'Communication' is a huge topic, so we need to narrow our focus a little. I want to concentrate on reporting, which while it could be dismissed as 'routine' is challenging because it involves understanding and communicating the behaviour of a complex, dynamic system – a whole organization – in near to 'real time'. Think of it doing the same job for an organization that a health-tracking app does for an athlete and her coach, providing a time ordered stream of mainly reassuring messages with an occasional 'alarm' identifying where there might be a problem or scope for improvement.

Although most of the things I will share can be applied to any form of visual communication, in this chapter I will not cover communication in the context of a 'deep dive' ad hoc analysis of data. Rather like medical diagnostic tests, this form of communication will vary in nature depending on the exact nature of the exploratory work required – the hypothesis being tested.

Figure 6.2:
Types of information

The key characteristics of the two main forms of performance communication.

	Communication	
	Reporting	**Analysis**
Frequency	Routine	Ad hoc
Form	Time Series	Context dependent
	Alerts	
Audience	Group	Personal/Group

Apart from its scope, the reporting process differs in another crucial aspect. Unlike analytic or feedback information, the audience for performance reporting is almost always a *group* of people who are required to act together in a collective manner. Performance reporting is embedded in a social process, which has implications for communicating information, as I discovered for myself recently.

In a parallel life to that of an author, I cofounded a business that provides forecasters with performance management. Our software helps them understand and analyse the quality of their forecasts and alerts them to problems with specific forecasts. When users access the system, they are directed to a dashboard that they customize to their needs. The dashboard summarizes the key performance variables for that part of the forecast process for which they are responsible and serves as a launchpad for detailed analysis and enquiry. So, the dashboard plays a reporting role and the rest of the system enables investigation to be carried out. Users spend most of their time in our system as it provides everything they need to inform and guide their own actions. But periodically they are required to contribute to meetings where representatives from different functions review plans for the business. As was mentioned briefly in Chapter 1, I discovered what this means for our software when I received a call from my key contact one day.

'Steve, how can I copy the bias graphs and tables from the dashboard into PowerPoint for the monthly demand review meeting?'

In response, I carefully and patiently explained how this could be done but encouraged him to use our application instead, because (in my mind) this is what it had been designed for. And after I put the phone down, I banged my head against the desk – the idiot! What is the point of having a sophisticated tool if you don't use it!

Later on, however, I realized that the real idiot was on my end of the phone.

What I had failed to appreciate was that the nature of the communication process in the review meeting was completely different to that for which our application was designed. A lesson that I think is sometimes lost on other designers of dashboard applications as well.

Our application had been developed to provide 'on demand' access to a wide variety of information in a way that catered for the needs of the individual. But many of the features that made it so useful to a forecaster in their everyday job were a positive handicap in the context of routine reporting to (part of) a group of people – the rest of the organization.

The demand review meeting comprised a group of people with a shared purpose but with varied perspectives and competencies, all of which were very different to that of the demand managers who we designed our application for. As a result, the information had to be carefully selected by demand managers and laid out in a way that would be consistently understood and interpreted by every member of the group. And in order to maintain cohesion and harmony within the group it was also important that they received exactly the same information at the same time. Cutting and pasting selected images from our application into PowerPoint slides and manually distributing 'hard copy' turned out to be a far more effective way of communicating to this audience than our performance analysis tool.

WHY PAPER (STILL) RULES

Perversely, the superiority of paper over 'sophisticated' IT tools like dashboards for supporting decision-making in businesses lies in the limitations of the medium of paper. Because it enables information professionals to control the messaging in a way that is not possible with more versatile media.

But I'm not arguing that paper is the best medium for communicating to groups of decision makers or that IT has no role to play. In fact, I believe there is enormous scope to improve the way that information is delivered and how decision makers interact with it.

The operations rooms used by the UK's RAF in the Second World War still set the standard for the effective delivery of information to decision makers. These were large rooms, buried deep underground, each responsible for directing and coordinating military activity in a defined 'theatre of operation' as part of a large network covering the whole country.

Decision makers typically stood in a gallery looking down on the action in the 'pit' where RAF personnel assembled relevant real-time information from a range of sources and presented it in large displays, using maps, models of aircraft and other easy to understand iconographic images and symbols carefully positioned in and around the room.

Because all the relevant information was on display, it was easy and quick to access the information needed to support whatever decision was under review. Operations rooms created an immersive environment in which groups of people were able to interact with information and with each other in a naturalistic way using a wide range of sensory input and almost all the available space.

Contrast this with the very personal view of a small two-dimensional screen or piece of paper that most decision makers in business have to work with today.

The military, and agencies such as NASA, routinely use IT-enabled operations rooms to manage operations. And it is interesting to see how the IT community has largely abandoned desks and meeting rooms, PowerPoint slides and Gannt charts for communicating within and between 'Agile' development teams. Instead they use 'stand-ups' in communal areas, walls that you can draw on, Post-it notes and other 'primitive' media.

But, as yet, very few businesses have gone down the route of using an immersive, multi-sensory environment for communicating performance, despite the advances in technology that could facilitate this, which is surprising.

Maybe virtual reality technologies will change this.

We will have to wait and see.

What this experience taught me is that, unlike many other forms of information, performance reports need to communicate meaning in a structured way. Information has to be carefully selected and tailored for a specific audience. Although the process of working out what to do based on performance reports is interactive, the process of communication itself should be carefully managed and largely one-way. While it is helpful to think of the process of uncovering meaning as a process of interaction with data, information professionals communicate not through dialogue but in a *broadcast*. As a result, the person producing a report needs to think and act like a journalist, simultaneously concerned with seeking meaning, crafting a message and working out how to best deliver it to their audience.

This doesn't mean that technology is irrelevant. Interactive dashboards and other analytical tools can play an important role in helping to *extract* meaning, in the way that we explored in Part 2, and there are many data visualization software tools on the market to support this. We can also use the insights of experts in dashboard design like Stephen Few to create more effective reports – as we shall soon discover – but there is no simple technological 'fix' that guarantees effectiveness, because judgement is crucial.

WHY THIS IS IMPORTANT

Before we dive into practicalities it is worth reflecting on what is at stake here.

Obviously, it is important that reports communicate their intended meaning effectively and efficiently. A shared perspective of reality is a prerequisite for purposeful collective action. But the role played by reporting is potentially more profound.

The latest theories of human consciousness suggest that our ability to recognize ourselves and our relationship to our environment is a product of interconnectivity in our brain – the ability to share, integrate and synchronize information generated by different cognitive systems.

When this connectivity in our brains breaks down, we lose consciousness. So – the theory goes – anaesthetic works, not by turning areas of the brain off but by supressing communication between them. The same thing happens to a less profound degree when we go to sleep. Our brains are still working when we sleep, and our autonomic systems continue to regulate the activity of physical systems such as the heart and lungs below the level of consciousness. We are still alive, but we are not aware of being alive. And we lose the capacity for voluntary action – to make choices and act upon them. We lose consciousness only to regain it again when the connections are restored as we 'reboot' in the morning.

I believe that 'reporting' and other processes that attribute meaning to data and share and integrate information from different perspectives help create a shared corporate consciousness. And by doing so they create an environment whereby individual components of the organizational system – its employees – can *self-organize* – come together to act in the interest of the whole without the need for detailed executive supervision.[3]

To fulfil the role of the creator of shared consciousness effectively we need to be able to communicate in 'high fidelity' – at speed and with the minimum loss of meaning. And to deliver this we need to learn how to effectively key into the perceptual system that we all share. The connection needs to be as direct as possible, so that the things we don't share, such as skills and experience, do not corrupt or distort the signal.

3. What is called 'situational awareness' is recognized by the military as being critically important in helping armies to maintain cohesiveness in the turbulent and uncertain environment of conflict zones. In his book *Team of Teams*, retired General Stanley McCrystal credits his ability to create 'shared consciousness' with their success in suppressing ISIS in Iraq; who had up to that point defied the might of the most technologically sophisticated armed force that the world had ever seen. He writes (my emphasis): 'the term "empowerment" gets thrown around a great deal in the management world, but the truth is that simply taking off constraints is a dangerous move. It should be done only if the recipients of newfound authority have *the necessary sense of perspective* to act on it wisely.'

So, to communicate effectively we need to understand how we – and most other human beings – 'see'.

Having set the scene, let's unpack the process of communication itself.

Figure 6.3:
Process of communication

In this context effective communication involves the faithful transmission of meaning, at the fastest speed consistent with the minimum distortion or loss of information. Note that this illustration oversimplifies somewhat, because in reality the audience are no more passive recipients than the information professional is when he or she interrogates data – they will be expected to attribute another layer of meaning to that which they receive. But, nevertheless, it is important that they start with a source of information that faithfully represents what the sender intended.

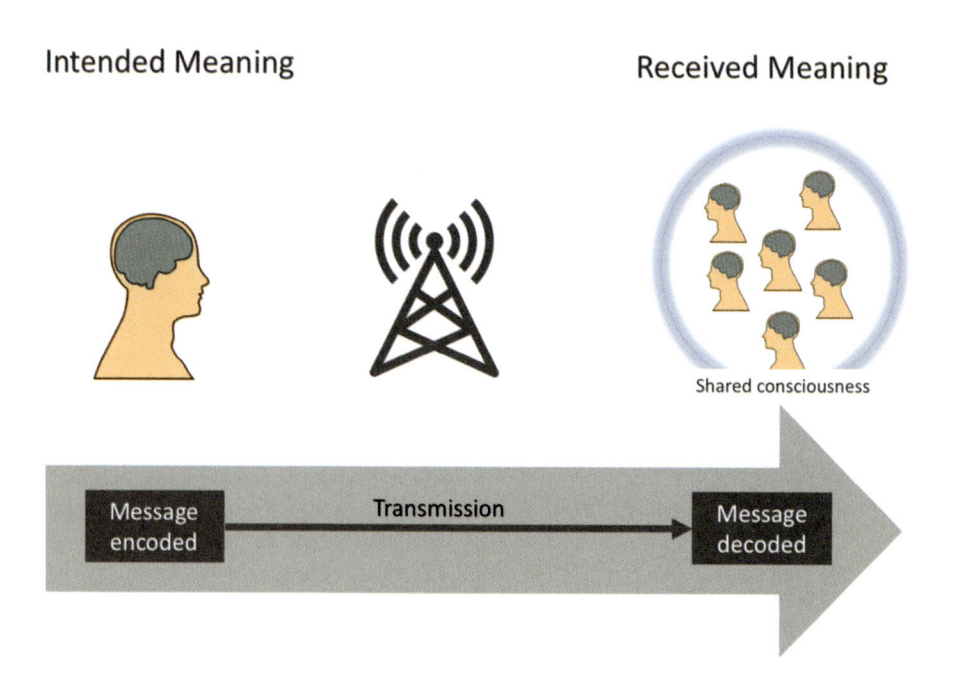

Communication, as Figure 6.3 shows, starts with an intended meaning, which is where Part 2 of this book left off. This meaning – the signal – is encoded in some form of language, transmitted and finally decoded by the target audience. When we communicate, our aim is to ensure that the signal is faithfully transferred from our brain to the brains of our audience, with minimal loss of meaning.

For me, it is best to start with the end. To understand how best to encode meaning, we need to understand how our brains decode a message. And given that our brains are dominated by the same visual circuitry we should focus on how to code messages using graphical means. Let's start by returning to the subject of how our brains work.

VISUAL THINKING PROCESSES

The term coding is most commonly applied to computer programming. Although it *is* a form of encoding, it is not the sort that interests us here. Our interest is in the process of transferring information (meaning) from our brain to a medium, of any sort. And decoding is the reverse – going from a medium into a brain.

Because we are taught to do it at school, we are familiar with encoding information symbolically by using words or numbers. As I write these sentences on my laptop I am encoding information. Words are good for encoding abstract concepts, but numbers are best for precisely encoding quantity, and in a way that enables it to be manipulated. But there are downsides to symbolic codes.

For communication to take place, senders and receivers must have a common set of coding rules – they need to use the same language. Ideally the sender's ability to encode should match the ability of the receiver to decode, but often the vocabulary of senders and receivers differ, particularly if the subject matter is technical.

Also, information that is encoded symbolically has to be transmitted sequentially to preserve its meaning, and this slows down the communication process. D–O–G has a different meaning to G–O–D – although my own pet West Highland White terrier doesn't seem to have received the message!

Numbers, however, can communicate quantities with great precision: but because it is not a language that our brains have evolved to use (beyond very simple numerical concepts such as, 'one', 'two' and 'many') there are enormous variations in the numerical literacy of audiences. This presents a particular problem for information professionals since we cannot be sure how the meaning that we have encoded in reports numerically will be 'read' by the recipients of those reports.

So, symbolic means have limitations. The other way that information can be encoded is visually – in the form of shapes, colours and so on. Visual coding of information is less precise and potentially more ambiguous than symbolic methods, but it does have one enormous benefit. Symbolic languages are relatively recent inventions; no more than a few thousand years old. Over many millions of years our brains have evolved into very sophisticated processors of visual information, for the simple reason that it was, and still is, critical to our survival.

I will take a lot of convincing before I hand over control of my car to Google; because the ability of our 3lb lump of nervous tissue sitting in our skull to make sense of visual signals dwarfs the mathematical sophistication that the world's largest companies can throw at it, now and in the conceivable future. Our eyes are home to 70% of our sense receptors, so it is no surprise that around half of our brain is given over to the processing of visual information – mostly below our level of consciousness. Our brains are essentially hugely sophisticated computers of visual data.

In Part 2 I referred to two different ways in which the brain can think.

'System 1' thinking is quick, powerful and works at an unconscious level to transform sensory input into something that we are capable of recognizing (literally 're-cognize'). As a result, we are able to deal with 'stuff' using our inherited or learned repertoire of mental routines, placing the very minimum burden on our limited attention. If our system of cognition fails, we make mistakes. And when we make mistakes, or fail to recognize something, our slower, logical, limited and conscious 'System 2' thinking system kicks in to resolve the problem.

I argued that we need to do a better job of using the power and speed of our System 1 processes to free up our System 2 brain to focus its limited but more flexible resources on defined subsets of data – where its peculiar strengths can be harnessed most effectively. In particular, because they stimulate and lock into our System 1 circuitry, graphical representations help us make sense of and communicate data more effectively than if the same data was represented using numbers alone.

Let me be clear. I am not advocating that we stop using numbers and words and use only pictures instead. Visual information processing will never completely replace symbolic methods, but we need to exploit our visual system's disproportionate share of the brain's resources if we are to extract meaning from the avalanche of data heading our way and communicate its meaning effectively and efficiently. Instead, we should use words and symbols to *supplement* visualizations; to do things that shapes alone cannot do like communicating context and (where necessary) precision in order to remove the ambiguity that is inherent in visual communication.

Up until now, we have talked about the workings of the brain at a conceptual level. But if we are to understand how to encode data visually precisely, we need to take a more forensic approach, at the visual equivalent of semantics and syntax. It is essential to understand something about how the brain processes visual stimulus at a detailed level to better understand and exploit its power. We have to understand how we 'see'.

HOW DO WE SEE?

We can think of 'seeing' as a four-stage process, as shown in Figure 6.4. Perception starts with our nervous system – specifically in this case our eyes – being stimulated. As I alluded to in an earlier chapter, sensing data is not the end of the matter – it is only the start. How sensation is translated into perception

Figure 6.4:
'Seeing' as a four-stage process

Perception can be thought of as a four-stage process: starting with (largely unconscious) sensation, content detection and pattern recognition, before being consciously processed in our visual working memory.

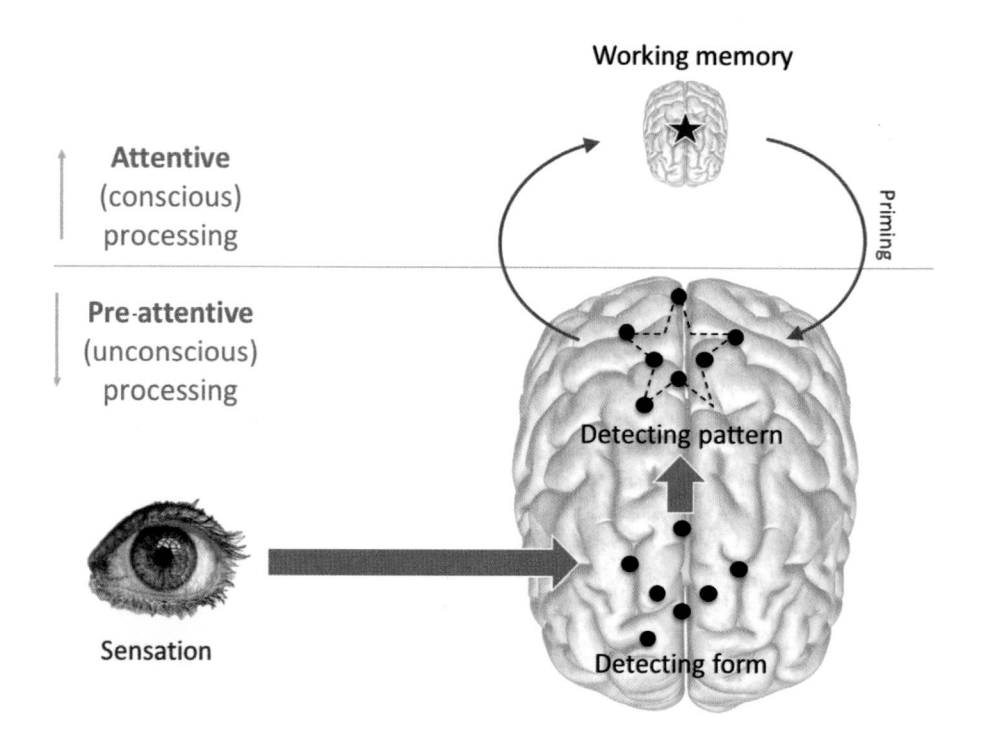

Communicating by Visual Means

is a fascinating process, which starts with the brain detecting content and then organizing it into patterns. All this takes place below our level of consciousness. It is only when it hits our working memory that we are able to consciously perceive the world. Let's work through each of the four steps in more detail.

Step 1 Sensation

Seeing starts with sensations that are triggered by photons hitting the back of our eye. These photons stimulate receptors that can only detect signals from the small part of the electromagnetic spectrum that we call visible light.

The receptors on our retina come in two types.

1. Cones, which are stimulated by what we call the colours red, green and blue. These are concentrated in the centre of the retina.
2. Rods, which can only differentiate between light and dark; but which are very sensitive to motion. (Having motion sensitive peripheral vision has obvious survival benefits.)

Our eyes may be a miracle of nature, but they have limitations that we need to recognize when we communicate visually.

One such limitation is our restricted ability to clearly differentiate between colours. Research suggests that, at best, we have a shared set of 12 colours that have agreed names and are far enough apart in colour 'space' for us to be able to use for encoding 'category' information.[4] But many of us can't even do that. For example, roughly 10% of men (but a smaller proportion of women) are red–green colour blind.[5]

In addition, although different colours stimulate our nervous system in different ways, colour cannot code for quantity. For example, green is clearly different to blue, but does it mean 'more' or 'less'? Our brain has no clue. It needs to be told that it has to translate colour into quantity by some other means (e.g. by using a legend) – which is a clumsy and slow way to communicate.

Because our brains have a very limited ability to sense and attribute meaning to colour, it is one of the *least useful* tools in our visual communication tool kit. Brightly coloured charts may excite our visual circuits, but they do a very bad job of communicating information – at least of the kind we are interested in.

Another limitation is a consequence of how our eyes collect data from the environment.

Sharp, detailed 20/20 colour vision is only available when light entering through the pupil is focussed on the area of our retina called the fovea, where the cones are packed most densely. But this comprises a very small part of our total visual field; an arc of roughly 1 to 2 degrees.[6] To get a sense of just how little visual data we capture in this way hold your arm out at arm's length – 1 degree is about the size of your thumbnail. Everything that we 'see' in detail is built up from 2-degree sized samples of the environment from eye movements called saccades. While our eyes move rapidly (around five times per second), what is clear is that there is thus

4. In reality colours don't exist: the electromagnetic spectrum is a continuum. We 'see' 7 colours in a rainbow because we have created that many named categories. In Russia they see 8 because they give different names to light blue and dark blue.

5. This is one reason why 'traffic light' systems of alerts need be used with caution – the other being that colours are interpreted through a cultural lens (red means 'happy' in China, for instance).

6. Research has proven that when we read text we can only see 10–15 characters at one time, the others on the page could just be a string of x's, and we wouldn't notice.

no way that the eye can gather precise data about everything in front of us. The stunning conclusion that scientists have come to is that, what we perceive – what we think we see – is largely *constructed by the brain* based on what it expects to see. The main job of visual perception is done by a 'generative model' in our brain. The role of our eyes is therefore simply to validate, flesh out and – only occasionally – refute the model of the world created by our brain.

Figure 6.5:
How our level of visual acuity varies across the retina of our eye

Our total visual field is about 180 degrees, but the sensitivity of our vision degrades very quickly away from the fovea – much more so in human beings than in other apes. So, 10 degrees away from the fovea our visual acuity declines ten-fold. The blind spot where the optical nerve enters the retina is about 15 times larger than the fovea, but we don't perceive this as a gap because our brain fills in the gap.

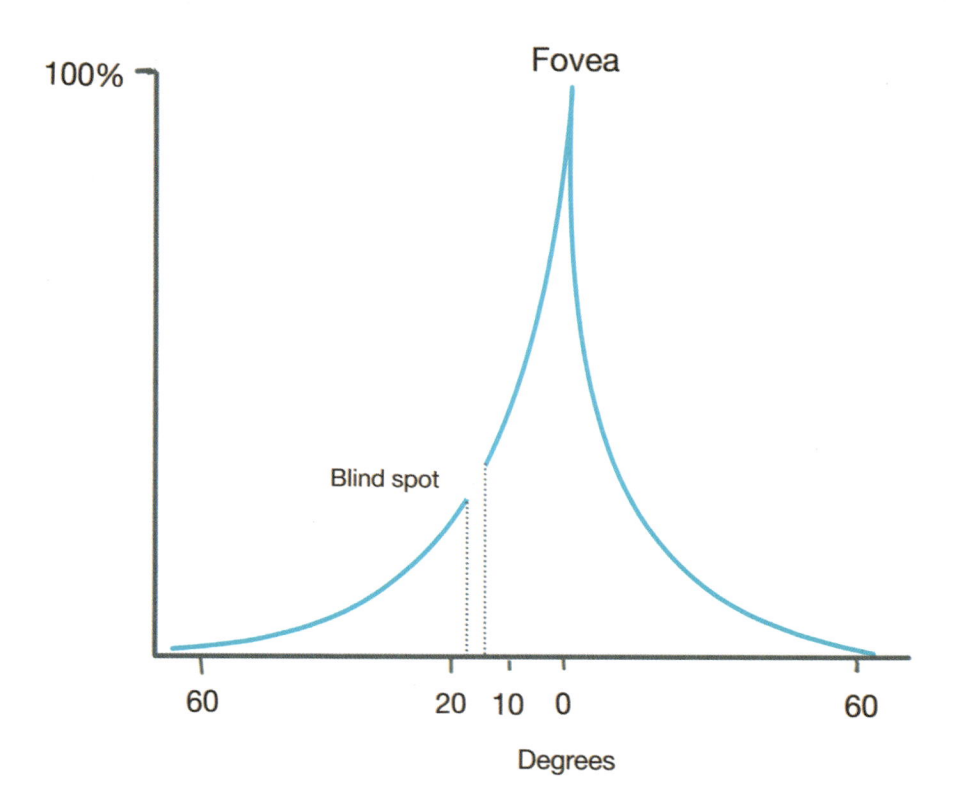

7. In writing this book I have come to realize that this is the reason why I have to leave at least a month between writing something and editing it. Any sooner and I see what I *thought* I had written rather than what I had *actually* written, so I miss what, to other people's eyes, are the most glaring typos. I literally become word blind.

This statement is so shocking it is worth repeating.

Although we think that what we perceive are rich full colour images across the entire visual field built up from data gathered by our eyes – in the form of photons hitting our retina – this is an illusion. Holding your thumb out at arm's length proves that this is literally impossible.

I'm sorry if you find this idea disturbing.

Get over it.[7]

Most of what we think we see is what we think we are going to see, based on our brain's hypothesis about the world. Our eyes help generate this hypothesis by providing cues for our brain, but after that their role is to test the brain's hypothesis by sampling the environment.

I hope this sounds familiar to you, because the strategy of rapid hypothesis generation and testing is exactly the same one that we use to make sense of data – that you met in Part 2. It seems that our brains never approach any phenomena with a blank slate – it is always populated with preconceptions (in the literal sense of the word) that our senses continuously test and refine. And when our

Communicating by Visual Means

mental models fail to satisfactorily explain the input from our senses (leading to a large number of prediction errors), our brain rejects them and searches round for something better.[8]

We are completely unaware of the limitations of this process (or extremely efficient high-speed detection process, depending on your point of view) but it is important to recognize its implications for designing reports (as well as for understanding how illusionists work!). Specifically, because of our eyes' narrow field of vision and their sampling role, it is important to provide our brains with the right cues (clues as to what you are trying to convey that trigger the right System 1 models) and concentrate the information that we want to communicate in as small an area as possible.

This is one reason why the 'one sheet of paper rule' works for communicating information.

Step 2 Detecting content

So, it is clear that most of the work of perception is done in the brain. Sensations – that is, data from the environment – play a supporting role by triggering associations in the brain and validating its interpretation of the world based on these models.

The second step in the process, which is entirely centred on the brain, involves the detection of 'content' or iconic features. Iconic features are the building blocks of visual perception, akin to the role that letters play in a language. At a higher level in our brain the distinction between perception[9] and cognition becomes blurred. But before sensory data gets there, it is processed by a special 'pre-attentive' system. This has its own 'rules', which we need to understand if we are going to do an effective job of feeding the brains of our audience.

According to Colin Ware, there are four basic types of visual 'content', which have different strengths and weaknesses when it comes to encoding information:

- **Colour.** This can be roughly divided into the qualities of hue and intensity. As we have already discussed, hue has limitations when it comes to encoding information. But intensity is more useful because it can communicate an impression of quantity. Probably because of our experience of dealing with concentrations in liquids, our brains naturally interpret dark as 'more' and lighter as 'less'.
- **Position.** Right and left can be used to encode time – if that is the convention used to prime the brain – up and down, which might encode larger or smaller. Even if we are restricted to a two-dimensional medium, we may also be able to make use of 'in front' and 'behind' to some degree.
- **Form.** We can use many kinds of shapes in isolation or in combination to encode information. Orientation, length, width, shape, size, marks and enclosure provide us with a rich set of 'letters' with which we can compose.
- **Motion.** The human brain is very sensitive to motion. However, our ability to exploit this directly is limited, given the abstract nature of what

8. This insight also informs the guiding principle of creating effective visualizations covered in the following pages: the elimination wherever possible of all graphical data (marks on a page) that is either distracting (noise) or irrelevant for the process of hypothesis creation or validation.

9. Not forgetting other sources of sensory data such as our ears (sound), skin (touch) and interoception (internal sensations).

we report on and the limitations of our technology; therefore, we will put this to one side for the moment.

Figure 6.6:
Types of iconic features

The building blocks of our (unconscious) perceptual system.

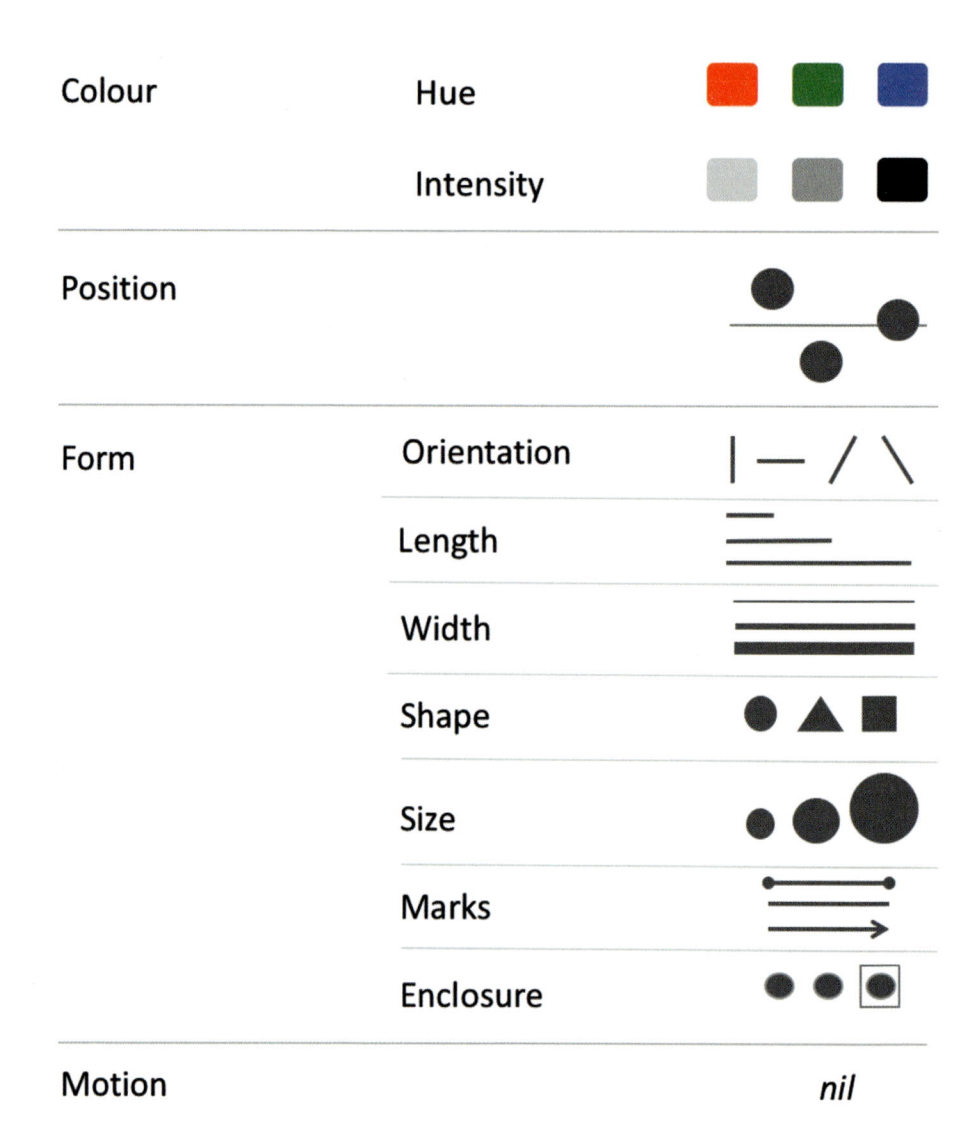

Colour	Hue	
	Intensity	
Position		
Form	Orientation	
	Length	
	Width	
	Shape	
	Size	
	Marks	
	Enclosure	
Motion		*nil*

Even having discarded hue and motion, what stands out for me from this analysis (Figure 6.6) is how many 'tools' we have at our disposal that we can use to stimulate our visual circuitry. Our challenge is to use them effectively.

Step 3 Pattern recognition
The third step in visual perception is pattern recognition.

When we dealt with signal detection in noisy environments in Part 2 we saw how. But our pattern hungry brain has us 'see' them in random noise – like faces in burnt toast – even when our rational brain 'knows' that these patterns are illusions.

It is difficult to overstate the importance of pattern recognition for animals like ourselves. It is what enables us to see camouflaged leopards lounging in the branches of a tree, and chairs and tables in a room rather than a collection of wood and plastic. This process is so quick and effective that the only time we are ever made aware of its existence is when it doesn't work.

Occasionally, like when we enter a poorly lit or unfamiliar environment, it might take a fraction of a second for us to identify and lock onto the features that help us work out where we are – but when we do 'snap', everything becomes clear in an instant. We don't slowly deduce where we are by assembling and analysing facts. We use a small amount of evidence to help us make a selection from a pre-existing library of archetypal objects. And we don't gradually assemble a montage of related objects to create this sense of place. Our pattern-seeking capabilities allow us to identify how iconic features (such as shapes, edges and colours) need to be grouped together to 'make an object' at lightning speed. This innate sense is so powerful that we are sometimes not capable of 'unseeing' the objects that we now recognize, even when we know that they are wrong.

Understanding the cues that trigger (correct) pattern seeking is critical to well-designed effective communication. Organizing these cues reduces the effort required to understand a piece of communication and the risk of misleading your audience. But when it is done really well, then everything becomes instantly obvious to the audience; to the extent that it is impossible to interpret things any other way.

Pattern recognition is a powerful tool but one that we need to learn how to use carefully. As we shall see, a very minor or subtle change in how the elements of a graphic are organized can make an enormous difference. The pattern-seeking process plays a similar role to grammatical rules in language. The cat sat on the mat pattern has a very different meaning to the mat sat on the cat. The structure of the phrase determines the meaning. In the same way, the organization of graphical objects in space suggests the nature of the relationship between them.

Fortunately, pattern seeking has long been the object of study, with many of the rules that our brains use having first been codified by the Gestalt School of psychology back in 1912 (Gestalt means 'pattern' in German). The rules describe how our brains see objects as linked, grouped or separated and how we can use them to design better charts and to organize them on a piece of paper or a screen.

According to Steve Few there are six Gestalt principles that are particularly useful to people building dashboards (and by extension reports). To us humans these might seem obvious but, because they are so familiar, we can forget that they are there, powerfully shaping the way that we perceive the world.

They are:

- **Proximity**: things spatially grouped together are perceptually grouped together.
- **Connectedness**: connections between objects can overrule other grouping principles.
- **Continuity**: smooth lines make connections easier to spot than angular ones.

- **Enclosure**: enclosed objects are grouped together.
- **Similarity**: similar objects are grouped together.
- **Closure**: a broken line is seen as an object and our brain tends to close gaps.

These Gestalt rules act like punctuation in a written language because they help us group related concepts. Unlike rules of punctuation, however, they are instinctive – we have inherited them from our genes – so we can be confident that something written using this 'language' will be understood in the same way by every recipient. There is no need to translate.[10]

The 'classical' Gestalt rules are, however, a small subset of the pattern-seeking rules used by our brain. For instance, our brains are tuned to recognize faces – new born babies don't have to be taught that the arrangement of eyes, nose and mouth in a particular way has a special significance. And we are predisposed to interpret the shape of objects based on their shadows – our brain assumes that the source of light is above an object – we don't have to learn it (Figure 6.8).

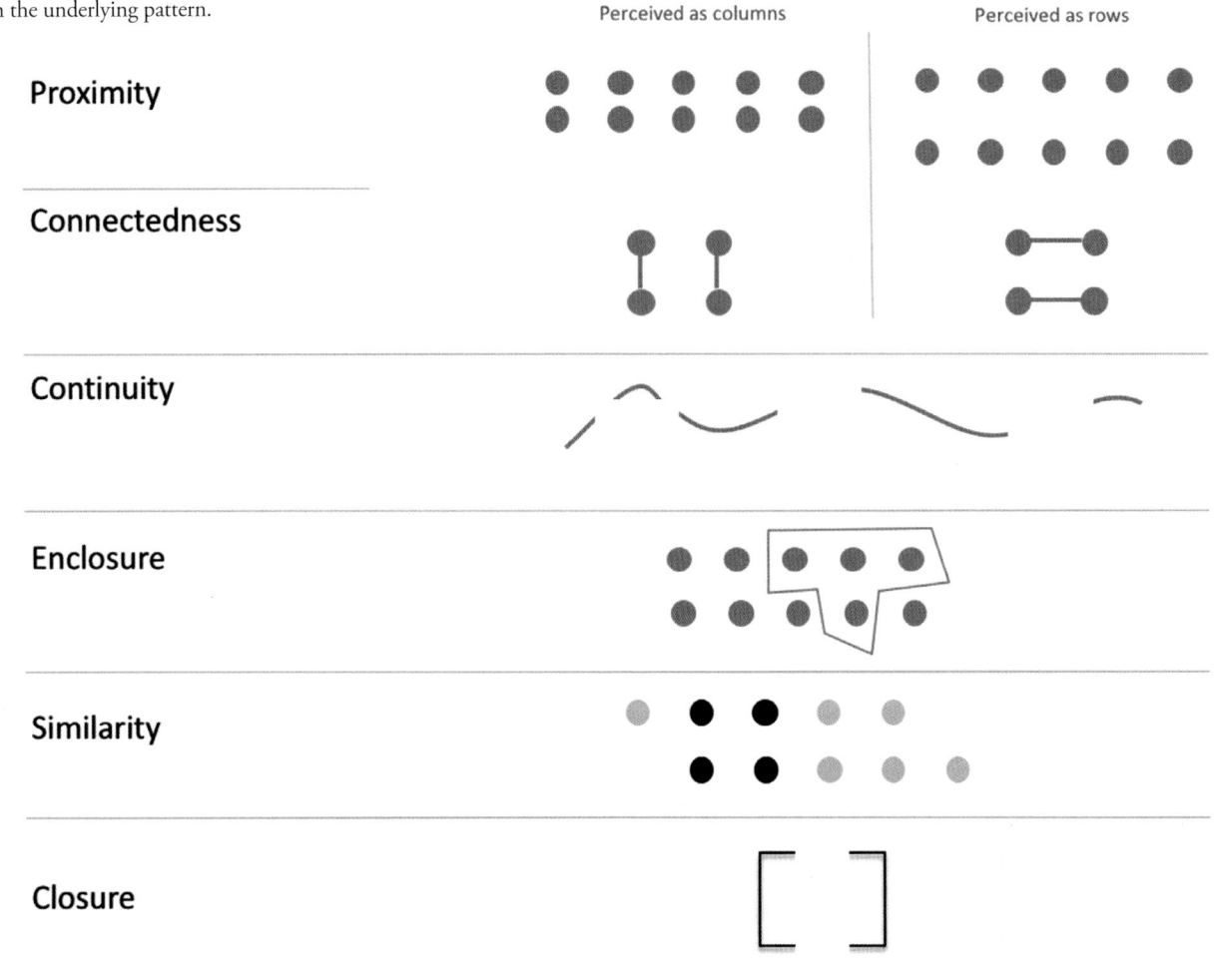

10. Lynne Truss wrote an unexpected bestselling book about grammar called *Eats Shoots and Leaves* (2003). In it she argued that a failure to apply the rules of grammar properly could leave a reader confused about whether the description applied to pandas or the actions of a gangster. In the same way, Gestalt principles (Figure 6.6) can be applied to enlighten or confuse. The difference lies in the skill of the writer or designer.

Figure 6.7:
Some Gestalt principles illustrated

Some examples of Gestalt principles in action.[11]

11. The power of Gestalt is illustrated by the fact that throughout this book I have created tables using only one horizontal line – that which helps you distinguish between column heading and their content. All other features of a table are created by the positioning of text and your brain's innate tendency to distinguish the underlying pattern.

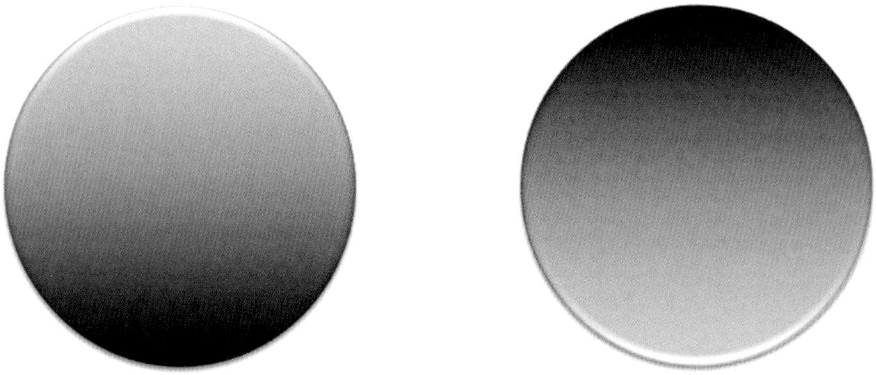

Communicating by Visual Means

Figure 6.8:
Button graphic

Because our brains have been programmed by evolution to expect light to come from above and for objects to cast a shadow, we see the first circle as a raised button and the second as a depression, despite the fact that the images are identical except that the second has been rotated through 180 degrees.

Although the basic rules we use to seek out patterns are unconscious and encoded in our genes, our subconscious brain can be primed by our conscious brain to recognize patterns that we have never encountered before in the world. In fact, you are experiencing this phenomenon right now.

Once you learn to read you acquire the ability to see patterns in squiggles on a piece of paper and attribute a meaning to them that is not inherent in the pattern. We do not 'see' letters – we 'hear' words and understand concepts. Once we have primed the brains of our audience – or, even better, exploited the way that they have already been primed in their everyday life – we can use this to craft much more effective communications.

A good example of how our visual systems can be primed are mapmakers. They have been training our subconscious pattern-seeking brain for centuries to recognize and ascribe meaning to abstract visual objects. What is no more than a collection of simple forms on a small two-dimensional surface can be used to communicate highly sophisticated understanding of a three-dimensional world.[12]

To be able to prime the brains of our audience, like mapmakers have done with theirs, we have to devise a set of graphical conventions that are aligned with our instincts but carry an extra level of meaning, and to apply them consistently. This brings us on to the fourth stage in the process of perception.

Step 4 Working memory

You are now aware that there is a lot of subtle and complex stuff involved in the process of perception, which we don't normally become conscious of 'seeing' until these organized sensations hit our brain's visual working memory. Everything up to this point is called 'pre-attentional', because it operates below our level of consciousness, just like our System 1 thinking system.

Neuroscientists believe that our visual working memory is distinct from, but closely coupled with, the verbal working memory where our logical (System 2) reasoning lives. Although it is separate to the logical central processing unit (CPU), it shares many similar characteristics; most notably it has a very limited capacity. In fact, it is even more puny than its verbal partner because it can only hold between three and five objects 'in memory' at one time. This means that we

[12]. There are signs that the advent of satellite navigation systems is eroding this capability in the young in particular. I know a few that are unable to 'read' maps at all. Without their phones, they easily become lost.

13. Computer engineers also struggle with small working memory. The pedestrian process of reading and writing to long-term memory (discs) is often the performance bottleneck, causing a phenomenon called 'thrashing'. This is why 'in memory' computing, *which* exploits the capacity of larger memory chips, is a trend currently sweeping the software industry.

need to be very careful about the level of demand we place on it if we want to communicate efficiently and effectively.

The 'objects' temporarily held in this tiny working memory trigger searches of the huge long-term memory for 'good matches'. Only when one is found can we literally *re-cognize* the object. When this happens the 'image' stored in the long-term memory as a pattern of neuronal connections is updated. This primes our pattern-seeking perceptual system in a process we call 'learning'.

Because its capacity is so limited, it is important that we learn how to use the visual working memory effectively.[13] One strategy our brain uses is 'chunking'. For example, we need to group visual data into more complex shapes – that is, chunks – that 'take up less space'. This has implications for use because we can exploit the priming process so that complex images are seen as a single object, rather than many. This helps to accelerate the process of perception and make it less effortful.

For example, the images in Figure 6.9 are made up of a number of simple shapes – circles, squares and triangles. However, our brain has been primed by prior experience to perceive them as a single shape.

Figure 6.9:
How 'chunking' graphical data works

What we see as two shapes are simply a combination of circles, triangles and squares that our brain has 'chunked' together and interpreted (with reference to 'archetypes' stored and recognized (by our brain) as a cat and dog respectively.

That's enough of the theory for now. Let's get down to business.

DESIGNING REPORTS FOR BRAINS – THE BASICS

Understanding the way our brain processes visual information gives us a handle on the things we need to do to communicate meaning efficiently and effectively by visual means. We can use this knowledge to define a set of design principles that are grounded in good science and easy to put into practice in a step-by-step fashion. I guarantee that once you have mastered this you will not need fancy data visualization software or any design flair to do a 'good enough' job.

Before I set out my recommended step-by-step process, let's lay out the design principles that inform it: a set of 'dos' and 'don'ts', with examples, based on our understanding of the science of perception that I have just described. I will group these using the same four headings.

Communicating by Visual Means

Sensation

COMPRESSION

DO compress information into as small a space as possible, to avoid the eye having to travel long distances and to lighten the load on our working memory (Figure 6.10). In practice this means using small objects and a small amount of 'real estate' – like a single sheet of paper – to display information.

GROUPING

DO group related items together to make best use of the highly constrained capacity of our working memory. It is obvious perhaps, but at least now you know why!

Figure 6.10:
The value of compression

Using a large chart (showing margins for the month of January) above detracts from its value as the eye has to jump around to take everything in. The same chart (lower panel, top left), if anything, works better when it is compressed, as the eye can take everything in at once. When it is presented next to margins for the year, the eye is drawn to compare the different patterns made by the bars, which helps the audience interpret the January numbers.

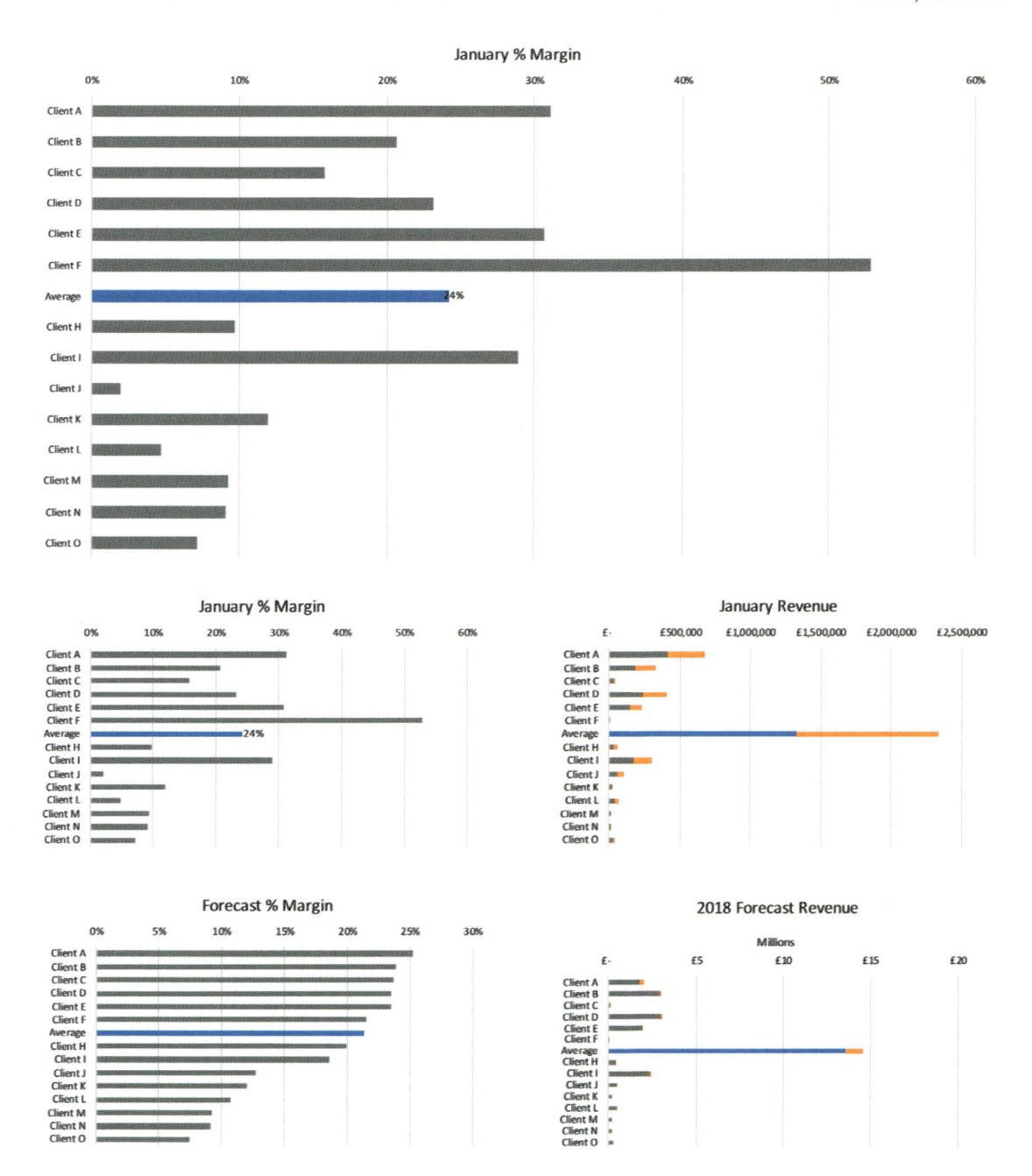

Features

Performance reporting requires us to broadcast a consistent message using a static medium, so we cannot use motion directly to encode our information. How do we make best use of the rest of our iconic toolkit?

Let's take a look at the type of information that we need to encode. We need to be able to represent five different characteristics of variables in performance reports:

1. The value of a variable or group of variables.
2. The movement of the value over time.
3. Categories of variables.
4. Their size.
5. Their significance (e.g. abnormal/normal).

Each characteristic is best encoded in different ways.

VALUE

- DO use position relative to something else, such as an axis or the value of other variables, to graphically represent the value of a variable (Figure 6.11).
- DO supplement position with a numerical value if precision is important.
- DON'T use three-dimensional charts. They should be banned for routine performance because representing objects in three-dimensional space is less precise, adds little information and can obscure other information (e.g. a data point on a representation of a plane can be hidden behind a 'hill').
- DON'T use colour to encode value, because the brain does not recognize that hue (colour) has a sequence.
- BEWARE when using intensity (shading) to convey relative value. Only use shading in this way when precision is not required, and you have five or fewer categories (because of the constraints of the visual working memory).

Figure 6.11:
Value of a variable

The simple unadorned bars on the left convey the impression of relative size well. Discrete axes and numbers give different levels of precision without compromising this effect.

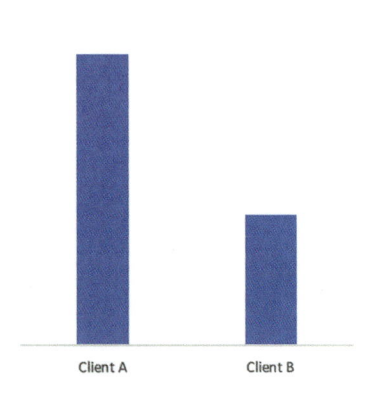

Communicating by Visual Means

MOVEMENT

In Part 2 of this book, I argued that movement is a critical neglected dimension of performance. This is where visual methods of communication come into their own. Although we cannot use movement directly[14], we can use lines to suggest motion, because our brains already 'understand' the idea of a trajectory (Figure 6.12).

- DO use lines in combination with orientation to encode for change over time. Sometimes marks (such as arrows) can help as well.
- DO use line markers (which is a position added to a line) if you need to be more precise about the value of a data point. If absolute values are important, you can use functionality like Excel data labels; but be sparing so as not to confuse the picture (they can be individually edited or deleted if required).
- BEWARE when using collections of shapes, such as bars, to represent movement over time. The jumps that the eye has to make when 'reading' bars can destroy the effect of continuity and flow and this makes it more difficult for the brain to detect changes in direction.
- DO use bars to signal a qualitative difference between different variables plotted on the same chart, or to help the eye separately track them.
- DON'T use smoothed lines to plot data that has been built up from discrete data points as it creates a misleading impression.

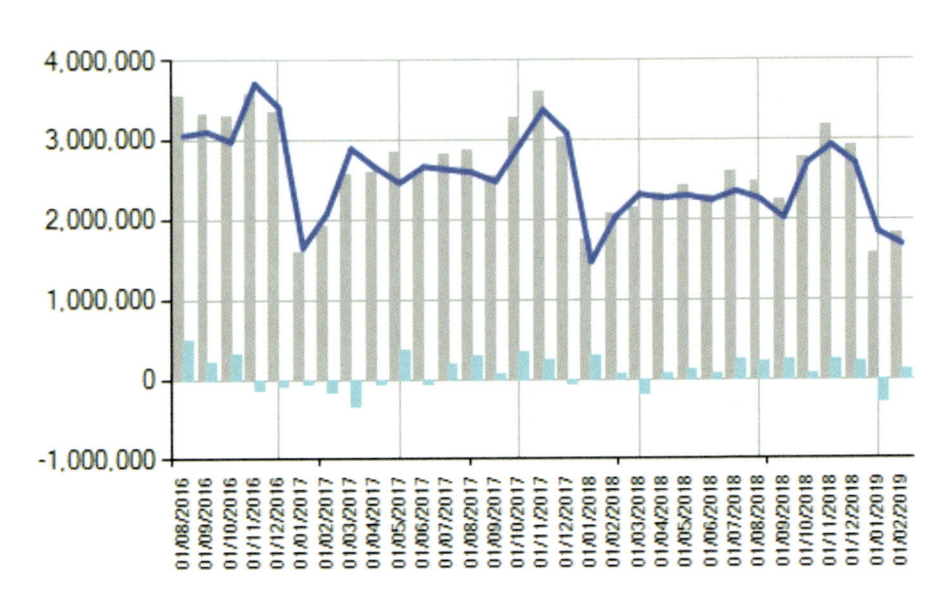

14. In fact, technically our eyes don't *see* movement directly. As we have discussed our eyes focus jumps around from one saccade to the next. Movement is what our brain infers from the change in position of an object over time. Arguably then a line representing a trajectory is no more 'artificial' than the 'movement' that we think we see.

Figure 6.12:
Different ways of encoding for movement

In this chart, copied from our forecast performance software application, sales are shown as an unbroken line since the phenomena is continuous – we only use monthly buckets to measure them. Notice how clearly this shows the periodic peaks and troughs in demand. Monthly forecasts (and the resulting errors) are qualitatively different as they are produced in monthly buckets and so are encoded using bars. Also, in this analysis we are not interested in the shape of the forecast, just how closely it captures actual demand, so nothing is lost by using bars rather than a line. Note that the pattern of errors does not follow the pattern of demand. Therefore, seasonality in the demand data is being captured by the forecast, but not the level, as most of the blue bars are above the X axis.

CATEGORIES

There are three ways in which category information can be encoded visually: colour, shape and enclosure (Figure 6.13).

- DON'T use any more than five colours or shapes to encode categories. Using more than five requires us to constantly refer to a legend,

Figure 6.13:
Encoding for categories

As the chart on the left demonstrates, trying to encode more than five categories using visualizations generates a great cognitive load. Either artificially compress the number of categories (in the chart) or use tables if all the category information is required.

because of the limitations of our working memory, which is slow and ineffective.

- DON'T use enclosure to encode for categories, because it provides only two options: in or out. It is possible to nest enclosures (such as a small box inside a large box) but beyond two nested shapes it gets difficult for the brain to keep track of the relationships.
- DO use tables rather than graphics when you need to encode more than five categories.

Sales by Client		
Client A	£	400,631
Client B	£	180,583
Client C	£	25,650
Client D	£	227,179
Client E	£	137,800
Client F	£	700
Client H	£	31,170
Client I	£	172,066
Client J	£	52,044
Client K	£	16,330
Client L	£	38,425
Client M	£	9,180
Client N	£	11,880
Client O	£	25,702
		£1,329,339

SIZE

There are two ways that you can represent size graphically: by the size of a shape (usually a circle or a rectangle) or the width of a line (Figure 6.14).

Figure 6.14:
Using shapes to represent size

The brain finds it easy to deduce the relative size of variables when squares and lines are used as in the chart on the left, but not circles in the pie chart on the right.

- DO use the width of lines, rectangles or circles to encode for relative size. Use numbers if precise distinctions are required.
- DON'T use pie charts for performance reporting. The brain finds it particularly difficult to estimate the area of circles and segments of circles, because it takes its cue from the vertical and horizontal directions and doesn't understand the concept of pi (no pun intended).

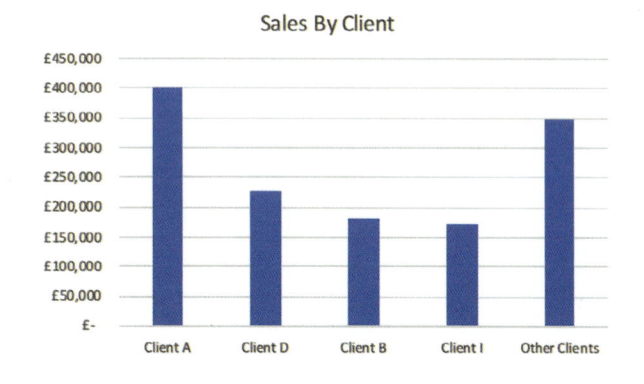

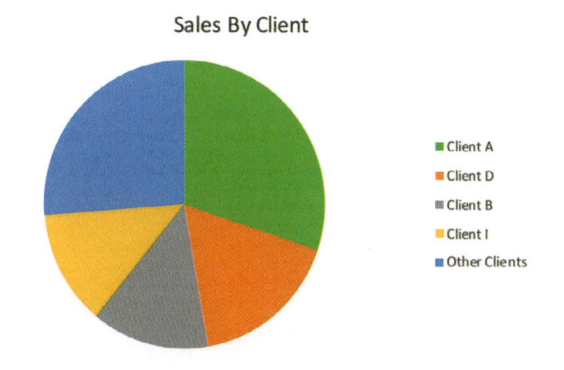

Communicating by Visual Means

SIGNIFICANCE

One of the qualities of a good report is that it quickly focusses our attention on the most important things. The most important distinction is between the marks on paper (or a screen) that encode information, which is where we want to direct attention, and those marks that don't. These 'non-coding' marks could provide useful contextual information, or they might be distracting 'junk'. We may also want to focus attention on particular variables.

The most common way to attribute significance is by using colour. But remember that there are two dimensions to colour: hue and intensity.

- BEWARE when using colour (hue). It can be problematic because of the incidence of colour blindness variation in the cultural meaning attributed to different colours.
- DO use intensity. It is by far the most effective way of highlighting significant attributes.

For our brain, intensity is a relative rather than an absolute phenomenon. What we 'see' is determined by the intensity of the object compared to the intensity of the background to the object. As a result:

- DO use high intensity to draw attention to information and its significance.
- DO use low-intensity background colours, such as white or black, to help these distinctions stand out.

I cannot over emphasize this point. If there is only one thing that you take away from this chapter, it should be that you must not spare the use of 'nothingness' in your reports. In particular the use of white in the background and low-intensity, neutral colours for 'marks' that don't code for information (such as title, axes etc.). This is why Edward Tufte, the statistical communication guru, advocates maximizing the 'data to ink' ratio. Neutral colours generate less visual noise, that would otherwise distract the brain, and as a result distinction between different elements of coded information are clear and things of special significance become more prominent.

And this doesn't just apply to graphical communication.

For example, compare this

As you can see from this paragraph, it is very important to ensure that there is enough **white space** surrounding the object that I want my brain to take notice of. If there isn't, then my brain has to work much harder to decipher the message. So, **what isn't imprinted on the surface of a piece of paper is just as important as what is.**

with this

As you can see from this paragraph, it is very important to ensure that there is enough **white space** surrounding the object that I want my brain to take notice of. If there isn't, then my brain has to work much harder to decipher the message. So, **what isn't imprinted on the surface of a piece of paper is just as important as what is.**

As these examples show, when it comes to communication, 'less is more'.

But it is not enough to use *any* restrained colour in the background. We need to use the *same* background colour consistently throughout, so we don't distort our perception of the foreground.

This is due to a feature of our perception called 'colour constancy', whereby our brain 'allows' for changes in the background. This is why yellow appears yellow in full sunlight and in shade, but it can distort our perception in artificial circumstances.

For example, in Figure 6.15 the two smaller grey squares in the centre of the larger ones are exactly the same colour. But the one on the left looks darker because it is placed on a lighter background.

Figure 6.15:
The impact of context on the perception of colour

The grey inner square is the same in both shapes but the dark background on the right makes it appear lighter to our eyes.

- DO use the same low-intensity background colour throughout the report.

We need to be particularly restrained in our use of high-intensity colour (Figures 6.16 and 6.17). As any adult that has walked around a toy store knows, using lots of saturated bright colours attracts our attention – to the point of migraine in my case!

- DO use unsaturated 'washed' colours to avoid overstimulating the brain.
- DO choose colour palettes that are properly calibrated. Pick colours with different intensities to direct attention, but not when the encoding needs to be neutral – for example, when it is used to encode category information. Certain colours go naturally together and enable us to encode without biasing our attention. Because they are visually neutral, we can easily switch our attention between them.

Communicating by Visual Means

- BEWARE how the background affects our perception of shade and colour. In our day-to-day life our ability to compensate for different light conditions is useful, since it means that yellow always looks yellow – it doesn't look brown when the light is dim. This can cause us problems when we use colour for encoding information because the same colour or shade in the foreground will look different if we use different backgrounds.
- DON'T use an image such as a photograph as background under any circumstances. This is detracting for our brain and plays havoc with our mental colour calibration processes.

(Top) Figure 6.16:
Hue and Intensity

Notice how the lower row of colours biases our attention and overstimulates our senses because of the different levels of intensity. The upper row uses the same hue, but the intensities have been adjusted so that no one tile stands out from the others.

(Bottom) Figure 6.17:
Intensity and making distinctions

Notice how in the upper row, because the intensity has been equalized, a clear distinction between pairs of tiles can be made with very subtle variations in hue and the highlighted tile clearly stands out. Contrast this with the lower row of saturated colours where the tile highlighted using the black border is not so clearly differentiated from its peers.

Pattern

Pattern recognition sits at the core of our brain's sense-making process, so it is crucial that we learn how to exploit it properly. We need to harness its power to communicate complex messages quickly and efficiently; and we need to eliminate anything that might trigger it unintentionally. This has many implications for the way that we encode information, but I will focus on a handful that I will call the five Cs:

1. Clarity.
2. Categories.
3. Comparisons.
4. Consistency.
5. Common language.

Clarity

The first, and most important, implication is that the patterns that encode information should be clear.

- DO emphasize the things that matter (information), and ruthlessly *eliminate or reduce distinctions that don't matter*, as these merely serve to distract the brain. We must pay as much attention to the background of our visual display as the foreground. Increase what Tufte calls the data to ink ratio; that is, the proportion of ink that contains information.

Some 'non-information' ink – Tufte calls it 'chart junk' – can't be eliminated because it provides the necessary context. For example, graph axes are needed if it is important to convey a value, and clear titles are essential. But a lot of stuff that appears on or in graphics does nothing except distract and confuse our brains and should be removed (Figure 6.18).

When I first applied this principle to my own software application, I was shocked to discover how many useless lines could be eliminated and pleasantly surprised by the impact it made. Out went borders and coloured backgrounds, most gridlines and lots of text.

Even more surprising was the impact that a series of other small and apparently trivial changes had. They dramatically improved the look and feel of the product without loss of meaning.

Users were quick to appreciate the difference. They described the new interface as 'clear' and 'clean'.

In contrast, our system had previously been described as 'old fashioned'. This shows how far the principles of good design have been taken up by software vendors and why many other people in the communication business – including information professionals – need to raise their game.

Figure 6.18:
Chart Junk

Chart junk – superfluous lines and fills – have been removed from the left-hand chart and context has been added to the one on the right. Note how much 'cleaner' and easier to interpret it is once the clutter has been removed and useful text added.

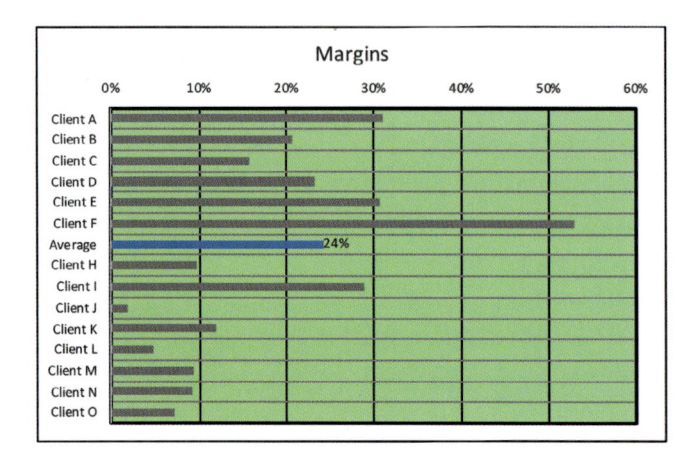

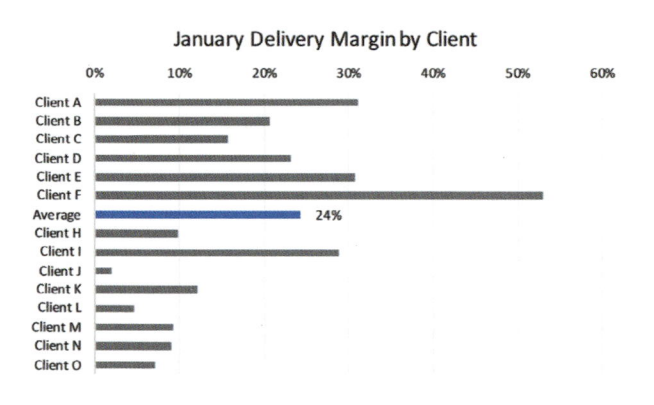

CATEGORIES

We have already seen how poor some visual methods are at encoding category information compared to others.

Communicating by Visual Means

- DO apply Gestalt principles to help differentiate between 'objects', rather than colour, for instance, which our brains find it more difficult to deal with.

This principle doesn't just apply to graphics. It is also important in the design of tables. For example, if we want users to read across rows, they need to be clearly differentiated from each other, ideally using white space. Similarly, if we want to encourage our audience to pay more attention to information in columns the gaps between them need to be bigger than the gaps between rows (Figure 6.19).

Figure 6.19:
Using white space in tables

Note how it is difficult to read these tables when rows and columns are either too tightly or widely spaced (top left and bottom right). In contrast, wide columns make it easy for your eyes to read down (top right), and wide rows guide your eyes along (bottom left).

Narrow Columns

Narrow Rows

Month	Sales	Cost of	Gross Profit	MA	Admin Costs	Profit
Jan-18	81.1	41.6	39.4	10.6	10.6	18.2
Feb-18	73.8	41.7	32.1	10.5	9.9	11.8
Mar-18	72.6	38.4	34.2	13.8	11.4	9.0
Apr-18	89.9	49.1	40.8	14.3	(3.0)	29.4
May-18	67.8	37.9	29.9	10.3	10.2	9.4
Jun-18	71.6	38.5	33.1	10.6	11.3	11.1
Jul-18	82.3	45.8	36.5	12.8	12.3	11.4
Aug-18	78.5	40.6	37.9	8.6	11.6	17.6
Sep-18	81.2	41.6	39.5	13.2	9.5	16.8
Oct-18	91.6	50.1	41.5	13.6	14.5	13.4
Nov-18	76.7	40.8	35.9	13.0	13.2	9.7
Dec-18	76.8	40.1	36.7	9.8	11.7	15.1

Wide Columns

Month	Sales	Cost of Sales	Gross Profit	MA	Admin Costs	Profit
Jan-18	81.1	41.6	39.4	10.6	10.6	18.2
Feb-18	73.8	41.7	32.1	10.5	9.9	11.8
Mar-18	72.6	38.4	34.2	13.8	11.4	9.0
Apr-18	89.9	49.1	40.8	14.3	(3.0)	29.4
May-18	67.8	37.9	29.9	10.3	10.2	9.4
Jun-18	71.6	38.5	33.1	10.6	11.3	11.1
Jul-18	82.3	45.8	36.5	12.8	12.3	11.4
Aug-18	78.5	40.6	37.9	8.6	11.6	17.6
Sep-18	81.2	41.6	39.5	13.2	9.5	16.8
Oct-18	91.6	50.1	41.5	13.6	14.5	13.4
Nov-18	76.7	40.8	35.9	13.0	13.2	9.7
Dec-18	76.8	40.1	36.7	9.8	11.7	15.1

Wide Rows

Month	Sales	Cost of	Gross Profit	MA	Admin Costs	Profit
Jan-18	81.1	41.6	39.4	10.6	10.6	18.2
Feb-18	73.8	41.7	32.1	10.5	9.9	11.8
Mar-18	72.6	38.4	34.2	13.8	11.4	9.0
Apr-18	89.9	49.1	40.8	14.3	(3.0)	29.4
May-18	67.8	37.9	29.9	10.3	10.2	9.4
Jun-18	71.6	38.5	33.1	10.6	11.3	11.1
Jul-18	82.3	45.8	36.5	12.8	12.3	11.4
Aug-18	78.5	40.6	37.9	8.6	11.6	17.6
Sep-18	81.2	41.6	39.5	13.2	9.5	16.8
Oct-18	91.6	50.1	41.5	13.6	14.5	13.4
Nov-18	76.7	40.8	35.9	13.0	13.2	9.7
Dec-18	76.8	40.1	36.7	9.8	11.7	15.1

Month	Sales	Cost of Sales	Gross Profit	MA	Admin Costs	Profit
Jan-18	81.1	41.6	39.4	10.6	10.6	18.2
Feb-18	73.8	41.7	32.1	10.5	9.9	11.8
Mar-18	72.6	38.4	34.2	13.8	11.4	9.0
Apr-18	89.9	49.1	40.8	14.3	(3.0)	29.4
May-18	67.8	37.9	29.9	10.3	10.2	9.4
Jun-18	71.6	38.5	33.1	10.6	11.3	11.1
Jul-18	82.3	45.8	36.5	12.8	12.3	11.4
Aug-18	78.5	40.6	37.9	8.6	11.6	17.6
Sep-18	81.2	41.6	39.5	13.2	9.5	16.8
Oct-18	91.6	50.1	41.5	13.6	14.5	13.4
Nov-18	76.7	40.8	35.9	13.0	13.2	9.7
Dec-18	76.8	40.1	36.7	9.8	11.7	15.1

Alignment is another way to communicate categories. For example, we might use different indents for different levels in a data hierarchy, as in the Profit and Loss account in Figure 6.20.

Figure 6.20:
Using indentation to communicate hierarchy

Notice how indentation, supplemented by judicious use of bars and fonts, allows our eyes to easily differentiate between numbers from three different hierarchical levels.

Figure 6.21 (opposite):
Indentation - text and numbers

In the first panel, text is left justified and numbers right justified; and as one decimal point is used consistently it is easy to get a sense of the size of the number from the size of the 'bar' that the numbers form. This is lost in the second panel because there is no consistency on the decimalization rule. In the final panel, everything is centre justified, so we lose the visual cues that help us differentiate between text and numbers and the size of the numbers.

Profit and Loss Account

			2018
Turnover			
	Sales	£	12,372,636
	Discount	£	(4,277)
Total Turnover		£	**12,368,359**
Cost of Sales			
	Attributable Costs		
	Delivery costs	£	(9,679,866)
	Expenses	£	(66,880)
	Other costs	£	**(66,880)**
	Total	£	(9,813,625)
	Acquisition Costs		
	Bid Management	£	(2,750)
	Recruitment Costs	£	(98,863)
	Referral Fees	£	(74,250)
	Delivery Fees	£	(830,174)
	Total	£	(1,006,036)
	Reclaimable Costs		
	Equipment	£	(547)
	Food Expenses	£	(112)
	Travel Expenses	£	(1,608)
	Exam and Exam Admin	£	(10,223)
	Hotel Expenses	£	(1,058)
	Total	£	(13,548)
Total Cost of Sales		£	(10,833,209)
Gross Profit		£	**1,535,150**

Justification within cells is also important. It helps our brains to quickly distinguish between text (left justified) and numbers (right justified). Right justification also provides our brains with visual clues about category values, since every decimal increment increases the size of the numeric string (providing we use consistent numerical encoding rules – such as the number of decimal points). This 'sense of size' is completely lost when we centre numerical information.

Communicating by Visual Means

Consistent Format		Inconsistent Format		Consistent Format	
Left	Right	Left	Right	Centre	Centre
Discount	(4,277.0)	Discount	(4,277.0000000)	Discount	-4277.0
Delivery costs	(9,679,865.9)	Delivery costs	(9,679,866)	Delivery costs	-9679865.9
Expenses	(66,879.7)	Expenses	(66,879.66)	Expenses	-66879.7
Bid Management	(2,750.0)	Bid Management	(2,750.000)	Bid Management	-2750.0
Recruitment Costs	(98,862.5)	Recruitment Costs	(98,862.50)	Recruitment Costs	-98862.5
Referral Fees	(74,250.0)	Referral Fees	(74,250.00)	Referral Fees	-74250.0
Delivery Fees	(830,173.6)	Delivery Fees	(830,173.62)	Delivery Fees	-830173.6
Equipment	(547.4)	Equipment	(547.35000)	Equipment	-547.4
Food Expenses	(112.2)	Food Expenses	(112.24000)	Food Expenses	-112.2
Travel Expenses	(1,607.5)	Travel Expenses	(1,607.5300)	Travel Expenses	-1607.5
Exam and Exam Admin	(10,223.0)	Exam and Exam Admin	(10,223.0000)	Exam and Exam Admin	-10223.0
Hotel Expenses	(1,057.5)	Hotel Expenses	(1,057.5300)	Hotel Expenses	-1057.5

COMPARISONS

- DO use Gestalt principles to help users to compare values or patterns.

We have already seen, in Figure 6.19, how varying the gaps between rows and columns of numbers in a table can guide the eye to look across or down. In the same vein, if you want to compare categories in two tables place them side by side (Figure 6.22).[15]

Vertical

	2018
Sales	$12,372,636
Discount	$ (4,277)
Net	**$12,368,359**

	2019
Sales	$18,149,533
Discount	$ (3,285)
Net	**$18,146,248**

Horizontal

	2018	2019
Sales	$12,372,636	$18,149,533
Discount	$ (4,277)	$ (3,285)
Net	**$12,368,359**	**$18,146,248**

15. In Figure 5.3, in Chapter 5, we compared categories in a chart by stacking them vertically, but, in this case, we were comparing two shapes that varied in the vertical dimension, which is why this alignment worked.

Figure 6.22:
Comparing categories in tables side by side

It is much easier to see the progression when numbers are placed side by side.

If you want users to compare the trends expressed in two line graphs, stack them on top of each other (Figure 6.23).

Figure 6.23:
Compare trends by stacking

It is easier to see how the change in margins for Client A and B is correlated in time when charts are vertically stacked. On the other hand, the relative size is easier to judge when they are placed side by side.

If it is important to determine the relative value of categories compared to peers arrange the categories in rank order (Figure 6.24).

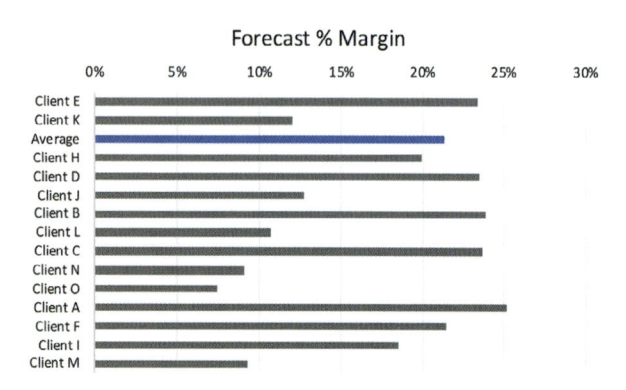

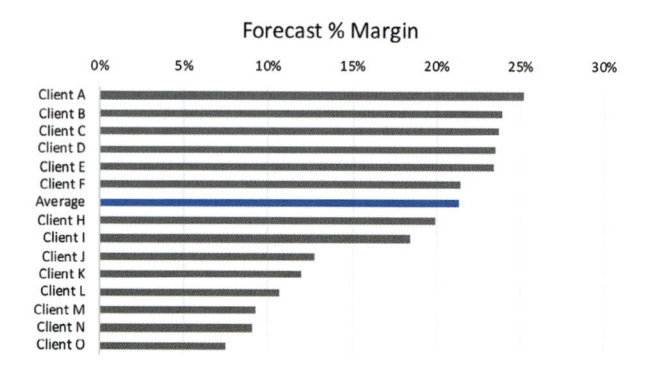

Figure 6.24:
Using rank order for comparing sizes

It is much easier to make judgements about the relative size of categories when they are rank ordered.

CONSISTENCY

The first three rules tap into our brain's innate – genetically programmed – pattern-seeking capabilities. But, as we saw earlier, we can also train our brain to recognize familiar patterns.

- DO exploit the ability of our conscious brain to prime the unconscious pattern-seeking brain so that it makes sense of what it 'sees' quickly, efficiently and correctly.

Communicating by Visual Means

	Sep-17	Oct-17	Nov-17	Dec-17	Jan-18	Feb-18	Mar-18
Region 1	13%	13%	13%	2%	25%	12%	12%
Region 2				30%	21%	21%	21%
Region 3		21%	22%	23%	26%	30%	
Region 4	32%	33%	31%	29%	28%	28%	27%
Region 5	20%	19%	18%	17%			
Region 6	29%	26%	19%				
Region 7	20%	19%	16%	16%	22%	25%	26%

Figure 6.25:
Organize times series data horizontally

It is easier, and more natural, to read continuous time series data from left to right.

	Region 1	Region 2	Region 3	Region 4	Region 5	Region 6	Region 7
Sep-17	13%			32%	20%	29%	20%
Oct-17	13%		21%	33%	19%	26%	19%
Nov-17	13%		22%	31%	18%	19%	16%
Dec-17	2%	30%	23%	29%	17%		16%
Jan-18	25%	21%	26%	28%			22%
Feb-18	12%	21%	30%	28%			25%
Mar-18	12%	21%		27%			26%

This is why it is important that as we use the elements of our visual vocabulary in a consistent way. If we used different colours to represent the same category in different graphs, for example, at best we would slow down the process of communication. At worst, our audience might jump to the wrong conclusion.

Here are some generic rules that I recommend you adopt.

- DO always arrange time series information horizontally from left to right in charts and tables. This taps into our learned behaviour (from reading) to assume that a sequence flows from left to right (at least, in the majority of Western languages).

Figure 6.26:
Use continuous lines for continuous data

It is easier to detect patterns in time series data when it is depicted as a line. The use of a continuous line, rather than discontinuous columns, also contains a cue for the brain about the nature of the process that is being depicted. Note how the chart on the right is easier to 'read' and conveys an impression of movement.

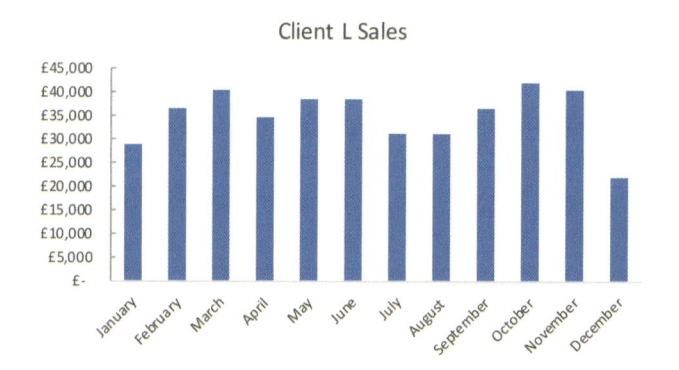

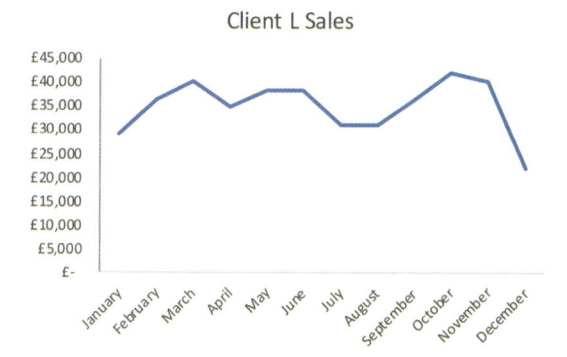

- DO use lines to encode time series data from a continuous process. For example, if you make sales every day but simply record them in monthly buckets, then use horizontal lines; but use bars for discontinuous data, such as sales forecasts, as they are produced once a period.
- DO organize category data (e.g. different products) vertically using the rows in a table or the X axis and bars on a chart (Figure 6.27) so that the brain can instantly recognize that this is category not time series data.

Figure 6.27:
Use rows or horizontal bars for category data

In the top chart category, data is plotted horizontally, using lines, which can fool the brain into thinking that this is continuous time series data rather than a cross section of categories. Instead, align categories vertically in either a table or a horizontal bar chart.

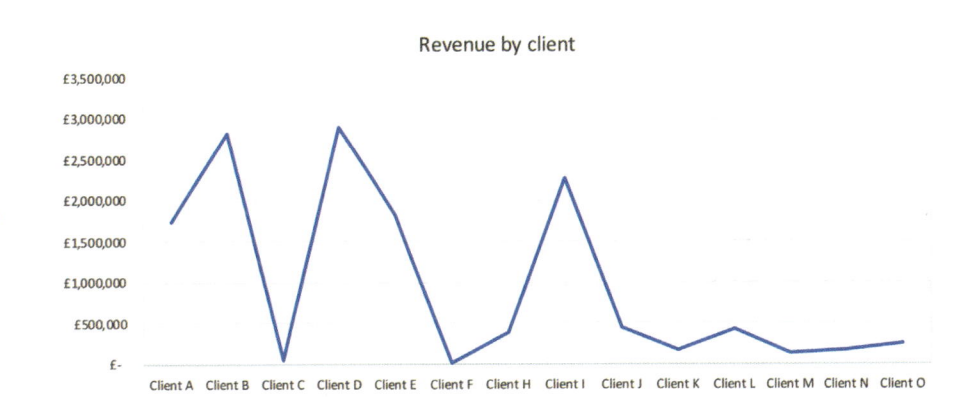

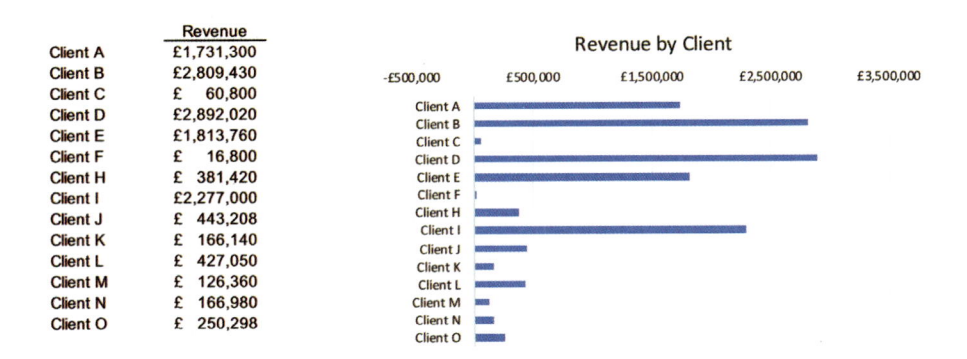

Revenue by client

[line chart plotting Client A through Client O with revenue values ranging from £- to £3,500,000]

	Revenue
Client A	£1,731,300
Client B	£2,809,430
Client C	£ 60,800
Client D	£2,892,020
Client E	£1,813,760
Client F	£ 16,800
Client H	£ 381,420
Client I	£2,277,000
Client J	£ 443,208
Client K	£ 166,140
Client L	£ 427,050
Client M	£ 126,360
Client N	£ 166,980
Client O	£ 250,298

Revenue by Client

[horizontal bar chart of Client A through Client O, axis from -£500,000 to £3,500,000]

- DO create 'coding' rules for yourself and use them consistently throughout your reports to prime your audience's brains.

Train your audience's brains to help them quickly attribute meaning to content on the page. Applying consistent rules means that your audience will not need to use their limited capacity working memory to hold a cross reference to a legend. Ultimately, if they become very familiar with the graphical language you are using, it might be possible to eliminate reference material altogether to further reduce the visual distractions.

Over time, using a consistent set of rules in a disciplined way helps us to communicate efficiently but it also builds your audience's expertise.

For example, my first degree was in Geography and, as a regular user of Ordinance Survey maps, I developed an enhanced ability to 'read' and interpret a map. As a result, whenever I look at a map, I can easily conjure up a mental image of what it is like on the ground and what forces have contributed to making the landscape. So, I can do much more than navigate from A to B. It sometimes almost feels like I can travel through time.

In the same way, with my software application I can understand what is going on with a forecast process at a glance, with no conscious effort on my part. This is because it uses a consistent set of rules for how different aspects of performance are represented on the screen.

Communicating by Visual Means

COMMON LANGUAGE

Another way to prime our brain's pattern-recognition system involves using a common language. By 'language' I mean the set of rules and conventions used for decoding information, whether that information is expressed symbolically using numbers of words or graphically. And by 'common', I mean that the same language is used by the person encoding the information and ALL of the recipients of the communication. If different rules are used, recipients will either literally not know what is meant or will interpret the same information in different ways.

But you don't have to invent a common language completely by yourself – it makes sense to exploit existing shared cultural norms.

For example, readers of English have been trained to read from left to right and this informs the way that we interpret sequences – what comes first. Also, we are conditioned to look for summary information at the top of a page, because that is where newspapers place their headlines. Lists of contents, on the other hand, are usually found in the left- or right-hand margin. Cultural priming also explains why traffic light icons are used by Westerners to encode meaning, and why this device doesn't work in many other parts of the world – particularly where there are no traffic lights!

Working memory

Finally, we have arrived at the working memory – the last leg of our journey through our system of perception.

As we have already discussed, our working memory has a very limited capacity. This means that 'reporters' like us need to encode information in the most efficient way so that we do not overload it – in the same way that the miniscule CPUs of early computers shaped the way that software was designed.

The implications for information professionals are obvious.

- DO restrict the number of visual categories to five or fewer, since this is the limit of what we can hold in memory at any one time. So, no more than five symbols or colours in a chart legend – got it?

Figure 6.28:
Using bubbles to represent size and significance

In Figure 6.28, the left-hand chart plots each client using two dimensions: revenue and margin. The right-hand chart adds two dimensions: the percentage margin (denoted by the size of the bubble) and its size in relation to a forecast (green is better, red is worse). The addition of the extra two data dimensions in the same space reveals a narrative that was otherwise hidden – that the larger clients (higher) generally have higher percentage margins (large) and are performing better than forecast (green).

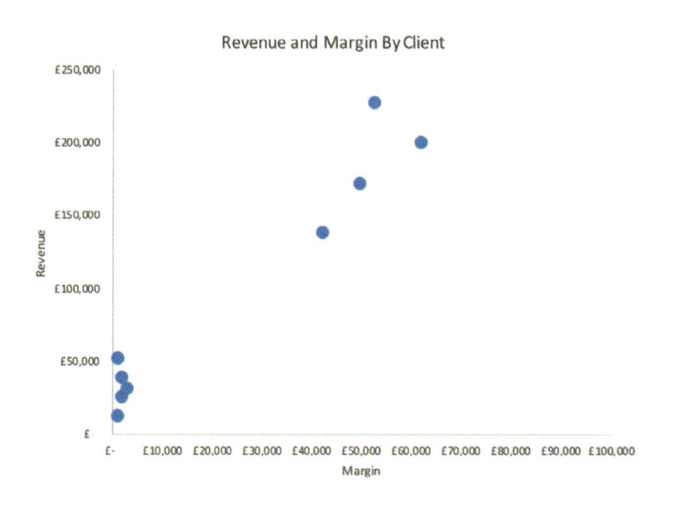

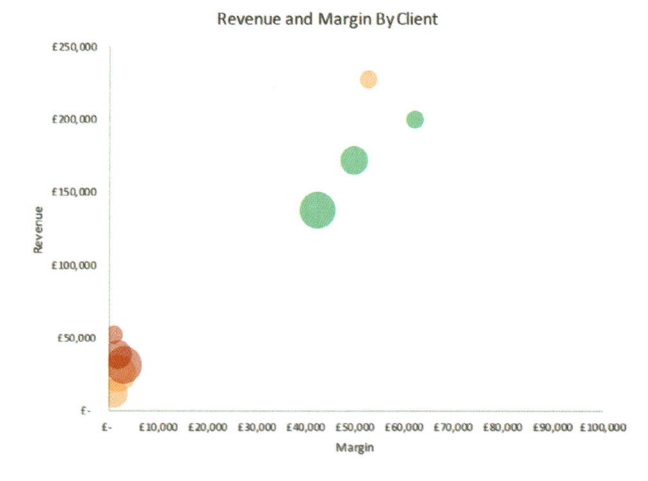

- DO get around this limitation in our working memory by chunking. Chunking involves collapsing as many different data dimensions as possible into a single object, so that it takes up one 'slot' in our memory rather than many. So, for example, using one symbol to represent the significance of a piece of data, and another to represent its size, takes up two of the five slots in working memory. Instead, use a coloured area to represent both size and significance, thus taking up only one precious slot.

This trick of collapsing data dimensions enables us to be more economical in the use of *any kind* of limited resource, be it our working memory or space on a page. And additional dimensions create the potential for new insights, providing you choose to present with care.

While the capacity of our working memory is limited, on the positive side of the equation, when it is engaged we become conscious of 'seeing'. This means that we can mobilize our conscious, logical brain. There is a limit to the amount of information that even the best graphics can convey, so expert communicators supplement graphical presentation with text (Figure 6.25). This helps direct attention, set a context or provide guidance if the content would otherwise be unclear or ambiguous.

- DO provide help and guidance to ensure that the recipients interpret the words, numbers or symbols used in a consistent and correct way. This is best done by adding text to images, providing that it does not obscure or interfere with the graphics

Figure 6.29:
Using text to add context and explanation

Here text is used to direct the attention of the audience and help them interpret (without help) what are potentially ambiguous results.

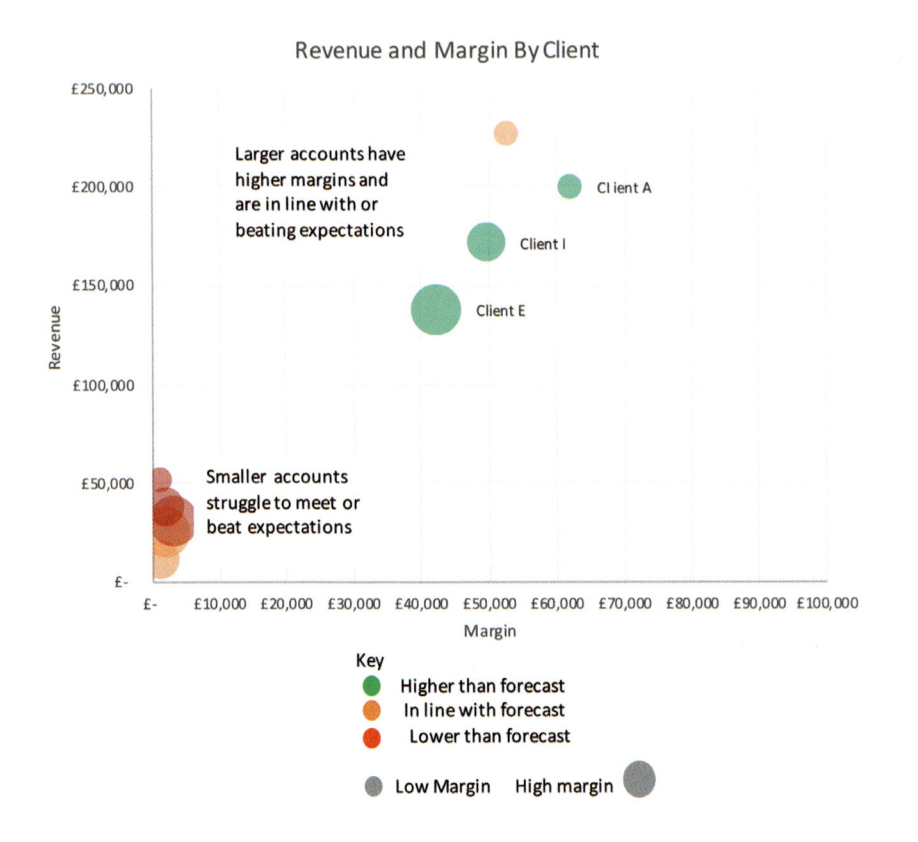

Communicating by Visual Means

PUTTING IT ALL TOGETHER

Now you have an insight into the neurological basis for how our brains assimilate information and some ideas of how to use this knowledge to design better reports. I'm guessing that much of this will just seem like common sense. But the fact that traditional practices flout many of these rules shows how easy it is to pick up bad habits and why we need to make the rules explicit. An understanding of the scientific basis behind our intuitive responses helps us break free of the dead hand of tradition.

However, it is difficult to internalize a list of dos and don'ts. Instead, I will lay out a step-by-step process to help you assimilate these ideas and apply them in practice. My aim here is to prime your brain to think about communications in a structured way and let your intuition do the rest. The list at the end of this chapter merely serves as a mental crutch when help is needed; literally an 'aide-memoire'.

The process I will describe has three steps, each with no more than four sub-steps each (since the brain likes small numbers). You could use this process to critique an existing report and give it a makeover or follow it when you are creating a new report.

In practice, however, it is likely that you will apply the process iteratively rather than in a strictly linear way, and you will have to make trade-offs. So, think of this as a set of guiding principles that reach the right place more often than not, rather than a set of hard and fast rules.

The three steps are as follows.

- **Step 1 Content** Deciding what to include in your report. It requires you to reflect on:

    o The *purpose* of the report.
    o What it should *include* for the report to fulfil its purpose.
    o The *needs* of your *audience* for the report, based on their roles, and their individual skills and competencies.

- **Step 2 Structure** Building the framework that will house your content:

    o on the page,
    o in the page and
    o between pages.

- **Step 3 Presentation method** The 'meat' of your report – the visualizations that carry the information. This builds on what we have already learned about the neurological foundations of perception. The key attributes of effective visual communication are:

o *Attenuation* – removing unnecessary or distracting 'ink'.
o *Condensation* – compressing information into as small a space as possible.
o *Contextualization* – providing the background necessary for the audience to make sense of the information.
o *Amplification* – directing the attention of the audience to the most significant features.

Let's now work through these three steps in sequence.

Step 1 Content

It is helpful to start with a clear idea of your objective. In this case we need to ensure that the meaning gleaned is properly and consistently assimilated by all the members of our target audience. We then have to help them to bring their disparate experience and knowledge to bear in order to decide what is the best thing to do; which might be 'nothing'. Here are some of the things that we should bear in mind when we are choosing what content to share.

PURPOSE

To start with, you should have a really clear idea of what the target audience's purpose is. Specifically, you need to know *what kind of decisions* they need to make.

In my experience, one of the most common mistakes report authors make – and I should know because I made them myself – stems from failing to clearly identify the target group for a particular piece of communication and their specific needs. This is sometimes because they don't have a clear idea of their collective purpose themselves; but often it is because the report author is trying to save time by using one report to serve the needs of different groups or individuals with very different needs. In these circumstances it would be far better to have a number of reports or multiples pages of reports that address different audiences. These might have much of the same content but organized in different ways.

It pays to be as specific as you can when you are trying to define the purpose of a group. For example, 'The purpose is to decide how much money we can afford to allocate to new projects'. This works well because it is likely to lead to a different report design than if the purpose was expressed in less specific terms – for example, 'to monitor project spend'. Vagueness is the enemy of effective report design. It leads to 'report bloat' as frustrated users often end up making more and more requests for information to compensate for their failure to specify their needs properly in the first place.

For run of the mill performance reporting the generic purpose is usually to decide whether and where intervention is required. Because this generic purpose is framed so broadly, extra discipline is required in designing reports. I find 'user stories' – a technique extensively used in 'Agile' software development – a particularly helpful tool because the audience's needs are stated in direct and personal terms, using the hooks 'I want' and 'So that I can'. In particular, I find

Communicating by Visual Means

Stakeholder	I want	So that	Priority
Managing Partners	To see the profitability of different contracts by month	I can determine who might need help	M
Account Principals	To see the profitability of my accounts by month	I can take corrective action if required	M
Operations	I want to compare actuals against forecasts	I can spot problems with actuals and reassure myself that my forecasts are reliable	S
Account Principals	To see what people are responsible for the costs and revenue charged to my accounts each month	I can ensure that everything has been properly accounted for	W
Managing Partners	To see a one page summary of key financial metrics continuously updated	I am reassured that everything is as it should be	C
Managing Partners	To see my cash and outstanding debtors position at all times	I can take steps to deal with liquidity issues (too little cash/too much in the wrong place)	M

Table 6.1: A set of user stories

The priority column uses the so-called 'MOSCOW' protocol, whereby you decide whether any particular features Must, Should, Could or Won't be provided as part of the next development cycle. Like modern software, performance reports should be in a continuous state of development as new needs are identified and redundant elements retired. This approach is also a helpful way of enforcing discipline on this process.

'So that I can' a helpful discipline to help strip out waffle, as the example in Table 6.3 demonstrates.

Resist the temptation to include information just in case, or (particularly when you have clever software tools) because you can. And don't try to anticipate the specific questions that may arise by adding extra 'routine' content. Routine reports should support routine decisions – don't try to anticipate ad hoc needs.[16] Instead, build information systems that make it easy to 'dig deeper' as and when the need arises.

COMPOSITION

Although any report is aimed at a group of people with a common purpose, every group will be comprised of individuals who have different perspectives and motivations. Therefore, it is important to ensure that the content of the report balances these different angles and is not skewed towards the concerns of any particular interest group. While the content needs to be unbiased as a whole, it may be helpful to use different pages to organize content from different perspectives. To avoid falling into the trap of breeding partisan behaviour, consider using some common content on different pages (e.g. shared performance 'headlines') and common layouts and conventions to provide a subliminal signal to the users that these are different views of the same phenomena, rather than competing versions of the truth.

CAPABILITY AND EXPERIENCE

Different group members will also differ in their ability to make sense of information. Although human beings are biased towards assimilating information through shapes and other visual artefacts, some people will be more comfortable with this than others. Certain individuals may have a high level of analytical skills while others may be frightened by information presented numerically and consciously avoid engaging with it.

As a general rule, avoid using technical terms, even if they are precise and 'correct'. It is important to explicitly define words that might not be properly

[16]. One particularly pernicious trap that accountants are liable to fall into is to build complex processes to apportion fixed costs to products or profit centres based on volume or revenue, for example. While this might help support ad hoc stock valuation or pricing decisions, treating fixed costs as if they were variable obscures the dynamics of a business, therefore making it more difficult to intervene intelligently.

understood by all members of the audience. Adopt the simplest methods capable of communicating what you mean faithfully and add explanatory text if the meaning of information in charts or tables could be missed or misinterpreted by any member of the audience.

SOME PITFALLS

The most common mistake I come across is falling into the trap of trying to do too much. I speak from personal experience! This might be because you have failed to precisely define the purpose of the group that you are serving, or the result of a well-intentioned but misguided attempt to meet all the needs of all its members. Or you might just be showing off.

You may feel like you are doing the right thing by giving everyone what they think they need. But if you provide content that is not germane to the purpose of the group you may fail to achieve your primary goal, which is to direct the attention of the business to the things that matter. The end result will be familiar to many readers – tens or hundreds of reports, most of which are rarely read or accessed. This is wasteful and confusing; but worse you open up the opportunity for people to select those perspectives that suit their purpose or prejudices, creating 'information bubbles' that foster division rather than cohesion.

My advice is to learn to think like a (high-quality) newspaper editor. Be sensitive to the needs of your readers but take care to maintain your editorial independence and push back against anybody who compromises the integrity of the meaning that you are charged with communicating. Even if a request to provide additional content is not politically motivated, avoid overloading reports with tangential reference data, particularly if it is readily accessible from other sources. Alternatively, publish reference data as an appendix – in the same way that financial newspapers provide tables of market information in a supplement.

Step 2 Structure

So, you have defined your audience and the kind of content they need. Now you need to work out the best way to structure the content to help them fulfil their purpose.

ON THE PAGE

Your first job is to allocate the page (or screen) 'real estate' to content.

An obvious way to structure the page is to use a grid with equally sized cells, but this doesn't work well. It provides few clues to the eye about the nature or importance of different items of content. Also, some cells will contain a lot of redundant white space while others would be too full of information ink.

But, while you should avoid laying content out on a strict grid it makes sense, from a Gestalt perspective, to align content along vertical or horizontal planes; and rectangles use two-dimensional space most efficiently. For these reasons, I recommend using rectangular shaped placeholders anchored on a subliminal grid structure, as all newspapers do (Figure 6.30).

Communicating by Visual Means

The relative size of content placeholders should reflect the role and importance of the information it contains, in the same way that newspaper headlines use larger font than the content of news stories. Also, since we have all been culturally primed by a lifetime of reading newspapers and magazines, there are a lot of cues that we can deploy to guide the reader. For example, you might use the top of the page for headline or summary information and the left-hand column for an index, as shown in Figure 6.31.

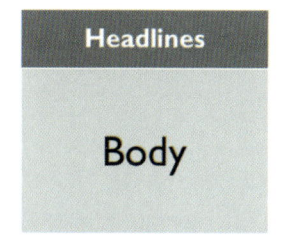

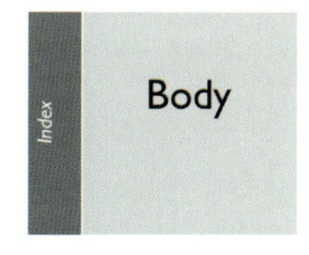

In the remaining space, position the most important content in the centre and top left of the page, since the eye will naturally look there first.

Because of the way that most of us have learned to read the least important 'real estate' on the page is in the bottom right-hand corner, so place less important content there or use it for variable or transitory content such as alerts or comments (Figure 6.31). This is where newspapers print their apologies for their mistakes and retractions, which is no accident!

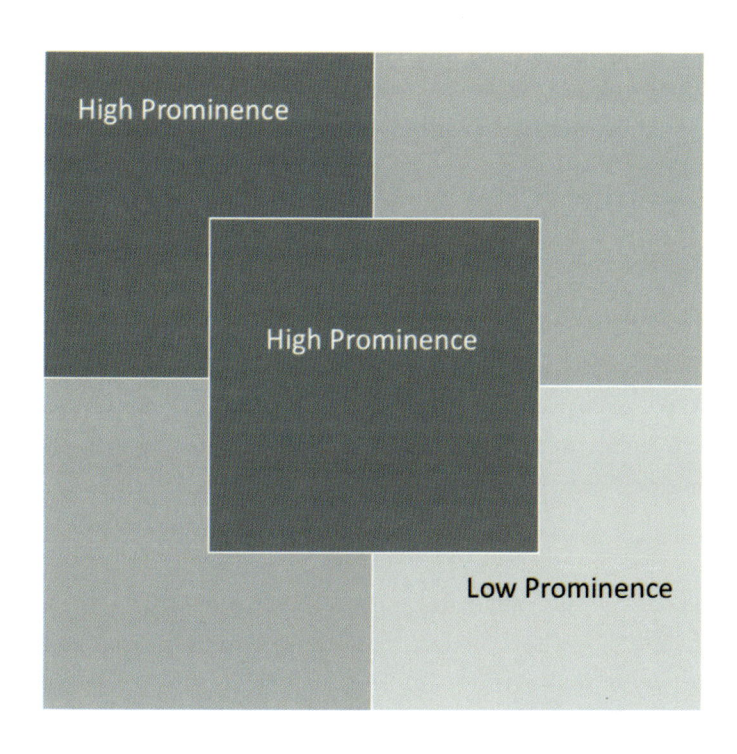

(Above) Figure 6.30:
Newspaper page showing how content is organized

Note how the layout of this newspaper page is informed, but not determined, by a rectangular grid – a Gestalt pattern that our brain 'likes'.

(Top left) Figure 6.31:
Some organizational conventions

Notice how we are primed to look for content below or to the right of contextual information.

(Left) Figure 6.32:
How to use 'real estate' on the page

Our brains are primed to look for important content at the top and centre of a page or screen. The bottom right is the least prominent because this is the last place a reader of Western script visits.

IN THE PAGE

Within these general guidelines be mindful of where you position related items of content (Figure 6.33). If you want to encourage users to make comparisons between time series data on two line charts, place them on top of each other so that the dates are vertically aligned. If you want to make it easy to compare different categories, organize them horizontally on the page so that the eye can easily read across. Likewise, if two items of content show information relating to two different steps in a process, place them side by side following the process flow.

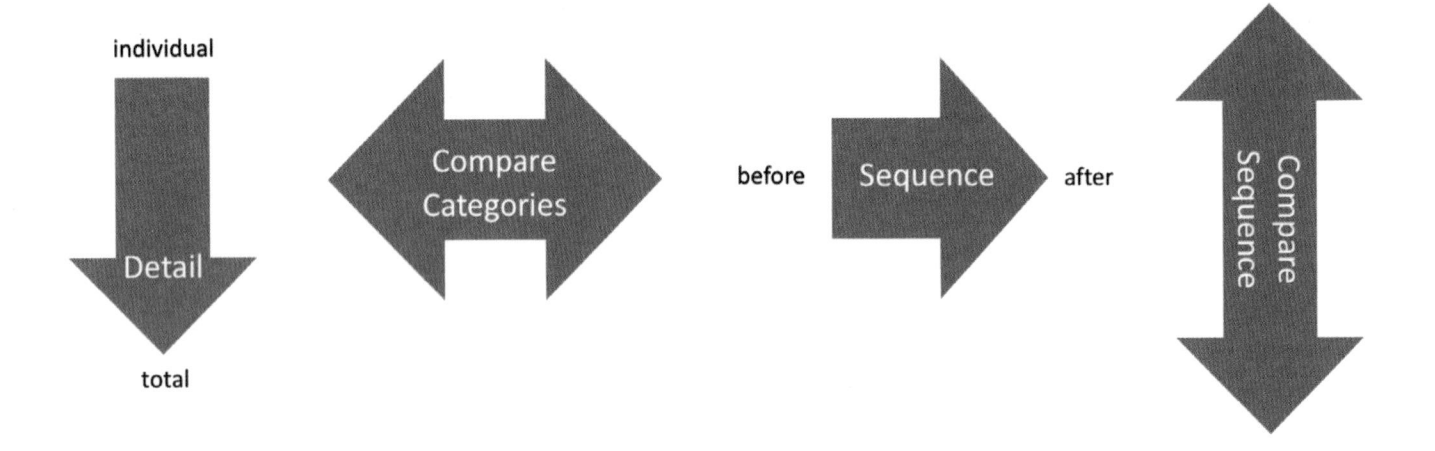

Figure 6.33:
Positioning related content

What we would like readers to do determines where we choose to position related content.

BETWEEN PAGES

It is particularly important to have a coherent and consistent structure when your report has more than one page (or screen). Try to use the same structuring rules on every page, so that the user gets a clear sense of the coherence of the message even if the content on each page differs. Using a consistent set of rules speeds up the process of communication because it primes the subconscious brain of your users, so they don't need to re-orientate themselves as they move through the document.

Step 3 Presentation method

Thus far we have dealt with context. Now we need to design our content – that is, the charts, tables and text that we use to communicate meaning. In keeping with the philosophy of this book, I don't intend to provide a list of rules and guidance about what type of chart to use and in what circumstances – it is unlikely you will be able to remember them all and there are many other sources that you can refer to.[17] Instead, I will walk you through the process in a simple step-by-step manner.

17. I would recommend *Show Me The Numbers* by Stephen Few (2004).

ATTENUATE

The first rule of communicating meaning through visual means is to eliminate, as far as possible, any visual artefact that does not contain information. And if you can't get rid of it altogether – perhaps because it provides essential context

Communicating by Visual Means

– reduce its prominence to make it subservient to the information content. In other words, get rid of visual noise.

At best, superfluous content will confuse and distract the brain. At worst it will distort the meaning or lead to misinterpretation (Figure 6.30). The pioneers of radio communication in the early 20th century used the word attenuation to describe what they did to dampen the noise that interfered with the transmission of radio signals, and I will use the same term to describe what we need to do to our reports.

Let's first look at attenuating the data itself.

As we discovered in Part 2 of this book there are two ways to attenuate data.

First, we can *summarize* it using familiar devices like totals and averages. This relieves our brains of the burden of trying to assimilate large amounts of data infected by an unknown level of noise. But, as we have seen, using summary statistics can lead to us losing potentially important information about patterns of behaviour (Figure 6.34).

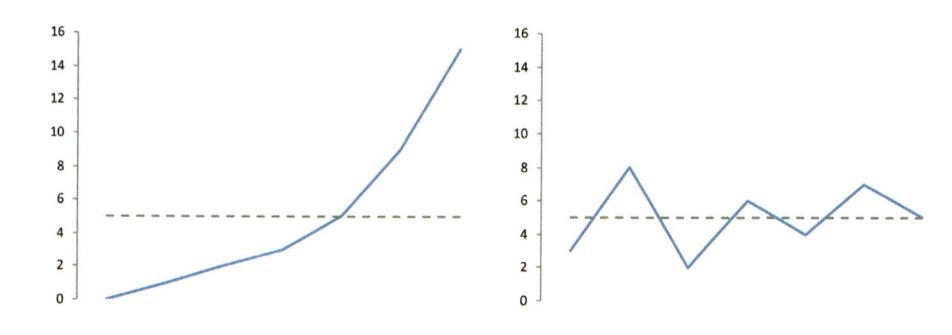

Figure 6.34:
How summary statistics can mislead: same average, different pattern

The two data series have the same average but contain very different 'messages'. Summary statistics attenuate data but can destroy important information.

Another way to attenuate to suppress unimportant or irrelevant data (noise) is to report only data points that represent exceptions to a prevailing pattern. This can be very effective, providing you use statistically sound methods like control charts or tracking signals to filter out noise and so identify the outliers.

Having attenuated the data by damping down noise, we need to communicate meaning without introducing new sources of noise. We have already touched upon three key attenuation strategies that we can use to make our communication more efficient and effective. They are eliminating unnecessary ink, reducing the use of distracting colours, and avoiding inconsistencies in encoding information.

ELIMINATE NON-DATA INK

In my experience, the single most effective way to improve the visual impact of reports is to eliminate as much non-information ink as possible.

Start by deleting *all* borders, gridlines, axes and fills to the point that the chart or table is almost meaningless.

Then carefully add contextual features back one at a time, only retaining those things that are essential for the communication of meaning. And make sure that what you do add back is visually subordinated to the information content. So, use less saturated colours, thinner lines and so on.

ELIMINATE DISTRACTING COLOURS

Colours can help to code category information – but use them sparingly. Don't use different colours where they do not communicate meaning, for example, axes, gridlines and so on.

If you are going to use colour, remember that the only requirement is that your audience should be able to quickly distinguish between categories, and that no category is more prominent to the eye than any other. Use muted colours and coordinated palettes – unless, of course, you want to draw attention to a specific category.

Also, remember that your working memory can only hold five objects at any one time. If you have more categories, consider using tricks like collapsing smaller categories into an 'other' category to avoid stressing the brain.

If you are concerned about losing important detail you could use a second graph for the minor items. Alternatively, use 'small multiples', as advocated by graphic visualization pioneer Steve Few. These are a set of small charts with identical formatting that contain different data (Figure 6.35). This can be a useful way of communicating a lot of data graphically while mitigating the cognitive burden.

ELIMINATE INCONSISTENCIES

The third way of attenuating is to eliminate inconsistencies in the way that information is coded. Use graphical objects and colours consistently to avoid unnecessary variety that might stress or distract the brain. Use the same type of graph or table to communicate the same type of information and, wherever possible, the same colours and formatting rules across graphical objects. Also, using consistent structures on different pages will help users to orientate themselves.

When you are presenting numerical data, use a consistent number of decimal points and choose a font where each number has the same width, to ensure that different numbers leave the same size footprint on the page. Use commas in a consistent way to break up long numbers into chunks that the brain can handle more easily. And consider using a consistent rule for attenuating the length of long number strings, so that none is longer than five characters, to respect the capacity of the working memory. So, 12,000,000 might be expressed as 12,000 (thousand), and 12,000,000,000 as 12,000 (million).

Reports always contain some text, and the same rules apply here as well. Use font types and sizes in a consistent way, varying them only when you want to signal something to your brain – for example, to distinguish a comment from a title.

Graphic designers obsess about fonts, and while it is not worth spending much time on the topic it is helpful to be aware of some of the issues involved.

Communicating by Visual Means

Figure 6.35:
Example of small multiples

Plotting the performance of 12 regions on the same chart produces a multi-coloured spaghetti that is impossible to interpret no matter how large the chart. Presenting the same information on 12 small graphs, using a restrained colour palette, is much clearer using only slightly more 'real estate'. Note how the average performance line and rough rank ordering makes it easier to interpret the results.

For example, Table 6.2 gives a summary of the recommendations made by a design consultancy that specializes in the dashboard design. This should give you a sense of the kind of choices you need to make.

If you are not familiar with the terms used:

- This is a sentence using a serif font called Adobe Garamond Pro (the serif being a reference to the curly bits on individual letters)
- and here is a sentence written with Calibri, a sans serif (i.e. without serif) font.

Most books (like this one) are written using a serif font as the minor flourishes on each letter are thought to help the eye flow across the page.

CONDENSE

Once you have removed unnecessary distracting detail from your report, the next step is to condense the remaining related information into as small an area as possible, without distracting or confusing the reader. Ideally, related

Table 6.2:
Analysis of text types and uses

Source: Juice
A suggested protocol for the use of different fonts in different parts of a report.

	Purpose	Size	Font	Colour	Style
Body	Clean readable text, 50-80% of your text will look like this	10-16 pts	Sans serif: Arial, Tahoma, Verdana Serif: Georgia, Times	Neutral	Normal. No bold, no italic. 1-2 line spacing
Header	Separate and name sections of your writing	150-200% of **body**	Same as **body** or flip serif/sans serif	Neutral	Normal, bold or italic. Whitespace above
Notes	Additional things a user should be aware of: data sources, calculations etc, that should fade into the background	85% of **body**	Same as **body**	De-emphasized, lower contrast	Normal. No bold, no italic.
Emphasis	Draws the eye to key points you want to make	Same as **body**	Same as **body**	High impact colour	Bold or italic.

content should be grouped together on a single page, to make it easy for your eye to take it in 'at a glance' (i.e. using a few saccades) and avoid the need to hold objects in working memory while you search for related information on another page.

There are limits to how much you can compress visualizations before they become illegible or the white space around them becomes too small to allow them to be easily distinguished from another. Once you have eliminated superfluous detail, however, my guess is that you will be surprised to discover how small you can make charts without the message being lost. This is because the meaning is often in the pattern, which is often easier to detect when it is small enough to be taken in at once.

Edward Tufte, the famous data visualization guru, invented a technique that takes miniaturization to an extreme. They are called 'sparklines', and you can find these in the charting tool bar in Excel. Sparklines are charts that are compressed into a single cell and are used to convey information about the pattern of behaviour of a variable – such as trend and variability – in a very small space. They are particularly useful when used in combination with charts that have complementary strengths, such as data tables (Figure 6.36).

Another way to compress information in charts is to increase the number of data dimensions – a dimension being an encoded variable or an attribute of it.

For example, using the same space to convey information about the position *and* the trajectory of a variable is more efficient than just coding for value at a point in time alone. Pie charts are particularly wasteful in their use of space, because they can only code for one variable at a time – the proportion of a whole made up by different categories.

Communicating by Visual Means

Margins By Region

	Sep-17	Oct-17	Nov-17	Dec-17	Jan-18	Feb-18	Mar-18
Region 1	13%	13%	13%	2%	25%	12%	12%
Region 2				30%	21%	21%	21%
Region 3		21%	22%	23%	26%	30%	
Region 4	32%	33%	31%	29%	28%	28%	27%
Region 5	20%	19%	18%	17%			
Region 6	29%	26%	19%				
Region 7	20%	19%	16%	16%	22%	25%	26%
Region 8	21%	22%	22%	22%	22%	24%	22%
Region 9	18%	17%	9%	6%	8%	7%	2%
Region 10	17%	13%	12%	12%	14%	18%	22%
Region 11	30%	29%	29%	27%	21%	18%	18%
Region 12	14%	14%	10%	9%	9%	9%	9%
Average	**26%**	**26%**	**23%**	**25%**	**22%**	**23%**	**24%**

Figure 6.36:
Sparkline example

In this example the sparkline is a small graph positioned in a cell to the right of the data in the table that it represents. The numbers in the table give precision, whereas the sparkline gives an immediate impression of pattern, and the red and green markers indicate the low and high points of the data series.

This is another reason why pie charts suck and why you should never use them.

In Figure 6.37, for example, a single stacked bar in the middle chart codes for all of the information in the pie chart (the contribution of parts to the whole) but it also has an axis, which allows us to judge absolute size. Additionally, it takes up much less space on the page and, because the shape is rectangular rather than a segment of a circle, it is easier for the brain to interpret. When we put a series of bars into a sequence, we also add an additional data dimension – time.

Figure 6.37:
Data compression using alternatives to pie charts

It is not difficult to improve on a pie chart. It uses a lot of space, encodes only one dimension and is difficult to interpret. A bar chart allows us to add the dimension of time and we can use a second axis to add another – in this case market share.

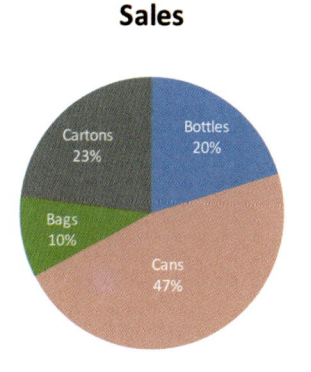

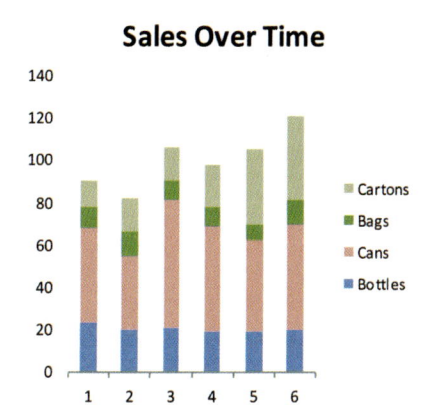

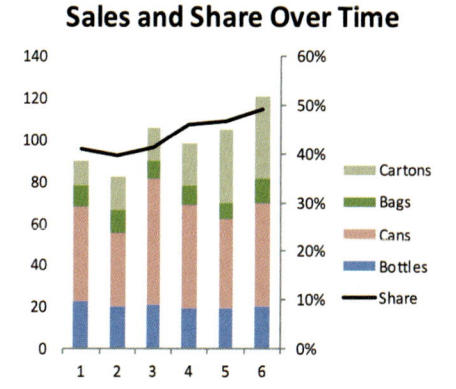

Figure 6.38:
An example of failing to encode different dimensions clearly

But we can do even better. The right-hand chart in Figure 6.38 shows how we can use a secondary axis to add a further dimension, in this case market share. So, we have got four times as much information in the same space; and in a way that is easier to interpret than a pie chart.

In this example, I have encoded size using area, trend by relative position, category using colour, and a secondary trend with a line. Using different graphical devices makes it easier to distinguish the different dimensions because our visual system can easily switch the focus of attention from one to another.

To illustrate why it is important to use different graphical objects for coding different things, compare the left-hand chart in Figure 6.38 where I have used a line to encode two variables, with the one on the right where I have used a line and a bar. See how much easier it is for the eye to 'read' the one on the right.

Another advantage of compressing multiple data dimensions into a single chart is that it makes more efficient use of another limited resource – our working memory. Table 6.3 is an example taken from my software product. The shape of the 'mushroom' symbol indicates the direction of forecast error (up being over forecast) and the colour its statistical significance (red signifying at least 95% biased). In this way, we can hold two dimensions in our short-term memory as a single 'chunked' object, because it keys into our neural circuitry that has evolved to treat a red apple as one object not two (the colour red, and the shape of an apple).

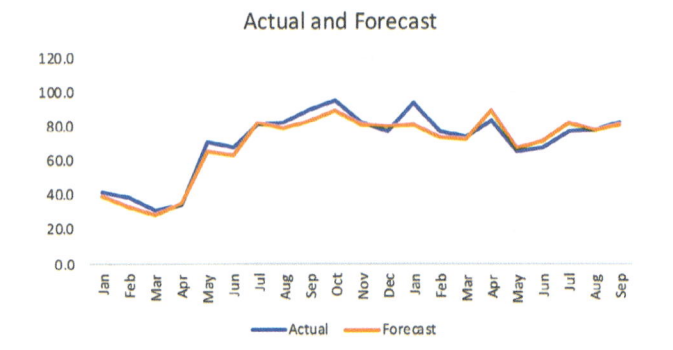

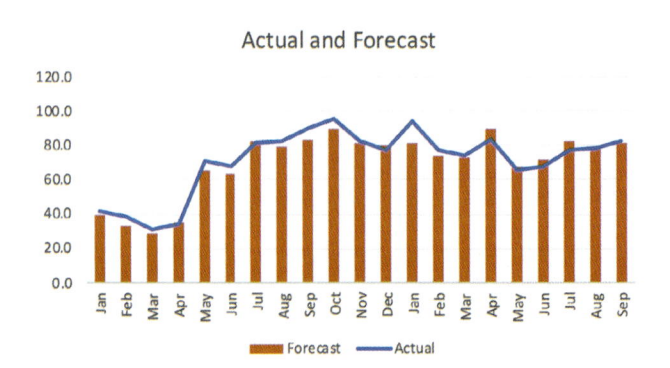

Table 6.3:
Example of using symbols to encode data

Here the symbol is used to encode two dimensions in a small space – the significance and direction of forecast bias.

If we are smart, it will be surprising how much information can be encoded in a single chart without overloading the brain. For example, Table 6.6 shows how to combine symbols that encode simple messages about the nature and relative size of forecast bias with a table that enables me to cram a lot of precise information into a small two-dimensional space.

Communicating by Visual Means

Class	Alarm	Time	Alarmed Impact		Total Impact	Bias
ANZP	🔺	●	62,699.64	▮	101,559.15	13%
EMEASA	🔺	●	47,503.94	▮	77,909.84	18%
UK	🔺	●	188,577.09	▮▮	294,831.98	13%
UK	🔺	●	118,236.66	▮▮	215,576.44	-10%
EMEASA	🔺	●	34,635.91	▮	72,139.10	-16%
NORTH AMERICA	🔺	●	55,658.21	▮	55,843.42	308%
3RD PARTY	🔺	●	352,309.21	▮▮▮	358,480.23	563%
ASIA	🔺	●	32,491.31	▮	41,251.76	47%
ASIA	🔺	◔	10,908.57	▮	20,077.17	-23%

Table 6.4:
Combining symbols and table

This table uses a mixture of text, numbers, symbols and small-scale charts to encode a lot of information. In adjoining columns, and by category, this table encodes for the direction and degree of bias (red symbol), the duration (small 'pie'), the precise size of the problem (alarmed impact), as a proportion of total impact (two tone blue bars), and as a percentage. Note also how the categories have been sorted by rank order of their 'total impact'. Although I think we have done a good job of compression in this table, there is probably more work to be done on attenuation by removing lines, solid blocks of colour and so on.

CONTEXTUALIZE

Here is some data that I would like you to interpret:

6.2
and
100,000

What do you make of them?

The answer is 'not much'. It is simply not possible to make any sense of numbers presented in isolation like this. We cannot interpret data in the absence of context.[18]

In this example, we don't know if the numbers represent two categories, different variables or one variable in a time series for a single category. We don't know whether the same units of measure have been used or whether the difference between them was the result of an unusual event.

Since numbers have no meaning without context, it follows that to be able to effectively convey intended meaning you need to pay attention to the background – the context – as well as the information in the foreground – the content.

At the most basic level, this means making sure that reports and the elements within them have proper titles (what, when, who). A good title might remove the need for a legend that would otherwise clutter up a chart. Also, arrange information on the page in a way that makes it easy to reference an appropriate comparator.

Add text or numbers to provide the contextual detail needed to quickly and easily draw the right conclusions from the content. This could be in an accompanying text box. In the example in Figure 6.34 I have edited a label in a single data point in Excel, to add helpful background information.

18. As we discussed in Chapter 5, goals effectively provide one form of context for the interpretation of actual performance. What conclusions we draw from any gap between the actual out turn and the goal will depend on the level of noise in the actual data, and whether the goal is meant to serve as a 'hard' target or a 'soft' guideline.

Figure 6.39:
Contextualizing - including editing data label

In this chart text has been used to provide context. Also, using labels has allowed me to dispense with a legend, which means that the eye does not have to jump to a different place for important category information.

TIP: The comment on the value for Region 3 in January was achieved by creating and then editing a data label for a single data point. Note how labelling each data series also removes the need for a legend.

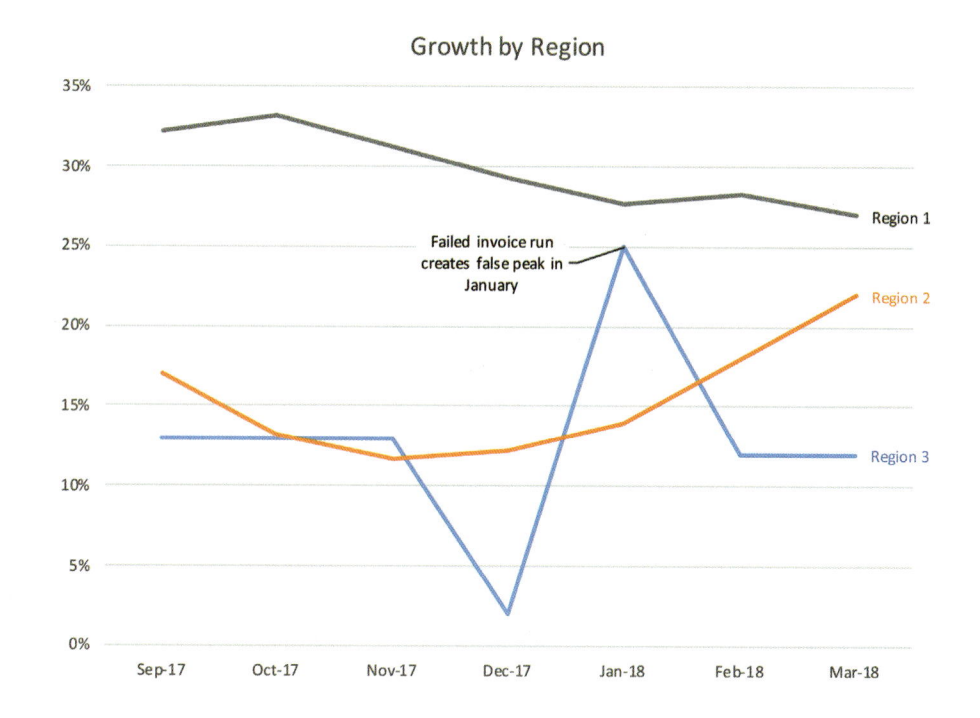

Growth by Region

AMPLIFY

Having organized, attenuated, condensed and contextualized the information that you need to convey your meaning, then – and only then – amplify what you want to draw attention to by adding back into your report just enough 'stuff' to emphasize the content that you want to stand out from the rest. As you have eliminated much of the junk that would otherwise distract your reader's eye, you need to do relatively little to amplify the most significant pieces of information.

There are a number of ways to amplify the impact of critical bits of content:

POSITION

Our visual systems implicitly assume that items at the top and centre of a page are more important than those located elsewhere on the page or screen; so place the most important items there.

SIZE

Make important objects bigger than less important ones. You can also use bigger text. For example, a single number that summarizes performance can become a graphic object in its own right, particularly if it is used to encode multiple data dimensions. In the example in Figure 6.35 colour has been used to signify the level of performance.

HIGHLIGHTING

Use bold type, thicker lines or enclosure.

Communicating by Visual Means

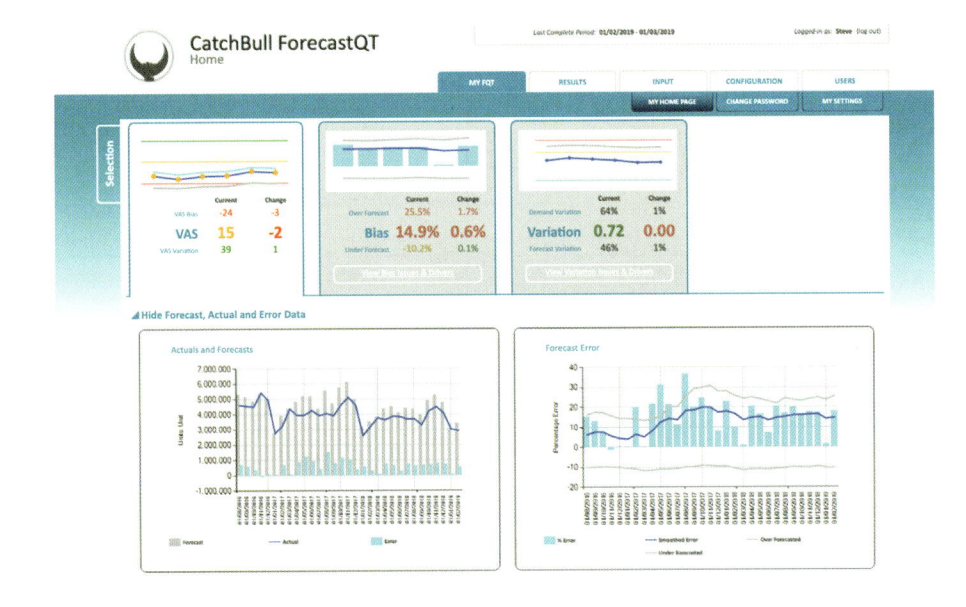

Figure 6.40:
Use ForecastQT headlines to show text size and colour to amplify

In this excerpt from the landing page in my software, note how the important data is positioned at the top in a 'headline row'. The larger numbers are the most important ones and the current status of the system is signified by the colour of text.

COLOUR

Use saturated colours to make items stand out.

ADDITION

Add symbols or marks to otherwise white space.

RANK

Order lists and tables in a meaningful way.

In the example of a football League table in Table 6.5, a range of different techniques have been used to highlight significant information.

Position	Team	Played	Won	Drawn	Lost	Goals For	Goals Against	Diff	Points
1	Chelsea	38	26	9	3	73	32	41	87
2	Manchester City	38	24	7	7	83	38	45	79
3	Arsenal	38	22	9	7	71	36	35	75
4	Manchester United	38	20	10	8	62	37	25	70
5	Tottenham Hotspur	38	19	7	12	58	53	5	64
6	Liverpool	38	18	8	12	52	48	4	62
7	Southampton	38	18	6	14	54	33	21	60
8	Swansea City	38	16	8	14	46	49	(3)	56
9	Stoke City	38	15	9	14	48	45	3	54
10	Crystal Palace	38	13	9	16	47	51	(4)	48
11	Everton	38	12	11	15	48	50	(2)	47
12	West Ham United	38	12	11	15	44	47	(3)	47
13	West Bromwich Albion	38	11	11	16	38	51	(13)	44
14	Leicester City	38	11	8	19	46	55	(9)	41
15	Newcastle United	38	10	9	19	40	63	(23)	39
16	Sunderland	38	7	17	14	31	53	(22)	38
17	Aston Villa	38	10	8	20	31	57	(26)	38
18	Hull City	38	8	11	19	33	51	(18)	35
19	Burnley	38	7	12	19	28	53	(25)	33
20	Queens Park Rangers	38	8	6	24	42	73	(31)	30

Table 6.5:
Other amplification techniques

Note how the teams qualifying for two different European competitions have been identified using a combination of shade and a horizontal line. Relegated teams are also identified using shading, but the position at the bottom of the table signals the significance attributed to the shading. Teams that have conceded more goals than they have scored are picked out in red. Finally, the winning team is denoted by bold type and my own team is highlighted using an enclosure. This is an example of where the assumed implicit knowledge of the readers (English football fans) relieves the author of the need to add explanatory text (context).

Table 6.6:

A poor example of table design

Team	Played	Won	Drawn	Lost	Goals For	Goals Diff	Against	Points
Chelsea (C)	38.0	26.0	9.0	3.0	73.0	41.0	32.0	87.0
Manchester City (CL)	38.0	24.0	7.0	7.0	83.0	45.0	38.0	79.0
Arsenal (CL)	38.0	22.0	9.0	7.0	71.0	35.0	36.0	75.0
Manchester United (CL)	38.0	20.0	10.0	8.0	62.0	25.0	37.0	70.0
Tottenham Hotspur (UC)	38.0	19.0	7.0	12.0	58.0	5.0	53.0	64.0
Liverpool (UC)	38.0	18.0	8.0	12.0	52.0	4.0	48.0	62.0
Southampton	38.0	18.0	6.0	14.0	54.0	21.0	33.0	60.0
Swansea City	38.0	16.0	8.0	14.0	46.0	-3.0	49.0	56.0
Stoke City	38.0	15.0	9.0	14.0	48.0	3.0	45.0	54.0
Crystal Palace	38.0	13.0	9.0	16.0	47.0	-4.0	51.0	48.0
Everton	38.0	12.0	11.0	15.0	48.0	-2.0	50.0	47.0
West Ham United	38.0	12.0	11.0	15.0	44.0	-3.0	47.0	47.0
West Bromwich Albion	38.0	11.0	11.0	16.0	38.0	-13.0	51.0	44.0
Leicester City	38.0	11.0	8.0	19.0	46.0	-9.0	55.0	41.0
Newcastle United	38.0	10.0	9.0	19.0	40.0	-23.0	63.0	39.0
Sunderland	38.0	7.0	17.0	14.0	31.0	-22.0	53.0	38.0
Aston Villa	38.0	10.0	8.0	20.0	31.0	-26.0	57.0	38.0
Hull City (R)	38.0	8.0	11.0	19.0	33.0	-18.0	51.0	35.0
Burnley (R)	38.0	7.0	12.0	19.0	28.0	-25.0	53.0	33.0
Queens Park Rangers (R)	38.0	8.0	6.0	24.0	42.0	-31.0	73.0	30.0

Compare this to the same table where the failure to attenuate and poor choice of amplification techniques make it difficult for a reader to grasp the salient facts (Table 6.6).

So, there you have it – a simple step-by-step approach to building and upgrading reports, involving:

- choosing content,
- structuring content and
- choosing method:

    o attenuating
    o compressing
    o contextualizing
    o amplifying.

Tools

Before we look at a real-life example of how to put these rules into practice, I would like to say a few words about a particular type of software, which many readers will have come across.

As I write, the last few years has seen the launch of a range of relatively cheap, flexible BI tools that have the rules of graphical grammar I talk about in this chapter 'hard baked' into them.

You might take my derogatory comments about dashboards to mean that tools like this are flippant or unnecessary. Far from it.

There is a need – which these tools fill – for business people to access and interrogate information for themselves, without a data person having to act as an intermediary. Every individual will have their own information needs, which cannot be met by a report that is designed for mass consumption. And giving people the ability to explore data for themselves helps build their System 1 muscles, which makes them a better-informed, more effective consumer of 'higher-level' insights into their organization, of the sort produced by information professionals.

The fact that the technology is based on recognized 'best practice' when it comes to effective visualization is very definitely a good thing.

Will technologies like this make the roles of the information professional redundant?

Absolutely not.

First, the information professional is usually the person who identifies what information the consumer needs. They then find the best source of data and design the reporting structures and dashboards that provide consumers with the ability to ask, and answer, the right kind of questions.

Second, and most crucially, out of the vast landscape of information that is potentially available to the modern business executive, the information professional is responsible for focussing the attention – the mental resources – of decision makers on those things that really matter. They must also help them to interpret the information that they are given in the right way – or at least to stop them misinterpreting it.

They might use paper as the medium for channelling their attention or a slide deck, but they could equally as well inform decision makers by giving them a conducted tour of the information 'landscape' using the BI tool. The content and the effectiveness of the communication are the most important things. The vehicle used is secondary.

PULLING IT ALL TOGETHER: A CASE STUDY

Over the last few pages I've given you a list of graphical 'ingredients' and some rules to help you combine them to bake an effective communication 'cake'. But, as the saying goes, 'The proof of the pudding is in the eating'. So, I'm guessing you will need a sample of something made this way to help these ideas 'stick'.

To demonstrate the impact that these ideas can make I will describe the process that we went through in redesigning the graphical interface for my own software application.

Because our tool is rather specialized, readers will struggle to understand the content, and the medium of communication is a computer screen rather than a piece of paper. Despite this, and the fact that the end result is not perfect, I think it provides a good illustration of how, with little practice or skill and general-purpose software, the simple principles I have described can dramatically improve the effectiveness of a performance report.

One reason why I wanted to share these insights is that I have paid for them in a very hard currency – my own failures. Trying and messing up has spurred me into finding out why things didn't work, and to search out sources of help. I'm hoping that after buying this book you don't have to go through the same pain.

I first became aware of the potential power of graphical communication in my professional life in 2001 when I saw an advert for Edward Tufte's book *The Visual Display of Quantitative Information* in a magazine. It showed what he claimed was the 'best chart ever made'. It wasn't the product of fancy software and wasn't in any way showy or colourful, but one glance was all I needed to convince me that there was some kind of magic going on, and that Tufte was the wizard that I needed to learn from.

The chart depicted the salient facts of Napoleon's doomed Russian campaign and had been drawn, by hand, over a century and a half ago. But its refined elegance and precision looked nothing like the clumsy graphs I had been using in my work. I bought all of Tufte's books and devoured them. Although they were undeniably beautiful, I initially struggled to see how I could apply his ideas in my everyday working life.

This all changed on the day I gave a software demonstration to a potential client from New Zealand.

We spent most of that web conference discussing the merits of the techniques I had used to analyse forecast performance; but towards the end of the meeting he made a throwaway comment that hit me like a slap on the cheek. 'Your biggest issue isn't the way you have analysed the data', he said, 'it just looks like it was produced 20 years ago'.

Up to that point, I realized that I hadn't given much thought to the way that the application might look to a user. The audience for these reports had been me! I had been too consumed by the technical details and seduced by my own cleverness to appreciate that the battle to sell our product – to sell the insights that would save our customers millions of pounds – depended more on the way in which different coloured pixels were arranged on the first screen than the clever analytical techniques we had used to generate them.

After the call I glumly reflected on his comment.

Looking at the landing page for our application with fresh eyes I could see what he meant. Our home page *did* look amateurish and I could see how it might easily create negative prejudices in the minds of potential users. I also recognized that even I was drawn to websites that 'looked good' and were easy to understand before I engaged with their content. It was all embarrassingly obvious. After all, when you buy a car, do you base your decision on its technical specifications or on how it looks?

And I was also aware that websites had got much better over the last few years, which couldn't have happened by accident – there must be some 'science' behind this shift that I wasn't aware of.

Just then, a presentation about dashboard design I had half dozed through at a conference some years before popped into my head. Fortunately, I remembered that the presenter had mentioned the name of the person who had inspired him: Stephen Few. And when I started to read Steve's work, I quickly worked out that what he had done was to make Tufte's beautiful ideas practical and implementable in an everyday business context. What particularly struck me was how much could be done using simple, easy to apply methods. There were few graphical gimmicks or 'sexy' charts. In fact, Steve's philosophy is that the more complex the graphic the more likely it is to fail the basic test of 'Does this make things

Communicating by Visual Means

obvious?'. Which is great, because it meant that even artistically-challenged people like me could easily apply his ideas.

Armed with what I learned from Steve's work, I began analysing our home page. I already knew that it wasn't pretty, but now I understood why. And since Steve had taught me the rudiments of graphical literacy, I began to see what I needed to do to improve things.

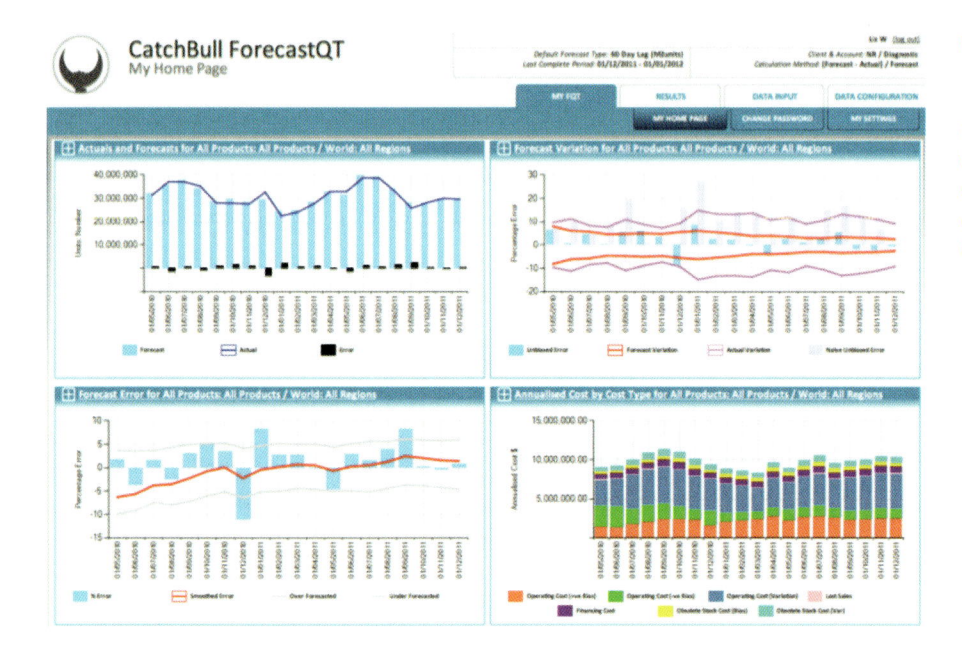

Figure 6.41:
Old home page

The old home page shown here has four panels, and the user can choose what graph is shown in each by clicking on the + sign in the top left-hand corner

Before you read my analysis, see if you can diagnose the problems with the screen in Figure 6.35a for yourself, armed with what you have already learned about:

- content,
- structure and
- method:
    o attenuate
    o condense
    o contextualize
    o amplify.

How did you get on? Compare your thoughts with the conclusions I came to.

Content

In its original form our home page was simply a collection of the 'favourite' charts. The page served no purpose other than making it quick for people who were already very familiar with the system (like me!) to find things that they might be interested in. I hadn't given any thought to what I was trying to communicate to whom and why. Indeed, the flexibility we gave to users to choose their own content virtually guaranteed that the biases of different users would be reinforced. Without realizing it, I had assumed that users understood what they needed to know and how to go about finding it and interpreting it, which was unlikely to be the case.

Structure
On the positive side, the top third of the page was given over to contextual information, using familiar graphical devices. Below that, however, the content was shoehorned into a simple grid. This structure provided no visual clues about the significance or meaning of the content. The strict rectangular grid is visually unappealing, and users are given no help in navigating from the home page to other report 'pages' in the system that might hold more detail or other context.

Method
Attenuate: Blue was the signature colour we used, reflecting our corporate branding, but there was obviously too much of it. As well as being visually overpowering, the heavy blue shading drew attention to the wrong things – to headings and contextual information rather than the content. In the charts themselves we used colours in an inconsistent way, with too little thought given to the meaning we wanted to convey. For instance, forecast error was sometimes encoded in black and sometimes in blue. We were right to use saturated dark colours to ensure that the small but important error bars were not overlooked; but the overall effect was confusing and placed too many demands on the user's attention. We also used far too much non-data ink: unnecessary words, lines and content.

Condense: By using smaller copies of charts used elsewhere in the system and sticking rigidly to the grid format for the home page, we compressed information, but not in an intelligent way. In particular, it was often difficult for users to extract key information, such as what the error was last period, from these small graphics, dominated as they were by too much non-data ink.

Context: On the positive side, there was plentiful information in the top right-hand corner and in the title bar for a user to know 'what', 'who' and 'when'. However, much of this was unnecessary, given that the home page is configured by the user and so would not change every time they used the system. There was also a lot of redundant contextual data in the body of the page, such as in the heading of each chart.

Communicating by Visual Means

Amplify: Because it was totally configurable, we couldn't use the home page to draw the user's attention to the salient features of performance – it relied on users working out what was important for themselves and selecting the most appropriate chart. The level of visual background noise on the screen also made it difficult to differentiate pieces of information from each other.

So, you can see we had plenty we could work on!

This analysis is not 'correct' or comprehensive because – just like the words on this page – there may be many equally effective ways of communicating. What it does demonstrate is that, although graphic design is ultimately a matter of judgement, it is easy to constructively critique a design armed with just a little knowledge of how the brain assimilates visual information.

But diagnosis is only the first step. Step 2 is redesign.

In Figure 6.42 you can see where we ended up after we gave the home page a makeover. This is not the finished article – nothing ever is – and this baby is probably due another overhaul to exploit the capabilities of new software and reflect what we have learned about how our customers actually use our system. But it does demonstrate how much effective reports owe to good visual design.

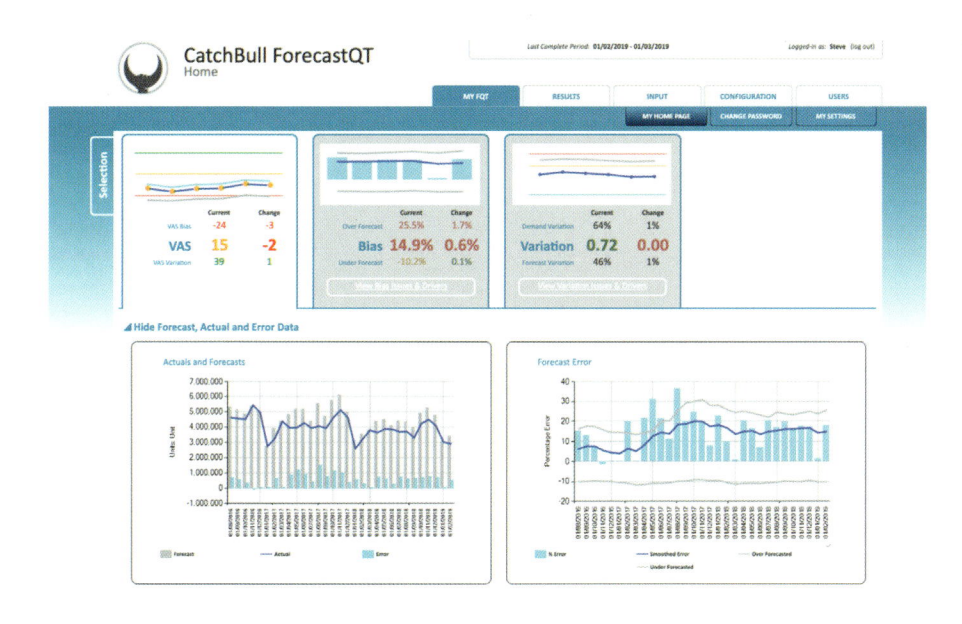

Figure 6.42:
New home page

After the 'makeover'.

Here are the major changes we made and the thinking behind them.

Content

We wanted to organize our new home chart to reflect a clear and consistent purpose. The primary purpose of the home page is to communicate the current level of forecast quality in a clear way, on three different but related dimensions: the value forecasting adds to the business, which is itself a product of how well it picks up the level and pattern of demand (bias and variation respectively). The results on these three perspectives are summarized in the headline strip, which also serves as a way of navigating between subsidiary reporting 'pages'. Because the headline strip is always visible, the context is preserved even when the content (on different pages) differs. While users are able to configure the home page so that it shows the results for the part of the business most relevant for them, the structure of the page is maintained.

Structure

The 'static' information strip at the top of the screen has been retained but it has been stripped of unnecessary clutter, so that the eye focusses on the most important dynamic content in the headline strip. The positioning of the headline strip keys into our newspaper-reading habits, which cause us to look for reference data (such as the date) at the top right and the most important summarized messages top and central. Below the headline chart the actual data and error charts (the data upon which all the analysis is based) are always shown below the headline strip, but other panels are hidden by default. The selection panel is also hidden but can be accessed by a tab on the left of the screen.

Method

Attenuation: The new home page uses fewer and more restrained colours, thinner lines, less shading and fewer words. Data colour coding is used in a consistent way throughout. So, for the error bars, we chose a shade of blue that is strong enough to be visible even where the error bars are small (as shown in the chart on the left of Figure 6.42) but not overpowering when they are larger (as in the chart on the right). Also notice how we use the same grey colour for under and over forecasting in the chart on the right, since the position of the grey lines codes for the meaning. Throughout the application, actual data and averages are encoded using lines that reflect their continuous nature. Any data generated periodically, such as forecasts, is encoded using bars, which signals that the underlying data is discontinuous (i.e. generated periodically in a batch).

Condensed: While the main medium of communication is graphical, in the headlines, we used numbers to provide a condensed summary of performance for the current period and the change from the last period. Note how we added an additional data dimension by colour coding the numbers to reflect the level of statistical significance and the direction of change respectively. The positioning and size of the numbers is also significant. For example, in the bias perspective, over forecasting is shown above the (larger and more important) net bias number, and under forecasting is shown below it. In support of the numbers we use a small 'thumbnail' summary chart with no axes or legends to provide a quick visual fix on how the pattern of performance has changed over the last six periods.

Contextualization: Since the headline summary of performance is always visible on the home page, irrespective of what perspective you are looking at, the context is never lost or hidden.

Amplification: The headline strip is bold and prominent, and the most important numbers are shown in large font and coded using colours. If performance is suboptimal or has deteriorated recently, the numbers are coloured amber or red. 'Neutral' performance is always shown using grey or black.

summary of part 3

What Have We Learned?

In Part 3 of this book I set out a step-by-step approach to improve the quality of your communication in formal reports.

The underlying premise is that the hallmark of truly effective communication is the ability to transfer an intended meaning to an audience quickly and faithfully. This requires information professionals to have a grasp of how the brain assimilates information. And given that the human brain is dominated by visual processing circuits, this means that we have to develop graphical literacy, based on an understanding of the grammar and syntax of visual communication.

Graphical designers make a living from their mastery of the medium, but the clumsiest analyst can produce 'good enough' reports following a simple procedure.

Focus first on purpose and content, then structure and only then on the method used to communicate meaning. And when considering method, first attenuate and condense your content to the bare minimum before adding context and amplifying that part of it which is critical to what it is you want to communicate. The overall objective is that it should be assimilated and faithfully understood by your audience with the minimum of effort on their part.

You know that you have succeeded if the impression that your audience have is that your reports are 'simple' and 'clear'. In this context, 'obvious' should be taken as a compliment. Things done well often just look easy.

Such faint praise might seem a meagre reward for the effort required to craft a good report. But the truth is that it is much easier to produce something dense and impenetrable, which might make you look clever, because you are the only one who understands it. While it is uncomfortable to admit to, many information professionals enjoy the power that comes with being the only ones who can navigate the labyrinth.

But, apart from the professional pride you will feel from a job well done, you will come to realize that no less responsibility – or power if you want to use that term – comes with the role of executing well-designed reports. This is because the apparent simplicity of delivery comes from information professionals selecting what data is relevant, attributing meaning to it and choosing how to communicate it.

What Have We Learned?

This places you, the information professional, in a privileged and responsible position, since you can shape what people understand to be the truth and therefore, to an extent, influence what is done as a result. You are not a dumb pipeline through which 'facts' flow. You are, in a real sense, an arbiter of what constitutes 'reality' for an organization – its consciousness of 'self' and its relationship to the world around it. This raises the important question of how this power should be used.

Learning	Reasons
Why it is important to learn to use graphical grammar.	To communicate effectively using visualizations you need to understand the rules, based on how the brain processes information coded visually – visual literacy.
What characterizes effective communication.	Communication is the process of transferring information between people using a medium in which meaning is encoded. Effective communication requires that recipients should be able to decode the encoded meaning, accurately and quickly.
How reports can fail to communicate.	Poor reports contain data that requires effort and extensive interpretation to try to determine what, if any, meaning it contains.
How reporting differs from analysis.	Unlike analysis, reporting tends to communicate information routinely in a consistent format, usually in a time ordered way. Crucially, it is almost always aimed at groups of people embedded within a social decision-making process.
Why digital dashboards have not replaced paper-based reports.	Paper (and slides) are a static 'broadcast' medium, thereby making it easier to ensure that recipients receive a consistent message. Software tools that enable individuals to explore and discover insights for themselves are complementary to static reports rather than replacements for them.
How BI software can enhance reporting.	BI software provides information professionals with an environment in which they can create crafted reports that users can interact with. This thereby enables them to combine control over communication process with an opportunity for recipients to actively learn and access relevant reference data for themselves.
Why visualization works for reporting.	Human brains have evolved to become highly efficient visual processing engines. Symbolic languages – particularly numbers – are an 'unnatural' cultural innovation, which some people are more skilled at using than others.

Learning	Reasons
When visualizations do not work.	Words and numbers are needed to provide the context and precision that visualizations alone lack.
How the brain perceives.	Our brain engages with visual sensations through the filter of our experience and expectations and then subconsciously scans them for form and pattern. We only become conscious of seeing and of 'doing work' when our working memory is engaged.
What implications the perception process has for how visualizations are used in reporting.	Use consistent rules of coding and organization across a report to prime our brains. Avoid the use of colours and circles to encode value and use shapes that provide clues about the phenomena that they represent, such as lines for continuous data. Position objects to suggest meaningful patterns and compress and chunk information to avoid overloading the limited capacity of our working memory. Use restrained colours and 'white space' to limit visual noise and guide the eyes.
How to design effective reports.	Decide what the report should contain, then how best to structure it before designing individual visualizations.
How to decide what a report should contain.	The content of a report is determined by its purpose, which is driven by the decisions that the audience of the report need to take and their individual knowledge and competencies.
What needs to be considered when structuring a report.	Consideration needs to be given to how content should be arranged on the page, in the page and between related pages. Look to exploit the way that our visual systems have been primed by the media that we come into contact with in our everyday life.
What qualities are required in a well-designed visualization.	Good visualizations should have a minimal amount of unnecessary 'ink' (attenuated). They must be contained in a small space (compressed) with a sufficient amount of background information to facilitate interpretation (contextualized) and with the most important information displayed prominently (amplified).

part 4
Action

action

/ˈakʃ(ə)n/
noun

1. the fact or process of doing something, typically to achieve an aim

chapter 7

Reporting is Reporting (Not Storytelling)

> In which I argue that information professionals should model themselves on news reporters, not storytellers.

At the end of Part 3 I posed the following questions:

1. 'What role should you, the interpreter of data and the designer of communication, play?'
2. 'What should guide your actions?'

You often hear people describing the process of performance reporting as being about 'storytelling', but I recoil from this thought. I understand why people think this, but I believe it is a dangerous idea.

Anthropologists have observed a phenomenon called 'Cargo Cults' in many 'underdeveloped' societies across the world that have sprung up where they have been exposed to an 'advanced' Western society that they don't understand. So, after the Second World War people in Melanesia who had observed supplies being dropped from planes to American occupying forces made 'control towers' out of wood and donned coconut shell 'headsets'. For them this made sense, because they had observed a correlation between these things and manna being dropped from heaven. They constructed a story that explained what they saw and a set of rituals to exploit what they thought they now understood.

This storytelling drive is deep within all of us and manifests itself most strongly whenever we are faced with situations that we cannot immediately make sense of. One of the qualities our brains crave most is 'coherence'. The need for coherence – the sense that everything fits together in a simple narrative with no ambiguity or loose ends – is a manifestation of our pattern-seeking drive. A story is just a pattern organized in time rather than in space, which is why human beings are storytelling animals. And as we have seen, the ability to discern patterns in a complex and noisy environment seems almost miraculous when it works; but it can equally lead us to make basic mistakes (such as seeing faces in clouds) or catastrophic errors.

In the same way, we can construct stories that can be compelling but completely untrue because they are based on flimsy or misinterpreted evidence. For example, people who believe in conspiracy theories usually have an entirely coherent internal model of the world – a story that hangs together that 'explains', for example, climate scientists' concerns about global warming or how autism is 'caused' by childhood vaccinations. In the latter case the problem is that these parents either are unable to assess evidence that suggests the contrary or are unwilling to accept it because they want to believe that someone or something is responsible for their tragedy.

In this context, it is worth thinking back to what we learned about the different ways in which our two hemispheres guide our attention. While the right hemisphere looks at the bigger picture, craves novelty and is comfortable with ambiguity, our left brain focusses, categorizes and compartmentalizes, often forcing a fit to reduce its sense of dissonance.[1]

This need for coherence, the desire for things to 'make sense' – even when we don't have the information to do more than make a guess – is the reason we like stories[2]. They neatly explain what happened and why, with simple cause and effect relationships, populated by 'goodies' and 'baddies' with simple motivations. We (or at least part of us) are uncomfortable with ambiguity and dislike suspending judgement or giving multiple competing interpretations equal weight. This is why intelligent people construct stories about 'why the market moved today' even when they and their audience know that they are just making things up. Understanding the motivation of even one person is difficult. How can anyone read the mind of thousands of market agents whom they have never met, particularly since many of them are machines. We want something that isn't possible in real life: absolute certainty. Even better if the story we create confirms our pre-existing opinions and prejudices.

Imposing order on and attributing meaning to a complex and fast-moving reality is the primary goal of information professionals. But it is at least as important – at the same time – to find ways to help your audience appreciate the highly provisional and contingent nature of any attempt to impose a simple explanation on a complex, dynamic and fundamentally unknowable world where ambiguity is rife.

And all of the traditional tools of the trade, like variance analysis, are already biased towards simple binary judgements that provide no scope for argument. Instead of finding new ways to drive out uncertainty, we should be encouraging people to perceive the world in a more holistic way and become more open to ambiguity. In particular, both learning and assessing risk – highly desirable traits in business – require us to take much more notice of things that *don't make sense* in the context of our current mental models.

This is the reason why I flinch whenever I hear people describing that they want information professionals to 'tell stories'. Granted, stories are powerful.

---

[1]. A famous example of this comes from research done in the 1960s on people who had had the corpus collosum that normally connects the two hemispheres of the brain surgically severed to treat their epilepsy. In one case a patient with a split brain is shown a picture of a chicken foot and a snowy field in separate visual fields and asked to choose from a list of words the best association with the pictures. The patient would choose a chicken to associate with the chicken foot and a shovel to associate with the snow; however, when asked to reason why the patient chose the shovel, the response would relate to the chicken (e.g. 'the shovel is for cleaning out the chicken coop'). Although accountants have not had their brains surgically modified my sense is that our focus on the minutiae of variance reports and the absence of context in our performance reports leaves us vulnerable to similar delusions.

[2]. It has been proven that the less we know the *more* confident we are of our opinions (the Dunning-Kruger effect) probably because it gives us more latitude to bend the 'facts' to fit our prejudices.

Reporting is Reporting (Not Storytelling)

They are clear and compelling. Too much so. They have a beginning and an end and a simple clear narrative that can only be interpreted in one way. Stories *tell* you what and why. There is no scope for alternative explanations or for doubt. And I think that is dangerous.

NEWS AND EVIDENCE

If we ever doubted the importance of having a capability to assimilate mountains of detail, synthesize it and present it in an accessible and balanced way, the storm around the recent reporting of political events has brought it home.

Despots have always exploited the ability to control news media in a world where facts are at a premium. So many tech entrepreneurs naïvely assumed that the instant availability of news and the proliferation of communication channels would provide us with a plurality of voices and views that would enable us to make up our own minds in a considered way, and help bring about a more tolerant, inclusive society.

Unfortunately, recent events have demonstrated how easy it is for the opposite to happen. Faced with an overabundance of data and opinion, we simplify matters by choosing a limited range of news sources; and in the process can too easily become trapped in a world of self-reinforcing views only loosely anchored in fact, where fake news is undistinguishable from reality.

On the unregulated news frontiers of our highly interconnected world we need the voices of trusted and reasoned judgement to be heard louder than ever before if we are not to revert to a tribal world where everyone retreats behind the palisades of their own prejudices.

In a different context, and on a smaller scale, this applies to organizations just as much as it does to societies. Information professionals have a key role in making sense of the world and communicating it in such a way that organizations come together around a measured and balanced view of the world. The alternative is a 'free' market where a dominant dogma swamps all other voices and competing interpretations.

Let me illustrate, in Figure 7.1, the communication challenge we face using the graphic that first drew me to Edward Tufte's work.
This chart was drawn by Charles Minard in 1869 and is a thing of great beauty on two levels. First, it is a wonderful example of how to communicate facts through graphics. Tufte claims that it is the best piece of graphical communication ever made – not bettered in over 150 years! And, armed with our new diagnostic skills, it is not difficult to see why he likes it so much.

Note the retained use of colour, the sensitive incorporation of contextual text and how it compresses multiple data dimensions (six!) onto a two-dimensional page. It tells the story of Napoleon's doomed Russian campaign in a way that words cannot. The chart succinctly illustrates the huge distances covered, the complex diversions and the shocking rate at which men perished in the bitter cold of a Russian winter while being harried by Russian irregular forces. It works

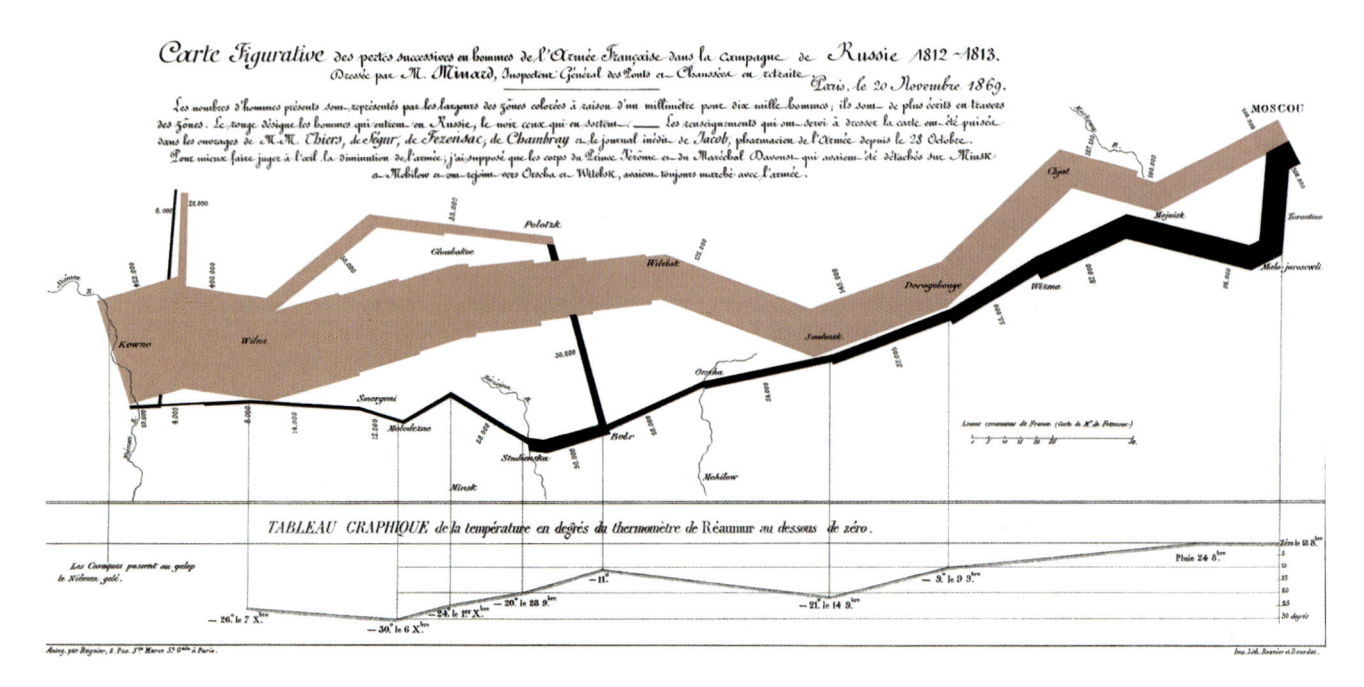

Figure 7.1:
Napoleon's Russian campaign graphic

The best chart ever?

Charles Minard's chart illustrating the history of Napoleon's 1812 winter campaign, used by Edward Tufte as an exemplar of good chart design. Source: Charles Joseph Minard, Tableaux Graphiques et Cartes Figuratives de M Minard, 1845-1869, Bibliothèque de L'École Nationale de Ponts et Chausées, Paris.

because it tells a performance story in an extremely efficient and effective way. But is it a model that we can emulate?

I don't think it is. Not just because the level of degree of skill and sophistication make it difficult to achieve in 'real time'. It is because I don't think that reporting is about telling stories at all; it is about *reporting*.

This chart demonstrates how it *is possible* to tell a coherent, simple story from the vantage point of a historian, in this case, 50 years after the event. Half a century afterwards, all the facts are known and a balanced judgement can be made with the full benefit of hindsight. But it is rarely possible to do this 'in the moment'. Indeed, sometimes the what and why may not even be clear many years after the event. Historians are still arguing over who 'won' the Battle of Borodino that immediately preceded Napoleon's long march back to France! In his great novel, *War and Peace*, Leo Tolstoy used the Battle of Borodino as an example of how we *impose a story* on events that are in reality confused and chaotic, because we find the messiness and meaninglessness of much of what happened difficult to cope with.

This is the reason I think information professionals should not aspire to be 'storytellers'. But as Phil Rosenzweig observes: 'management is about taking action, about doing things. So what can be done?'. He argues that as a first step we should 'set aside the delusions that color so much of our thinking about business performance. To recognize that stories of inspiration may give us comfort but have little more predictive power than a pair of coconut headsets on a tropical island.'

Next, I would argue that information professionals should think of themselves not as storytellers but as reporters. A good model for what they do is the war correspondent attempting to make sense of what is happening on the ground in a conflict situation. Their job is to present a balanced report, recognizing that we don't have access to all the facts and the events that are being reported on can be interpreted in different ways. A reporter's role is to communicate the relevant facts in order to help us form *our own opinions*. A good reporter doesn't promote a particular version of the truth. That is called propaganda. History can only be told after the event; it cannot be observed in real time.

Even though the performance reporter doesn't have the job of 'telling the story', the role still carries great responsibility. While any report can be interpreted in a number of different ways, what a reporter chooses to include and exclude and how information is communicated has a big influence on the psyche of the audience and how they respond to what they learn. And with power comes responsibility, so it is important that performance reporters have a sense of their duty to the 'truth', in so far as it is possible, guided by a clear set of principles to steer their activities.

This is not the place to explore the role and ethics of performance reporting in detail, but I think there are at least four key duties.

The duty of clarity

Performance reports should be clear. The intended meaning must be communicated in a way that can be quickly assimilated by the intended audience. Data that confuses or distorts the message needs to be excluded where possible. Significant data that would otherwise be hidden or obscured should be emphasized.

The duty of balance

A reporter has to make choices about what is, and what is not, 'said'. These choices must be made in a way that does not favour the interests of any constituency in the business. The message should neither reinforce received wisdom nor challenge it merely to be provocative. Communication should, as far as possible, be balanced and free from bias.

The duty of requisite ambiguity

Communication needs to be clear, balanced and nuanced – simple but not simplistic. The collective knowledge and experience of the audience is always greater than that of an individual performance reporter. So, it is important that he or she provides sufficient contextual information to allow the audience to validate or challenge the message, or to come up with an alternative interpretation of the facts, particularly if they have contextual knowledge that can be brought to bear. Reports therefore have to contain a degree of redundancy (slightly more information than is needed to support the intended message), even to the point of ambiguity, since the 'truth', if such things exists at all, is only obvious in hindsight.

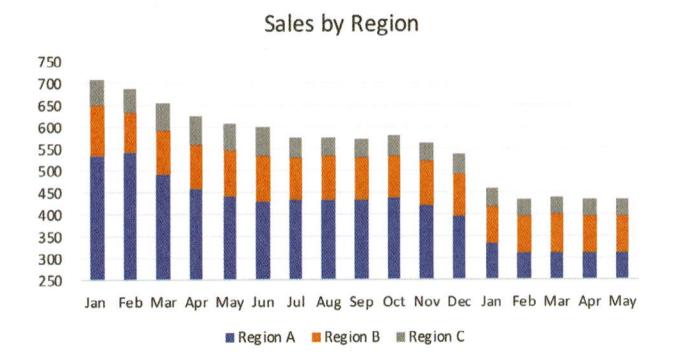

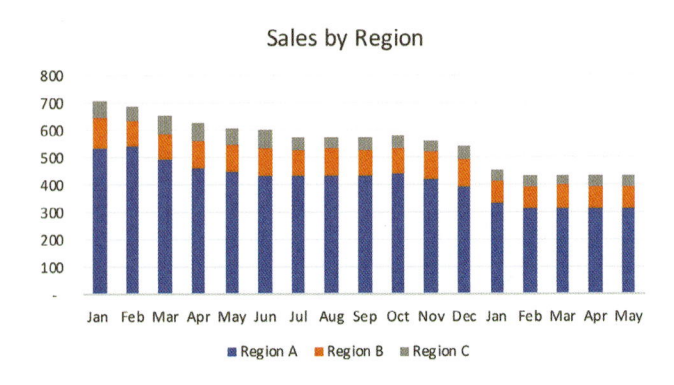

(Above) Figure 7.2:
Misleading use of chart areas

The bar chart on the left does not start the Y axis at zero, which fools our eye because it is triggered by area. The magnitude of the change is overstated, and the contribution of Region A is understated.

(Right) Figure 7.3:
Misleading trends

The right-hand chart overstates the magnitude of the change by tampering with the aspect ratio as well as the origin of the Y axis.

(Bottom) Figure 7.4:
False correlations

Dishonestly juxtaposing two unrelated data series and tampering with the scale of the secondary axis creates a misleading impression of correlation. Unless of course you think that eating more cheese causes death by bedsheet![3]

3. Read more about this and other spurious correlations in Tyler Vigen's book of the same name. Taken at face value, they suggest that Nicolas Cage should be stopped from releasing movies, as they're linked with deaths in swimming pools (correlation coefficient +0.67), and that America should ban the import of Japanese cars, as they're associated with suicide by car crash (correlation coefficient +0.94). This illustrates as well as anything can the dangers of setting loose 'learning machines' on large data sets.

The duty of integrity

Finally, reports should not mislead, intentionally or otherwise. In particular, reporters need to ensure that:

- Areas faithfully reflect the size of the variable that they represent. So, for example, Y and X axes of bar charts should, wherever possible, intersect at zero (Figure 7.2).

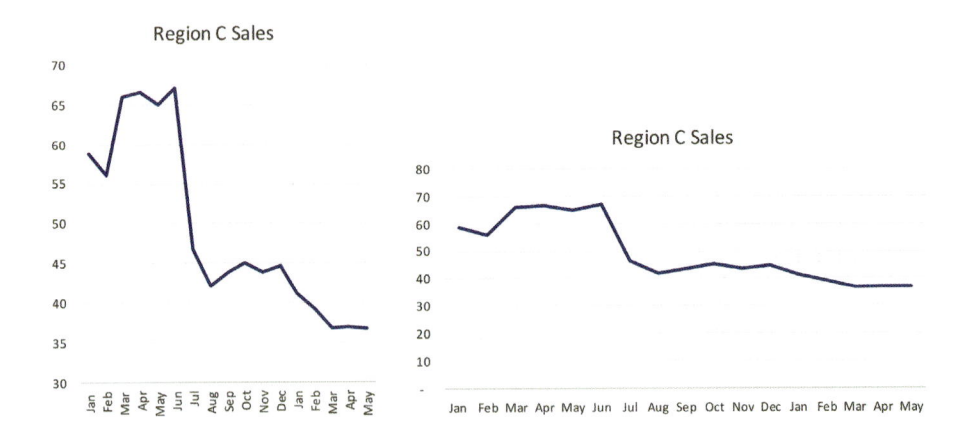

- Trends are not presented in a way that magnifies or suppresses them (Figure 7.3). Thus, for instance, the aspect of line graphs should have consistent aspect ratios, ideally around 1 to 1.5 (height to width).

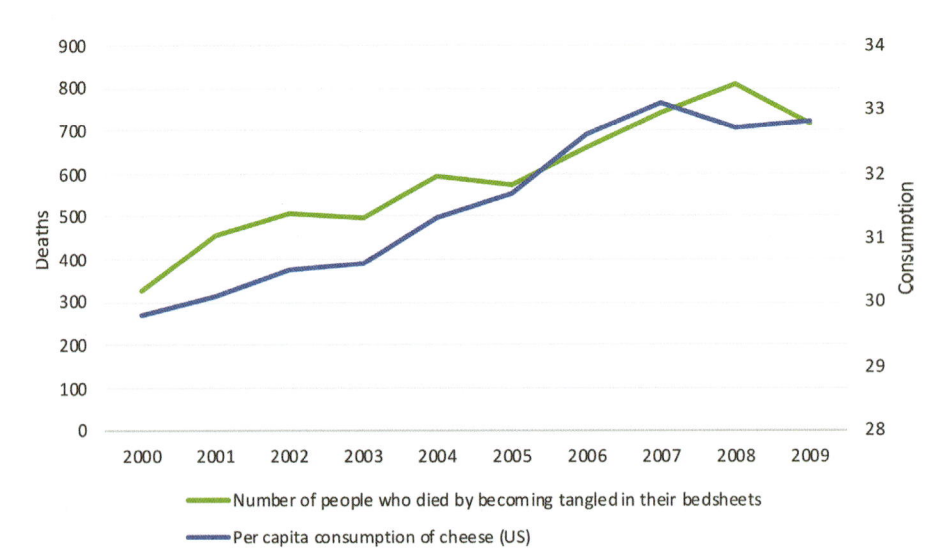

Reporting is Reporting (Not Storytelling)

- Information is presented in a way that does not invite false correlations to be made. This involves careful consideration of the scales used, particularly when a single chart has a secondary scale (Figure 7.4).

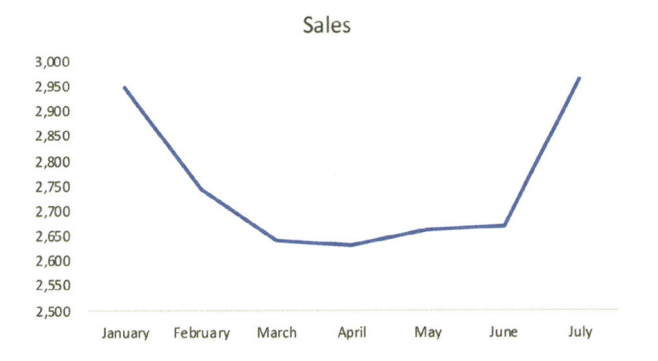

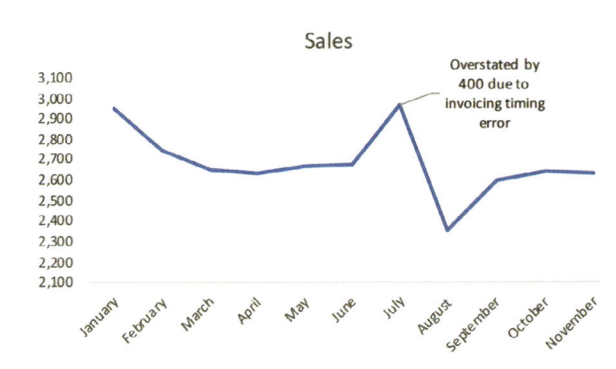

- Anything that is presented that could easily be misinterpreted is highlighted (Figure 7.5). For example, a reporter might add a comment to a data point if it is known to be unrepresentative of the series – perhaps because of an exceptional event or a data collection issue.

Figure 7.5:
Missing context

Selective presentation of the historical context on the left creates a false impression. On the right we can see that the apparent rapid decline and 'bounce back' is better interpreted as a steady decline interrupted by a false 'spike' associated with a data recording incident.

Although being 'right' all the time is a noble aspiration, it is unattainable. Instead, what reporters should strive for is to be respected – for their skills – and trusted – for their judgement and impartiality.

Sometimes the best, and perhaps the only, thing that you can achieve in the limited time available to you is to direct the attention of the right people in the business to the right things, and help them ask the right questions.

Learning	Reasons
Why 'storytelling' is a bad analogy for performance reporting.	Unlike the world of stories, the real world is complex and ambiguous with no simple cause and effect, beginning and end. Nor do performance reporters have the time or knowledge to form neat conclusions. Reporting the news is a better example to follow. In this case, the reporter acts as a filter, directing the attention of the audience to those things that they need to take into account when forming their own opinion.
What principles should guide the actions and behaviour of performance reporters.	Performance reporters have the duty to present the 'news' with: • clarity, • balance, • requisite ambiguity and • integrity.

chapter 8

Now What?

> In which I share a practical framework to help readers work out how best to facilitate changes in their organization.

There is one question that authors like me dread when we present our stuff to an audience. It usually goes something like this:

> 'I buy most of what you say; but you haven't given me any advice about how to do it'.

It is difficult to dismiss this kind of challenge for the simple reason that the people asking it are right. Knowledge only has value if you can apply it.

The problem I have is that, if I try to answer the question directly or use a case study to illustrate how these ideas can be applied, the riposte is often 'My company/the situation I am facing isn't like that'. Which is also right, because everyone starts from a different place, has different aims and different levels of influence and power.

How can we avoid this catch-22 situation?

I've come to appreciate that you cannot solve everyone's problems for them, at least not from a distance. The best you can do is to provide them with a set of general principles to help them work out what to do for themselves in their specific context.

In my experience, there are two basic types of situations faced by those promoting change in an organization.

Scenario one is where it is widely recognized that large-scale change is needed. Perhaps a new Chief Financial Officer (CFO) has come into a business and wants to make her mark by sweeping away the tired and bureaucratic reporting processes she has inherited. Maybe business teams are drowning in a sea of numbers and are crying out for help. There could be a political crisis at the top of the business that has led to different factions subverting corporate information processes by producing their own versions of 'the truth'.

In these circumstances, change can be tackled in an open and deliberate manner. And you can either design your own change programme or bring someone in to help you. In this situation, the challenge is one of execution.

Scenario two is where it is not possible, or perhaps even desirable, to make changes in an open, explicit and structured manner – a much more common situation in my experience.

Maybe the change agent has lots of great ideas but doesn't have the organizational power to make sweeping changes. Perhaps the organization as a whole is distracted by other 'more important' projects and it doesn't think it has the capacity or the will to take on another. It might be that the people who need to approve any new project *are* the problem; perhaps their thinking is out of date or they are using the current dysfunctional processes to protect their own interests.

In this scenario, creating the conditions for change in an organization is usually more of a challenge than actually making the changes themselves. This is certainly true for performance reporting, where the techniques I have presented can be executed using standard desktop software and plugged into processes that already exist.

The resistance to change that you encounter could be because people in the organization have an investment in the status quo. Perhaps it is the inertia of familiarity or that traditional ways of working are just easier – tables are straightforward in Excel, but graphs take more work. Or maybe they are worried about losing power or influence. This is particularly so for the finance function, because established practice follows the traditional financial model very closely – as evidenced by the pre-eminence of financial metrics, the use of fixed targets providing binary answers (good/bad), simple arithmetic, tabular presentation methods and so on.

But, in my experience, the source of resistance is much more difficult to spot and overcome because it is a consequence of the way that people *think* – their assumptions about the world and their beliefs about the motivation of the people that inhabit it.

For example, if you do not recognize the existence of 'noise', believe that the world is perfectly predictable and that human beings have to be motivated to do the right things by setting targets and being 'held to account', then traditional variance analysis is the obvious – perhaps the only – way that performance can be measured and managed.

Only when people recognize for themselves that these assumptions are questionable will they be able to conceive of a different way of doing things. Which is tricky, because often the individuals are not aware that they are making these assumptions – they don't know that they don't know. Just as often, people talk about uncertainty and ambiguity but act as if they don't exist. They set targets and chase down variances without recognizing the disconnect between what they say and how they actually behave.

So, this isn't always straightforward. Is there any hope?

When I am thinking about how to facilitate change (which includes writing this book) I usually refer to a simple approach that I call the change formula. While it isn't the 'right' or only way to go about things, it is simple, subtle and flexible enough to enable change agents to design a coherent approach in a wide variety of situations – including the two scenarios I have just outlined.

According to this formula, these are the conditions required for any successful change:

$$D \times V \times S \geq R$$

In a nutshell, what this tells us is that a precondition of successful change is that people are sufficiently unhappy, inspired by a vision of the future and clear about the practical first steps needed to overcome the forces of resistance to that change.

Let's take each of the terms in turn:

D STANDS FOR DISSATISFACTION

It is the received management wisdom that change requires a 'burning platform' – an emergency that puts the organization in peril. While it is unlikely that the current state of the reporting process is 'life threatening' for any business, it is true that it is very difficult to bring about change unless there is a widespread recognition that there is a problem that needs fixing. Just ask anyone who has tried selling something to someone who is satisfied with what they have already got.

A big part of the secret of successful change involves making invisible problems visible, and helping people to appreciate why they are important enough to do something about. Even when people don't like the status quo, they have often learned to live with it. They tell themselves that there is 'no alternative' or things 'will always be this way'. Therefore, one of your jobs as a change agent might be to shock them out of their passivity and fatalism.

So, one of the most important, and relatively easy, steps to mobilize an organization for change is to force people to confront their misery. In the words of William Bridges, author of *Managing Transitions*, as a change leader you need to 'sell problems, not solutions'.

V STANDS FOR VISION

Vision is a picture of the future that is capable of inspiring people.

Getting the vision right is a matter of balance.

If a vision is made too concrete and detailed it is unlikely to be inspiring. But if it is insufficiently clear and tangible people may find it difficult to commit to it.

It is also important to get the right level of 'stretch'. If a vision is too far-fetched it will be difficult to get people to believe that it is achievable. If it is too much like current reality it will be difficult to generate enough enthusiasm, because there is no challenge.

Clearly it is great if the leaders of the business publicly commit to the vision; but it doesn't have to come from the top. The authentic passion of the individual promoting it, and their ability to inspire others (perhaps even the 'official' leaders) is often more important than their job title.

Also remember that organizations never change – only people in them do. The vision must resonate with what people really care about, and these might not be the same things that motivate the CEO.

S STANDS FOR FIRST STEPS

If the vision has the right amount of stretch – challenging but not implausible – it is unlikely that you will be able to specify everything that needs to be done in detail at the start.

Even if it were possible, issuing a set of instructions to be followed could disenfranchise the very people that you need to enrol in the process for it to succeed. People only really commit to what they help create. So my advice is to 'design to 50%' and let others – and the lessons you learn from doing things and not getting it quite right – look after the other half.

AGILE (AGAIN)

This is another area where we can use 'agile' style development methods.

In an agile project, once you have checked that what you are attempting to do and how you plan to do it are technically and economically feasible, you proceed by a series of incremental steps.

The process starts with a set of needs (often expressed as 'user stories'), prioritized based on the size of the benefit and how easy it is to achieve, or the opportunity it gives to learn something important to the ultimate success of the project (e.g. how easy it is for non-technical people to use this software).

The project team is then responsible for addressing the most important 'user stories' in the next timebox - which could be a day, a week or a month depending on the nature of the project.

After each sprint (as these timeboxes are sometimes called) progress is reviewed, needs reassessed and the prioritized list for the next iteration is drawn up. Critically, users are deeply involved in the process of creating the prioritized lists and reviewing progress.

In this way, meaningful change can be rapidly and effectively delivered without there being a need for a plan in the conventional sense of the word.

R STANDS FOR RESISTANCE

Resistance to change can take many forms.

It might represent an individual who sets out to block or undermine efforts to bring about change. More likely, however, resistance comes in the form of FUD:

fear (e.g. 'I'm not sure that I can do this'), uncertainty (e.g. 'How will this affect me?') and doubt (e.g. 'Will this work?').

In physical systems, such as cars, resistance (in the form of friction or inertia) is passive. In social systems, like organizations, we call passive resistance to change apathy, but we are as likely to encounter active resistance to change. In a physical system, such as a stationary car, increasing the pressure for change (pushing it) will ultimately overcome resistance. But organizations are populated by biological systems called human beings that behave differently to the application of force. Anyone with children knows that simply increasing pressure can increase the resistance, so dealing with resistance requires more than just the application of force. The best strategy is to reduce resistance – or avoid it altogether – rather than to try and overcome it. Even a child can move a frictionless car.
So that's the change equation. How can we make it work for us?

At a high level, this model tells us that to bring about change the value of the product of the terms on the left-hand side of the equation must be greater than the forces of resistance on the right. It is not enough to have a 'burning platform' or a 'compelling vision'. These are necessary but they are not sufficient.

The equation also tells us that you need a value for every one of the terms on the left.

If the 'vison' term is zero, no one will follow you, since they do not know where they are going. If the perceived level of dissatisfaction is small, there will be no energy for change; people will be satisfied with the status quo. If the 'first steps' is blank then 'S' is zero and nothing will happen because if no one knows what to do next the commitment to change will soon ebb away – even if there is energy and a sense of purpose.

Equally, if you fail to manage the forces of resistance effectively your efforts to bring about change will be frustrated.

For those facing scenario one who adopt an explicit, systematic approach to change, the lessons are clear.

First

Start by identifying the problems that people have or believe they have (D). Then, picking away at them as if they were a scab, make the problems bigger and more painful. The scope of what you can achieve and the resources that you can mobilize are driven by the perceived size and urgency of the problem you solve for the organization. More pain, more gain.

Second

Identify those things or people that could frustrate your ambitions (R) and understand the source of the resistance. It is easy to assume that those who disagree with you are stupid or bad, but the source of their misgivings might be innocent and easy to resolve. Perhaps they have misunderstood or suspect your motives; maybe they don't understand what you are trying to achieve; or they could be scared or intimidated by the prospect. Perhaps they need to be helped to see that how they think is what stops them recognizing the problem or coming up with a solution. Once you have identified the resistance, do what you can to eliminate or reduce it – ideally by education or persuasion rather than by hiring a hit man!

THEN

Having surfaced the problems and neutralized potential resistance, you can now set out the vision and devise your implementation strategy. In framing the vision, express it in a way that is meaningful to those you want to inspire. And in planning what to do first, choose something that is easy, and that has a relatively large, visible and positive impact. Nothing attracts support better than success.

With scenario two – where it is not possible to elicit support for a 'full-frontal assault' on a recognized problem – you have to start from a different position. You cannot be as open about what you would like to achieve either, because the forces of resistance are too great or there is not widespread recognition of the problem. It may be that you don't even know yourself because you don't have all the answers.

In these circumstances it is best to adopt guerrilla tactics rather than attempt a full-frontal assault. Instead of confronting them, avoid sources of resistance and attract support by 'doing' rather than persuasion. When what you do comes to be recognized as valuable you will be able to build a supporting coalition and make a case for change more explicitly. Even if your victories are small or not widely appreciated, you will gain the confidence and the permission to make further incremental changes. In time, the world will come over to your side.

This iterative, incremental approach to change begs the following questions:

- Which of the innovations I have described in this book would it be best to tackle first?
- What changes are likely to give the biggest visible benefit and engender the least resistance?

This is the order in which I would place them – all other things being equal (which they never are):

1. GRAPHICAL COMMUNICATION

Improving the quality of communication through better design is the easiest thing to 'sell', precisely because it doesn't need much selling. You probably don't even need to ask permission to make changes and, if you do it well, it is unlikely that you will encounter any resistance. After all, who is going to object to you making their life easier, particularly if you don't ask them to let go of anything that they believe is important to them? Having control over what and how information is presented gives you the power to influence the perceptions of the audience and so, over time, shift their behaviour in subtle ways.

2. Dynamic measures

In my experience, techniques like MATs are easy to introduce because they are simple and intuitive. And, as the audience becomes more comfortable with this way of presenting information, they will become less reliant on crude and misleading target-based measures of performance, which will help loosen the grip of the damaging obsession with financial periods. In Unilever, we stopped collecting the detailed phased budgets necessary for corporate level variance analysis without anybody noticing (not even the Corporate Controller!) until we pointed it out some months later – which shows how little value they had.

Had we (myself and the Head of FP&A) asked for permission to ditch the process, I'm sure that it would have been refused.

3. Tracking against targets

Once users have become comfortable with a dynamic perspective on performance, it is not a big leap to replacing period end 'fixed point' with moving targets and tracking performance against them. In turn, over time, this will help undermine the belief that managing business performance has to involve a big set piece annual process generating a raft of targets. Although the tracking method I describe in Part 3 is statistically rigorous, users do not need to understand anything about the mechanics of the calculations used, since the results are intuitively easy to grasp and lend themselves to being presented in a familiar form – as traffic light type alarms.

4. Statistical filtration

There is no doubt that statistically-based tools like control charts are the most challenging innovation to introduce into organizations.

But as businesses collect more and more data they cannot continue to duck the challenge of making sense of noise in data sources by pretending the problem doesn't exist or outsourcing it to 'experts'. It is impossible to exploit the potential of the large data sets that most businesses now have using traditional analytical methods based on simple arithmetic, where numbers are usually just added, subtracted and occasionally divided. Sooner or later businesses will be forced to accept that they need to add more sophisticated analytical techniques to the toolkits that they use to routinely analyse performance data. And information professionals need to get on board the bus and start driving it or risk irrelevance.

I'm not talking AI or fancy algorithms here. The world of business is far too complex for someone armed only with a mathematics PhD!

Statistical filtration techniques like control charts have a big part to play because they augment rather than replace the human being in the process. They do this without being too complicated for normal human beings to understand – after all they predate electric calculators by half a century. These techniques enable a more sophisticated approach to the assimilation and analysis of large data sets without the need to educate the consumers of information in the statistical niceties of the method – the only requirement is to be able to 'read' a chart, which is easy.

While the consumers of information can be spared the statistics, this approach does require information professionals brought up in an arithmetical world to re-orientate their thinking – even if they do not perform any of the statistical calculations themselves. Some things need to be unlearned before new ways of thinking can be learned, and this will not happen overnight. Introducing even simple statistical techniques like this on a large scale will require investment in tools and education.

Looking further ahead, it is clear that we are at the early stages of a revolution in analytical practices that rely on much more sophisticated statistical algorithms such as those that drive Machine-Learning technology. Better start sooner rather than later with small-scale local experimentation and learn how best to exploit the power of statistics before being forced to embark on anything more ambitious.

5. Reframing the meaning of performance

Arguably the biggest opportunity associated with letting go of stale techniques, like variance analysis, is that it enables us to break free from the narrow-minded and intellectually indefensible practice of using arbitrary fixed 'point' targets to manage performance. But breaking out of this self-imposed straitjacket and embracing a dynamic perspective requires us to reframe the meaning of performance.

This is a really fundamental change – much bigger than the challenge associated with the adoption of new tools and techniques. It requires us to rethink our ideas about how businesses are organized and managed, along with the thinking and behaviour of those that work in it, from first principles. Within the scope of this book, I have done little more than expose the questionable nature of many of the assumptions that underpin conventional thinking on how performance should be managed. If you want to explore this topic further, I suggest you start by dipping into the companion volume to this book, *The Little Book of Beyond Budgeting*.

Now What?

Learning	Reasons
How to go about creating the conditions for successful change.	Successful change requires that there should be dissatisfaction with the status quo, a vision for the future and some idea of what to do first – and that the energy these create should be greater than the forces of resistance.
What process to follow in managing a successful change project.	First amplify the dissatisfaction with the current situation, then identify the things that could frustrate change and either weaken or avoid them. Finally, enrol people in a vision and start implementation, focussing on those things that yield visible benefits, quickly.
How to tackle the process of changing performance reporting when you don't have an explicit mandate.	Make those changes that you can make without the need for corporate endorsement and build a case for change by demonstrating the effectiveness of alternative approaches rather than argument.
In what order changes should be made.	The order is determined by the likelihood of resistance, practical ease and the immediacy of the perceiver benefits. This would have us introduce visualizations first, followed by dynamic measurement and performance monitoring. The introduction of statistical filtration techniques and finding alternatives to traditional fixed targets are more challenging and are best tackled when an organization has more maturity and confidence.

epilogue

A Reflection

I started the intellectual journey that led to me writing this book with a simple idea. The idea that conventional variance analysis of the kind that I was taught to use didn't work, and that we needed an alternative.

I was driven by my personal experience as a practitioner and the uncomfortable feeling that my professional pride in churning this stuff out – accurate and on time – was misplaced. I was trying to process the uncomfortable feeling that much of what I had done in my professional life – particularly when I got my hands on the reigns of sophisticated IT systems – was the wrong thing, just more efficiently and more quickly.

Perhaps I am being too hard on myself. The sins I committed are the same as those of over 99% of my peers in what one might loosely call the business information professions. Ironically, probably the only people that weren't fooled were the amateurs – the simple-minded people I wrote off as being numerically illiterate. The kind of people who didn't use fixed targets and variances to manage their personal finances and saw no reason to use them at work.

We, the information warriors, were – are – prisoners of our inherited mental models forged in the early years of professional management, in an age dominated by mechanical machines. This taught us that there was only one way to go about producing anything in an efficient and consistent way. Break a complex process down into its constituent parts and engineer each one before putting them back together to create a complicated whole by the repetition and combination of simple tasks.

This approach works well in a simple world. It even works well in complicated situations like manufacturing, providing the input and the environment can be tightly controlled and the desired output of the process properly specified. And, for the want of a better way of doing things and the technology needed to do anything different, managers from the 1920s onwards have applied this approach to measuring and managing organizations.

But this approach does not work well in a complex world. The level of detail is overwhelming and ever changing; and simple cause and effect relationships of engineered machines don't exist. Ironically, most of the complexity that we now face was created directly or indirectly by another kind of machine – the electronic computer.

It is now clear to everyone who thinks deeply about organizations and how best to structure and manage them that we have to think and act in a different way. We must rid ourselves of machine metaphors, or at least relegate them to the background, to be brought out when we are faced with a task that they are suited to.

Instead, we need metaphors for management and organizations that are grounded in biology to guide the development of management thinking and practice. Only organic life has the ability to survive and thrive in a complex and dynamic environment. And the only organic life that has learned the trick of adapting without the messy business of evolution by selective extinction are human beings, because they have access to a unique and special organ – their brain. It is the brain that should inspire our thinking about how to make sense of the world. And, at a practical level, we need to exploit the power of our brain where it does things well (like spotting patterns in visually rendered data). We also have to find ways of compensating where it does less well, like noisy environments where we need to use probabilistic reasoning.

This book has explored the implications of these ideas for information professionals at a practical level. For working out how best to make sense of the work and for communicating it to those we work with who are charged with making the decisions that impact the entire organization. In the process we create the shared consciousness that is a prerequisite for effective and efficient collective action.

Some people believe that we are standing at a threshold of a revolution in the application of cognitively inspired technologies to the business of management, powered by machine learning and fed by Big Data. Some of the things that have started to make their way into our everyday life, like voice recognition systems, were regarded as science fiction only a few years ago. But I'm not going to make any brave predictions about how these will change the nature of management. The flickering shadows of many false dawns haunt the history of AI, and I'm sure that there are plenty more hurdles we have not yet faced that will make progress more challenging than the current crop of technological evangelists imagine.

But even if self-driving cars go the way of expert systems and readers of this book never touch anything more sophisticated than an Excel spreadsheet, I am convinced that the results of applying this thinking and the approaches I have described in this book can be transformative. And here is the best bit. By using approaches that are more in tune with the way our brains are structured – our intuition – even as the world gets more complex, the solutions will look and feel simple.

It is nearly 50 years since the systems scientist Stafford Beer published *Brain of the Firm*, where he derived the principles of the functioning of the human nervous system and applied them to the structure and functioning of 'exceedingly complex systems' such as social organizations. What is new is that technologies are now being built that have the capability to enact ideas like those that Beer described.

But I'm jumping ahead of myself. These ideas are for another time and place. For the moment, thank you all for accompanying me this far on the journey. And be sure to enjoy yourselves by creating something great.

Reading List

ACCOUNTING, MEASUREMENT AND GOALS

Bosgnes, B. (2016). *Implementing Beyond Budgeting: Unlocking the Performance Potential.* John Wiley & Sons.

> A practical down to earth guide to the challenges and opportunities from implementing Beyond Budgeting for someone who has been there, done that and got the tee shirt.

Kay, J. (2011). *Obliquity: Why our Goals are Best Achieved Indirectly.* Profile Books.

> To my knowledge there is almost nothing written on the subject of goals and goal setting outside the traditional (and to my mind) discredited literature. This is one, from an unusual source - an academic economist. Its thesis is that the world is so dynamic and complex that we can never know enough to set precise meaningful goals in advance. Instead we need to set 'proximate' goals that help us navigate towards our ultimate goals, often in an oblique fashion. Well worth a read.

Johnson, H. T. (1992). *Relevance Regained: From Top-Down Control to Bottom-Up Empowerment.* Free Press.

> Tom Johnson is perhaps the first and most trenchant critic of the dominant paradigm of what he called 'management by remote control' - that is, financial variance analysis.

Morlidge, S. (2017). *The Little Book of Beyond Budgeting: A New Operating System for Organizations: What it is and why it works.* Matador Press.

> A short introduction to the ideas and principles of Beyond Budgeting. This book was originally conceived of as providing a solution to the measurement challenge in the Beyond Budgeting framework, but grew into something bigger.

Wheeler, D. (2000). *Understanding Variation: The Key to Managing Chaos* (2nd ed.). SPC Press.

A classic. Short, to the point and practical.

Wheeler, D. (2003). *Making Sense of Data*. SPC Press.

A more detailed exposé of measurement practices and noisy environment. For the enthusiasts only.

COGNITIVE SCIENCE

We are lucky that we live in an era where serious scientists are prepared to expend time and energy communicating their ideas to a lay audience. Many of these books are excellently written and the science is progressing at a rate that, however well informed you think you are, there will always be something that surprises and delights you.

Here are a few of my favourites.

There are a number of concise, readable introductions to recent developments in brain science. I would recommend the following:

Eagleman, D. (2011). *Incognito: The Secret Lives of the Brain*. Canongate.
Frith, C. D. (2007). *Making up the Mind: How the Brain Creates Our Mental World*. Blackwell.
Seth, A. K. (2014). *30-second Brain: The 50 Most Mind-blowing Ideas in Neuroscience, Each Explained in Half a Minute*. Icon Books.

The more academically minded might enjoy:

Clark, A. (2016). *Surfing Uncertainty: Prediction, Action, and the Embodied Mind*. Oxford University Press.

Although I have focussed on the interrelationship between visual perception and explicitly rational cognition in this book, there is increasing evidence of the important role that feelings and emotion play in the way that we make sense of the world.

To discover more read:

Damasio, A. R. (2006). *Descartes' Error: Emotion, Reason and the Human Brain*. Vintage.
Feldman Barrett, L. (2017). *How Emotions Are Made: The Secret Life of the Brain*. Picador.

Finally, it is clear that the brain operates as a network, rather than a collection of localized modules with distinct functionality. There is also a history of the role of left/right hemisphere divide being distorted in pop psychology. Nevertheless, there is evidence that there is some differentiation in their roles, which is relevant in the context of this book. To discover more read:

McGilchrist, I. (2009). *The Master and His Emissary: The Divided Brain and the Making of the Western World*. Yale University Press.

DATA VISUALIZATION

Although most practitioners are only vaguely aware of it, this field has made rapid advances in the last decade or so. And there are many books from authors out there that (like me!) have 'seen the light'. But I think it is difficult to beat the work of the pioneers.

In particular I would recommend the work of Stephen Few who, in my opinion, has struck the right balance between intellectual integrity and practicality. In particular I recommend the following:

Few, S. (2006). *Information Dashboard Design: The Effective Visual Communication of Data*. O'Reilly.
Few, S. (2012). *Show Me the Numbers*. Analytics Press.

For a more theoretical 'design-orientated view,' read Edward Tufte's work, particularly:

Tufte, E. R. (2001). *The Visual Display of Quantitative Information* (2nd ed.). Graphics.

But if you want to 'deep dive' into the theory try:

Ware, C. (1999). *Information Visualization: Design for Perception*. Morgan Kaufman.

OTHERS

Here are some other books that readers might enjoy.

Christian, B. and Griffiths, T. (2017). *Algorithms to Live by: The Computer Science of Human Decisions*. William Collins.
Kahneman, D. (2011). *Thinking, Fast and Slow*. Penguin.

I have grouped these two together because they view decision-making (and therefore cognition) from completely different perspectives. Christian and Griffiths looks at how computer scientists have tackled some of the problems that the brain has faced, thereby giving us insight into why the brain is 'engineered' the way that it is. Kahneman famously describes how we actually often think in a way that is not strictly rational, thereby providing us with the awareness of and the ability to compensate for our biases.

Meadows, D. (2009). *Thinking in Systems: A Primer.* Earthscan.

A classic, easy to read introduction to system modelling by one of the pioneers.

McChrystal, S. A., Silverman, D., Fussell, C. and Collins, T. (2015). *Team of Teams: New Rules of Engagement for a Complex World.* Penguin.

A fascinating and surprisingly thoughtful book about how a military leader came to understand why creating a shared consciousness for a fighting force was superior to conventional command structures.

Pink, D. H. (2011). *Daniel H Pink: Drive. The Surprising Truth about What Motivates Us.* Canongate Books.

A readable summary of recent research on motivation at work.
Last and not least, here are two excellent books that provide us with valuable insights into the process of making evidence-based judgements:

Rosenzweig, P. M. (2007). *The Halo Effect… and the Eight Other Business Delusions That Deceive Managers.* Free Press.

This outlines the logical traps that business academics and authors fall into when they try to describe and explain the performance of different businesses.

Silver, N. (2013). *The Signal and the Noise: The Art and Science of Prediction.* Penguin.

Nate Silver has become famous for applying rigorous analytical technique to complex real-life issues. In particular, it provides a practical and simple explanation of how and why Bayesian inference works.

End Piece

You can read this book on at least two levels

At one level it describes a set of ideas and tools to fill in, what I see as, shortcomings in the traditional education of information professionals. It provides practical help to 'get people started' and a guide to other sources of support, with which most time pressed business folk will be unfamiliar. Even if few readers will have the opportunity to put most of these ideas into practice, I hope that, after reading this, those responsible for educating the next generation of professionals will stop teaching new recruits management methods that are fundamentally flawed and start introducing them to using 21st-century ideas and tools.

At another level, drilling into the practice of reporting, as one of the fundamental pillars of information management, helps expose the rotten core at the heart of the existing management paradigm. The methods that I, and many hundreds of thousands who have followed me, have used to manage organizations do not stand up to scientific scrutiny. They lead to dysfunctional behaviour and have unintended consequences, very often diametrically opposed to the espoused goal. And, at the level of the individual, they fail to exploit the potential and meet the needs of those that they purport to help.

At this point I also need to give a big thank you to everybody who has helped or inspired me.

To my colleagues and work mates in Unilever, over a career of more than 20 years. One of the joys of working there was that, while the organization was not immune to collective stupidity, it was rare to come across an individual who was not clever, decent and honest. After more than a decade later I still refer to the organization as 'we' which says a lot about the loyalty and respect that the organization commands.

To the Beyond Budgeting community past and present, who – more than anyone else – are responsible for my liberation from intellectual and economic slavery. It is invidious to name names, but I owe a particular debt to Jeremy Hope and Peter Bunce, who sadly are no longer with us. Fortunately, I am still able to personally thank long-standing fellow travellers like Robin Fraser, Bjarte Bogsnes,

Anders Olesen, Professor Franz Roosli, Rikard Olsson and Dag Larsson, but they deserve a mention in print as well.

The biggest intellectual influence on my life has undoubtedly been the late Stafford Beer and his work on the cybernetics of viable systems. Although I rarely acknowledge them, his ideas run right through this and every other book I have written, because they shape the way I think about everything. One day I hope to bring these to a general audience. In the meantime, I can only acknowledge my debt to him here, and to those who have helped me to understand his work, like my wonderful PhD supervisor, Angela Espinosa.

The work of W Edwards Deming is rather better known than that of Stafford Beer, but in this book it has been just as influential. Before I encountered Deming's work – mainly through interpreters such as Donald Weaver – I had no idea how flawed my understanding of data and how to interpret it was. Particularly given the transformative effect that these ideas have had over the last 50 years in the manufacturing sector, it is little short of a disgrace that these works do not figure prominently in the curricula of business schools and professional bodies. More recently I have been influenced by the work of John Seddon, who has reinterpreted Deming's ideas in applying them to service organisations.

Happily, two other more recent innovators in the field of graphical communication have had an impact on organizational life that is more widely appreciated. Edward Tufte was for many years a lonely pioneer in the field of graphical communication of information. But his work has been picked up on and operationalized by many other people – it infuses our modern world. I would particularly like to acknowledge Stephen Few, who has done an especially good job of building on the foundation laid by Tufte and making it practical and implementable. Much of Part 3 of this book is a straight lift from Steve's work, which I am happy to own up to because I am one of his biggest fans. At a personal level I am grateful to Steve because he has been open and supportive of my efforts, when he could easily have been guarded, which shows what a big and generous person he is.

At a practical level I would like to thank everyone who has helped in the rather tortuous process of getting this book to the finishing line. This includes those who have read early drafts and helped me squash some of my stupid ideas. This includes all members of the Beyond Budgeting core team and other supporters such as Professor Sebastian Becker and Axel Guoni Ulfarsson. I am also indebted to Anil Seth, Professor of Cognitive and Computational Neuroscience and head of the Sackler Centre for Consciousness Science at Sussex University, and particularly his research student Manuel Baltieri who selflessly read through the manuscript to make sure that I didn't take any liberties with the science. The staff at Matador Books have again done a terrific job of helping me to produce another book to my rather idiosyncratic and exacting specifications. And Steve Player, my partner in crime in the US who has consistently over many years supported and encouraged my efforts to share what I have learned.

Finally, I need to thank my family, and particularly my wife, for allowing me to indulge my nerdy passions.